THE
CARIBBEAN

Survival, Struggle and Sovereignty

By
Catherine A. Sunshine

An EPICA Publication

Acknowledgements

We are indebted to many people who helped make this book possible, and our acknowledgements must necessarily remain incomplete. In every Caribbean country we visited, we were assisted by friends who shared their reflections, ransacked their files, arranged interviews and provided hospitality for our stay. To all of them, we express our deepest gratitude and hope that our work may contribute in some way to the success of their efforts as well.

Organizations we particularly wish to thank include the Caribbean Conference of Churches at its Barbados headquarters and subregional offices; the Center for Ecumenical Action and Planning (CEPAE) in the Dominican Republic; the National Ecumenical Movement of Puerto Rico (PRISA); the Caribbean Project for Justice and Peace in Puerto Rico; SAC, Ltd. in Jamaica; and Projects Promotion in St. Vincent and the Grenadines.

Many persons read and critiqued portions of the manuscript. We are grateful to: Tony Bogues, Hopeton Dunn, Kris Eppler, Todd Jailer, Kim Johnson, Tim Hector, Ralph Gonsalves, Fritz Longchamp, James Millette, William Minter, Roy Neehall, James Phillips, Rickey Singh, Claudio Tavarez and Hilbourne Watson.

Several individuals deserve special mention. EPICA interns Leslie Wade and Janet Theiss worked on portions of the manuscript and helped in many ways. Vicky Surles did the drawings which begin each section and James True assisted with graphic design and maps. This book could not have been written without the support and assistance of Philip Wheaton, director of EPICA, who conceived the idea for the book and helped guide its evolution. Special thanks to Phil for contributing the chapters on the Atlantic coast.

Finally, we are grateful for funding assistance from National Community Funds of the Funding Exchange, the United Church of Canada, the Women's Division of the Board of Global Ministries of the United Methodist Church, and the Jesuit Centre for Social Faith and Justice in Toronto, Canada.

Catherine Sunshine

Typesetting: Grimwoods'

Front cover photo: Grenadian fishermen © 1973 by Flora Phelps

Back cover photo: Trinidadian workers on strike © 1980 by
Transport and Industrial Workers Union of Trinidad and Tobago

ISBN: 0-89608-304-7 paper
ISBN: 0-89608-305-5 cloth

Manufactured in the United States of America

An EPICA publication, distributed by:
South End Press   116 St. Botolph St.   Boston MA 02115

Contents

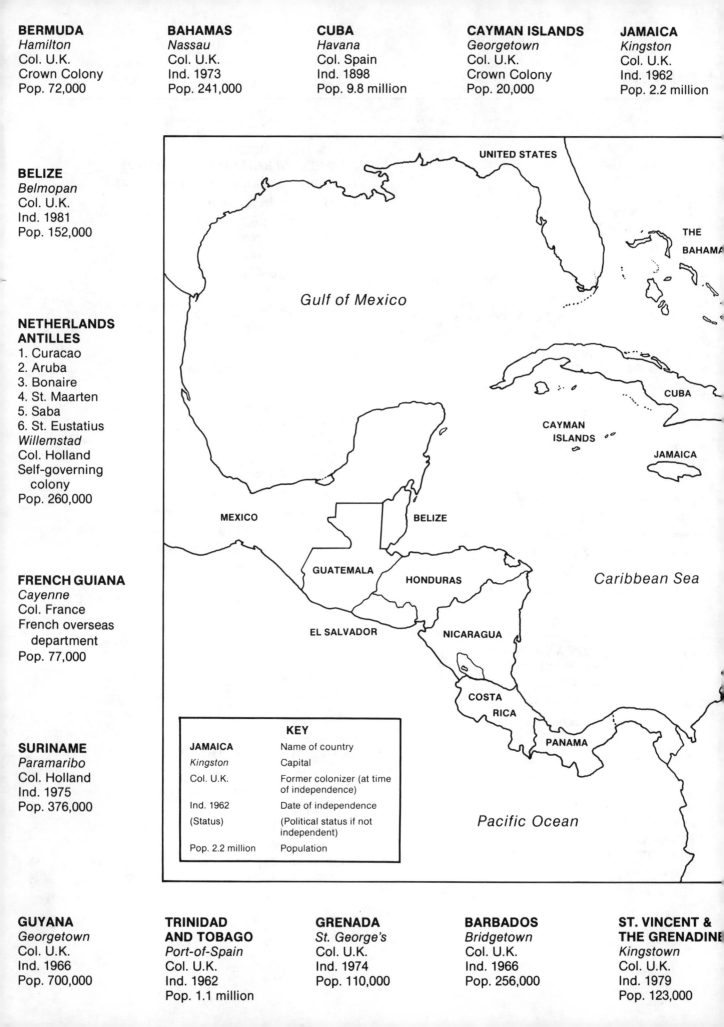

BERMUDA
Hamilton
Col. U.K.
Crown Colony
Pop. 72,000

BAHAMAS
Nassau
Col. U.K.
Ind. 1973
Pop. 241,000

CUBA
Havana
Col. Spain
Ind. 1898
Pop. 9.8 million

CAYMAN ISLANDS
Georgetown
Col. U.K.
Crown Colony
Pop. 20,000

JAMAICA
Kingston
Col. U.K.
Ind. 1962
Pop. 2.2 million

BELIZE
Belmopan
Col. U.K.
Ind. 1981
Pop. 152,000

**NETHERLANDS
ANTILLES**
1. Curacao
2. Aruba
3. Bonaire
4. St. Maarten
5. Saba
6. St. Eustatius
Willemstad
Col. Holland
Self-governing
  colony
Pop. 260,000

FRENCH GUIANA
Cayenne
Col. France
French overseas
  department
Pop. 77,000

SURINAME
Paramaribo
Col. Holland
Ind. 1975
Pop. 376,000

UNITED STATES

THE BAHAMAS

Gulf of Mexico

CUBA

CAYMAN
ISLANDS

JAMAICA

MEXICO

BELIZE

GUATEMALA

HONDURAS

Caribbean Sea

EL SALVADOR

NICARAGUA

COSTA
RICA

PANAMA

Pacific Ocean

KEY	
JAMAICA	Name of country
Kingston	Capital
Col. U.K.	Former colonizer (at time of independence)
Ind. 1962	Date of independence
(Status)	(Political status if not independent)
Pop. 2.2 million	Population

GUYANA
Georgetown
Col. U.K.
Ind. 1966
Pop. 700,000

**TRINIDAD
AND TOBAGO**
Port-of-Spain
Col. U.K.
Ind. 1962
Pop. 1.1 million

GRENADA
St. George's
Col. U.K.
Ind. 1974
Pop. 110,000

BARBADOS
Bridgetown
Col. U.K.
Ind. 1966
Pop. 256,000

**ST. VINCENT &
THE GRENADINES**
Kingstown
Col. U.K.
Ind. 1979
Pop. 123,000

TURKS & CAICOS
Grand Turk
Col. U.K.
Crown Colony
Pop. 8,000

HAITI
Port-au-Prince
Col. France
Ind. 1804
Pop. 5.2 million

DOMINICAN REPUBLIC
Santo Domingo
Col. Spain
Ind. 1844
Pop. 6.3 million

PUERTO RICO
San Juan
Col. Spain/U.S.
U.S. possession
Pop. 3.2 million

BRITISH VIRGIN IS.
Road Town
Col. U.K.
British dependency
Pop. 13,000

The Caribbean

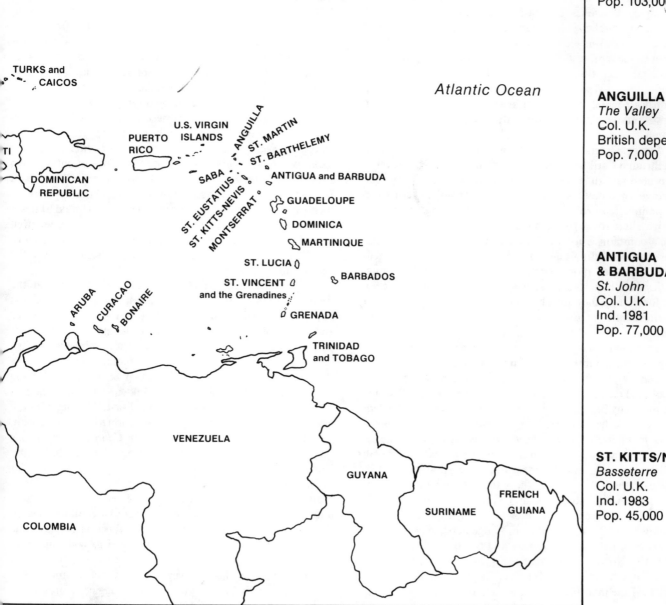

Atlantic Ocean

U.S. VIRGIN IS.
1. St. Thomas
2. St. Croix
3. St. John
Charlotte Amalie
Col. U.S.
U.S. territory
Pop. 103,000

ANGUILLA
The Valley
Col. U.K.
British dependency
Pop. 7,000

ANTIGUA & BARBUDA
St. John
Col. U.K.
Ind. 1981
Pop. 77,000

ST. KITTS/NEVIS
Basseterre
Col. U.K.
Ind. 1983
Pop. 45,000

ST. LUCIA
Castries
Col. U.K.
Ind. 1979
Pop. 119,000

MARTINIQUE
Fort-de-France
Col. France
French overseas
  department
Pop. 303,000

DOMINICA
Roseau
Col. U.K.
Ind. 1978
Pop. 74,000

GUADELOUPE
Pointe-à-Pitre
Col. France
French overseas
  department
Pop. 328,000

MONTSERRAT
Plymouth
Col. U.K.
Crown Colony
Pop. 12,000

Introduction

By Philip E. Wheaton
Director of EPICA

The subtitle of this book—*Survival, Struggle and Sovereignty*—was chosen to reflect three themes which dominate the history of the Caribbean and its reality today.

Survival is a word increasingly on the lips of Caribbean people as the economic crisis of the 1980s tightens its grip. Unemployment rates of 15-40% throughout the region, spiraling food prices which put a minimum diet beyond the reach of working-class families, crowded and unsanitary housing, and deep cuts in public services such as health care spell out the issue of survival in harsh personal and family terms. Highlighted by mass protests in the Dominican Republic, Haiti and Jamaica, desperation has neared the breaking point in some societies and is steadily building in others. The fact that the majority are merely surviving means that every year thousands do not survive; many of these deaths are of infants and children.

Struggle refers to that thread of hope and meaning which runs through Caribbean history. Popular resistance to slavery, indentured servitude and the racism of the colonial system set the stage for today's struggles against neocolonial economic and political control. This includes a continuing search for creative alternatives to the old structures and an attempt to forge a common vision of a new Caribbean. The Cuban and Grenadian revolutions, denounced and derided in the United States, are taken more seriously in a region where existing realities seem hopeless and alternatives few. If people have no hope for change, they quickly or slowly cross the threshold into despair, lashing out in disorganized and often frustrating street riots.

Sovereignty was supposed to have been won with political independence from the colonial powers. But real sovereignty has been fragile and today is overshadowed by the growing neocolonial dominance of the United States, which filled the vacuum left by British withdrawal from the region. The United States claims the Caribbean as its own "backyard," and its efforts to militarily secure the region as part of its empire represent a rejection of Caribbean peoples' desires for regional self-determination, non-alignment and peace. Although rooted in the past, these U.S. attitudes have found extreme expression in the policies of the Reagan administration since 1980. Indeed, some regional observers speak of the Reagan policies as the "recolonization" of the Caribbean, a huge step backward from the dream of national sovereignty and Caribbean unity.

Many North Americans have visited the Caribbean as tourists and businessmen, but relatively few of them have penetrated the invisible walls which surround the tourist and transnational enclaves in the islands. Posh hotels, private beaches and yachts, limbo dancers and pseudo-Voudou performances, ersatz calypso and Continental cuisine—the essence of Caribbean tourism is artificiality, isolated from the real lives and concerns of Caribbean people. Decades of such tourism and pass-through business trips have barely scratched the surface of North American ignorance about the region. But if Americans find it easy to ignore or misunderstand the Caribbean, precisely the opposite is true in terms of the Caribbean perception of the United States. In the region, Caribbean people are reminded every day of the power, proximity and politics of the superpower to the north. The smallest political or economic change in Washington is scrutinized for its potential impact on the Caribbean—an impact which often is major. As one Caribbean leader said, "When the U.S. economy sneezes, the dependent economies of the Caribbean catch a severe case of pneumonia."

In the 1980s, however, it is becoming less easy for North Americans to ignore the Caribbean or view it simply as a tropical playground. The region has moved center-stage as a focal point for right-wing politics in this country. Two successive administrations—of Presidents Carter and Reagan—have made the Caribbean "Basin" the keystone of their hemispheric policies, the arena where the United States is making a dramatic show of force in the context of a renewed Cold War. Centered today in the Central American isthmus, this U.S. military aggression is casting its shadow over the Caribbean islands as well.

The U.S. invasion of Grenada in 1983 signalled the Reagan administration's determination to turn back socialist efforts in the Caribbean through the use of direct military force and to consolidate the region as an anticommunist bastion of U.S. influence. As part of this strategy, the administration also has sought to create an economic and ideological model for the region by restructuring the Jamaican economy under the conservative Seaga government. Held up as a showcase in 1981, Jamaica today is an economic disaster, laying bare the bankruptcy of "Reaganomics" as a solution for the Caribbean.

The crisis of U.S. intervention in Central America has focused tremendous attention on that region, prompting many North Americans to examine its past and present realities for the first time. The same process must begin for the Caribbean—not in the deceptive and self-serving ways which followed the Grenada invasion, but out of a genuine concern for the problems and aspirations of Caribbean people. While the Caribbean is not now an arena of armed struggle, suffering is so acute that explosive protests are bound to increase. This challenges concerned North Americans to develop a movement of solidarity with Caribbean popular struggles, a movement that has begun but is still embryonic. The black community in the U.S. has been key to this growing solidarity, pointing the way to an expanded interchange between North Americans and Caribbean people.

How We Have Organized Our Material

The Caribbean is a unique region embracing some 27 coastal and island territories, four linguistic groups and a kaleidoscope of races, cultures and histories. This complexity makes writing about the region as a whole a difficult task. The organization of this book is neither chronological nor geographic, but primarily thematic. Our four major thematic divisions are: history of the region, alternative models of development, the current social and economic crisis, and U.S. dominance versus Caribbean desires for regional unity and sovereignty. In building these themes, we have drawn examples from the English, Spanish, French and Dutch-speaking territories, although we could not include every country. Our main emphasis is on the Commonwealth (former British) Caribbean because of the growth of U.S. influence there. We focus secondarily on the Spanish-speaking Antilles, cradle of U.S. imperialism since the days of gunboat diplomacy. We have also included the Atlantic coast of Central America, which is historically and culturally tied to the insular Caribbean.

Parts One and Two examine the **history of the Caribbean** from colonial conquests to the present, including slavery and indentured servitude, post-emancipation struggles, and the roots of U.S. imperialism in the region. We trace the genesis of the Caribbean progressive movement in Pan-Africanism, labor organizing and socialist currents, and show how the contemporary Caribbean left emerged from these indigenous movements. We examine the failure of the U.S.-imposed "Puerto Rican model," and attempts to create alternative models in Cuba, Jamaica and Trinidad.

Part Three looks at a phenomenon which has had a major impact on the life of the Caribbean: **outmigration from the region.** This is illustrated through the experiences of various Caribbean communities abroad, including: West Indians in Britain, the Netherlands and France; Puerto Ricans in the United States; Caribbean peoples in Brooklyn; Cuban exiles in Miami; and the Haitian "boat people" fleeing the repression in their homeland.

Part Four examines the **Cuban and Grenadian revolutions** as alternative models in a region desperate for creative change. Through a realistic understanding of these experiments, we can appreciate both the problems and the potential of attempts to build more socially just, economically viable Caribbean societies. We believe that while the tragic end of the Grenada revolution must be studied with care in terms of the lessons it holds for the left, the revolution itself scored many positive achievements which must be valued for their contribution toward evolving a progressive model of change.

Part Five looks at various **control mechanisms the U.S. has used** to maintain its dominance over the Caribbean. Ranging from gunboat diplomacy and labor subversion to banking structures and the media, these methods have varied over time, although the basic strategy has remained the same. These shifting patterns of domination came full circle with the U.S. invasions of Cuba, the Dominican Republic and Grenada, demonstrating that the United States has never abandoned the practice of military intervention in its "backyard."

Part Six, **the Caribbean in Crisis,** profiles fifteen Caribbean societies to show the depth of social and economic problems facing the region today. These case studies include seven independent countries of the English, Spanish and French-speaking Caribbean; three colonial groups wrestling with the question of eventual independence; and five Central American countries whose "Atlantic coast" populations form a human link with the Caribbean.

Part Seven focuses on the **Caribbean in the wake of the Grenada invasion.** Attacks on the regional left, the advance of conservative forces, divisions within the Church community and setbacks for regional unity are the bitter legacy of this aggressive action by the United States. We examine the political, military and economic underpinnings of the Reagan administration's Caribbean policies and show how these policies have further frustrated the region's long unfulfilled dream of regional unity and sovereignty.

The Caribbean: Survival, Struggle and Sovereignty draws on EPICA's fifteen years of work on Caribbean/Central American issues and on our close collaboration with a wide range of Caribbean popular organizations, including religious and ecumenical groups, trade unions, women's and peasant organizations and others. In small yet fundamental ways, they are carrying out what we consider to be the heart of the struggle for Caribbean unity, dignity and self-determination. At the same time, this book was written with a North American audience in mind, particularly those who are beginning to understand that the United States' own liberation is tied up with liberation struggles in Central America and the Caribbean. We believe that it is only through North-South dialogue and solidarity that the injustices and crimes of the past can be challenged and new relationships created for the future.

In the long view of Caribbean history, one is struck by the unbroken domination of foreign powers in the region—and yet also by the fact that, one by one, these powers have declined or left the region, leaving Caribbean people to deal with colonialism's legacy of poverty and division. In the short view, one sees present contradictions escalating toward a social crisis, proving that U.S. domination has not provided any better solution. We affirm that the Caribbean is nobody's "backyard" in spite of North American presumptions. We also affirm that only the Caribbean people themselves can forge alternative models of development, justice and peace in the region. ■

The stone had skidded arc'd and bloomed into islands:
Cuba and San Domingo
Jamaica and Puerto Rico
Grenada Guadeloupe Bonaire

curved stone hissed into reef
wave teeth fanged into clay
white splash flashed into spray
Bathsheba Montego Bay

bloom of the arcing summers . . .

The islands roared into green plantations
ruled by silver sugar cane
sweat and profit
cutlass profit
islands ruled by sugar cane

Excerpted from "Calypso"
by Edward Braithwaite, Barbados

PART ONE
Caribbean Peoples' Unity
History and Culture

Vicky Surles

Brief History of the Caribbean Through Emancipation

When Queen Isabella of Spain sent Christopher Columbus across the Atlantic Ocean in 1492, his official mission was to discover a new trade route to Asia and Christianize the "heathens" who lived there. But Columbus and the Spanish *conquistadores* who followed him made little secret of their real interest: gold. When Columbus landed in the Bahamas and saw the native Arawaks adorned with gold trinkets, he was convinced that mythical "El Dorado"—the Golden Land— must be nearby. For years, the conquistadores pushed farther and farther into the Americas, driven by their greed for precious metals.

They were driven also by a lust for power. Many were *hidalgos,* or knights, who hoped to grab enough land and wealth in the New World to join the Spanish ruling class. Once the land had been claimed for Spain through conquest, the Spanish monarchy awarded them *encomiendas*—rights to rule—over areas of land inhabited by Amerindians.[1] The Spaniards forced the Indians into slavery in gold mines and on their colonial farms and ranches.

Destruction of the Arawaks by the Spanish; Carib Resistance to the British and French

When the Spanish arrived in the Caribbean, there were two Amerindian peoples living there: the Arawaks, centered in the Bahamas and the Greater Antilles, and the Caribs, in the Eastern Caribbean. Both had come from the tropical rain forest areas of northeastern South America, with the more aggressive Caribs gradually pushing the Arawaks northward.

The Indians were subsistence farmers and fishermen, growing corn, cassava, sweet potatoes, cotton and tobacco. They navigated among the islands in dug-out canoes capable of holding up to 80 people, which they used for inter-island trade, and in the case of the Caribs, to raid the Arawaks for goods and slaves.

The Arawaks whom Columbus encountered included three major subgroups: the Lucayanos, living in the Bahamas; the Borequinos in Puerto Rico; and the Tainos in Cuba, Jamaica and Hispaniola (now Haiti and the Dominican Republic). Though not warriors like the Caribs, the Arawaks made a brave effort to oust the Spanish from the Greater Antilles. Their resistance was crushed by the Spaniards' superior weaponry, vicious fighting mastiffs and armor-covered horses. The Spaniards' system of forced labor completed the destruction of the Arawaks, who died from starvation, abuse, and new European diseases, especially smallpox. Unable to successfully enslave the Amerindians, the Spanish turned to African slaves supplied to them by Portuguese traders.

England, France and Holland refused to recognize Spain's claim to "ownership" of the entire Caribbean,[2] and in the early 17th century, after years of warfare with Spain, the French and British began to colonize the Lesser Antilles. The Caribs living on those islands put up a fierce and prolonged resistance to the European invaders. Early attempts to colonize Grenada and St. Lucia had to be abandoned because of Carib ferocity, and later settlements on St. Kitts, Antigua, Montserrat, Grenada and St. Lucia were attacked repeatedly by the

DEATH OF HATUEY

Hatuey, an Arawak chief on the island of Hispaniola, fled to Cuba where he was captured by the Spaniards and burnt alive as an example to other Indians who resisted colonization.

From Bartolome de las Casas, *Very Brief Account of the Destruction of the Indies, 1552.*

Caribs. In Grenada, the Caribs fought the French for three years and finally hurled themselves into the sea rather than submit to French domination.

By the mid-17th century, the Europeans' superior fire-power had forced the Caribs back into Dominica and St. Vincent. These mountainous islands were natural fortresses, and the Europeans recognized them as under Carib control in a treaty signed in 1660. From their strongholds, the Caribs continued to raid the European settlements for the rest of the century.

From Small Farms to Sugar Estates: The Big Planters Take Over

Barbados was uninhabited when the Europeans arrived, and a British colony there quickly grew and flourished. The colonists originally tried to make their fortunes growing tobacco, as pipe-smoking was a new fashion in Europe. Even these small farms required a cheap labor force, so the colonists brought in white indentured laborers from Europe. These were often convicts or debtors who signed themselves into servitude with the hope of some free land after a few years' bonded labor.

By the 1640s tobacco was no longer very profitable, so the settlers on Barbados turned to growing sugar cane, setting a pattern that was soon to be followed in all the French and British islands. The turn to sugar transformed the colonies and signalled the start of an era of exploitation which was to bring misery to hundreds of thousands of people. Unlike tobacco, sugar had to be grown on large plantations and required costly investment in buildings, equipment, and labor. Wealthy entrepreneurs steadily bought out or drove out the small farmers and consolidated their holdings into large sugar estates. Many of these big planters became "absentee land-lords" who left the running of their estates to attorneys and overseers while living luxuriously in England on the profits from sugar.

The plantations required an endless supply of labor. Plantation work was so grueling that few people would voluntarily sign themselves into this kind of servitude; so the governments of Britain and France forcibly transported to the colonies thousands of convicts, paupers, and political or religious dissidents. But even these were not enough. Because the white laborers were Europeans, it was harder for the planters to rationalize the use of cruelty to keep them subdued. Africans, on the other hand, were a non-European race, and had already been slaves on Spanish and Portuguese planta-tions. Spain, France and Britain readily embraced the idea of an enslaved African workforce kept in submission by bar-barous and inhuman methods.

The Dutch initially controlled the slave trade. From com-mercial bases on the islands of Curaçao and St. Eustatius, Holland kept the Spanish, British and French colonies supplied with slaves as well as food and other goods. After the ocean journey in the hold of a slave ship, the Africans were held in walled-in slave camps on Curaçao before being reshipped to other colonies. At the height of Holland's "Golden Age" in the mid-1600s, these camps often held more than 15,000 people at a time.[3]

African Resistance to Slavery

The dominant theme throughout the slavery era was the continuous struggle between the planters' coercive power and the slaves' determined resistance. Everything was pitted against the Africans: cruel torture devices on board the slave ships, the whips and guns of the planters and overseers, posses of soldiers and dogs sent out after runaway slaves. By 1700, slaves greatly outnumbered Europeans in most Caribbean colonies, and the planters lived in constant fear of a slave insurrection. They thus resorted to horrible punishments and executions of "trouble-makers" to keep the slaves from rising against them.

But the slaves did revolt, repeatedly and often violently. There were hundreds of mutinies or attempted mutinies by slaves during the "middle passage" across the Atlantic. On the islands, especially Jamaica, slaves organized large-scale upris-ings in which plantations were burned and the slave-masters killed. Some of the leaders of these revolts are remembered in

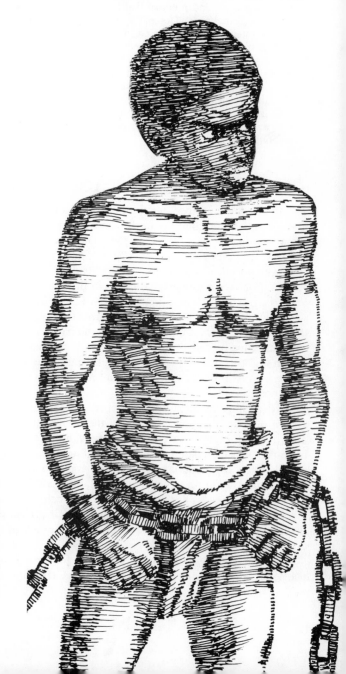

Courtesy Belize Government Information Service

the Caribbean for their daring: Cuffy in Guyana, Nanny and Tacky in Jamaica, and Morales in Cuba, among others.

In certain colonies, large numbers of slaves escaped from the plantations and set up independent communities beyond the reach of the planters. This was possible only where the terrain provided protection for the runaways, as did the mountainous interiors of Jamaica, Dominica, and St. Vincent, and the jungles of Guyana and Suriname. In Jamaica, the Maroons—as the rebels there were called—waged two long wars against the British, forcing the colonists to strike treaties recognizing them as free men. In Guyana and Suriname, they were called "Bush Negroes" since they lived in the wild interior:

> . . . Their villages were built on circular pieces of ground cleared of bush. The huts were hidden by planting fruit trees, yams and plantains and the whole area was defended by a wide ditch filled with water which covered sharp stakes. False paths were laid to lead enemies away from the underwater firm paths into the village.
>
> From their hidden homes the Bush Negroes raided the European plantations and forced the Dutch to send expeditions into the interior to attempt to crush them. These expeditions were costly in soldiers' lives and probably helped future runaways, for the Europeans took slaves with them who thus learned of the pathways through the bush. Rather than continue with the wars the Dutch Governor made treaties in 1761 and 1767 with the two main groups of Bush Negroes. The treaties were modeled on those with the Jamaican Maroons and gave the Bush Negroes freedom in return for an agreement to return any new runaways.[5]

Mercantilism: Consolidation of the Colonial System

In the mid-17th century, France and Britain had little interest in the moral niceties of the slavery issue because the economic logic for slavery was so strong. The transportation of slaves to the Americas formed one side of a three-legged "triangular trade." Slave ships would load up with guns, ammunition, and manufactured goods in British and French ports, then sail to Africa where the cargo was exchanged for slaves. Then came the middle passage across the Atlantic, and the sale of the Africans in the Caribbean and North American colonies. Finally, the ships loaded up with colonial sugar, cotton and tobacco and sped back to England and France, where the raw produce was refined and re-exported to other countries.

The triangular trade was one aspect of the mercantilist system of economic policy becoming the dominant view in England and France.[6] According to mercantilist theory, a nation could accumulate wealth by controlling colonies which would supply raw materials for industry, and also provide a captive market for the goods produced. Mercantilism depended on monopoly. For instance, the British colonies could buy only British goods and had to ship all their produce in British ships. In return, they were given a monopoly of the sugar market in England.

The system produced enormous profits for the colonial planters, the slave traders, and the merchants who financed the

trade and processed the sugar. Many spin-off industries also profited: shipbuilders, iron-mongers (who made the handcuffs and leg irons), and the industrialists who manufactured the goods sent to Africa. In both Britain and France, these interests used their wealth to buy political influence, keeping the colonial system entrenched for over 100 years.

The Caribbean became an arena for imperialist rivalry. France and Britain first fought three wars to drive the Dutch out of the Caribbean and reserve the lucrative slave trade for themselves. Then they turned on each other. Disputes which began in Europe were fought in the Caribbean with the colonies as pawns. French and British warships would attack and ravage each other's colonies, or seize and occupy them; in the latter part of the 18th century many of the islands flip-flopped back and forth between French and British ownership. Tiny Dominica, an extreme example, changed hands twelve times.

Revolutionary Surge at the Turn of the Century: Slave, Maroon, and Carib Revolts and the Haitian Revolution

For over a century, France and Britain exploited their colonies to extract every last cent of sugar profits. The results, by the end of the 1700s, were depleted soils, an enraged slave population, and prohibitively expensive sugar. As France and Britain were swept up in the Industrial Revolution, West Indian sugar lost its economic importance. The colonies entered a period of economic and social crisis, culminating in the Caribbean's only successful slave revolt, the Haitian Revolution.

HORRORS OF THE MIDDLE PASSAGE

The slaves were collected in the interior, fastened one to the other in columns loaded with heavy stones of 40 or 50 pounds in weight to prevent attempts at escape, and then marched the long journey to the sea, sometimes hundreds of miles, the sickly and weak dropping to die in the African jungle . . .

On the ships the slaves were packed in the hold on galleries one above the other. Each was given only four or five feet in length and two or three feet in height, so that they could neither lie at full length nor sit upright. Contrary to the lies that have been spread so pertinaciously about Negro docility, the revolts at the port of embarkation and on board were incessant, so that the slaves had to be chained, right hand to right leg, left hand to left leg, and attached in rows to long iron bars. In this position they lived for the voyage, coming up once a day for exercise and to allow the sailors to "clean the pails." But when the cargo was rebellious or the weather bad, then they stayed below for weeks at a time. The close proximity of so many naked human beings, their bruised and festering flesh, the foetid air, the prevailing dysentery, the accumulation of filth, turned these holds into a hell. During the storms the hatches were battered down and in the close and loathsome darkness they were hurled from one side to another by the heaving vessel, held in position by the chains on their bleeding.

. . . They died not only from the regime but from grief and rage and despair. They undertook vast hunger strikes; undid their chains and hurled themselves on the crew in futile attempts at insurrection. What could these inland tribesmen do on the open sea, in a complicated sailing vessel? To brighten their spirits it became the custom to have them up on the deck once a day and force them to dance. Some took the opportunity to jump overboard, uttering cries of triumph as they cleared the vessel and disappeared below the surface.

— C.L.R. James, *The Black Jacobins*[4]

The French colony of St. Domingue (now Haiti) was the biggest sugar producer in the Caribbean. It epitomized the repressive and decadent plantation societies found all over the region, and was rigidly stratified according to skin color. As elsewhere in the Caribbean, the planters had made a practice of sexually using the slave women on their plantations. The mulatto or "colored" children of these unions were born into slavery, but often were freed by their fathers and sometimes inherited property. Especially in the French colonies, some free colored became relatively wealthy, owning estates and even slaves. Despite this, however, they were still denied full social and political equality by the white ruling class.

The French Revolution of 1789, with its promise of freedom and equality for all men, sent shock waves through the Caribbean—most of all in St. Domingue. The uprising began as a revolt by the free colored to gain full equality, but soon escalated into an island-wide slave revolution under the dynamic leadership of the slave named Toussaint L'Ouverture. Toussaint's black troops first soundly defeated a large British army sent out from Jamaica to seize St. Domingue. Next, the slave army defeated and massacred the mulatto military forces who wanted to set up a separate colored republic. In 1799, France recognized Toussaint's total control over St. Domingue and made him Governor-General of the island.

Toussaint, about 1801 or 1802, came to a conception for which the only word is genius. He wrote a constitution for San Domingo and he didn't submit it to the French government. He declared in the constitution that San Domingo would be governed by the ex-slaves. French officials asked him: what is the place of the French government in this constitution? He replied, "They will send commissioners to talk with me"—and that was all he would say.[7]

Meanwhile, however, the French Revolution had fallen into the hands of Napoleon Bonaparte, who plotted an invasion to restore slavery in St. Domingue. Toussaint was captured and killed by Napoleon's trickery, but the momentum of the Haitian Revolution continued. In 1803 slave armies led by Dessalines and Christophe defeated Napoleon's fever-ravaged army and set up the first independent republic under black control.

The success of the Haitian insurrection gave courage to subjugated peoples all over the Caribbean. Revolts broke out, incited in some cases by agents of the French Revolution, but drawing their force from the volcanic uprising of the black and colored masses. In Guadeloupe and St. Lucia, the slaves helped repel British invasions so as to keep the islands under French revolutionary control. In Grenada and Dominica, the slaves, free colored, and resident French joined in a struggle to overthrow the British rulers of the islands. There was a major slave revolt in the Dutch colony of Curaçao. On St. Vincent a group known as the "Black Caribs" revolted under the leadership of their chief Chatoyer. The British defeated the uprising and deported the surviving Black Caribs from St. Vincent to the Bay Islands off the coast of Honduras.

The revolutionary surge in the Eastern Caribbean coincided with a second major war by the Jamaican Maroons against the British. Although the Maroons were finally subdued and many deported to Nova Scotia, they exhausted the British forces and thus contributed to the British defeat by Toussaint in St. Domingue. Several years later the Maroons on Dominica joined the Dominican slaves in revolt. While all of these rebellions were eventually defeated, the cost to Britain was high. From then on, the British stood on notice that the viability of the slave system was nearing its end.

Declining Profits and Rising Violence
Force the Emancipation of the Slaves

The idea that the moral pressure of the British abolitionists alone ended slavery is a myth. The slaves in the French and British colonies were emancipated when the slave system became unprofitable—and not until then.

As the Trinidadian historian Eric Williams argues in *Capitalism and Slavery,* it was the wealth the slaves created which finally destroyed the slave system.[8] The profits from the West India sugar trade had been steadily reinvested in British banking, finance, and industry. By the end of the 18th century, the Industrial Revolution was in full swing and new British industries were mass-producing goods for export around the world. Britain traded these manufactures for raw materials— cotton from the United States and India, coffee from Brazil, and most of all, *sugar,* from huge new producers like Brazil, India, and Cuba. Obviously, this system could not work if the West Indies kept their monopoly making them the only ones who could sell sugar to Britain.

It was also a question of price. The West Indian islands were small, their soils exhausted and production costs were high. Meanwhile the world market was flooded with cheap sugar from the new producers and from beet sugar, a growing industry in France. Powerful industrial and financial interests in Britain who had previously supported slavery now wanted to put the West Indian planters out of business so that Britain could buy this cheaper sugar. To attack the West Indian monopoly, Britain abolished the slave trade (but not slavery) in 1807. With the West Indian colonies no longer profitable, the way was cleared for the abolitionists to turn public opinion against slavery for moral and humanitarian reasons.

The second crucial factor was the slaves themselves, whose increasingly violent demands for freedom left the slave owners little choice but to get off the "powder keg" they were sitting on.[9] The slaves were acutely aware of the abolition debate in England and of the planters' resistance to ending slavery. Many slaves in fact believed that the French and British governments had already ordered emancipation, and that the planters were illegally withholding freedom.

Britain and France tried to defuse the situation through a reformist strategy: improving treatment of the slaves, sending money and missionaries to the colonies, liberalizing the system slightly. It failed. The West Indian slaves refused to wait any longer and the islands exploded one by one in revolt. In Guyana, 12,000 slaves on fifty plantations rose up demanding unconditional emancipation. Slaves on Barbados angrily claimed that "the island belonged to them, and not to white men." Sam Sharpe's Montego Bay revolt in Jamaica was crushed by British troops, leaving hundreds dead. There were four major rebellions on previously placid Martinique in the space of eleven years. In the Danish Virgin Islands, the slaves delivered an ultimatum: freedom by four o'clock or they would burn the capital to the ground. Freedom was granted. Finally,

Members of the plantocracy out for a stroll with their servants on the grounds of a private estate in Barbados. Note the Victorian style of dress which was stifling in the tropical heat.

Moorland-Spingarn Research Center, Howard University

on August 1, 1834, all the slaves in the British colonies were declared free, followed by emancipation in the French islands in 1848.

The Planters Turn to Immigrants to Avoid a Free Labor Market

After emancipation, the planters tried every possible scheme to keep the ex-slaves tied to the plantations. The slaves were not actually freed in 1834; instead, they became "apprentices" obliged to perform 40½ hours of unpaid labor each week. The slaves were outraged by this hypocrisy and rioted violently in some colonies, and by 1838 the impractical apprenticeship system was abandoned. As soon as the slaves were released the local island assemblies passed laws aimed at keeping them on the plantations by making "vagrancy" and unemployment punishable crimes.

Everywhere, the freed slaves looked for ways to leave the hated plantations and become economically independent, but this was only possible in some colonies. In Barbados, Antigua, and St. Kitts, which are flat, virtually all the land was under sugar cane and there was nowhere for the ex-slaves to go. They stayed on or near the sugar plantations, working for a small wage.

In the mountainous Windward Islands the situation was different. These islands had never been ideal for growing sugar, and many of the smaller estates were abandoned when the market for West Indian sugar collapsed. Thousands of ex-slaves left the plantations to buy, rent, or squat on abandoned estates or idle land in the hills. They formed the beginnings of an independent peasantry which pioneered the introduction of new export crops to replace sugar: cocoa and nutmeg in Grenada, arrowroot in St. Vincent, limes in St. Lucia and Dominica, cotton in Nevis and Montserrat. They also grew food crops which they sold to the estates or to neighboring islands.

Jamaica and Guyana, where land was relatively abundant, saw the fullest development of the free peasant society. Under pressure from the planters, the British government would sell land only in large tracts so as to keep the ex-slaves from buying. But the freed slaves circumvented this restriction by pooling their savings and buying land jointly, either forming cooperatives or parceling out individual plots to families. Missionary societies also purchased land for the ex-slaves, especially in Jamaica. By 1865, two-thirds of Jamaica's freed slaves had left the sugar plantations and were living in free villages.

These villages had their own internal governments which built and maintained roads, settled disputes, and helped to market crops. In some cases former slaves took over the entire operation of abandoned sugar estates. In a radical departure from the plantation system in which almost all food was imported, the free peasantry concentrated on growing food for local consumption. The surplus was sold to nearby estates in order to have money to pay taxes. They also grew crops for export, so that within several generations, Jamaican peasant farmers were producing a large portion of the island's national income.

The sugar planters liked to wail to the British government that the ex-slaves had deserted the plantations and brought about the financial ruin of the colonies. In fact, the best arable land remained under planter control, and many freed slaves had no choice but to remain on or near the estates as tenant farmers or sharecroppers. By charging steep rents for houses and house lots, the planters kept the ex-slaves in perpetual debt and ensured that those who remained in their homes on plantation land would have to perform wage labor on the plantation.

The planters could not use rents to extract labor from the residents of the free villages, so they used taxes. The colonial government greatly feared the growth of a self-reliant peasant economy, and levied punitive taxes to keep it in check. To pay these taxes, most of the villagers had to perform some wage labor on nearby estates. But their base of independent production gave them considerable latitude in deciding when and where to work, and the planters furiously resisted negotiating on a basis of equality with the ex-slaves for their labor.[10]

To avoid a "free" labor market where the workers could bargain for better wages and terms, the planters brought in indentured laborers from India, Asia, Africa, and Europe. Although most of them signed limited indentureship contracts voluntarily, these laborers were under the control of the planters once they arrived in the West Indies, and could be used as a weapon against the demands of the free workers.

Indentureship had the greatest impact in Trinidad and Guyana, where the sugar industry continued to flourish after it had declined in other islands. In Guyana, the freed slaves formed work gangs which moved from estate to estate, negotiating for short-term labor. They sought the best-paid, most highly skilled tasks, and bargained hard for favorable wages and terms, not hesitating to withhold their labor at crucial points in the crop cycle. When the Guyanese planters actually *reduced* wages in the 1840s, corresponding to a fall in the price of sugar, the free workers backed up their demands with strikes.[11]

The Guyanese planters used indentured labor to break the strikes. In 1845 and 1846, they brought in 6,000 Portuguese from the Madeira Islands, 4,000 laborers from India, and 2,000 Africans captured from foreign slave ships. With this new labor force, the planters were able to break the second and more serious sugar strike in 1848.[12]

Except in Haiti, Santo Domingo, Puerto Rico, and Barbados, the Caribbean islands underwent a demographic revolution in the 1800s as a result of this new immigrant labor. To the old black/white/colored structure were added East Indians, Chinese, Javanese, Portuguese, Africans, poor Europeans, and even a few Japanese. East Indians dominated the influx: more than half a million of them came to the Caribbean, primarily to Trinidad and Guyana. These two societies became biracial, with populations nearly evenly divided between people of African and East Indian descent. Not surprisingly, the planters' use of immigrants to control the free laborers left a legacy of animosity between the two groups, despite the fact that all were victims of the same exploitative system. ■

Collaborative Role of the Colonial Church
... and challenge from the Afro-Christian cults

Christianity came to the Caribbean as part and parcel of Spanish, French, British, Dutch, and finally, North American colonialism. The Church went on to assist these powers in building colonial societies: it endorsed slavery, and helped to entrench racial and class divisions after emancipation. Neither the prophetic role of a few church leaders nor the individual sincerity of the faithful altered this long history of religious collaboration with the colonial system.

Spanish colonization of the Caribbean had as its double weapon the sword and the cross. Its very justification for conquest was to convert indigenous peoples from their "heathen" beliefs. Fray Bartolome de las Casas, the Spanish priest, tried to defend the Amerindians from the Spanish onslaught, but his belated appeal for a few thousand Indians came after tens of thousands had already been killed or died of foreign diseases. It was not the Church which prevented the total genocide of the Indians, but the fact that the Spanish turned to importing African slave labor.

The Church gave its blessing to slavery. In 1685, the Council of the Indies in Spain decreed that the slave trade was lawful "where there was no danger of the Faith being perverted."[1] Meanwhile, Catholicism was imposed with almost complete disregard for the bloody crimes being committed against the Church's new converts. This produced a faith which was hardly more than skin-deep for the vast majority of its enslaved "converts."

The Church explained slavery as the result of a "divine judgement" or curse on the black race; or alternatively, as part of a divine plan for the betterment of mankind through the Christianizing of heathens and the enrichment of the planters. A French intellectual writing in 1675, for example, defended the slave trade on grounds that . . .

> inhuman though it might appear, the Christian merchants were enabled by its means to retrieve from a cruel slavery in Africa people who were idolaters or Muslims, to transport them to a milder servitude in the West Indies, and to confer upon them there a knowledge of the true God and the way of salvation by the teachings of priests and ecclesiastics who took pains to make them Christians.[2]

The Catholic Church actively assisted in institutionalizing slavery in the Spanish and French colonies. The French *Code Noir,* or Black Code, served as a means of enforcing both Church strictures and social control of the slaves:

> The Code, like the Spanish legislation of the preceding century, was permeated with the spirit of Roman Catholicism. All slaves were to be baptized, only Roman Catholics could have charge of slaves, slaves were not to be worked or go to market on Sundays or holy days, marriages among them were to be encouraged, consent of father and mother being replaced by consent of the owner.[3]

In the case of the British colonies, where Anglicanism and Protestantism were dominant, the Church's role focused on subduing and assimilating the Africans. Originally, there was little interest in Christianizing the slaves, and the few early missionary efforts which did reach out to blacks were marked by racism and elitism. Count Zinzendorf, a Moravian leader, said in 1739:

> God punished the first Negroes by making them slaves, and your conversion will make you free, not from control of your masters, but simply from your wicked habits and thoughts, and all that makes you dissatisfied with your lot.[4]

This led to an ironic situation in which those blacks who became Christians often prayed for their white oppressors, saying in one case: "Father, forgive them, for they know not what they do . . . Buckra (the master) left him God in England, and the devil in Jamaica stir him up to do all this wickedness. Poor thing! Him eye blind, and him heart hard."[5]

In fact, the impact of this early Christian teaching remained superficial, since African religious beliefs and practices continued to dominate the plantation until the 1830s. In the slave world people turned to African religions such as Shango and Kumina, or to *obeah* (sorcery) for spiritual and practical help. Through the dances and drumming, masks and rituals, the slaves realized a link to their ancestral home. At the same time, these practices were used to provide protection against the planters. The obeah-man or woman could give the slave a charm to be worn to protect him against the cruelty of the overseer. Charms and potions could also be used to take revenge on fellow slaves who collaborated with the Europeans. The planters' fear of obeah magic was one reason they finally allowed the slaves to be Christianized:

> In short, I know not what I can do with him, except to make a Christian of him! This might induce the negroes to believe that he [the obeah-man] has lost his infernal power by the superior virtue of the holy water . . . [6]

Kumina or myalism, strongest in Jamaica, stemmed from an ancient Ashanti ancestor possession cult. Through a ritual dance, the spirit of the ancestor takes control of the dancer's body to communicate hidden knowledge to the living. By the 1780s, Kumina had incorporated some Christian elements as a result of the coming to Jamaica of black Baptists from the southern United States. As these "Native Baptists" spread their faith, Kumina absorbed key elements of the Baptist religion, including belief in possession by the Holy Spirit—similar to the African belief in ancestor possession—and baptism by immersion in water. For the next 40 years, membership in the cult grew rapidly, so when missionaries in Jamaica in the 1830s tried to convert the slaves to Christianity, they had to compete with the powerful and entrenched Kumina/Native Baptist complex.

Baptist missionaries baptizing Jamaicans in the sea in 1843.

When it became clear that emancipation was inevitable, the colonial authorities encouraged the churches to help assimilate the blacks. The Anglican, Dutch Protestant, and French Catholic churches were favored for this role over the non-conformist Moravian, (English) Baptist, and Methodist churches.* By 1830-31, the churches were allowing blacks into their worship and had begun to open up parochial schools to teach them to read and write. The goal of this education was not enlightenment toward social freedom, however, but preparation for servile roles in the colonial church and planter-dominated society. The ruling class . . .

> demanded and obtained [an agreement] that the school would not be used to affect adversely the supply of manual labor on the plantation, nor to encourage the coloured people to wish to rise too quickly up the social ladder.[7]

The Baptists, Methodists and Moravians played a more positive role, forming an alliance with the freed slaves to help them become independent from the planters. In Jamaica, where a majority of the ex-slaves left the plantations and moved to the hills, the non-conformist churches provided thousands of acres of land bought with church money. As a result, these denominations were initially seen as "liberators." The Methodist Church in Jamaica doubled its membership between 1831 and 1841, while the Baptists' tripled from 10,000 to 34,000 during the same period.[8]

Even among these churches, however, the white leadership made clear that its task was not to arbitrate between master and former slave. The Church was forbidden to meddle in "social and political questions," its task being to pacify the rebel spirit in the blacks through education and Christian teaching.[9] Thus just a few years after emancipation, missionaries reported with pride that:

> cunning, craft, and suspicion—those dark passions and savage disposition before described as characteristic of the Negro—are now giving place to a noble, manly, and independent, yet patient and submissive spirit.[10]

Rise of the Afro-Christian Cults

Such "success" blinded the missionaries to the real process taking place: black disenchantment with the white churches and the steady growth of Afro-Christian syncretic religions. Mistaking church attendance for assimilation, the missionaries failed to realize that the blacks were merely allowing the practice of Christianity to co-exist and blend with their African religious beliefs.

The racial, class and color bias of colonial society was scarcely affected by emancipation. The failure of the mission churches to challenge these social attitudes drove many blacks away within a decade after emancipation. For one thing, the churches discouraged the baptism of illegitimate children, which meant that at least 70% of the population was barred from full privileges of membership in the Church. Governed by a Victorian, white European morality, the missionaries regarded the reluctance of the blacks to marry as evidence of "deep cultural defects which would take a long time to remove."[11]

Also disturbing to many blacks who converted to Christianity was that the training of black leaders—primarily in the non-conformist churches—did not mean oversight of a congregation, much less denominational leadership. Rather, blacks became deacons (servants), teachers and preachers *within* the congregation. These new positions had a social impact in terms of providing jobs, but they were confined to service roles in support of the white missionaries. The training

---

*Called "non-conformist" because they refused to conform to the rules and practices of the Church of England (Anglican Church).

of native leaders and lay agents within these churches facilitated the entry of blacks into service occupations in the larger society, such as clerks, subordinate estate managers, and school teachers.

This gradual social integration was not accompanied by a lessening of racist attitudes, but by their intensification, as blacks moved closer to whites in the social spectrum. As in the post-reconstruction period in the U.S., it became common in the Caribbean to hear blacks referred to as "niggers." As late as 1870 the West Indian Anglican Church was publicly asserting that blacks had the right to "spiritual equality" with whites, but not cultural equality.[12]

As a result of these attitudes and practices, between 1842 and 1865 the mission churches in Jamaica lost up to half the members they had gained since 1831. Black children dropped out of the church schools. Many blacks trained as native ministers (especially Baptists) left to pastor their own African and Afro-Christian churches.

While the European churches preached deference to the system, the essence of the black religions was resistance. Native Baptists figured prominently in the Montego Bay revolt just before emancipation, and afterward, the Kumina/Native Baptist movement became the core of resistance to the hardship of the post-emancipation years. In 1841-42, the connection of the cult to plantation work stoppages led the planters to outlaw Kumina, and the movement went underground.

As with other elements of West Indian mass culture, however, the attempt to suppress Kumina only led to its resurgence in a stronger, if altered form. In the early 1860s, the mission churches in Jamaica launched a united assault on black religion, aimed at a sweeping conversion to "pure" Christianity. But their attempt to stir up a Christian religious frenzy in Jamaica produced unexpected results: the revival turned African in form, with oral confessions, trances, dreams,

prophecies, spirit seizures and wild dancing. This marriage of myalism and Christianity came to be called Pocomania—the strongest of the Jamaican native religions until the emergence of Rastafarianism in the 1930s.

A similar syncretic process produced Haitian *Vodou*. Many Haitian slaves came from the Dahomey region of Africa, where they had worshipped gods called *voduns*. The French planters suppressed this practice through the Catholic Church, which held total control over the slaves' religious life according to the French Code Noir. To get around this, the slaves used Catholicism as a cover for the practice of Vodou. Latin liturgical rituals meshed with the traditional rites of dancing and drumming until Vodou became an Afro-Christian religion, widespread at all levels of Haitian society as a form of popular resistance to domination by the European/Christian value system.

A third example of syncretism is the Shango/*santería* complex, variants of which exist in Trinidad, Cuba, Puerto Rico, the Dominican Republic, and Brazil. It is based on the polytheistic religion of the Yoruba, who were transported to the Spanish and Portuguese colonies in great numbers. The Yoruba believed in multiple gods called *orishas*. As the dominance of the Catholic Church in the colonies gradually transformed the religion, the Yoruba gods merged with the Catholic saints. "During the course of their captivity," explains a Puerto Rican writer, "the Yorubas started to recognize their gods behind the white facade of the Catholic images."[13] Thus the orisha Chango (Shango), god of fire and storms, is identified with Saint Barbara. Olorun-Olofi, the creator, represents the Crucified Christ. Oggun, god of iron and war, is Saint Peter; and so on. The orishas are credited with supernatural powers, and followers of santeria practice a complex magic with herbs and ritual objects for the purpose of healing or casting spells. Although it originated as an Afro-Christian cult, many of the white Spanish and Portuguese settlers also became involved with santería, and today it is widespread throughout the Spanish-speaking Caribbean.

* * *

As if floating on a higher plane, the colonial Church remained aloof and defensive toward these challenges. Its contributions to justice and liberation were minimal, while its collaboration with the power structure of colonial society was a self-conscious and chosen role. It was as if the Church couldn't see the forest of its own biblical revelation for the trees of its forms, fashions, and filial relationship with the colonial system.

It was the black majority which constantly called out for the Church to hear and respond. The emergence of the Afro-Christian religions was the first major challenge to the colonial Church. It set the stage for the 1920s and 30s, when black religiosity would be a seminal influence in the explosive popular rebellion against the Church, the colonial powers, and the established social order. ∎

Batá drums of Cuba, used in ceremonies worshipping Yoruba orishas.

Unifying Themes in Caribbean Cultures

The overwhelming cultural characteristic of the Caribbean, taken as the sum of all its parts, is heterogeneity. In race, in culture, in language and religion, it is one of the most diverse geographic areas in the world. But this larger regional picture should not be mistaken for the social reality at the national level. While the Jamaican nationalist slogan and myth—"Out of Many, One People"—suggests an equal contribution from numerous ethnic groups, the truth is that Jamaica is an Afro-Caribbean nation, with 95% of its population black or brown. Other Caribbean countries are bicultural, notably the African/East Indian societies of Trinidad and Guyana. Still others are truly multi-ethnic—the quadrilingual mosaic of Curacao, for example.

A cultural map of the Caribbean reveals almost impassable barriers and omnipresent, interconnecting links. The primary barriers are the ones imposed by colonialism, which carved the region into Spanish, British, French and Dutch empires. These divisions have persisted into the era of political independence. Thus the English-speaking Caribbean is a world unto itself, Anglicized, and more recently, Americanized; the Spanish-speaking islands consider themselves part of Latin America; the French *départements* look only toward France; and the Dutch Antilles are mired in confusion, torn between African, Amerindian, Dutch, Venezuelan, and U.S. influences.

The linkages are more subtle. Despite the colonial divisions between Caribbean societies, their histories are parallel and intertwined. What unity there is rests upon this shared experience: of African or Asian origins (for the majority), of slavery and indentured servitude, of colonial domination, and of a present status on the periphery of the world economy. These historical connections link people in a way which sometimes transcends the colonial barriers. French-based *patois,* for instance, is understood not only in Haiti, Guadeloupe and Martinique, but also in the neighboring English-speaking islands of St. Lucia and Dominica which were colonized first by the French.

The Spanish-speaking countries of the Greater Antilles stand somewhat apart from this variant of the Caribbean experience. They had plantation slavery, but it developed on a large scale only after two centuries of Spanish settler colonialism. Over generations, the Spanish, the African slaves, and the surviving Arawak Indians blended together. Cuba and Puerto Rico developed as light-skinned *mestizo* (Spanish/Indian) nations, with the Spanish racial influence dominant. The Dominican Republic, on the other hand, became predominantly mulatto (African/European) because of the large number of slaves and the flight of most of the Spanish settlers during the country's occupation by Haiti from 1822 to 1844.

Dancing the merengue in the Dominican Republic: Afro-Latin roots.

El Nuevo Diario

The Spanish-speaking islands have a cultural unity arising out of their own historical links. The ties between Cuba and Puerto Rico are particularly strong. Their independence struggles from Spain were jointly planned in the 1860s by the Cuban patriot José Martí and the Puerto Rican doctor Ramon Emeterio Betances; many Puerto Ricans fought and died in Cuba's war to free itself from Spanish control. The North American takeover of Spain's colonies in 1898 created a barrier to this growing Cuban/Puerto Rican unity, but the nearly identical flags of the two countries testify to the closeness which once existed.

As elsewhere in Latin America, the struggle against colonial Spain did not mean a rejection of Spanish culture for the people of Cuba, the Dominican Republic, and Puerto Rico. This is particularly true in the Dominican Republic, where the dictator Trujillo promoted Latin culture as a way of rejecting the country's experience under Haitian rule. Because of this, Dominican culture contains strong elements of anti-black racism, even though most Dominicans are themselves mulattoes of mixed Black/Spanish descent.

But cultural links do exist between the Spanish Caribbean and the West Indies. Fidel Castro shocked many in the Latin world when he declared Cuba to be an Afro-Latin country, but he was recognizing a reality which exists throughout the Spanish-speaking Caribbean. Many Cubans are black or mestizo, although the urban middle class is predominantly of Spanish descent. African elements are strongly evident in the country's music and dance, and there is even a distinctive Afro-Cuban dialect of Spanish. African influences also are present in Puerto Rico and the Dominican Republic, although they do not receive official recognition. Black Puerto Ricans living along the island's coasts, where the slave plantations once were located, still perform the African dances of *la bomba* and *la plena*. La bomba has Ashanti origins, and is similar to dances in Jamaica and Haiti. Dominican blacks and mestizos in the countryside perform drum dances called *los palos;* a festival involving this dance was outlawed by Trujillo in his campaign to eradicate African influences from Dominican culture.

The one thing all Caribbean societies have in common is a colonial past. Through its components of racism, migration, and class oppression, colonialism gave rise to three themes woven throughout the Caribbean cultural tapestry. They are the *class basis* of Caribbean cultures, their use of creative *synthesis,* and *culture as resistance.*

The Class-Color-Culture Triangle

The correlation between skin shade and social class has become a truism of Caribbean life. White (with admixtures of Syrian, Jewish, and Chinese) equals upper-class; mulatto or brown is middle-class; while the black and East Indian majority occupies the base of the social pyramid. But within these broad parameters exists a more complex stratification resulting from social mobility through education, property ownership, and marriage.

. . . The class-colour correlates of the West Indian social structure are real. But they are not the absolutes of a rigid caste system. Skin colour determines social class; but it is not an exclusive determinant. There are many fair-skinned persons who are not upper-class, and many dark-skinned persons who are. The real divisions of the society are the horizontal ones of social class rather than the vertical ones of colour identification.[1]

These horizontal class divisions, pegged broadly to color, carry with them a host of cultural implications. The European identification of the elite—the British mores of Jamaica's "21 families," or the Frenchness of Martinique's native white *békés*—sets the standard for the society, becoming the goal toward which the middle class aspires. Even in the Spanish-speaking islands, where cultural blending has been greater, "*La Madre Patria*" (Spain the Motherland) is a theme primarily stressed by the light-skinned urban class. Historically, Caribbean societies have looked down upon the culture of the popular classes. Yet as Gordon K. Lewis argues, it is here that the vibrancy and creativity of the Caribbean finds expression; it is here that the region comes closest to creating an identity of its own.

For if there is a common West Indian culture, it has been created, first and foremost, by the social classes at the bottom... They, more than any others, have been the culture carriers, for the higher rung groups have been inhibited by the hybrid forms of European culture they have imbibed from playing that role.[2]

Puerto Rican farm worker, 1945.

20

SOME AFRICAN WORDS IN CONTEMPORARY JAMAICAN SPEECH

Caribbean slaves belonged to many different African ethnic groups, each with its own language. Many African words are incorporated into West Indian creole speech, especially from the Twi language in Jamaica, and from Yoruba in Trinidad and Cuba.

Jamaican	Twi	
Afu	Afuw	A species of yam.
Bankra	Bonkara	A wicker basket.
Bobo	Booboo	Someone who is lazy, dull, or silent.
Bufu-bufu	Bofoo	A fat person.
Cuffie	Kofi	A common man's name in the West Indies. In Twi, the name for a man born on a Friday.
Kas-kas	Kasakasa	To talk loudly, argue.
Nana	Nana	A title of honor and endearment.
Nyaka-nyaka	Nyaka-nyaka	To work in a sloppy fashion.
Obeah	Obayi	Witchcraft.
Ono	Ono	Third-person pronoun.
Patu	Apatu	Owl, with supernatural significance.
Senseh	Asense	A type of fowl, used to detect witchcraft.

Adapted from Leonard Barrett, *The Sun and the Drum: African Roots in Jamaican Folk Tradition*

The use of language reflects class divisions. The languages and dialects of the region form a continuum, with Caribbean variants of "standard" English, French and Spanish at one pole, and the patois or creole tongues at the other. Many gradations exist in between. The continuum correlates roughly to class, most strongly so in the French islands. In Haiti, Martinique, and Guadeloupe, the majority of the population speaks only *kréyòl* (Creole) and does not understand French. Yet French is the official language used in the schools, the government, courts of law, etc. In the English-speaking islands the contrast is not as great, but being able to speak standard English is still considered the mark of an educated person. Reflecting the strength of popular culture, however, it is generally true that everyone native to a given country, including the middle and upper class, understands the local patois and often uses it in private situations. This process has been carried farthest in the Dutch Antilles, where Papiamento (a blending of Portuguese and African elements) has emerged as the national language. While higher education is still in Dutch, Papiamento has largely replaced Dutch for daily spoken use, and is increasingly the language of the national literature and the press.

Religion is another class "marker," reflecting the historic competition between the colonial churches and the African cults. Jamaican author Leonard Barrett tells of the division in his own family between his mother's relatives, who belong to the brown middle class, and his father's family, black Jamaicans from a rural background. The former are Christian churchgoers, while the latter follow the Afro-Christian Pocomania cult.[3] As people move up the social ladder, they tend to leave the cults in favor of mainline denominations such as the English Baptists, Methodists, and Presbyterians. Each country also has its "high-status" denominations historically associated with the colonial ruling class: Anglicanism in territories colonized by Britain, Catholicism in those colonized by the French and in the Dominican Republic, U.S. Protestantism in Puerto Rico, and Dutch Protestantism in the Dutch Antilles.

The "official" view of popular culture, however, has changed somewhat in recent years. With political independence, the new black and brown leadership has turned to the people's culture as a reservoir of authenticity in the struggle to forge a national identity. The international commercial success of Caribbean creations such as Carnival, steelband, calypso and reggae has been an added impetus. Carnival, which began as a sedate French Lenten celebration, exploded onto the cultural scene when the black working class of Trinidad took it over after emancipation. The festival's spectacular costumes and parades now draw visitors to Trinidad from all over the world. Likewise, calypso, steelband, and reggae—now highly commercialized—were born in the poverty of Port-of-Spain and Kingston slums. When the Trinidad government discovered that Carnival and steelband made good tourist attractions, it gave them official sponsorship and new respect, which also served to bring them under closer control.

Synthesis and Resistance

A second theme which marks Caribbean cultures is *synthesis*—the seamless blending and transformation of elements from sources as diverse as Africa, Spain, Elizabethan England, France, and 20th century America.

> From its opening moment of *jour overt* and the "ole mas" costume bands to its finale, forty-eight hours later, in the dusk of Mardi Carnival, the Trinidadian populace gives itself up to the "jump up," the tempestuous abandon of Carnival . . . Port-of-Spain becomes a panic of mob art: the Sailor Bands, sometimes of five thousand or more . . . the Seabees groups, mocking their original United States Navy inspiration with their exaggerated high-ranking officer titles and overblown campaign ribbons . . . impertinent personifications of, variously, Texas Rangers, French Foreign Legionnaires, British Palace Guards and Nazi High Command officers . . . [4]

And underneath it all runs "a powerful undercurrent of Shango, bamboo-tamboo, canboulay, of the secret Negro cults of the Americas."[5] Similarly, the Jonkonnu Christmas parade which once flourished in Jamaica, Belize, Bermuda, and the Leeward Islands integrated African elements such as the horsehead, cowhead, and devil costumes with masked caricatures of British kings and queens.

The West Indian music known as calypso is another example of how Caribbean people have borrowed from diverse sources to create an original art form. Originating in Trinidad in the 1800s, calypso has roots in the African oral tradition. Early calypso lyrics were in French-based patois, then shifted to English toward the end of the century. Musical influences on calypso included French and Spanish music (from those colonial periods in Trinidad), East Indian drumming, and Revivalist spirituals. During World War Two, with hundreds of U.S. soldiers stationed in Trinidad, calypso absorbed influences from rhythm and blues, swing, and bebop, along with an increasing degree of commercialism.

The same blending process underlies the Afro-Latin cultures. The national dance of the Dominican Republic is the *merengue,* which was originated by the Dominican peasantry using African instruments and drums. The upper class traditionally scorned the merengue, preferring to dance the waltz. But gradually a synthesis occurred: Spanish instruments such as the *tres* and *cuatro,* the accordion and the *bandeon* were incorporated into the merengue alongside the African drums. This Europeanized merengue was called *merengue de salon,* or "parlor merengue." It became popular with the middle and upper class in the towns, and merengue is now a national passion spanning all classes in the Dominican Republic.

Closely intertwined with the theme of synthesis is the theme of *culture as resistance* which runs through Caribbean history. By borrowing elements of European culture and subsuming them into new, original forms, Caribbean people fought back against cultural domination. This is often done in the form of satire—in the ribald parodies of the Carnival masquerade, for example, or the grotesque white-face masks of Jonkonnu. Such irreverent humor has its roots in the slavery era, when one form of slave resistance was subtle mockery of the ruling class.

In West Indian cultural resistance, the drum has always held pride of place. Drums were used in Africa for long-distance communication, and Africans on the Caribbean plantations continued this practice. Fearful of any communication or organization among the slaves, the planters outlawed the drum. The ban continued after emancipation, since the planters and the missionaries considered drumming subversive and an obstacle to the assimilation of the blacks. But they could never totally suppress it. In the late 1800s, West Indians beat out rhythms on the ground with cured bamboo sticks, a practice called *bamboo-tamboo.* In the 1930s and 40s, young men in the urban slums of Trinidad turned to using metal biscuit tins and old oil drums, and the modern steel band—"pan"—was born.

In the Spanish-speaking Caribbean, culture has served less as resistance to the original Spanish colonialism than as resistance to the North American imperialism which replaced it. This is particularly true in Puerto Rico, where political annexation of the island has meant heavy pressure to assimilate U.S. culture. To retain their identity as a people, Puerto Ricans have drawn on the indigenous culture of the *jíbaro,* or Puerto Rican peasant, and on their Latin heritage. Pride in the Spanish language itself has become a form of resistance for Puerto Ricans. ∎

PAN RECIPE

First rape a people
simmer for centuries

bring memories to boil
foil voice of drum

add pinch of pain
to rain of rage

stifle drum again
then mix strains of blood

over slow fire
watch fever grow

til energy burst
with rhythm thirst

cut bamboo and cure
whip well like hell

stir sound from dustbin
pound handful biscuit tin

cover down in shanty town
and leave mixture alone

when ready will explode

— John Agard, Guyana

Links to Central America: The Atlantic Coast

Most North Americans think of Honduras, Nicaragua, Costa Rica and Panama as Latin or mestizo nations—as indeed, in terms of their population majorities, they are. But the traveler who journeys to the isolated, sparsely-populated Caribbean or Atlantic coast of Central America is in for a surprise. Spanish place names are interspersed with towns like Bluefields, Nicaragua; Brewers, Honduras; Livingston, Guatemala; and Stann Creek, Belize. Goods imported from England line store shelves and cater to the tastes of a population more West Indian than Spanish in its cultural identification. The coastal population is primarily of African and Amerindian descent; people speak more English than Spanish, and Protestant religion dominates over Catholicism.

Early British Colonization

Although Spain laid claim to all of Central America in the 16th century, the absence of precious metals, the lack of a large indigenous work force, and the difficult climate and topography kept the Spanish from maintaining a physical presence along the Atlantic coast of the isthmus. But for British pirates, the swampy coastal lagoons and rivers were perfect supply and refuge sites; and there were valuable timbers to be harvested. In 1655, after capturing Jamaica from Spain, Britain moved into the Atlantic coast to challenge Spain's nominal claim. Based at Providence Island and Cape Gracias a Dios, the British founded settlements all along the coast as far north as British Honduras (present-day Belize).

English colonization of the Atlantic coast took on two distinct forms. With the Indians living along the Miskito Coast of Nicaragua, the British traded firearms and metal tools for turtle meat, lumber and fish. They formed alliances with the Miskito Indians, using them as guerrilla forces to counter Spain's occasional attempts to regain control. The British even set up a Miskito monarchy of British-educated "kings" who presided over the area, loyal to the British Crown.[1]

In Belize, Bluefields, and the Bay Islands off Honduras, on the other hand, English settlers cut logwood and mahogany or grew indigo, sugar and bananas. These industries required a large labor force, so the British brought in African slaves captured from the Spanish or purchased in Jamaica. In Belize, slaves accounted for 71% of the settlement population by 1745, leading to many slave revolts and escapes requiring intervention from the British naval forces based in Jamaica.[2] In these areas, then, the Caribbean colonial/slavery model dominated.

Garífuna drummers in Belize.

Belize Government
Information Service

23

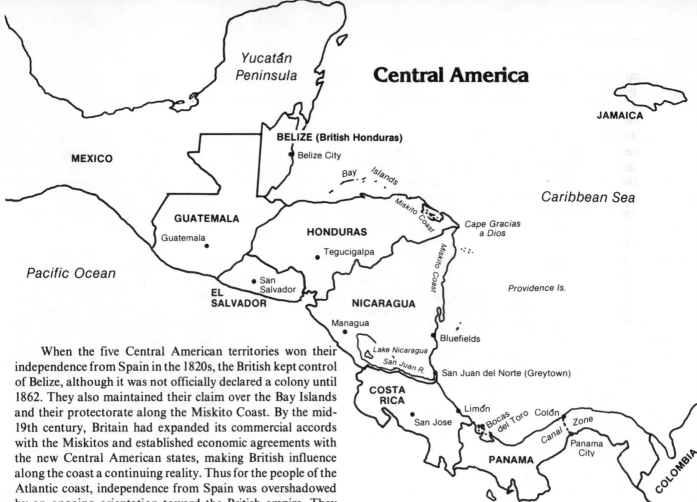

Central America

(Map labels: Yucatán Peninsula, MEXICO, BELIZE (British Honduras), Belize City, JAMAICA, Bay Islands, Miskito Coast, GUATEMALA, Guatemala, HONDURAS, Tegucigalpa, Cape Gracias a Dios, Caribbean Sea, Pacific Ocean, San Salvador, EL SALVADOR, Miskito Coast, Providence Is., NICARAGUA, Managua, Bluefields, Lake Nicaragua, San Juan R., San Juan del Norte (Greytown), COSTA RICA, San Jose, Limón, Bocas del Toro, Colón, Zone, Canal, Panama City, PANAMA, COLOMBIA)

When the five Central American territories won their independence from Spain in the 1820s, the British kept control of Belize, although it was not officially declared a colony until 1862. They also maintained their claim over the Bay Islands and their protectorate along the Miskito Coast. By the mid-19th century, Britain had expanded its commercial accords with the Miskitos and established economic agreements with the new Central American states, making British influence along the coast a continuing reality. Thus for the people of the Atlantic coast, independence from Spain was overshadowed by an ongoing orientation toward the British empire. They imported British goods, spoke English and acquired Anglo customs, setting them apart from the dominant Spanish-mestizo cultures in the central regions and on the Pacific side of the isthmus.

Yet this British influence represented not a fully developed colonialism, but a limited, *enclave* model of foreign domination. It laid the basis for a continuing exploitation by foreign governments and corporations (mostly British and North American) which occupied areas of Central America with little regard for either the sovereignty or boundaries of states. This model led to both the underdevelopment of the enclave areas and their isolation from larger national societies, contributing to the historic impoverishment of the Atlantic coast region.

The Trans-Isthmian Enclave

The British presence was soon to be challenged by the emerging power to the north, the United States. In 1823, President James Monroe announced what came to be called the Monroe Doctrine, warning the European powers against further colonization in the western hemisphere, while leaving the way open for future U.S. expansion.

By the 1840s, the United States had reached its western continental limit, California. Beginning in 1846, Americans stampeded west to claim land in the Oregon territory, and in 1848 the California Gold Rush began. Both made it profitable for business interests to provide a fast route to the west coast, as the overland crossing by covered wagon was slow and

dangerous. The preferred route was around the continent by steamship, requiring a passageway across the Central American isthmus.

One such route was through Panama, then a department of Colombia. U.S. financiers first provided passage across Panama by horse-drawn carriage, and in 1855 completed the construction of the Panama Railroad. The presence of the railroad and of North American travelers required protection along the passage strip, so a Texas Ranger named Ran Ruggles was hired to organize a police force, while U.S. Marines intervened in Panama five times between 1856 and 1865 to put down protests or strikes along the route.[3]

A shorter route lay to the north in Nicaragua. Here a traveler could board a boat at Greytown (San Juan del Norte) on the Atlantic coast, sail up the San Juan River into Lake Nicaragua and across the lake, leaving only a twelve-mile trip over land to reach the Pacific. This passage was controlled by the Accessory Transit Company owned by U.S. railroad magnate Cornelius Vanderbilt.

But the mouth of the San Juan River was part of the British protectorate over the Miskito coast, and Britain quickly challenged the right of the U.S. to monopolize transit through the area. The issue was temporarily resolved by the Clayton-Bulwer Treaty of 1850, in which it was agreed that neither the U.S. nor Britain would unilaterally build a canal through Central America. The treaty also prohibited either side from attempting to occupy or rule any part of the isthmus, so Britain eventually gave up its protectorate over the Bay Islands and the Miskito Coast.

In Nicaragua too, the presence of U.S. interests encouraged bids for political control. This was temporarily realized in the 1850s by a North American filibuster (adventurer) named William Walker, who was invited into Nicaragua by the Liberals to aid in their fight against the Conservatives. Heading a small mercenary army and backed by the Accessory Transit Co., Walker gained control over all of Nicaragua and became president in 1856.

The slave states of the U.S. South, fearing that their plantation days were numbered, saw Walker's activities as a beachhead for the expansion of slavery into all of Central America and thus a way to bolster their weakening position. Walker did reinstitute slavery in Nicaragua, hoping for southern support to counter the U.S. government's rising opposition to his role. But he was defeated on May 1, 1857 by the combined armies of other Central American states (who feared the filibustering model) and by an epidemic of cholera among his troops.[4]

The Panamanian and Nicaraguan passageways represented a continuation of Britain's enclave approach by the U.S., which sought to control limited strips of territory for specific economic and political ends. Once they had served their purpose, however, these enclaves and their inhabitants often were abandoned without a second thought. When the first transcontinental railroad across the United States was completed in 1867, the Panama Railroad fell into bankruptcy. San Juan del Norte on the Miskito coast became a backwater, undeveloped and forgotten for a hundred years.

The Banana Company Enclaves

By the 1890s, U.S. interests had moved into the Atlantic coast region to begin large-scale banana exports, along with lesser exports of cocoa, sugar and timber. One of the first was a U.S. railroad magnate, Minor Keith, who acquired land in Colombia, Panama and Costa Rica to plant bananas. Keith's holdings in Bocas del Toro, Panama and Limón, Costa Rica formed a single large operation and later led to disputes between Costa Rica and Panama as to where the border between them actually lay.

In Honduras, the hundreds of small traders exporting bananas to the United States between 1870 and 1890 shrank to twenty as the great fruit trusts began expanding overseas. By 1894, their number was reduced to three: the Boston Fruit Company, which also had holdings in Cuba, Jamaica and Puerto Rico; the Cuyamel Fruit Company; and Vacarro Brothers (later Standard Fruit). In 1899, Keith merged his holdings with those of the Boston Fruit Company to form the United Fruit Company, which came to control 80% of the U.S. banana market.[5]

United Fruit built its Honduran operation into a vast infrastructural enclave. Honduras, seeking a railroad to improve internal transportation, agreed to give the company 15,000 acres of land in exchange for building the Tela Railroad. But the railroad did not link the capital of Tegucigalpa to the coast, nor even the coastal towns to one another; rather, each segment linked a banana plantation to an Atlantic coast port. In thirty years, only 50 miles of "national" railroad was completed, while United Fruit built 900 miles of crisscrossed rails connecting its land holdings.[6]

The Canal Enclave

Competition between the United States and Great Britain for control of the Caribbean temporarily slackened during the last quarter of the 19th century. England's imperial might was waning, and the U.S. was bogged down with its Civil War and postwar reconstruction. Into this vacuum stepped the French, fresh from their successful completion of the Suez Canal. In 1878, France obtained a concession from Colombia to build a canal, and in 1880 the digging began.

But the narrow strip of land turned out to be far more formidable than anyone had imagined: a "geologist's nightmare" of volcanic bedrock, mountains, jungle and swamp. The French attempt was a costly failure, with thousands of deaths among the West Indian contract laborers who did the digging. The French bid spurred the United States to undertake a canal quickly lest some European power establish such a crucial foothold in the U.S. "backyard." The canal also was seen as essential to the United States' continued commercial expansion, including a link to the markets of the Orient. President Rutherford Hayes said in 1880:

> The objective of this country is a canal under American control. The United States cannot consent to turning over this control to some European power nor to some combination of European powers . . . Our commercial interest in the canal is greater than that of other countries, while its relationship to our means of defense, our unity, peace and security is a matter of primary importance for the people of the United States.[7]

The Spanish-American War of 1898 provided the final motivation for the canal: a strategic defense rationale based on the need to move U.S. warships from the Pacific to the Atlantic without sailing around Cape Horn. The U.S. first attempted to negotiate with Colombia for rights to build and control a canal. When this was rejected, the U.S. orchestrated a Panamanian revolt against Colombian control and promptly concluded a "treaty" with the newly-independent state. The treaty was signed on Panama's behalf by a Frenchman, Bunau-Varilla, a representative of the bankrupt French Canal Co. which hoped to recoup some of its losses by selling the remaining French interests in the canal to the U.S. No Panamanian signed the Panama Canal Treaty of 1903.

The great majority of construction workers on both the Panama railroad and the canal were contract laborers from the West Indies. During the French attempt to build the canal, some 38,000 workers were brought to Panama, including 18,000 Jamaicans and 8,000 Haitians.[8] When the U.S. took over the project, the Panama Canal Company recruited another 45,107 workers, of whom 31,071 came from the Caribbean. Most of these came from Barbados, Guadeloupe and Martinique.[9] Because these migratory waves arrived in a sparsely populated, primarily campesino society, the Panamanian working class essentially developed as a result of this foreign immigration.

Belize: The British Enclave

The exception to this pattern of expanding U.S. influence was British Honduras, the only formal British colony in Central America. Renamed Belize in 1966, the colony developed along lines which largely paralleled the history of the British West Indies, but with important differences. The basis of the Belizian economy was timber, which was less important to Britain than its sugar production in the Caribbean. Also, there was a large indigenous population of Mayan Indians which was not, as in the West Indies, completely destroyed. Instead, the foreign settlers pushed the Indians farther and farther into the interior, where they lived isolated from the settler economy along the coast.[12]

Within the slave-based colonial society, however, there were many parallels. As in the West Indies, the Africans in Belize continuously resisted their servitude. Slave uprisings in the 1760s culminated in a large revolt in 1773 which was put down by a British naval force from Jamaica. The last revolt occurred in 1820 under the leadership of two slaves named Will and Sharper. There was also a continuous movement of runaway slaves into remote areas of interior Belize and neighboring Mexico, Guatemala and Honduras.

Another link to the islands were the Black Caribs, known in Belize as the Garífuna. They were descendents of Carib Indians who intermarried with escaped African slaves on St. Vincent. After they rebelled in 1795, about 5,000 Garífuna were exiled by the British to the Bay Islands off Honduras, from which some migrated to Belize. The settlers used the Garífuna as another source of slave labor in the mahogany camps.

After emancipation in 1838, Belizean blacks, like their West Indian counterparts, entered a new period of hardship. The situation of land ownership and wage labor paralleled that in the West Indies. The mahogany cutters owned the best land; in fact, most of the privately-owned land in Belize belonged to an elite group of twelve families. Through anti-squatting laws

WEST INDIAN WORKERS ON THE PANAMA CANAL

The construction of the Panama Canal is commonly depicted in history books as a North American achievement, the fruit of U.S. engineering and medical advances. Those were important factors, but it was the people of the Caribbean, along with other foreign laborers, who actually built the Canal between 1881 and 1914. Driven by economic need, they labored and died in the Panamanian jungle so the United States could realize its grandiose dream.[10]

Many of the workers during the French period of construction came from Jamaica, but there were also Cubans, South Americans, Europeans, Chinese, and blacks from the United States. This ill-fated group labored under horrifying conditions. Before the canal could be dug, the men had to hack their way through thick tropical jungle and swamps infested with poisonous snakes and stinging vermin. Panama's oppressive heat and humidity made the work a nightmare, especially during the rainy season, which lasted eight months of the year. There was little fresh food or pure drinking water, and the terminal towns of Colon and Panama City became sinkholes of diseases including dysentery, pneumonia, tuberculosis, typhoid, yellow fever and the bubonic plague. Once the digging began into the mountainous core of the isthmus, landslides added a new element of danger. It is estimated that 20,000 workers died during the disastrous French attempt to dig the canal.

After the United States took over the project, the government of Jamaica refused to allow any further recruiting of canal workers. But recruits flooded in from the other depressed, overcrowded islands of the British and French West Indies, especially Barbados, where the lack of available land and high unemployment made many people desperate for income. Some 20,000 Barbadians left for work on the canal during the construction years—40% of the adult male population of the island.

The workers were given free passage to Panama and guaranteed repatriation after 500 working days. Wages were 10 cents an hour for heavy labor such as digging out rock with a pick and shovel. While the black workers thus made about $24 a month—considered good money at the time—salaries for the white Americans working as overseers and technicians averaged $87 a month. The black laborers received their pay in Panamanian silver coins, the North Americans in gold.

A caste system permeated every aspect of life in the Canal Zone. Housing, schools, hospitals and mess halls were segregated into "silver" and "gold," which became code words for black and white. While the North American workers lived comfortably in modern housing provided for them, the West Indians were crowded into the slums of Colon and Panama City, or lived in makeshift jungle camps.

Due to improved sanitation and the eradication of disease-carrying mosquitos, only about 5,600 deaths occurred during the U.S. phase of the project. However, black workers died at a rate four times that of the white workers. Many others were maimed by accidents or disease. Visiting a black hospital ward, one observer wrote:

> Some of the costs of the Canal are here. Sturdy black men in a sort of bed-tick pajamas sitting on the verandas or in wheel chairs, some with one leg gone, some with both. One could not help but wonder how it feels to be hopelessly ruined in body early in life for helping to dig a trench for a foreign power that, however well it may treat you materially, cares not a whistle-blast more for you than for its old worn-out locomotives rusting away in the jungle.[11]

and high land prices, the British kept the freed slaves from forming independent farming communities, leaving them with no choice but to perform contract labor in the mahogany camps.

Meanwhile, the Mayan Indians underwent the final phase of their subjugation by the British. In 1848, the Indians in the Yucatan peninsula in Mexico rebelled against the Spanish, and in the resulting chaos, thousands of Indians and mestizos fled south to Belize. These refugees formed farming communities which grew rice, corn, vegetables and sugar for subsistence and export. In fact, Indian sugar production was so successful that the big landowners of Belize decided to take it over. With their land and capital, they set up sugar plantations using steam machinery on which they forced the Indians to work as wage laborers.

By 1866, some Mayan refugees had migrated into central Belize where they founded independent villages near the mahogany works. In 1867, three hundred British soldiers invaded the principle Mayan village and burned it to the ground, along with the Indians' crops. The Mayan chief, Marcos Canul, fought the British for five years but was finally defeated in 1872. From then on, the Indians were incorporated into the colonial structure as a dispossessed and dominated minority.

Because of this resistance in the interior, the British focused their attention on the coast, with most of the population concentrated in Belize City. However, the spirit of resistance was strong among the blacks as well. In 1894, a group of mahogany workers demanded higher wages and upon being refused, looted the properties of the merchants and contractors. Troops from a British warship stationed off the coast were landed to quell the rebellion, and most of the leaders of the uprising fled into the interior or into Mexico. Belize entered the 20th century a stagnant colonial enclave, with the majority of its people living in poverty along the coast or isolated in the undeveloped interior. ∎

National Archives

Laborers loading holes with dynamite at the Culebra Cut, October 10, 1913.

Roots of U.S. Imperialism in the Greater Antilles

Decline of Spanish Colonialism Leads to U.S. Penetration

Following the "horror and the glory" of the Spanish conquest, the Spanish Caribbean took a back seat to the riches of Mexico and Peru, falling into more than two centuries of controlled neglect. This stagnation was interrupted in 1799 by the Haitian Revolution, the first major challenge to colonial rule in the Caribbean. Not only was Toussaint L'Ouverture's slave army powerful enough to defeat the French and British forces; but once independent, Haiti went on to seize the western part of Hispaniola from Spain in 1822.

With this challenge to European domination came the first bid by the United States to exert its influence over the region. The U.S. coveted the Caribbean trade, but was not ready to overtly challenge the European powers. Opportunity appeared with the sudden independence of Haiti and then Santo Domingo, which freed itself from Haitian control and became the Dominican Republic in 1844. Haiti, facing economic isolation, needed North American markets to survive. Toussaint therefore signed two agreements, one with the U.S. and another with England, granting them commercial and maritime rights that opened up Haiti to economic penetration.[1] In the Dominican Republic, the emerging middle class, anxious to secure its weak independence, turned over Samana Bay to the U.S. as an economic base and finally attempted to annex the whole country to the United States in 1877, a motion which failed in the U.S. Senate by only one vote.[2] Economic necessity in the case of Haiti and middle-class opportunism in the Dominican Republic thus opened the door to the United States long before the U.S. was strong enough to take over the islands by force.

During the 19th century, Spain tried everything to hold on to its restless Caribbean empire: troops, treaties, settlers. Ironically, the influx of Spanish settlers into Cuba, Puerto Rico and Santo Domingo after 1815 led to the formation of a nationalist middle class on each island which eventually challenged Spanish control.[3] In Cuba, the *autonomistas* joined with freed Cuban slaves to fight for independence in a decade-long war (1868-78) spearheaded by the black brigadier-general Antonio Maceo. Spain was steadily forced to yield ground to these internal independence movements, granting autonomy to Cuba and Puerto Rico in 1897.

Proximity and a vastly larger market made the United States a far more advantageous trading partner for the Spanish Caribbean than was Spain itself. U.S. firms moved steadily into the Greater Antilles during the 1870s and 1880s to grow and export sugar and bananas. By 1877, exports from Puerto Rico to Spain totalled only 709,000 pesos, while those to the United States were valued at 4,702,000 pesos.[4]

U.S. flag raised over San Juan, Puerto Rico on October 18, 1898.

National Archives

It was within this context that the United States forced Spain to sign the Commercial Treaty of 1891, facilitating U.S. trade with Cuba and Puerto Rico and in effect handing over economic supremacy in the Spanish Caribbean to the U.S. This agreement was the handwriting on the wall which virtually guaranteed some form of U.S. military challenge to Spain. The Spanish-American War broke out only seven years later.

The Expansionist Dream

Until the 1870s, most North Americans were anti-colonialist and anti-imperialist in spirit, believing themselves morally superior to the colonial exploiters of Europe. This was

to change, however, as the United States' evolving capitalism began producing more goods than the domestic market could absorb. By the 1880s, this overcapacity had led to economic depression, and U.S. business interests began searching for ways to acquire new markets and areas for investment abroad.

In government, business circles, and the press, many influential voices argued for a southward expansion. "The day is not distant," one senator proclaimed, "when the dominion of the United States will be extended . . . to every part of the American continent—British America, Mexico, Cuba, Central America, and the islands on our coast."[5] U.S. businessmen and politicians organized the American Annexation League in 1878 to push for the annexation of territories in Latin America and Canada.

This drive toward empire was cloaked, however, in pseudo-scientific and moralistic rationalizations. One such concept evolved out of Charles Darwin's *Origin of the Species* and came to be called Social Darwinism. According to this thesis, if the United States was not to perish in the struggle for survival of the fittest, it must compete fiercely with other nations, taking over or controlling weaker lands. Reinforcing this theory was blatant racism—belief in an inherent Anglo-Saxon superiority which supposedly gave the United States the right and duty to "bring civilization" to other lands. One newspaper declared:

> The miserable republics of Central America, peopled by a degraded half-race of humanity, will yet bow to the rule of the Anglo-American . . . [and Americans will carry] moral and material well-being to the disintegrating communities and decaying races of Spanish America.[6]

These ideas all formed part of the credo known in the U.S. as "Manifest Destiny," meaning that God had intended white North Americans to take over and control the entire hemisphere.

A second rationalization arose from Captain Alfred Mahan's famous *Influence of Sea Power on History* (1890) which defined naval power as the key to national supremacy. Mahan stressed the relationship between overseas expansion and U.S. economic growth: "Whether they will or no, Americans must begin to look outward. The growing production of the country demands it . . . "[7] Mahan made clear that this expansion depended on a strong U.S. Navy and on control of the strategically located Caribbean territories of Cuba, Puerto Rico and Panama.[8] His ideas had a major impact on leaders such as John Hay, Theodore Roosevelt, and Henry Cabot Lodge, as well as on the North American public, paving the way for direct U.S. intervention in the Caribbean Basin over the next thirty years.

Shifting Caribbean Paramountcy: From Great Britain to the United States

Before this expansionist dream could be put into practice, the dominant Caribbean power—Great Britain—had to be somehow edged out of the region. Despite the Monroe Doctrine of 1823, the Caribbean was still basically considered a British lake. The West Indies were studded with British strongholds, and British warships outnumbered the American fleet by seven to one. The United States hardly dared challenge England on the high seas, but by the 1840s, the U.S. was signing treaties with Britain which politely signaled America's imperialist intent.

The issue of the British presence came to a head in 1895 in relation to a boundary dispute between Venezuela and the colony of British Guiana. The British stronghold at the mouth of the Orinoco River in Venezuela was strategically placed to control the Amazon and the entrance to the Caribbean at the southern tip of the Windward Island chain. It was here that the U.S. chose to make a decisive challenge. Venezuela wanted the British out, and the United States, while not openly siding with Venezuela, delivered a powerful message to the British literally ordering them to resolve the matter. When the British refused, the issue of the Monroe Doctrine was drawn, implying the ominous possibility of war with the United States.

The crisis was resolved when the United States softened its terms slightly and the hesitating British backed down. An Anglo-American agreement was signed setting the terms for a treaty between Great Britain and Venezuela. In effect, England had given in peacefully to U.S. pressures and yielded paramountcy in the region. As one historian wrote:

> In the Caribbean, Britain's surrender of 1896 proved to be only the beginning of a process which within a decade converted the hitherto British-dominated sea into a primary defense zone of the United States.[10]

The Spanish-American War of 1898

By the 1890s the independence struggle in Cuba was far advanced, drawing its ideological leadership from the Cuban nationalist intellectual José Martí. In 1894 the United States imposed a duty on Cuban sugar exports, which until then had been duty-free by agreement with Spain. This blow to the island's economy triggered renewed armed rebellion within the context of the Cuban independence movement. Insurgents roamed freely through most of the country, while Spain controlled Havana, the seaports, and the larger towns. Some of the property held by the insurgents was U.S.-owned and the rebels began setting fire to sugar cane fields, hoping to provoke an American intervention on their behalf.

North American business interests were by then entrenched in Cuba with around $50 million in investments, mainly in sugar production. They hoped for a peaceful settlement of the crisis, since the war was hurting profits. In 1894, U.S. exports to Cuba were worth $20 million, but by 1898 they had fallen to $10 million. U.S. imports from Cuba sank from $76 million to $15 million in the same period.[11]

The Liberals in Cuba replaced the Conservatives in 1897 and seemed to offer a chance for compromise. Spain granted "autonomy" to Cuba and Puerto Rico, hoping to defuse the issue. But the Spanish loyalists in Havana, furious about the grant of autonomy, rioted on January 12, 1898, crushing U.S. hopes for a quick end to the conflict. To the United States it now seemed that Spain could no longer keep control in Cuba; and conversely, that the Cuban rebels could not win independence from Spain without a prolonged and costly war.

At that moment, an event occurred which changed the course of history: an explosion sank the battleship *USS Maine* in Havana harbor, killing 260 crew members. Stunned American reaction turned on Spain as responsible. At the time, an investigation indicated that the *Maine* had been blown up by a Spanish submarine mine. The U.S. Congress immediately approved a defense fund of $50 million to be used at the discretion of President McKinley.

The destruction of the *Maine* coincided with a shift in opinion on the part of the U.S. business community, which had come to see U.S. intervention as the quickest way to resume business as usual in Cuba. For these interests, the blowing up of the *Maine* was suspiciously opportune. One of the most influential protagonists of war with Spain, newspaper magnate William Randolph Hearst, sent a reporter to Havana to cover

MARTI'S WARNING

José Martí, the Cuban poet-journalist who led his country's independence movement from Spain, warned Latin Americans against trading Spanish colonial control for dominance by the United States. While Martí admired many traits of the North American people, whom he came to know during his years in New York, he clearly saw the road down which the growth of monopoly capitalism was taking the United States in the crucial decade of the 1880s. On the eve of the U.S.-controlled "Pan-American Congress" in 1889, Martí repeated his dark predictions of North American imperialism masquerading as Pan-Americanism, and made a futile call for the Latin nations to demand a true and unified independence:

Dangers must not be recognized only when they are upon us, but when they can be avoided. In politics the main thing is to clarify and foresee. Only a virile and unanimous response, for which there is still time without risk, can free all the Spanish American nations at one time from the anxiety and agitation—fatal in a country's hour of development—in which the secular and admittedly predominant policy of a powerful and ambitious neighbor... would forever hold them . . .[9]

a "big story." Shortly before the explosion, the reporter cabled back: "Everything is quiet . . . there will be no war. I wish to return." Hearst replied, "Please remain. You furnish the pictures and I'll furnish the war."[12]

More recently, an investigation by Ret. Rear Admiral Hyman Rickover has concluded that the explosion was caused by a bomb placed inside the hull of the *Maine* in an intentional act of sabotage. Whatever the truth of the matter, the blowing up of the *Maine* triggered a decisive shift in public and Congressional opinion in favor of war. On April 13, Henry Cabot Lodge stated:

> All men in this country are agreed today . . . that this situation must end. We cannot go on indefinitely with this strain, this suspense, this uncertainty, this tottering on the verge of war. It is killing to business.[13]

Days later, Congress passed a resolution declaring the people of Cuba "independent" and ordering Spain to evacuate the island. War was declared on April 25, 1898. Under the battle cry "Remember the *Maine!*", U.S. Marines invaded Spain's remaining overseas colonies—Cuba, Puerto Rico, and the Philippines—and took control of all three countries. Puerto Rico and the Philippines became U.S. possessions, while a puppet government was established in nominally independent Cuba. Under the "Platt Amendment" which the United States wrote into Cuba's constitution, the U.S. retained the right to intervene militarily in Cuba and to maintain the Guantanamo naval base on the island until the year 2000. The United States, born in revolution and anti-colonialism, had itself become an imperial power.

Gunboat Diplomacy and Economic Expansion

The War of 1898 opened a new era in the Caribbean Basin as the full might of North American imperialism descended like a tempest upon the countries of the region. Military interventions and corporate land takeovers became commonplace as the United States now assumed the role of regional policeman, judge and executioner.

> Chronic wrongdoing, or an impotence which results in the general loosening of the ties of civilized society . . . in the Western hemisphere . . . force the United States, however reluctantly . . . to the exercise of an international police power.
>
> — President Theodore Roosevelt, 1904

In the name of "prosperity" and "order," U.S. Marines invaded independent countries of the Caribbean 33 times in as

Cartoon from around 1910 portrays President Theodore Roosevelt and his "Big Stick" of American military intervention. The U.S. invaded independent countries of the Caribbean dozens of times during the gunboat diplomacy years.

many years, remaining in five countries—Cuba, Nicaragua, Panama, the Dominican Republic, and Haiti—for prolonged periods. The official justifications for these interventions fell into several categories:

- To protect American property and interests or American lives
- To "promote peace and government stability"
- To prevent revolution
- To create or maintain neutral zones or cities.

Officially, President Roosevelt's justification for intervention was to maintain "law and order"; President William Taft's goal was to contain the "malady of revolutions that produce financial collapse"; while President Woodrow Wilson's stated purpose was to reform and educate "backward" societies in the image of America.[14]

These ideals notwithstanding, the cold reality of U.S. interventions involved extensive corporate land takeovers. Under the protection of the Marines and the new laws they imposed, U.S. corporations moved in and seized peasants' lands, turning them over to export production. Before 1898 the invaded countries had grown much of their own food; now they became dependent on imported foreign products.

To better organize this empire-building, the U.S. government and business leaders held a hemispheric "economic planning conference" in 1915 in Washington, D.C. To get the edge on the British, the conference was deliberately held at a time when England was tied down by its involvement in the First World War. Financial initiative shifted from London to New York, and by 1929, the United States had taken over economic leadership in the hemisphere.[16]

U.S. Marine Interventions in the Caribbean Basin Between 1899 and 1934[15]

Cuba	1898, 1906-09, 1912, 1917-1933
Puerto Rico	1898 and thereafter
Nicaragua	1898, 1899, 1910, 1912-25, 1926-33
Colombia	1902, 1904, 1912, 1903-14
Honduras	1903, 1907, 1911, 1912, 1919, 1924, 1925
Dominican Republic	1903, 1904, 1914, 1916-24
Haiti	1914, 1915-34
Mexico	1913, 1914-17, 1918-19
Guatemala	1920
Panama	1921, 1925

The Human Impact: Examples from Cuba, Puerto Rico, and Panama

There were three principal consequences of the U.S. expansion:

- The takeover of large tracts of land and removal of local property holders through force, cheap payoffs, or legal trickery;
- The elimination of tens of thousands of subsistence farms which fed local populations;
- U.S. government and business alliance with the conservative sectors of national bourgeoisies against the working-class and peasant majority.

Cuba. The United Fruit Company entered Cuba in 1901, as soon as the U.S. conquest was complete. The company quickly acquired large tracts of land through the implementation of U.S. Military Order No. 62, which legalized *de facto* occupation of land by North American corporations. United Fruit's technique was to draw up a possession lien on a given property and then use that lien or actual occupancy against legal challenges in the Cuban courts. To carry out this occupation, the company had to first remove the peasants who had lived on and worked the lands for years.

One such case involved an area called El Cristal in the municipality of Mayari. Cuban authorities, unable to counter United Fruit or in collusion with the company, ordered the police to clear the land of its inhabitants. The peasants expelled from El Cristal appealed their case in court, declaring:

We protest before said judges and authorities the threats, charges and repressive acts to which we have been subjected . . . they (the UFC) have made charges against us for the crime of "usurping land and damaging property and products" . . . Even after we managed to get free under bond, the authorities detained us illegally and we have been held prisoner for 72 hours . . .[17]

After the removal and arrest of peasants, United Fruit would then bring in Haitians to cut the sugar cane on the plantations, so that the dispossessed peasants could not even secure wage labor on their former farm plots.

Puerto Rico. In 1898, Puerto Rico had a balanced agricultural economy: 41% of the total arable land was used for coffee cultivation, 32% for edible foods, 15% for sugar, and 1% for tobacco. Puerto Rican farmers owned 93% of the existing farms, and a large number owned their own homes.[18]

Immediately after the 1898 invasion, U.S. companies arrived in Puerto Rico to set up large-scale sugar and tobacco industries. Four U.S.-owned sugar mills were established: Central Aguirre in 1899, South Porto Rico Sugar Company in 1900, Farjardo Sugar Company in 1905 and Loiza Sugar Company in 1907. Puerto Rico's small farms were swallowed up, and the peasants lucky enough to get work on the plantations received at most 80 cents per day during the six months of cane cutting. Once a self-reliant agricultural country, in the space of a decade Puerto Rico had become a foreign-owned, foreign-run plantation.

Puerto Rican rum on San Juan docks awaiting shipment to the United States.

By 1929, the situation of Puerto Rican peasants, called jíbaros, was desperate. Luis Muñoz Marín, future governor of Puerto Rico, wrote an angry indictment of U.S. colonial rule:

> By now the development of large absentee-owned sugar estates, the rapid curtailment in the planting of coffee—the natural crop of the independent farmer—and the concentration of cigar manufacture into the hands of the American trust, have combined to make Puerto Rico a land of beggars and millionaires, of flattering statistics and distressing realities. More and more it becomes a factory worked by peons, fought over by lawyers, bossed by absentee industrialists, and clerked by politicians. It is now Uncle Sam's second largest sweatshop.[19]

Panama. Between 1904 and 1925, the United States virtually ran Panama. North Americans held key posts in bureaucracies such as the National Police, the Public Works, and General Education. A Panamanian petty bourgeoisie was developing, but they had very little capital and sought to acquire more power as landlords of slum housing in Colon and Panama City. To bolster their position, in 1925 they pushed through a new law raising taxes by 5% on all property in the two port cities. This increase was then used as an excuse to raise rents by 25-50%. The tenants revolted in what has become famous in Panama as the Gesta Inquilinaria (Renters' Protest).

The tenants formed a Renters' League under the leadership of the General Workers' Union, and rallied people through a series of public meetings which were finally outlawed by the mayor of Panama City. The League then called for a

THE CHURCH AND THE "AMERICANIZING" OF PUERTO RICO

The historic Protestant churches based in the United States played a key role in socially legitimizing and institutionalizing North American domination over Puerto Rico after 1898. Shortly after the Marines took over, six Protestant denominations began working in Puerto Rico, dividing up the island into separate geographic areas reserved for exclusive evangelization by each church body.

Encouraged by U.S. officials and facilitated through "freedom of worship" statutes, the new churches quickly gained access to the rural areas where the Catholic Church had weak roots. The Protestants grounded their evangelistic efforts in social action by founding schools—virtually taking over public education at the primary level—as well as hospitals, orphanages, medical clinics, small agricultural projects and technical training centers. In this way they undercut the Catholics' social base and established strong ties to the people, although their leadership and funding was almost entirely North American.

The end of Spanish control and the shift to U.S. colonialism produced a deep dislocation within the Roman Catholic Church as its official recognition and privileges came to an end. To compensate, Rome replaced Spanish prelates with Irish Catholic bishops from New England, who brought with them North American clergy, customs, catechism, hymnology and theological attitudes. This new Catholic leadership also helped to Americanize Puerto Rico. However, many Spanish priests and nuns stayed and resisted this "foreign" process, remaining sympathetic to Puerto Rican autonomist or independence forces. This produced a split within the Puerto Rican Catholic Church between pro-American and pro-Hispanic tendencies which intensified over the years.

But it was the Protestant churches which expanded rapidly while the Catholic Church struggled merely to hold its own. The new denominations promoted baptism and membership as a sign of Puerto Ricans' becoming "good Americans" and "true Christians"—reflecting both their colonizing role and the competitiveness which developed in relation to the Catholic Church.[24]

mass meeting on October 10, 1925, but attempted to cancel it at the last moment when it became evident that the police planned to provoke violence. But the leadership could no longer stop the hundreds of Panamanian workers who poured into Santa Ana Park to demand lower rents. The first speaker at the rally was shot by police when he rose to urge the crowd to go home. This triggered a barrage of gunfire from the surrounding police, resulting in three deaths and ten injuries. On October 12, U.S. troops entered Panama City to "guarantee independence and sovereignty of the Fatherland"—thus beginning the U.S. practice of siding with Panama's upper class.[20]

Training U.S. Surrogates: The National Guard Model

The practice of gunboat diplomacy met with resistance everywhere. Charlemagne Peralte of Haiti led a people's army which held one-fifth of the country before being defeated by U.S. Marines in 1919. In the Dominican Republic, resistance in the eastern flatlands was continuous between 1916 and 1924, when it was finally crushed by Rafael Trujillo's brutal repression under Marine supervision. The uprising of Sandino's peasant-worker army in Nicaragua was never defeated, even after five years of fighting the Marines (1927-1932).

Other opposition was non-violent, such as the workers' strikes in Honduras and El Salvador during the 1920s. A growing middle-class protest emerged through the national congresses of the region, weak and elitist as they often were. An Anti-Imperialist League created by middle-class businessmen in Central America and the Spanish Caribbean found sympathetic support in Europe and even in the United States itself.

The unpopularity and injustice of gunboat diplomacy gradually penetrated North American consciousness. In 1928, the Clark Memorandum attempted to eliminate interventionism as a principle from the Monroe Doctrine, while preserving the ability of the U.S. to intervene in practice. President Hoover opposed the idea of a global American empire; yet his warning about the "specter of Bolshevism" signaled the new propaganda that would rationalize U.S. interventions in the future.[21] Financier Thomas Lamont was less theoretical and more pragmatic, and it was his argument which finally convinced the United States to change its tactics. He said: "The theory of collecting debts by gunboat is unrighteous, unworkable, and obsolete."[22]

But the United States could not maintain its empire without some means of controlling local resistance in the exploited countries. So began the process, in the late 1920s, of training and installing local militias and national guards as U.S. surrogates. The first example of this new strategy appeared in the Dominican Republic when the Marines set up a National Guard and prepared Generalisimo Rafael Trujillo to lead it. Another occurred in Nicaragua where the U.S. created and trained a National Guard and placed Anastasio Somoza García in charge. In Haiti, the Marines trained the "Guarde d'Haiti" to take over when they left. These forces were not intended to be independent national armies, but praetorian guards of the United States.

It was only when these surrogates were in place that President Franklin D. Roosevelt could introduce his non-interventionist diplomacy called the "Good Neighbor" policy. The United States, he said, would now return to its "traditional Jeffersonian *de facto* recognition" of the independence of other states. The Marines left Nicaragua on January 2, 1933, and on March 4, President Roosevelt stated:

> The essential qualities of a true Pan-Americanism must be the same as those which constitute a good neighbor, namely, mutual understanding, and . . . a sympathetic appreciation of others' point of view.[23]

While Roosevelt was willing to forego the practice of armed intervention in the Caribbean—and withdrew the last Marines from Haiti in 1934—he also admitted subsequently of Nicaraguan dictator Somoza that while "he is an S.O.B., he's *our* S.O.B." The same was initially true of Trujillo, whose cruelty had become legendary after only four years in power.

Despite rumblings of internal revolt in the Caribbean and war abroad, the United States sailed into the 1940s on the lofty words of good-neighborly Pan-Americanism. Under this banner, a General Maximiliano Hernández Martínez could murder 30,000 peasants in 1932 in El Salvador, and Trujillo could murder 20,000 Haitians in the Dominican Republic in 1936 while Washington hardly blinked an eye. The Marines had come home, but the U.S. corporations and their new gendarmes remained in tight control. ∎

U.S. Marine officer inspecting rifles of the Haitian National Guard, 1919.

The West Indies: Middle-Class Ambivalence, Workers' Revolt

The extreme poverty and exploitation of West Indian workers led to the upsurge of Marcus Garvey's black nationalist movement after World War I and, subsequently, to the organized labor movement in the West Indies. For a while, from 1919 through the early 1930s, the two movements were closely linked. As the confrontation between the ruling class and the people intensified, however, it was middle-class leaders who were able to mediate and speak "on behalf" of the masses. This opened the way for a middle-class cooptation of the labor movement and the eventual abandonment of its more revolutionary goals. Garvey's radical Pan-Africanism, excluded from this process, helped inspire Rastafarianism, a religion rooted in social protest but one which refused to play an active part in formal "politics."

Rise of the Middle Class

The Sugar Equalization Act of 1846, which revoked the West Indies' monopoly of the British sugar market, meant bankruptcy for many planters. Many left the islands, and their lands were taken over by London firms and banks. But planters, their attorneys, and rich merchants still dominated the political life of the colonies, occupying all the seats in the local legislative assemblies. This led to a struggle by the native-born middle class for the political power they felt was rightfully theirs.

This emerging class was formed of two strands. On the one hand were the mulatto (or "brown-skinned") descendents of the unions between planters and slaves. They rose by inheriting property, often using their assets to go into business as merchants. On the other hand, a substantial number of blacks moved up through education, with the most successful leaving the colonies to study abroad on scholarship. They rose socially through the professions, becoming doctors, lawyers, teachers, journalists, and clergy. The more affluent individuals from these two groups began to stand for election to the local assemblies, where they challenged the entrenched position of the planter class.

Meanwhile, the British were becoming alarmed that the dwindling white plantocracies could no longer control the black majority in the colonies. These fears were confirmed by a riot in Jamaica in 1865 led by Paul Bogle, a black Native Baptist preacher, and George W. Gordon, a colored Baptist leader. The freed slaves in Jamaica, as elsewhere, had suffered decades of harassment since emancipation: arbitrary evictions, high taxes, and harsh penalties for "trespassing" were all used to deny the ex-slaves access to land. The Morant Bay rebellion was an outburst of pent-up anger by the Jamaican peasantry against these conditions. The governor overreacted to the riot and his colonial troops killed 439 blacks, flogged another 600, and burned more than 1,000 homes to the ground. Bogle and Gordon were arrested and hanged.[1]

Convinced that the planters were losing control of the situation, the British government persuaded a willing Jamaican Assembly to give up its authority and allow Jamaica to become a Crown Colony. By 1870, all the British colonies except Barbados had followed Jamaica's lead. Crown Colony government meant a return to direct imperial rule. Instead of local assemblies which made laws, each colony was to be ruled by a governor who answered directly to the Colonial Office in Britain. The governor was "assisted" by two local councils which essentially served to rubber-stamp his decisions.[2]

The middle class was dismayed by this turn of events, since it cut short their growing political influence. Through their professional organizations and local newspapers, they agitated for "self-government" in which they would play a leading role. Especially after 1920, this campaign often took the form of protest to the colonial authorities over the plight of the poor. T.A. Marryshow of Grenada and Arthur Cipriani of Trinidad were leading spokesmen for this liberal tendency.

The petty reforms won by the middle class—allowing themselves to be elected to the powerless councils—were all but meaningless to the masses. The middle class wanted to speak *for* the poor, but recoiled in horror from the idea of a universal suffrage which would allow the poor to speak for themselves. Like the ruling class they emulated, the middle class viewed the poor black majority from a paternalistic, color-conscious perspective heavily conditioned by two hundred years of colonial rule.

The Marcus Garvey Movement

This societal racism and complacency was soon to be challenged by a rising social movement, one with roots both in the intellectual tradition of Pan-Africanism and in black religion [see pp. 38-39].

Even before the turn of the century, West Indians had put forth new concepts of Africa which refuted the racist theories of the day. Edward Blyden, born in the Virgin Islands in 1832, emigrated to Liberia and became a high official in the Liberian government. He focused on West Indian-African historical links, urging West Indians to emigrate to Africa. J.J. Thomas, a Trinidadian scholar, wrote a book refuting the racist opinions of the Englishman J.A. Froude, and emphasized the need for black unity to accomplish the "true purposes" of the African race. H.S. Williams, also born in Trinidad, convened the first Pan-African Conference in London in 1900 which formed a Pan-African Association with branches in many countries.

All these figures were overshadowed by the fame of one man, Marcus Garvey, who successfully consolidated Pan-Africanism as a dynamic mass movement. Garvey was born in Jamaica of humble peasant origins. In 1910, he traveled up the Atlantic coast of Central America, where he was outraged by the exploitation of black workers on the banana plantations and railroads and on the Panama Canal. Between 1912 and

Members of Garvey's Universal Negro Improvement Association line the streets of Harlem for the parade preceding their annual convention in 1924.

1914, Garvey lived in London and worked on the *Africa Times and Orient Review,* a Pan-Africanist paper. Upon returning to Jamaica he formed the Universal Negro Improvement Association (UNIA), aimed at uniting "all the Negro peoples of the world into one great body to establish a country and Government absolutely their own."[3]

Garvey's formation of the UNIA coincided with the period of the first serious labor organization in the West Indies. After 1900, labor disturbances had become frequent on the estates and in the towns, but they were generally spontaneous and unorganized. World War I marked a turning point. Some 15,000 West Indian men served in the West India Regiment of the British Army, and many returned home radicalized by their first exposure to the outside world and by their experience of discrimination in the segregated military. After the soldiers came home in 1919, a wave of strikes and riots swept the region. The uprisings drew their philosophical inspiration from the new racial consciousness of Garvey's UNIA, and UNIA members figured prominently in the disturbances.

The returning soldiers also gave a strong push to the formation of trade unions. But except for Hubert Critchlow's British Guiana Labour Union—recognized in 1919 with the help of the British Labour Party—the fledgling unions remained unrecognized and unprotected through the 1930s. Picketing was illegal, and employers could sue strikers for damages or simply call on troops and police. Strikes were

quickly crushed by the colonial forces.

Garvey ultimately met with frustration in Jamaica, where colonial ideas of white superiority were deeply ingrained. The middle class hated and feared him, and even many of the workers and small farmers were not yet ready for Garvey's open affirmation of their blackness. He moved to the United States, where his ideas caught fire among thousands of blacks driven by poverty into the slums of the northern cities in a massive post-war migration. The UNIA took root as a grassroots movement in New York City's Harlem section, and soon expanded to include branches in 40 countries and an estimated 2 million dues-paying members.

The UNIA's impact on West Indian affairs was almost immediate. Garvey's agents traversed the area establishing branches and spreading the word of nationalism and anti-colonialism. Some were deported from, and/or refused permission to land in certain territories.

(It was) a genuine Pan-Caribbean mass movement, cutting across political and linguistic barriers. Cuba had more branches (52) than any other territory in the West Indies, and indeed more than any country other than the United States. Trinidad had at least 30 branches, Jamaica had 11, British Guiana 7, and the Dominican Republic 5.[4]

At its height, the UNIA ran a far-flung network of centers called Liberty Halls which provided social services and credit

Marcus Garvey

to black communities. Garvey also started a visionary but financially unsuccessful steamship venture, the Black Star Line, in order to link black peoples around the world and carry blacks who wished to repatriate back to Africa.

The theme of repatriation was a powerful element of Garvey's message. His slogan, "Africa for the Africans, those at home and those abroad," resounded around the world as the colonial powers completed their scramble for Africa. Garvey defied the whole system of white domination, at the same time challenging blacks to build themselves up as a self-reliant, proud people. His movement soon incurred the enmity not only of white America but also of the black intelligensia, which feared the strength of his openly race-based appeal. He was arrested by U.S. federal marshalls on trumped-up mail fraud charges, imprisoned for two years in Atlanta and deported to Jamaica in 1927.

1930s: The People Revolt

Conditions had worsened in the Caribbean during the years of Garvey's absence. While the middle class was politely pursuing constitutional reform, the workers were becoming desperate over their low wages, unemployment, and the near starvation of their families. Wages for unskilled workers ranged from 28¢ to 60¢ per day throughout the West Indies.[5] Where sugar was still "King," as in Barbados, so little local food was grown that laborers and their families had to subsist on imported rice and cornmeal.[6] Living conditions for the poor were typified by this report from Jamaica:

> At Orange Bay the Commissioners saw people living in huts the walls of which were bamboo knitted together as closely as human hands were capable; the ceilings were made from dry crisp coconut branches which shifted their positions with every wind. The floor measured 8 feet by 6 feet. The hut was 5 feet high ... In this hut lived nine people, a man, his wife, and seven children. They had no water and no latrine. There were two beds. The parents slept in one, and as many of the children as could hold on in the other. The rest used the floor.[7]

The people's health and strength were sapped by malnutrition and diseases like hookworm, tuberculosis, and malaria. In Barbados—patronizingly called "Little England"—217 of every 1000 babies died before their first birthday, compared to 58 of every 1000 in "Big England."[8]

Garvey returned to a triumphant hero's welcome from Jamaican workers. "No denser crowd has ever been witnessed in Kingston," proclaimed the *Daily Gleaner* upon his arrival.[9] He formed the People's Political Party, the first anti-colonial party in Jamaica's history. It contested the 1929 council elections on a platform which included a minimum wage, an 8-hour work day, workmen's compensation, land reform, rural housing construction, and judicial reform.[10] He also started a trade union, the Jamaica Workers and Labourers Association.

Even before he arrived back in Jamaica, the colonial authorities had mounted a campaign to suppress Garvey's influence. His newspaper *Negro World* was widely banned, and Garvey was denied visas to visit other islands. Active Garveyites were persecuted under obsolete laws. Garvey's failure in Jamaican electoral politics, however, had more to do with the fact that he needed the support of the black and brown petty bourgeoisie—since the poor could not vote and had no money—but this group remained ambivalent, excluded from the power structure but still unwilling to upset the system.

The Great Depression severely eroded the financial base of Garvey's movement. He left in 1935 for England, where he died five years later. But the hardship of the Depression had just begun to have its impact on the Caribbean. As production fell off in the U.S. and England, imports from those countries became expensive and scarce. The world market for sugar and bananas collapsed, meaning higher unemployment, falling wages, and increased taxation for Caribbean workers. To make matters worse, the United States stopped admitting West Indian emigrants in 1927, and countries where many West Indians were working—Cuba, the Dominican Republic, and Central American countries—began deporting the migrants, who swelled the ranks of the impoverished in their home countries.

As the Depression deepened, a wave of mass strikes and violent demonstrations erupted across the region. The first was in St. Kitts, where all the land was under sugar cane and cane cutters earned at most 36¢ per day.[11] The planters' refusal to raise wages in 1935 led to a widespread strike and violent police reaction which left three workers dead. In St. Vincent, where wages averaged 28¢ per day, riots broke out when the government attempted to raise taxes on imported food. In the coaling port of Castries, St. Lucia, coal stokers were joined in protest by the unemployed. In Belize, a labor revolt closed down the sawmill owned by the Belize Estate and Produce Company, which was by then the largest employer in the colony. All of these uprisings were swiftly crushed by armed colonial police and British Marines.

As the riots spread, contradictions emerged between the desperate actions of the starving workers and the reformist strategies of the middle-class politicians. In 1933, oilfield workers in Trinidad organized a hunger march to protest their starvation wages, but the march was called off by Cipriani because the government promised to pass a minimum wage bill. The bill was passed but never enforced, leaving the workers worse off than before and disillusioned with liberal strategies for change. They had only two years to wait before a leader emerged from their own ranks. In 1935 Tubal Uriah Butler, a Grenadian-born oilfield worker, led a ragtag band of 120 poor people on a hunger march from the southern oilfields straight into the Trinidadian capital of Port-of-Spain. Butler's dynamic leadership gave Trinidadian workers a self-confidence and unity they had never known before. On June 19, 1937, every Trinidadian oil worker laid down his tools, and the strike quickly spread to the other major labor sectors, the sugar cane cutters and the urban workers. This was too much for the government, and it foolishly tried to have Butler arrested as he addressed a public meeting. The crowd reacted with fury, and in the resulting violence both workers and police were killed. As elsewhere, the uprising was finally quelled when the governor called in a British destroyer and a contingent of British Marines.

Middle-Class Takeover:
Adams, Bustamante, and Manley

As the uprisings spread, a pattern emerged which was to have a definitive impact on the future of West Indian politics. The strikes which were initiated and sustained by the workers were used by middle-class leaders to win a popular following.

In Barbados, for instance, the deportation of a radical Butlerite, Clement Payne, sparked riots in which hundreds of workers were arrested and imprisoned. Many of them were defended by a liberal lawyer named Grantley Adams, who emerged as the champion of the people. From this base Adams went on to form the Barbados Labour Party and the Barbados Workers Union: labor-based organizations under middle-class control. From them emerged the two parties which dominate Barbadian political life to the present day.

It was the famous Jamaican uprising of 1938, however, which illustrated this process most clearly and became a symbol of the region-wide upheaval. In 1935, unemployment in Jamaica stood at 11%, while another 50% were employed only part of the year. Employers followed a system of "rotational employment" in which they would take on a worker for two weeks, then fire him to make way for another.[12] By 1936, Jamaican workers were organizing under the leadership of Hugh Buchanan, an ex-Garveyite and the first Jamaican Marxist, and G.S. Coombs, a union leader. Throughout the next year "the whole country rumbled with huge marches and strikes" involving banana workers, sugar workers, ex-servicemen, dockworkers, and other groups.[13] By 1938 things had come to a head. Estate after estate went out on strike, protesting not only low wages but also the burden of rents, and thus zeroing in on the key question, control of land. In May, workers struck at Frome, the largest sugar estate in the

Banana workers in rural Jamaica around the turn of the century. The United Fruit Company gained a virtual monopoly over the Jamaican banana trade after 1900, forcing many independent peasants off their lands to become wage laborers on the company's plantations. The poverty in rural Jamaica under the thumb of United Fruit made banana workers the most militant group in the 1938 strikes.

Moorland-Spingarn Research Center,
Howard University

Photos facing page: National Library of Jamaica

country, which was owned by the British company Tate & Lyle. The strike was crushed by the police, who charged the crowd with fixed bayonets.

As demonstrations rippled across the island, a leader emerged in the person of Alexander Bustamante, a near-white member of the lower middle class (he was a petty money-a leading who had assisted Buchanan and Coombs. Together with a leading Garveyite, St. William Grant, the charismatic "Busta" thrust himself to the head of the workers' movement.

Early next morning, the 23rd of May, the city of Kingston was in the hands of the working population. Groups of workers moved from place to place and dislodged others from their stations. Street cleaners, power station workers, pumping station employees, and municipal workers joined the throng of people who surged through the street. Traffic was halted, business places closed. Shops were invaded. Passing cars were stoned.

. . . As the military moved in on the crowd, Bustamante in a dramatic gesture bared his chest and declared, "Shoot me if you want, but spare the poor defenceless people." The police drew nearer. Bustamante called upon the audience to sing the national anthem. As the strains of "God Save the King" were raised, the Police were forced to stand at attention, and could advance no further. Bustamante then moved away with the large crowd following him.[14]

Bustamante was the man of the hour. His arrest and imprisonment by the authorities triggered a cataclysmic public fury which paralyzed Kingston. But his cousin, an upper middle-class lawyer named Norman Manley, arranged for Bustamante's release, and the two men proceeded to negotiate a settlement between the workers, the employers, and the government. While this settlement had some favorable provisions, it was by no means revolutionary. The outcome was clear: middle-class leaders had assisted the workers in their struggle but compromised on their demands.

LABOUR LEADERS IN COURT

BUSTAMANTE And St. William Grant, The Arrested Labour Leaders, Looking Fit And Well As They Left The Central Police Station Yesterday Under Guard For The Court.

Never before had Jamaican workers tried to organize at a national level to negotiate with the ruling class for change. It was this inexperience, in part, which led them to eagerly accept the leadership of Bustamante, who brought the resources of his class into the fight on the people's behalf. But while he was dedicated to winning immediate gains for the workers, Bustamante lacked a political strategy for structural change. Norman Manley, on the other hand, had a clear anti-colonial perspective, but his nationalism did not include radical social change within Jamaica.

The 1938 revolt laid the basis for Jamaica's future political system. In the aftermath of the strikes, the popular movement came under the umbrella of two new organizations: the Bustamante Industrial Trade Union (BITU), headed by Busta, and the People's National Party (PNP) headed by Manley. The colonial authorities feared the militancy of a working class which could not be divided by race (as had been done in Trinidad and Guyana), and they feared the radical anti-colonialism of Marxist leaders within the PNP. They therefore contrived to split the movement. Under the influence of the colonial governor, Sir Arthur Richards, Bustamante broke from Manley in 1943 and formed the Jamaica Labour Party (JLP) to compete for the loyalty of the workers.

Although the PNP and the JLP were ideologically different at first, the groundwork had been laid for a "Tweedledum-Tweedledee" two-party system. Each party was dominated by one politician, a "big man" whose influence was overwhelming. Over the next ten years, external forces worked on Manley to persuade him to force the radicals from the PNP, culminating in the expulsion of the four leading Marxists from the party executive in 1952. Over the next two crucial decades, the JLP and the PNP moved steadily closer in ideological terms. But the working class was split into two warring political "tribes" which blocked popular unity on real social issues. ∎

RASTAFARIANISM

The refusal of the colonial Church to bend on its commitment to a white, middle-class value system, and its failure to challenge the racism of the larger society, continued to fuel the growth of black religion. The Revivalist and Native Baptist churches welcomed anyone: black and poor, married or unmarried, legitimate or illegitimate. Moreover, poor people felt that the black church was with them in their historic and continuing search for freedom from slavery, poverty, and oppression. This search is the source of the eschatological fervor which marks black religion in all its Caribbean variants: the belief in a coming "redemption" as a means of enduring the pain of the present.

The religious basis for this hope is found in the Old Testament, particularly in the story of the Exodus, and in the Book of Revelations of the New Testament.

> The comparison of African traditional religion and the Old Testament indicates a link between black religion and biblical religion. The search for freedom in history runs like a black thread between both worlds.[1]

To the Revivalists there was no contradiction between biblical religion, including a belief in Jesus, and the West African myalist belief in a world peopled by spirits who have the power to help the living. The Bible was the most important element of the Revival service. These services were held in house yards, where a pole would be erected with a banner attached and an ark (of the covenant) placed on top. The "mother" of the service wore a belt with a pair of scissors (to "cut clean") evil spirits, a whistle (to warn the spirits) and a key (to open the door of salvation). The drum was central to the ceremony, which also included Bible readings, prayers, spirit possession, public testimonials and baptism by immersion.[2]

Alexander Bedward, the "Father of Revivalism," was a poor estate laborer in Jamaica who became a founder of the Native Baptist Free Church. In 1920, Bedward declared himself to be the incarnation of Jesus Christ. Thousands of Jamaicans sold their lands and houses and traveled to Kingston to see the Messiah:

> Bedward gave to the people a hope that in him a deliverer had emerged for blacks. Addressed at first as "Shepherd" by his followers, he changed his title to "Incarnation of Jesus Christ" in 1920, with the promise that he would ascend to heaven on December 31, 1920, thereby destroying the rule of white people and establishing the kingdom of Bedwardism on earth.[3]

The messianic focus of Bedwardism set the stage for Marcus Garvey, whose vision of the liberation of Africa from colonialism and a world-wide empire of black people was a new incarnation of the continuing search for societal deliverance. Garvey linked this search to the biblical

...and the search for freedom in black religion

doctrine of creation, asserting that since God had created all equal and provided space for all peoples, Africans must claim the continent God had given them.[4] He backed this apocalyptical promise with concrete action in the historic present in the form of his attempt to build a world-wide black organization, the United Negro Improvement Association.

Garveyism also found its theological basis in the Old Testament, equating the enslaved Israelites with the black race and the promised land with Africa.

> As children of captivity we look forward to a new, yet ever old, land of our fathers, the land of God's crowning glory. We shall gather together our children, our treasures, and our loved ones, and as the children of Israel, by the command of God, face the promised land, so in time we shall also stretch forth our hands and bless our country.[5]

Garveyism in turn provided the theological and philosophical base for the new movement which emerged among the Jamaican poor in the 1930s. Garvey is reputed to have said, "Look to Africa where a black king will be crowned, for the day of deliverance is near." When King Ras Tafari of Ethiopia was crowned Emperor Haille Selassie I in 1930, he was proclaimed by a growing cult of Jamaican followers to be divine, a messiah sent by God to liberate Africans from colonialism. Selassie was the "Lion of the tribe of Judah, the Root of David" (Rev. 5).

Echoing the anthem of Garvey's UNIA, "Ethiopia, Thou Land of Our Fathers," the Rastafari asserted that Ethiopia is the real Zion referred to in the scriptures. At the same time, they point out that Ethiopia is the only African country never under colonial domination (except for a brief incursion by Italy). This joining of the biblical with the concrete historical extends to their interpretation of the entire New Testament. For the Rastafari, the true children of Israel are the blacks, and the exile their diaspora to the New World; and the exodus will be a return to Ethiopia, the promised land.

> Within the Bible itself, and particularly in the Old Testament, there were gifts of tongue and a conception of the life and history of the black people of Jamaica. Were not African enslavement and plantation cruelty the same as The Scattering of the twelve tribes of Israel and the Exile in Babylonian captivity? Surely, then, the Return to the Promised Land for the Jews must be the Return to Africa for the Jamaican Blacks![6]

Some of the early Rastafari had been active Garveyites, and the Rasta movement regarded Garvey himself as a prophet, sometimes identified with John the Baptist. Garvey's dream of black repatriation to Africa was also the focal aim of the Rastafarian movement. As one Rasta said:

We say repatriation is rede[...] redemption for us, not black p[...]

The Rastas argue that each ra[...] own, and that by enslaving o[...] lands, the white race has brou[...] can only be erased when each [...] its rightful home. Unlike Garvey, however, [...] saw this deliverance as the fruit of determined human effort and organization, the Rastafari believe that it will come by divine intervention of Selassie, and that their role is to believe and wait.

> Repatriation will come, though I don't know the time. Not even the birds that fly high knoweth the time appointed by His Majesty.[8]

Taken on its own terms, therefore, Rastafarianism is an apocalyptical faith rather than a political movement. Yet its political impact on the Caribbean and on Jamaica in particular has been immense. By giving biblical and religious underpinnings to the Pan-African themes of black pride and unity, Rastafarianism called into question the entire structure of white-dominated colonial society.

The Rastafari regard the white Church as an integral part of the structures which hold them in captivity, and thus the movement challenges the Church directly.

> We don't business with religion! A colonial thing that! That is what the white man bring down here to enslave the black man![9]

From a theological standpoint, the Rastas denounce the Church for teaching that God is outside man or "in the sky," rather than on earth in man. They accuse the Church of a preoccupation with death and the afterlife rather than life on earth. Indeed, at the heart of the challenge posed by black religion to white church/society is the idea that deliverance and salvation are not individual and in the afterlife, but rather, *collective* (societal) and *in the foreseeable future.* When the slaves in the U.S. south sang "Swing low, Sweet Chariot," they were referring to escape northward, not heavenly ascent.[10] According to Jamaican theologian Noel Erskine, this joining of the concrete historical and the eschatological underlies the role of black religion in the struggle for black freedom and equality.[11]

The reaction of the Church to Rastafarianism, not surprisingly, was one of social rejection and religious belittlement. Any possibility of a prophetic message in the Rastafarian creed was summarily dismissed. But the marriage of black religion, black nationalism, and anti-colonialism continued to disturb and challenge the Caribbean Church until the 1960s, when the thunderbolt known as the Black Power movement finally forced the Church to come face to face with the social realities it had helped create.

...or's Challenge Ends
...n the Failure of Federation

The Second World War effectively brought a halt to the labor revolts of the 1930s. England demanded, and received, full cooperation from her West Indian colonies in the war against Nazi Germany. The war was also used to squelch radical elements of the labor movement, as the more forceful leaders—Bustamante, Butler—were jailed on the pretext that they "hindered the war effort." After the war, England turned to a strategy of social reform based on the recommendations of the Moyne Commission which toured the West Indies in 1938-39, confirming the awful poverty of the West Indian masses and recommending palliative measures in health care, housing, education, and wages. This social welfarism was one element in the gradual weakening of labor's demands for reform.

Anti-colonial politicians close to the labor movement, such as Norman Manley, did use their new power to extract certain concessions from England. These included universal suffrage and approval for a Federation of the West Indies, which would be a group of self-governing states constituting a new nation within the British Commonwealth. Trade unions also won the crucial right to legal recognition and protection. As a result, during the 1940s, strong unions sprang up all over the British West Indies and joined the new regional labor body, the Caribbean Labour Congress (CLC). At its conference in Kingston, Jamaica in 1947, the CLC decided to push for a West Indies Federation which would implement socialist planning on a regional basis.[1]

Most of the new unions included a "political committee" which became the nucleus of a party closely linked to the union. Thus the Belize General Workers Union, formed in 1939, gave birth to the People's United Party in 1950. The St. Kitts-Nevis Trade and Labour Union, formed in 1940, gave rise to the St. Kitts-Nevis Labour Party in 1951. From the Dominica Trade Union emerged the Dominica Labour Party; from the Antigua Trades and Labour Union came the Antigua Labour Party; and so on all over the English-speaking Caribbean. When Britain granted universal suffrage to her colonies in the early 1950s, the working-class voters going to the polls for the first time swept these labor-based parties into power.

World War Two created powerful pressures on Britain to relinquish its hold over its colonial empire. At U.S. insistence, Prime Minister Winston Churchill joined in signing a 1941 charter in which the U.S. and England agreed to "see sovereign rights and self-government restored to those who have been forcibly deprived of them."[2] As soon as the war ended, strong nationalist movements in Britain's eastern colonies—particularly India and Egypt—demanded independence, signaling the imminent disintegration of the British empire and prompting Britain to seek a more gradual and controlled independence process for her Caribbean colonies. To this end, a new British government under the Labour Party promised in 1947

to "guide" the British West Indies to "self-government." In fact, Britain's strategy was a delaying process aimed at establishing a neocolonial structure in the islands before they received independence.

Despite their electoral victories, therefore, the labor leaders did not hold complete authority in their respective territories. Colonial administrators still controlled key areas, particularly finance. To groom a class of neocolonial politicians who would be ready to take over at the time of independence, Britain filled the colonial civil service with educated, middle-class West Indians who tended to see government service primarily as a means of advancing themselves financially, socially, and politically.[3]

Once the labor heroes held political office, moreover, their own attitudes began to change. They now had some power to protect, and were reluctant to agree to anything which might weaken their political base. In the larger territories of Trinidad and Jamaica, the rush was on to industrialize in the 1950s. This meant that the islands were competing for foreign capital, and it also made Trinidad and Jamaica unwilling to link themselves to the weaker economies of the small islands. Together these factors spelled doom for the West Indies Federation.

Negotiations leading up to the formation of the regional body gradually stripped it of all but token powers over the member states. When it was finally launched in 1958, the Federation was barely a shadow of the united and progressive new nation which the labor movement had envisioned in the 1940s. By 1961, after first Jamaica and then Trinidad pulled out to "go it alone" to independence, the Federation collapsed.

> The old colonial system consisted of insular economies, each with its financial and economic capital in London. A federation meant that the economic line of direction should no longer be from island to London, but from island to island. But that involved the breakup of the old colonial system. The West Indian politicians preferred the break-up of the Federation.[4]

The United States Moves Into
the Caribbean As Britain Withdraws

The Second World War was pivotal in consolidating U.S. military presence in the Caribbean. During the war, the United States enlarged its existing military bases in Panama, Cuba, and Puerto Rico. U.S. strategic thinking centered on guarding access to the Panama Canal, and for this reason the U.S. had purchased the Virgin Islands from Denmark in 1917 in order to establish a naval base at St. Thomas harbor.

The war also meant U.S. military expansion into a new area: the English-speaking Caribbean. Under a "land-lease agreement" with Britain, the United States traded 50 old destroyers to the British Navy in return for 99-year leases of land for military bases on Antigua, St. Lucia, Jamaica, Guyana, and Trinidad. The largest U.S. base was built at

A U.S.-run sweatshop in Puerto Rico in the 1950s.

Chaguaramas, Trinidad. This deal between Britain and the United States was strongly opposed by the West Indian governments, especially that of Eric Williams in Trinidad.

Rising U.S. influence in the region was also economic and social, corresponding to Britain's gradual withdrawal from the scene. In 1942 the United States participated in an "Anglo-American Caribbean Commission," a development which signalled Britain's willingness to have the U.S. involve itself in the economic affairs of British colonies. The war also brought a North American cultural invasion as the presence of thousands of U.S. soldiers on the bases caused "Yankee" pop music, clothing styles and food tastes to become fads in the West Indies. This was especially true in Trinidad, both on account of the huge Chaguaramas base and because of U.S. oil companies which moved into Trinidad during the war. In the islands where U.S. bases were built, this new economic sector drew many people off the land to seek high-wage work with the Americans. At the same time, social contradictions were reinforced as many of the U.S. troops regarded West Indians with open racism.

The Puerto Rican Model

The end of the war saw the newly-powerful United States restructure the international economic system, with the U.S. dollar replacing gold as the new world currency. At the Bretton Woods conference in 1944, the World Bank and the International Monetary Fund (IMF) were set up to provide economic support to postwar Europe and supervise an international system of "free trade" necessary to U.S. economic expansion.

In this context, the United States introduced in the late 1940s what it touted as a new model of development for the Caribbean. Launched in Puerto Rico in 1947, the plan was for U.S. corporate investment to create new industries in the Caribbean to replace the moribund plantation system. Led by investment in minerals, manufacturing, and tourism, whole new sectors appeared in Caribbean economies almost overnight.

The underlying principle of the Puerto Rican model was the same as that of old-fashioned colonialism, however. The Caribbean was to shape its productive system according to

43

what the industrialized countries needed. Management, capital, and technology would continue to be imported, and the end product exported from the region. In Puerto Rico, this meant offering incentives to U.S. firms to set up branch plants on the island for the assembly of consumer goods. These so-called "screwdriver factories" brought in all of their inputs from abroad—machinery, raw materials, half-finished components—and used cheap Puerto Rican labor to complete the assembly process. The finished goods were then sent back to the U.S. for shipment to world markets.

One believer in the Puerto Rican model was Sir Arthur Lewis, a St. Lucia-born economist. Lewis urged the English-speaking Caribbean territories to copy the model on a regional, cooperative basis. During the 1950s, the larger territories of Trinidad and Jamaica did attempt to industrialize by offering investors tax holidays and other incentives—what Lewis called "a period of wooing and fawning upon" foreign capitalists.[5] However, they did so not on a regional basis as Lewis had proposed, but individually, with each island competing for investment.

The decade of the 1960s brought a radical transformation to Caribbean economies as North American firms moved into the region on a large scale. With the U.S. economy booming, capital was going "transnational"—seeking low-wage labor, cheap raw materials and new markets around the globe. Prominent among the firms which entered the Caribbean were U.S. aluminum multinationals mining the rich bauxite ore of Jamaica, Guyana and Suriname. Tourism controlled by North American investors mushroomed in Jamaica, Barbados, and the Dominican Republic, and became important to the economies of the smaller islands, particularly Antigua. In manufacturing, U.S. firms sought to transfer their labor-intensive operations to branch plants on the islands to escape minimum wage laws and other workers' gains in the United States.

Industrialization went farthest and fastest in Puerto Rico, Trinidad, and Jamaica. The latter countries have the largest domestic markets in the English-speaking Caribbean, and some of their industrialization was therefore geared toward producing goods for the local market. On the other hand, the smallest and least developed islands such as Grenada, St. Vincent, and Dominica had little infrastructure and were ill-positioned to attract foreign investment. They remained heavily dependent on agricultural exports, especially bananas.

Proponents of the Puerto Rican model argued that although the strategy depended on low wages, the firms' profits would be reinvested locally and industrial skills and technology transferred to the Caribbean. The results were not so glowing. As it turned out, the multinationals repatriated their profits and invested hardly anything back into the local economies. Indeed, repatriated profits sometimes even exceeded incoming investment flows, as in Jamaica between 1966 and 1976, representing a net *export* of capital from Jamaica to the U.S.[6] Technically skilled jobs were filled by foreigners, while West Indian workers received low wages for mindless assembly-type work.

The multinationals made clear that to come into the Caribbean they required guarantees of labor peace. Many refused outright to deal with unions. To satisfy the companies, governments passed repressive legislation curtailing the rights of workers to strike—for example, the Industrial Stabilization Act (ISA) in Trinidad, which workers dubbed "Is Slavery Again." Despite these concessions, companies frequently packed up and left the Caribbean as soon as their ten or twelve-year tax holiday expired, or if wages were raised.

The new industries were integrated not with the economies of the Caribbean host countries, but with the economies of their home countries where their headquarters were based.[7] They depended on duty-free imports of machinery and spare parts from abroad. Decisions were made in foreign corporate boardrooms with little concern for the needs or development of the Caribbean. Even Caribbean governments could exert little influence over the decisions of their powerful guests. Often the investors literally wrote their own package of incentives which was then relayed to the appropriate minister to sign.

The other side of this dependency process was a growing Caribbean reliance on imported food and consumer goods. With the emphasis on building an infrastructure to attract foreign investors, agriculture was allowed to stagnate, and not enough food was produced for local consumption. At the same time, advertising by foreign producers seeking Caribbean markets helped change people's food tastes away from local products and toward products available only as imports. The beneficiaries of this process were primarily North American. The Caribbean became dependent on the U.S. for virtually all of its wheat flour and corn, and for much of the meat, milk, and other products consumed in the region.[8]

By the end of the 1960s, the Caribbean had traded its old colonial dependence on Europe for a new dependence on the United States. Caribbean politicians had little connection to the productive system in their own countries, and thus went straight from colonialism to neocolonialism without ever holding real control over their economies.[9] Political independence finally came to the Caribbean nations one by one, but economic independence and regional unity remained an elusive dream. ∎

NOTES TO PART ONE

Brief History of the Caribbean

1. *Amerindians* refers to those peoples who inhabited the Americas before the arrival of the Europeans. *West Indians* are people born in the West Indies in the post-Columbus era. *East Indians* trace their ancestry to India.
2. Spain based its claim on a Papal Bull which divided the world between Spain and Portugal along an imaginary line west of the Azores. Spain was to rule everything west of the line and Portugal everything east of it.
3. J. Hartog, *Curacao: Short History* (Aruba: De Wit Stores, 1979), p. 17.
4. C.L.R. James, *The Black Jacobins* (New York: Vintage Books, 1963), pp. 2-3.
5. William Claypole and John Robottom, *Caribbean Story* (Essex: Longman Group Ltd., 1980), Book One, p. 148.
6. Mercantilism was associated with the rise to power in England of Oliver Cromwell, who represented the interests of the emerging commercial bourgeoisie. Under Cromwell's "Western Design," Britain attempted to seize Spain's Caribbean possessions, capturing Jamaica from Spain in 1655.
7. C.L.R. James, *Spheres of Existence* (London: Allison & Busby Ltd., 1980), p. 182.
8. Eric Williams, *Capitalism & Slavery* (New York: University of North Carolina Press, 1964).
9. *Ibid.*, p. 207. A member of the British House of Commons said, "The planter was sitting, dirty and begrimed, over a powder magazine, from which he would not go away, and he was hourly afraid that the slave would apply a torch to it."
10. Walter Rodney, *A History of the Guyanese Working People, 1881-1905* (Baltimore: Johns Hopkins University Press, 1981).
11. *Ibid.*, Chap. 2.
12. *Ibid.*, p. 33.

Collaborative Role of the Church

1. Eric Williams, *From Columbus to Castro: The History of the Caribbean 1492-1969* (New York: Harper & Row, 1970), p. 203.
2. *Ibid.*, p. 203.
3. *Ibid.*, p. 183.
4. Idris Hamid, *Troubling of the Waters* (Trinidad: Rahaman Printery, 1973), p. 63.
5. James M. Phillippo, *Jamaica: Its Past and Present State* (London: Unwin Brothers, 1843), p. 158.
6. M.G. Lewis, *Journal of a West Indian Proprietor* (New York: Houghton Mifflin, 1929), p. 124.
7. Keith D. Hunte, "The Church in Caribbean Development," in David I. Mitchell, *With Eyes Wide Open* (Barbados: CADEC, 1973), p. 143.
8. Philip D. Curtin, *Two Jamaicas: The Role of Ideas in a Tropical Colony 1830-1865* (New York: Atheneum, 1970), p. 162.
9. Noel Leo Erskine, *Decolonizing Theology: A Caribbean Perspective* (Maryknoll, NY: Orbis Books, 1981), p. 74.
10. Phillippo, p. 253.
11. Lilith M. Haynes, *Fambli* (Guyana: CADEC, 1971), p. 40.
12. *Ibid.*, p. 36.
13. Migene Gonzalez-Wippler, *Santeria: African Magic in Latin America* (New York: Julian Press, 1973).

Unifying Themes in Caribbean Cultures

1. Gordon K. Lewis, *The Growth of the Modern West Indies* (New York: Monthly Review Press, 1968), p. 20.
2. *Ibid.*, p. 28.
3. Leonard Barrett, *The Sun and the Drum: African Roots in Jamaican Folk Tradition* (Jamaica: Sangster's Book Stores, Ltd., 1976), pp. 11-12.
4. Gordon K. Lewis, pp. 30-31.
5. *Ibid.*, pp. 31-32.

The Atlantic Coast

1. Center for Research and Documentation of the Atlantic Coast, *Trabil Nani: Historical Background and Current Situation on the Atlantic Coast of Nicaragua* (New York: Riverside Church Disarmament Project, 1984), p. 12.
2. *The Road to Independence* (Government of Belize, 1981), p. 7.
3. Dalva Acuna de Molina, "Repercusiones de la Trajada de Sandia," in *Relaciones entre Panama y los Estados Unidos* (Panama: Ministry of Education, 1974), pp. 136-139.
4. Robert E. May, *The Southern Dream of a Caribbean Empire* (Baton Rouge: Louisiana State University Press, 1973), pp. 85-110.
5. Humberto E. Ricord et al., *Panama y la Frutera: Una Batalla Contra el Colonialismo* (Panama: Editorial Universitaria de Panama, 1974), p. 11.
6. "Banana Diplomacy: The Development of U.S.-Honduran Relations," *El Salvador Bulletin,* Vol. 2, No. 7, May 1983 (Berkeley, CA: U.S.-Salvadoran Research and Information Center), p. 4.
7. EPICA, *Panama: Sovereignty for a Land Divided* (Washington, DC: EPICA, 1976), p. 12.
8. Luis A. Diez Castillo, *Los Cimarrones y Los Negros Antillanos en Panama* (Panama, 1981), pp. 71-72.
9. *Informe de la Comision del Canal Istmico, 1914.* Cited in Xabier Gorostiaga, "La Zona del Canal y su Impacto en el Movimiento Obrero Panameno," *Tareas* (Panama), #32, July-Aug. 1975, p. 34.
10. The main source for this section was David McCullough, *The Path Between the Seas: The Creation of the Panama Canal 1870-1914* (New York: Simon & Schuster, 1977).
11. *Ibid.*, p. 582. Quote is from Harry Frank, *Zone Policeman 88. A Close Range Study of the Panama Canal and Its Workers* (Century, 1913).
12. The main source for this section was *The Road to Independence, op. cit.*

Roots of U.S. Imperialism

1. Jose L. Franco, *Historia de la Revolucion de Haiti* (Havana: Instituto Cubano del Libro, 1966), pp. 272-274.
2. Juan Bosch, *Composicion Social Dominicana* (Santo Domingo: Impresora Arte y Cine, 1970), Chs. 19 and 20.
3. Gordon K. Lewis, *Puerto Rico: Freedom and Power in the Caribbean* (New York: Monthly Review Press, 1963), p. 58.
4. Juan Angel Silen, *Historia de la Nacion Puertorriquena* (San Juan: Editorial Edil, 1973), p. 112.
5. Philip S. Foner, ed., *Inside the Monster: Writings on the United States and American Imperialism by Jose Marti* (New York: Monthly Review Press, 1975), p. 40.
6. May, p. 5.
7. Alfred T. Mahan, "The U.S. Looking Outward," *Atlantic Monthly* LXVI (1890), p. 816.
8. Alfred T. Mahan, "The Strategic Features of the Gulf of Mexico and the Caribbean Sea," *Harper's New Monthly Magazine,* Vol. XLV (October 1897), pp. 680-691.
9. Jose Marti, "The Washington Pan-American Congress," in Foner, p. 340.
10. Arthur Whitaker, *The United States and Latin America: The Northern Republics* (Cambridge, MA, 1948), p. 160.
11. U.S. Bureau of the Census, *Historical Statistics of the United States, Colonial Times to 1957* (Washington, 1961), pp. 550-552.
12. Hugh Thomas, *Cuba: The Pursuit of Freedom* (New York: Harper & Row, 1971), p. 340.
13. *Congressional Record,* 55th Cong., 2nd sess. (April 13, 1898), p. 3781.
14. William Appleman Williams, *Empire As A Way of Life* (Oxford: Oxford University Press, 1980), pp. 130-136.
15. *Ibid.*, pp. 136-142.
16. Norman Bailey, *Latin America in World Politics* (Walker & Co., 1967), p. 50.
17. *United Fruit Company: Un Caso del Dominio Imperialista en Cuba* (Havana: Editorial de Ciencias Sociales, 1976), p. 54.
18. Manuel Maldonado-Denis, *Puerto Rico: A Socio-Historic Interpretation* (New York: Vintage Books, 1972), p. 75.
19. Cited in *American Mercury,* Vol. XVI, No. 62, February, 1929.
20. EPICA, *Panama: Sovereignty for a Land Divided,* p. 14.
21. William A. Williams, p. 153.
22. *Ibid.*, p. 155.
23. J. Lloyd Mecham, *United States-Latin America Relations* (New York: Houghton Mifflin Co., 1965), p. 115.
24. Moises Rosa Ramos, "Analysis of the Church in Puerto Rico" (Church and Theology Project of the National Ecumenical Movement of Puerto Rico, 1985).

The West Indies

1. EPICA, *Jamaica: Caribbean Challenge* (Washington, DC: EPICA, 1979), pp. 21-23.
2. Patrick Emmanuel, *Crown Colony Politics in Grenada 1917-1951* (Barbados: ISER, University of the West Indies, 1978).
3. Amy Jacques-Garvey, ed., *Philosophy and Opinions of Marcus Garvey* (New York: Atheneum, 1969), p. 126.
4. Tony Martin, "Marcus Garvey—A Caribbean, Not Jamaican Hero," *Caribbean Contact,* April 1979.
5. Eric Williams, *From Columbus to Castro,* p. 444.
6. *Ibid.*, p. 449.
7. *Ibid.*, p. 453.
8. *Ibid.*, p. 454.
9. *Daily Gleaner,* December 12, 1927. Cited in Rupert Lewis, "Political Aspects of Garvey's Work in Jamaica 1929-35," *Jamaica Journal,* Vol. 7, No. 1-2, p. 32.
10. *Ibid.*, p. 34.
11. Eric Williams, *From Columbus to Castro,* p. 444.
12. *Ibid.*, p. 446.
13. Trevor Munroe and Don Robotham, *Struggles of the Jamaican People* (Jamaica: Workers Liberation League, 1977), p. 110.
14. BITU, *Jamaica 1938: The Birth of the Bustamante Industrial Trade Union* (Jamaica: BITU, 1968), pp. 7-8.

Rastafarianism

1. Erskine, p. 38.
2. *Ibid.*, pp. 99-100.
3. *Ibid.*, p. 98.
4. *Ibid.*, p. 108.
5. Jacques-Garvey, p. 121.
6. Joseph Owens, *Dread: The Rastafarians of Jamaica* (Jamaica: Sangster's Book Stores Ltd., 1976), p. xiii.
7. *Ibid.*, p. 195.
8. *Ibid.*, p. 190.
9. Owens, p. 82.
10. Erskine, p. 55.
11. *Ibid.*, p. 55.

Political Independence Without Economic Independence

1. Gordon K. Lewis, *Growth of the Modern West Indies,* pp. 346-347.
2. Samuel B. Bemis, *A Diplomatic History of the United States* (New York: Henry Holt & Co., 1942), pp. 863-864.
3. C.L.R. James, "The West Indian Middle Classes," in *Spheres of Existence,* pp. 131-140.
4. *Ibid.,* p. 155.
5. W. Arthur Lewis, "Industrialization of the British West Indies," *Caribbean Economic Review,* Vol. 2, 1950.
6. Ransford W. Palmer, *Caribbean Dependency on the United States Economy* (New York: Praeger Publishers, 1979), pp. 66-69.
7. *Ibid.,* p. 41.
8. *Ibid.,* p. 38.
9. Jay R. Mandle, *Patterns of Caribbean Development* (New York: Gordon & Breach Science Publishers, 1982), p. 62.

PART TWO
Rising Contradictions in a Troubled Time: 1959-1980

Failure of the Puerto Rican Model

The new economic thrusts of the 1950s and 60s created high expectations that the problems of poverty and unemployment would finally be solved. These hopes were not fulfilled. Instead, the failure of the Puerto Rican model in Puerto Rico and elsewhere set the stage for a period of upheaval in the 1970s, when the region's economies declined and new social forces emerged to seek alternative models of change.

Disaster in Puerto Rico

Starting in 1947, U.S. corporations were invited to open factories in Puerto Rico with promises of a low-wage work force, freedom from U.S. income taxes, and tax-free repatriation of profits. "Operation Bootstrap," as it was called, was advertised as an attempt to build a modern industrial state on the ruins of Puerto Rico's sugar economy. Its deeper purpose was to bring the Island into the U.S. economy as an industrial enclave supplying U.S. firms with cheap labor.

Incentives were only part of the reason firms located in Puerto Rico, however. The other reason was the Island's special status as a U.S. colony—not stated in so many words, but a reality nonetheless behind the title of "freely associated state." This colonial relationship meant that firms could expect compliant local authorities and a "stable" political climate, while enjoying low wages typical of the Third World. It also meant U.S. federal subsidies were available to build highways, port facilities and other infrastructure needed by foreign investors.

Operation Bootstrap was touted as an economic miracle, and for a while, it appeared to be. Its results included:

- Average growth rates of 6% in the 1950s, 5% in the 1960s, and 4% in the 1970s.
- U.S. capital investment increasing from $1.4 billion in 1960 to $24 billion in 1979.
- Second highest per capita income in Latin America.
- Literacy and life expectancy approaching that of the U.S.
- Extensive port and highway development.
- Highest per capita level of imports from the U.S. in the world, and 34% of total U.S. direct investment in Latin America.[1]

But behind these glowing figures lay an alarming reality. Puerto Rico's rapid industrialization was accompanied not by rising employment, but by relentlessly rising *unemployment.* Official unemployment figures stood at 12-14% in the mid-1960s; by 1975 it had risen to 20%, and this was considered an underestimation of true joblessness.[2] At the same time, Puerto Rico became hopelessly dependent on subsidies from the U.S. federal budget. These subsidies, which stood at $119 million per year in 1950, soared to $3.1 billion by 1979![3]

The Bootstrap model made Puerto Rico dependent on foreign capital—capital which became increasingly mobile and elusive as transnational corporations broadened their reach. In the first years of Bootstrap, labor-intensive light industry entered Puerto Rico to take advantage of its low wages. These were mainly firms manufacturing consumer goods like shoes, clothing, and glassware from parts or raw materials brought in from the U.S. In the mid-1960s, however, the 15-17 year tax exempt period in the initial contracts of these companies began

to expire. At the same time, wages on the island had risen partly due to successful labor organizing and partly due to the arrival of new, capital-intensive industries which employed few people but paid higher wages. The result was that many of the assembly factories closed their Puerto Rico operations and relocated to cheaper wage havens such as Haiti, the Dominican Republic, and the Far East.

Petroleum refining and petrochemicals dominated investment in the Island from 1965-1972.[4] These "heavy" industries used huge amounts of land, water, and energy, but provided relatively few jobs. Companies like Exxon, Mobil, Shell, and Union Carbide were attracted by Puerto Rico's cheap water and land, and by the willingness of local and federal authorities to ignore environmental standards. But after 1973, when world oil prices rose, this sector too went into a slump.

The next wave of investment came from chemical and pharmaceutical firms in the 1970s. Every major drug company built a plant in Puerto Rico, giving the Island the highest concentration of pharmaceutical factories in the world. Like the refineries, the drug companies are heavy polluters but provide relatively few jobs.

The pharmaceutical companies stayed in Puerto Rico but they exacted a grim price. The Island became the United States' toxic waste dump, where pollution unacceptable in the U.S. could be transferred by runaway firms. Communities in heavily industrialized areas of Puerto Rico began to register high rates of respiratory problems, cancer, leukemia, and other illnesses.[5]

While these successive waves of industrialization were taking place, jobs were being lost in the rural areas due to the virtual abandonment of agriculture. This was part of the Bootstrap plan: Puerto Rico would export manufactures, while importing all the food and consumer items it needed from the United States. But the labor force displaced from the

"Yes, in my house we also think that things go better with Coke."

countryside was too large to be absorbed by the new industries, especially after the labor-intensive assembly firms began moving out. The result was growing unemployment and dependence on imported food. Today about 90% of what Puerto Ricans eat is imported.[6]

Bootstrap's failure to reduce unemployment was particularly striking in light of the fact that two concurrent programs were imposed to reduce the size of the Puerto Rican work force. One was officially sponsored emigration, resulting in the exodus of 40% of the Island's population to the United States. The other was a heavily-promoted program of "voluntary" female sterilization which reduced the birth rate from 160 per 1000 women in 1941 to 102 per 1000 in 1970.[7] Without these population control measures, Operation Bootstrap's failure to provide enough jobs would have been even more glaring.

As the factories closed their doors, the U.S. government increasingly had to subsidize the standard of living in its colony. By 1975, 50% of the Puerto Rican population was receiving food stamps, while others survived on welfare payments and distribution of U.S. surplus foodstuffs.[8] To relieve unemployment, workers were added to inflated government payrolls underwritten by U.S. subsidies.

By supporting the Puerto Rican work force at a minimum level, this welfare safety net allowed firms operating on the Island to pay lower wages. U.S. federal payments to Puerto Rico thus became a subsidy by U.S. taxpayers to runaway U.S. firms. Built on the shifting sands of transnational investment, the Puerto Rican model turned out not as a miracle of development, but a model for dependency and disaster.

The Puerto Rican Model in Jamaica

Three North American aluminum companies—Reynolds, Alcan, and Kaiser—began exploiting Jamaican bauxite in the 1950s, using U.S. government subsidies under the Marshall Plan. They bought up vast tracts of land, and bauxite soon replaced sugar as Jamaica's main source of income.

The aluminum companies, however, processed all of the bauxite outside Jamaica. The island received only taxes and royalties paid on the raw ore. These were kept low through a device called "transfer pricing," in which the aluminum firms "sold" the Jamaican ore to their U.S. parent companies at an artificially low price, which was then used as the basis for taxation. The result was that Jamaica received less than 2% of the value of the finished aluminum in the world market.[9] Nor did the bauxite sector have much impact on unemployment. A mechanized industry, bauxite mining provided a small number of relatively highly-paid jobs.

Other industries which boomed along with bauxite included construction, transportation, cement and clay production, manufacturing, banking and tourism. All were dominated by North American and British capital, with Jamaican capitalists playing a growing role as local managers and partners for the foreign firms. This local elite was drawn largely from Jamaica's upper class of 21 white, Chinese and Syrian families, including the Matalons, Ashenheims, Harts, Henriques, and others.

The Jamaican economy's swift growth, averaging 6.7% per year from 1950 to 1968,[10] primarily benefited this elite and a growing urban middle class. Conditions for the black majority, on the other hand, grew steadily worse. Agricultural stagnation displaced many from the rural areas, so that unemployment, after dropping in the 1950s due to emigration, rose again. By 1967, 18% of the work force was unemployed and many more under-employed.[11] Their desperation grew as Jamaica's "development boom" left a majority of the population behind.

Trinidad

Dr. Eric Williams took office in 1956 a firm proponent of the Puerto Rican model, which had been launched in Trinidad by the preceding government of Albert Gomes. Under the "Pioneer Status Act," foreign firms were encouraged to set up branch plants in Trinidad to assemble consumer goods such as automobiles, televisions, and refrigerators for the local market. Many multinationals established subsidiaries in Trinidad, seeing it as a good regional base in the Eastern Caribbean.

The Trinidad economy was dominated by oil refining and sugar, both under foreign control. The oil sector was exploited by U.S. multinationals, notably Texaco and W.R. Grace, while the sugar industry was owned by Caroni Ltd, a subsidiary of the British firm Tate & Lyle. Mounting labor struggles against these multinationals in the 1960s caused Williams to reverse his early pro-labor posture in favor of a policy of repressing labor struggles.[12] In March 1965, a major strike in the sugar industry threatened to produce an unprecedented unity of African and East Indian workers behind the militant, Butlerite trade union leader George Weekes. Using the strike as justification, Williams declared a state of emergency and hastily passed an Industrial Stabilization Act which outlawed strikes in various industries and replaced union negotiation with arbitration by a government-controlled industrial court.

As in Jamaica, economic growth surged ahead in the early years, with real gross domestic product growing by 8.5% per year from 1951-1961.[13] But unemployment also rose, standing at 14% in 1966 with another one-third of the work force under-employed.[14]

Rising Anger

By the end of the 1960s, it was clear to many in the Caribbean that "Industrialization by Invitation is really the absentee owner transferred from agriculture to industry."[15] The old colonial structures were replicated in the new society. While political power was now in black and brown hands, economic power was still largely controlled by whites, primarily foreign corporations, with the participation only of local elites consisting mostly of white, mulatto, and other non-black minorities. The "trickle-down" theory of the Puerto Rican model—that growth would automatically improve conditions for everyone in the society—proved wrong. While consumption levels soared for a privileged few, the majority of farmers, workers and youth were worse off than ever before.∎

The Cuban Revolution

From the dawn of the 1800s through the year 1958, the extremes of colonial and imperial domination found their expression in Cuba. After the Haitian Revolution of 1795, Cuba replaced Haiti as the sugar bowl of the world, becoming the ultimate example of a deformed monocrop economy. King Sugar

SOMOS CUBANOS
HOY MAS QUE NUNCA
ORGULLOSOS DE SERLO
AHORA Ó NUNCA
VIVA CUBA LIBRE
ADELANTE, CUBANOS

Mario Garcia Joya, courtesy of Center for Cuban Studies

"We are Cubans, and today more than ever, proud to be. Now or never, long live Free Cuba. Forward, Cubans!"

absorbed all the human labor, sapped the fertility of the soil, and razed the island's forests of precious woods. A Havana-based sugar aristocracy indulged its tastes for European luxuries, while the peasants were thrown off their small plots and slaves labored on the plantations.[1]

"In Cuba, sugar was the knife, imperialism the assassin," writes Latin American historian Eduardo Galeano.[2] When the world price of sugar fell to 4¢ a pound in 1921, U.S. interests bought up many bankrupt sugar mills, as well as many banks, including the Banco Nacional. By 1948 Cuba was sending almost all of its sugar north, supplying one-third of all the sugar consumed in the United States.[3] U.S. companies controlled about 75% of Cuba's arable land, along with sugar mills, railroads, ports, mines, banks, and even the country's telephone and power systems.

Washington had helped install the neo-fascist dictator Gerardo Machado in 1925, and when a nationalist revolt erupted against him in 1933, maneuvered Fulgencio Batista into power as army chief of staff. Batista forged an early alliance with U.S. crime interests. Miami crime boss Meyer Lansky contracted with Batista to supply Cuban molasses for a mob-run bootlegging operation during Prohibition, and Cuba was also the principle entry point to the U.S. for the Mafia's Chinese heroin network. After Batista was forced to resign and flee Cuba in 1944—because President Franklin Roosevelt found him too accommodating toward the left—the Cuban's powerful friends came to his aid. In the early 1950s, Meyer Lansky bribed then-Cuban president Carlos Prio to let Batista back into Cuba, where he seized power in a coup and proceeded to realize Lansky's dream of turning Cuba into the hub of a syndicate empire in the Caribbean.

Havana in the fifties became the capital city of organized crime, an anything-goes Disneyland run by the mob and a major conduit for the narcotics flowing into the United States. Alongside the rocketing casino trade, fueled by mob-organized junkets from the mainland, the satellite rackets—prostitution, narcotics, and wholesale abortions—spun in profitable orbit. Cuba's government officials and favor-brokers got a piece of everything, twice: once from the syndicate, and once again from the government treasury, where the cashflow of the poverty-ridden island was diverted into gold-lined pockets.

. . . Batista kept the mob in the driver's seat, and Washington kept Batista in power through economic and military aid. In Washington two of Batista's most devoted supporters were Florida senator "Gorgeous George" Smathers and his good friend and later Vice President Richard Nixon.[4]

Prerevolutionary Havana glittered with expensive hotels and casinos, many of them, like the luxurious Havana Riviera Hotel and Casino, operating as joint ventures between the mob and the Batista government. This was the Havana North Americans knew. In the countryside, however, the Caribbean's largest country was a stagnant backwater, where there was one doctor for every 2,000 people; where less than 10% of dwellings had electricity and only 15% running water, and more than half had no toilet of any kind; where only 4% of the peasantry ate meat on a regular basis, and only one family in ten could give their children milk to drink.[5] In his famous court defense,

History Will Absolve Me, the young lawyer Fidel Castro traced these ills to the reality of foreign control:

> Eighty-five percent of the small farmers in Cuba pay rent and live under the constant threat of being dispossessed from the land they till. More than half of the most productive land belongs to foreigners. In Oriente, the largest province, the lands of the United Fruit Company and West Indian Company join the north with the south coast. There are two hundred thousand peasant families who do not have a single acre of land to till to provide food for their starving children. On the other hand, nearly three hundred thousand *caballerias* of cultivable land owned by powerful interests remain uncultivated.[6]

Under these circumstances it was not surprising that three-quarters of the guerrilla fighters who joined Castro's revolutionary army were drawn from the rural sugar workers.[7]

Batista's second period of rule was far more fascistic and brutal than his first. There was no freedom of speech; the army and police regularly rounded up potential opponents and turned them over to court-martials and the firing squad. This repression helped fuel a broad-based opposition to the dictatorship. An intellectual and student movement centered at the University of Havana grew during the fifties, relating the goal of social justice to socialism and an end to foreign ownership of the economy. Strikes by labor unions in the cities and the sugar sector became frequent after 1955. Opposition finally spread to the urban middle class and even many businessmen and landowners—everyone who did not have their hand directly in the till of Batista's corruption. By the end of 1958 the government was crumbling under pressure from the growing guerrilla movement and its own internal decay, and top Batista military men fled into exile.

The revolution which swept the rotten remnants of Batista's regime from the National Palace on January 1, 1959 was a fundamentally nationalist and anti-dictatorial movement. It sought a return to constitutional rule. More than that, however, it sought to cleanse the country of corruption and end U.S. domination of the economy: send the Mafia back to Miami (in fact, they fled with their casinos to the Bahamas) and realize the historic Cuban dream of independence from colonialism. In June 1959, Castro's new government passed the first Agrarian Reform Law returning foreign-owned sugar, tobacco, and cattle estates to national control.

For more than fifty years, the Greater Antilles of Cuba, Puerto Rico, Haiti and the Dominican Republic had been outposts of U.S. capitalism, controlled directly through military occupation or indirectly through U.S.-backed dictators. The Cuban revolution was the first break in this control. What became known as the "Cuban model"—health and education for all, racial and economic egalitarianism, a priority on the needs of the poor—stood as proof that social justice was possible once a country freed itself from imperial control [see Part IV, Ch. 1]. The nearby Puerto Rican example, with its neocolonial reliance on foreign ownership, was not the only path to development. This knowledge combined with rising racial and political consciousness elsewhere in the Caribbean to forge a new progressive movement which would alter the face of the region. ∎

New Progressive Movement Emerges

Two social forces came together during the 1960s and coalesced in a way which had never before happened in the West Indies. On the one hand were Caribbean intellectuals, many educated abroad, who for the first time turned to the study of their own societies and the search for radically new models of development. On the other hand were workers and a burgeoning population of unemployed youth, fed up with the old system and ready to fight for any change offering hope for the future. Erupting in a wave of protests at the end of the decade, the progressive movement took shape after 1970 as new political groups and parties whose first experience with state power came with the Grenada revolution of 1979.

Intellectual Roots of the Movement

Progressive intellectuals began organizing in Guyana in 1963, calling themselves the New World Group. The group acquired branches in Trinidad and Jamaica and began to publish a journal, *New World Quarterly*. Consisting primarily of scholars associated with the University of Guyana and the University of the West Indies (UWI), New World challenged the assumptions of traditional Caribbean social science. The economists of the group, including Maurice Odle and Clive Thomas in Guyana, Lloyd Best in Trinidad, George Beckford and Norman Girvan in Jamaica, compared the economic dependency of the plantation system to that of the Puerto Rican model. Political scientists like James Millette in Trinidad and Trevor Monroe in Jamaica focused on the failure of West Indian politicians to alter the colonial power structure after independence. Historians Walter Rodney, Woodville Marshall and Douglas Hall reinterpreted the region's history, not from the perspective of the colonizers but from that of the Afro-Caribbean; while sociologist Orlando Patterson analyzed the effects of colonialism and slavery on the "Caribbean Man."[1]

These scholars and others like them were the product of an educational system which selected the brightest individuals for advanced training at universities in Europe and North America. Upon their return to the Caribbean, graduates traditionally would move into coveted civil service, professional, and academic posts, ensuring their absorption into the upper middle class and their identification with the status quo. This pattern began to splinter with the second generation of intellectuals when some made the unprecedented choice of siding with the popular classes. This reflected, on the one hand, their experience of racism abroad: brown-skinned persons who drew a social advantage from their fair complexion in the West Indies found themselves labeled black in Europe, with all the racism that entailed. The second and more important factor was their exposure to the anti-colonial and Pan African movement in Paris, London, and the United States.

The intellectual roots of this movement went back to Marcus Garvey, and flowered anew in the 1950s around the struggle to decolonize Africa. A seminal influence in the fifties was the writing of Frantz Fanon, a Martiniquan psychiatrist practicing in colonial Algeria who became involved in the Algerian war of independence from France. Fanon focused on the destructive effects of racism and colonialism on the personality of a colonized people, calling for violent resistance as the only way in which the colonized could liberate

themselves from this oppression. Even more shocking at the time was Fanon's criticism of the black intelligentsia for failing to lead an active anti-colonial struggle—thus calling into question the whole decolonization process which passed power gradually into the hands of a black and brown elite.

In London, West Indian and African intellectuals came together in the International African Service Bureau, founded in the 1930s by Trinidadian George Padmore. Its members included figures who would later lead Africa to independence: Kwame Nkrumah, Julius Nyerere, and Jomo Kenyatta, among others. The Bureau's journal, *International African Opinion*, was edited by another Trinidadian, C.L.R. James, whose articulation of an independent black marxism was to be a key ideological influence on the Caribbean left. James envisioned a kind of direct democracy built on local citizen assemblies, drawing inspiration from historical models such as the Greek city-states and contemporary examples such as the workers' councils of the 1950s in Hungary and Poland.[2] He argued that the worldwide struggle of blacks was independent of the socialist struggle led by Marxist parties and trade unions, but that it was also a powerful contributor to that struggle.[3]

James and Padmore both spent years in the United States and helped link the civil rights struggle there to the anti-

Frantz Fanon

colonial movement. As the Black Power movement took shape in the 1960s, it counted among its leaders Caribbean-Americans such as Stokely Carmichael, born in Trinidad, and Malcolm X, whose mother was Grenadian. The travels of these and other Black Power spokespersons helped tie the movement together as it developed in the four separate but connected "poles" of Africa, the West Indies, Europe, and the United States.

While these trends were developing in relation to the English and French-speaking Caribbean, the Spanish-speaking Caribbean provided the first example of a country to actually implement radical change. The Cuban revolution's impact on the English-speaking left was primarily symbolic in this early era. For the people of the Dominican Republic, on the other hand, suffering under the Trujillo dictatorship, Cuba was a concrete model and inspiration. The Dominican popular movement which organized after the death of Trujillo was not directed by Marxists, as Washington portrayed it; but young Dominicans, especially university students, did see the Cuban reforms as a model of how positive change could occur.

For people throughout the Caribbean, but especially in the Greater Antilles, the U.S. invasion of the Dominican Republic in 1965 and the war in Vietnam had a powerful impact. They contributed to a deepening awareness that the United States was taking over from the colonial powers in denying self-determination to Third World peoples. The positive formulation of this theme came out of the Cuban revolution's calls for "Tri-Continental Unity" between the people of Asia, Africa and Latin America. The negative side developed fully after the Marines had landed on the shores of Santo Domingo, leading to a clear anti-imperialist ideology among all the progressive forces in the Dominican Republic.

Youth, Students and Rastafari

While these political currents were shaping the movement, winds of change were blowing through a new Caribbean generation coming of age. The youth population had expanded at a phenomenal rate: in some territories, 60% of the population was under 25 years old. Since secondary education had become generalized in the colonies during the 1950s, the mid-'60s saw the first wave of educated, unemployed youth hit the streets. They did so just as tourism was expanding in the English-speaking Caribbean following the cut-off of U.S. tourism to Cuba. To black youth, the tourist industry symbolized the foreign domination of the society and their own subservient place in it. They bristled at the spectacle of Caribbean people acting as waiters, bellhops, and chauffeurs for rich foreigners. Whereas the older generation tended to be resigned to the status quo, the youth refused to passively accept racial and economic stratification as a fact of life.

In this context, Rastafarianism broadened its appeal as a social philosophy proclaiming the roots of Caribbean oppression in the system of white supremacy. Most numerous in Jamaica, the Rastafari were heavily repressed in the 1950s and '60s by the Jamaican government. Despite their social isolation, the Rastas' emphasis on Africa and their assertion that blacks are a "chosen people" shook the color-conscious

Walter Rodney

Caribbean to its foundations.

The late 1960s saw the fusion of elements of Rastafarianism with the Black Power movement of workers and students. University of the West Indies students and graduates in various islands proclaimed themselves Rastafarians, broadening the cult from its original base in the urban poor. Pan-African symbolism was evident in the names of newspapers published by newly-formed progressive groups, often centered at regional campuses of UWI. These included *Abeng* in Jamaica (*abeng* is the Ashanti word for the conch shell blown by slaves to signal an insurrection); *Moko* in Trinidad (referring to the Moko-jumbie, an African spirit figure); and *Ratoon* in Guyana (referring to the growth of sugar cane).

In the same period, intellectuals and civil servants in the Eastern Caribbean islands of St. Lucia, St. Vincent, Dominica and Grenada were organizing "Forums" to discuss social change. These small discussion groups were the forerunners of left parties which would emerge in the next decade.

1968 Explosions: Jamaica and Antigua

Intellectual leader of the Black Power movement in the Caribbean was Dr. Walter Rodney, a Guyanese historian then teaching at UWI's Jamaica campus. Rodney, a scholar of African history, defined Black Power as follows:

> First, a break with imperialism which is historically white racist. Second, the assumption of power by the Black masses in the islands. Third, the cultural reconstruction of the society in the image of Blacks.[4]

This message from the respected Rodney was immensely threatening to the Jamaican power structure. In 1968, the JLP government took a step which was to provoke a major backlash: it banned Rodney from Jamaica. Riots broke out instantly, followed by demonstrations in Trinidad, Barbados,

May 30, 1969: Workers at the Shell Oil Refinery in Curacao prepare to strike.

Amigoe

Guyana, and among West Indians in New York and Montreal.

That same year, workers in Antigua staged a general strike which nearly brought down the government of premier Vere C. Bird. Development during the 1960s had made tourism virtually the only industry in Antigua, and it was mainly in the hands of U.S., Canadian, and European entrepreneurs. Although Bird had risen to power via trade unionism and headed Antigua's main union, the workers perceived his government as selling out to the employers—a natural consequence of the island's dependence on granting concessions to foreign investors. When the general secretary of Bird's union, George Walter, formed a new, more militant union, the workers transferred their allegiance overnight.

Bird's refusal to recognize the new union sparked a mass demonstration on February 11, 1968 in which some 22,000 out of Antigua's population of 60,000 marched through the streets of the capital, St. John. While recognition of the new union was the main demand, the protest went farther, embracing popular anger over the foreign-dominated economy. The leadership of Walter's union included Tim Hector, an Antiguan teacher who had studied in Canada. He and other organizers held dozens of public meetings around the island in the weeks which followed, and on March 19, Antiguan workers launched a general strike. The government responded by declaring a state of emergency: workers and youth battled police in the streets, the British were called in to mediate, and Bird offered to resign.

Whether Walter was persuaded by the British mediators that Hector was "communist," or whether he simply feared losing personal control to the radical wing of the workers' movement, in the end Walter turned down Bird's resignation, tossing away victory. This led to a split between Walter and Hector and to the emergence of a new group under Hector's leadership, the Afro-Caribbean Liberation Movement.

Curaçao: The "May Movement"

From 1917 until well into the fifties, the economy of Curaçao was dominated by the giant Royal Dutch Shell refinery which sprawls across the port of Willemstad. Supplied by crude oil from neighboring Venezuela, the refinery initially opened up jobs for Antillean workers. Real economic power, however, remained in the hands of the Dutch and a local elite consisting primarily of whites of Dutch descent, mulattos, Lebanese, and Jews. This sector included most of the ruling Democratic Party which controlled the Central Government of the Netherlands Antilles and stayed in power through economic aid from Holland.

Beginning in 1957, automation sharply reduced the number of jobs at the refinery, from 11,000 in 1952 to 4,000 in 1969.[5] Shell also turned over many of its functions to subcontractors who paid much lower wages than Shell itself. At the same time, the Central Government imposed a wage freeze in hopes of attracting tourism and industrial investment. This shrinking economy brought into sharp focus the contrast between the workers' socio-economic position and that of highly-paid expatriates and the local ruling class.

As in Antigua, the catalyst for protest was the emergence of new grassroots leadership comprising militant trade unionists (in this case the head of the port workers) and radical intellectuals. The latter included Curaçaolenes who had returned from studies in Holland and were publishing a newspaper in Papiamento called *Vitó* (Plantation Overseer) which put forth a class and racial analysis of local labor problems. From mid-1968 onward, labor unrest spread through the island. The flashpoint came on May 30, 1969 with a wage dispute between 400 organized workers and WESCAR, one of Shell's Dutch subcontractors. Within hours, the protest was transformed into a violent riot as at least 5,000 striking and unemployed workers marched from the refinery into the heart of Willemstad, where their anger exploded in looting, vandalism and arson. Holland rushed in 300 Marines who helped local police and the 250 Dutch Marines stationed in Curacao to quickly crush the uprising.

Threatened with a general strike, the Central Government resigned five days later on June 5, 1969. A new political party was formed, the "Frente Obrero i Liberacion 30 di Mey 1969" (May 30, 1969 Workers and Liberation Front). But although it was the first worker-led party in the island's history, when elections were held that September the Frente won only 3 out of 12 seats, and the ruling DP returned to power. This defeat reflected the spontaneous, unorganized and minority character of the May movement. While the majority of Curaçaolenes could identify and sympathize with the strikers' grievances, many people were taken aback by the violence, and the Frente was perceived as having no real ideological consensus, organizational base or political plan.[6]

The May movement put the ruling class on notice that reforms were needed if the system was to survive. The government began treating the labor movement as a political force: wages went up by 20-30% in the lower brackets, and a minimum wage law was passed. A process of "Antilleanization" began as Shell and its subcontractors hastened efforts to replace expatriate managers and technicians with Curaçaolenes, and a similar process took place in the civil service. Steps were taken to introduce Papiamento into the schools. These nationalistic reforms paved the way for the emergence of the MAN party which came to power with a social-democratic agenda in 1979.

Trinidad 1970

Just as the Jamaican riots became the symbol of labor's revolt in the 1930s, Trinidad's "Black Power" uprising came to symbolize the protests which convulsed the region at the close of the decade of the sixties.

In 1969, a group of Trinidadian and other West Indian students at the Sir George Williams University in Montreal were arrested for destroying the university's computers during a protest against the racism of a Canadian professor. Back in Trinidad, students at the University of the West Indies organized in support of the arrested students, demanding that the Trinidad government provide legal assistance. When the Canadian governor-general arrived in Trinidad on a visit, the UWI students barred him from the campus in protest.

These organizing activities led to the formation of the National Joint Action Committee (NJAC), spearheaded by UWI student Geddes Granger. NJAC soon grew beyond its university origins to encompass some two dozen grassroots organizations, including the progressive wing of the trade union movement. Eric Williams' introduction of the repressive Industrial Stabilization Act in the mid-1960s had split the trade unions into a pro-government and an anti-government camp. A transport strike in open defiance of the ISA strengthened links between NJAC and radical union leaders such as George Weekes of the Oilfield Workers Trades Union and Clive Nunez of the Transport and Industrial Workers Union.

The social backdrop was one of rising unemployment and economic domination by a racial elite. Of the executive and managerial staff of major firms, only 4% were black, while 53% were white and the rest mulatto, Chinese and East Indian.[7] Trinidad differed from the other West Indian societies, however, in that the working class was divided between blacks (in the oil and industrial sector) and East Indians (in the sugar sector). The possibility of a link-up between these two groups, especially under the leadership of the radical unions, was immensely threatening both to the pro-government union leaders and to the government itself.

On February 26, 1970, Geddes Granger and about 200 students began a march through Port-of-Spain to protest the government's handling of the Sir George Williams University affair. Unexpectedly, the crowd swelled as thousands of unemployed youth ran to join its ranks. The marchers turned first upon the visible symbols of Canadian imperialism, the Canadian banks in downtown Port-of-Spain, then moved on to the Chamber of Commerce and the Roman Catholic Cathedral. For 55 tense days, Trinidad reverberated with the angry chants of the marchers as they struck out at the establishment of business, Church and state. The Rev. Roy Neehall, then head of the Caribbean Conference of Churches at its Port-of-Spain office, recalls the protest:

> They used the symbols and the language of the Black Power movement, but it was certainly far more than something that had to do with the color of their skin. It grew and grew until they started challenging everything in the society that represented established power and privilege. They challenged the Church too, because the Church seemed to be very much linked up with the government, and to be a place where distinctions were made between those who were privileged and those who were poor.[8]

The march had begun with "Black Power" as its slogan, but soon the organizers had to confront the implications of defining their protest in racial rather than class terms. In an attempt to manipulate the old black/East Indian split, the Williams government labelled the march "anti-Indian." On March 12, the protesters marched to Caroni, in the heart of the sugar district, in an announced act of solidarity with the East Indian sugar workers then locked in struggle with the reactionary head of their union, Bhadase Maraj. The plan was that the sugar workers would march to Port-of-Spain where they would join black unions in a general strike—the black/Indian unity which the ruling class so feared.

It was at this point that the Williams government broke its silence and declared a state of emergency, ordering the detention of Granger and the other leaders. That same day, a mutiny broke out in Trinidad's 700-man army in support of the demonstrators, but Williams called in U.S. and Venezuelan warships which sat offshore while a dawn-to-dusk curfew was imposed and the protest subsided.

> They probably could have achieved a good deal more if they had been given enough time to unite the urban folk with the rural sugar workers. But because political power had been based on the divisions within the society, including racial divisions, the government realized that any unity between East Indians and people of African descent would be the end of

power for anybody who depended on that division to retain power. It was that movement toward the unity of the two groups that led to the declaration of the state of emergency and ultimately to the structures of extreme oppression against all those who were calling for change.[9]

After the riot, governments around the region took measures to stamp out potential Black Power influence in their own societies. The government of Barbados banned NJAC leaders from the island, and in Jamaica writings by Black Power leaders such as Malcolm X and Eldridge Cleaver were confiscated. In Belize, two members of the United Black Association for Development were charged with seditious conspiracy for calling for an end to "economic colonialism"; while in tiny Grenada, premier Eric Gairy announced that he was doubling the island's police force and creating a new paramilitary squad to deal with potential unrest.

The New Jewel Movement

Out of the social protest movements of the 1960s emerged the leaders and embryonic organizations of the contemporary Caribbean left. In the years which followed, most of them attempted to move beyond the racial confines of "Black Power." The Afro-Caribbean Liberation Movement, for example, became the Antigua Caribbean Liberation Movement. Most of these groups initially rejected participation in electoral politics, seeing the British Westminster system as excluding the people from real economic and political power. They styled themselves "movements" or used similar non-party designations, such as the Youlou Liberation Movement in St. Vincent, the Workers' Liberation League in Jamaica, or the Working People's Alliance in Guyana.

One such group was the Movement for Assemblies of the People (MAP), started in Grenada by two young British-educated lawyers, Maurice Bishop and Kenrick Radix. In February 1970, Bishop was on his way home from England and passed through Trinidad at the moment of the Black Power uprising. Back in Grenada, he and other young intellectuals organized a sympathy protest which also attacked the corrupt and incompetent government of then-premier Eric Gairy. Gairy responded with harsh repression, including the formation of a paramilitary squad called the "Mongoose Gang."

In November of that year a group of Grenadian nurses led a peaceful protest to highlight the appalling conditions at the St. George's hospital. Gairy's police reacted violently, beating, tear-gassing and arresting the demonstrators. The arrested nurses were defended by Bishop and Radix in a trial which attracted regional attention.

Two years later, Bishop, Radix, and Jacqueline Creft formed MAP, which proposed a new grassroots democracy based on village assemblies inspired by the Marxian populism of C.L.R. James. Around the same time, a young U.S.-educated economist named Unison Whiteman started JEWEL—Joint Endeavor for Welfare, Education and Liberation—in a rural parish of the island. In March 1973 the two organizations merged to form the New Jewel Movement (NJM).

Maurice Bishop

The NJM resembled other embryonic, Marxist/populist political groups, but there was a difference: Gairy's repression. Gairy was a pariah among the region's governments, considered the shame of the Caribbean. At home he was an eccentric tyrant kept in power by rigged elections and a bloated military armed by Pinochet's Chile. Whereas outbursts of protest elsewhere were channeled into reformist social gains, in Grenada the confrontation between the people and the government continued to deepen. Because of the repression and Gairy's personalized corruption which also affected the middle class, the young NJM activists were able to build a durable opposition which cut across class lines.

The repression forced the NJM to be a well-organized party with a clear strategy for building a grassroots base—something other fledgling left groups lacked in the early 1970s. It organized clandestinely, going door-to-door and holding house meetings to discuss an agenda for social change. In November 1973, Gairy's Mongoose Gang attacked six NJM leaders and beat them nearly to death, enhancing their popular image as heroes. Soon after that "Bloody Sunday," a coalition of businessmen, clergy, and other elite figures joined Grenadian workers in an island-wide strike which fell just short of bringing down the Gairy government.

Because of this broad-based opposition, the NJM was able to move relatively early to become a party and contest Parliamentary elections. It formed a tactical alliance with the other non-Gairy party, the Grenada National Party, to contest the 1976 election. The election was blatantly fraudulent and produced another Gairy victory, but the NJM became the

Eric Gairy, right, meets Chilean dictator Augusto Pinochet.

leader of the Parliamentary opposition, giving the party legitimacy and a forum from which to denounce Gairy's corruption.

This same need for legitimacy spurred a number of other radical Caribbean groups to declare themselves parties toward the end of the decade. This formalized their participation in the political system, but it also put them at a disadvantage in terms of competing in an arena largely controlled by the ruling parties. Some groups suffered by attempting to contest elections without first having built a strong popular base as the NJM did before 1976.

Ideologically, the left within the English-speaking Caribbean was still in a process of exploration. They had come out of the racially-oriented Black Power movement but were attempting to move beyond it to forge an actual agenda for social and economic change. The central role of university intellectuals infused a strong interest in Marxism and Marxism-Leninism, but there was no consensus on how these concepts should be applied to the Caribbean. Initially, the interest in Cuba was primarily an emotional admiration for a small Caribbean country which dared to stand up to foreign domination. Serious analysis of Cuban socialism did not occur until Michael Manley came to power in Jamaica and used Cuba as a model for some of his reforms. ∎

THE NEW PROGRESSIVE PROGRAM

As new progressive groups emerged in the early 1970s, the changes they advocated coalesced to form a kind of progressive "platform." Although it was not formally defined and the specifics varied, this vision of change was consistent in its basic themes. It formed the basis for Manley's democratic socialism in Jamaica in the 1970s, and for the New Jewel Movement's policies in Grenada after 1979. Common themes included:

In agriculture . . .

DIVERSIFY AGRICULTURE to reduce dependence on one-crop economies. GROW FOOD LOCALLY to reduce food import bills. DEVELOP AGRO-INDUSTRY based on locally-grown crops. MODERNIZE THE FISHING INDUSTRY. Support start-up of COOPERATIVES in agriculture, fishing, crafts.

In the economy . . .

MAKE LOANS AVAILABLE to small producers such as farmers and fishermen through a nationally-owned bank. ENCOURAGE INVESTMENT IN PRODUCTION by the private sector, not just commercial activities. DIVERSIFY FOREIGN TRADE and sources of aid and loans. INTRODUCE PLANNING into the economy. CREATE PUBLICLY-OWNED INDUSTRIES where the private sector does not invest. CONTROL PRICES on basic necessities such as rice, flour and cement.

In social services . . .

MAKE EDUCATION FREE through the high school level. IMPLEMENT LITERACY DRIVE to wipe out adult illiteracy. SECURE UNIVERSITY SCHOLARSHIPS from diverse sources abroad. EXTEND HEALTH CARE to rural areas and make free care widely available. EXTEND RUNNING WATER AND ELECTRICITY to rural areas as rapidly as possible.

In political life . . .

DEVELOP ORGANS OF LOCAL GOVERNMENT such as village and parish councils. LEGISLATE WOMEN'S RIGHTS, including equal pay for equal work, maternity leave, and state-funded day care centers. IMPLEMENT MANDATORY TRADE UNION RECOGNITION LAW.

Religious Opening in the 1970s

... and creation of the Caribbean Conference of Churches

After World War Two, the mainline Catholic and Protestant churches in the Caribbean became more broadly middle-class in constituency and attitude. Besides their primary evangelical thrust, they continued their educational and social service activities for the poor. But they remained dominated by expatriate clergy and approached the poor in a paternalistic manner, preaching deference to authority which reinforced the status quo.

The reformist political process of the 1950s and '60s did not profoundly affect the Church. The failed West Indies Federation did not bring regional unity, industrialization did not eliminate unemployment or poverty, and political independence left many of the colonial attitudes in the society untouched. Instead, it was the grassroots protest against these unchanged conditions which shook the Church and forced it to begin dealing internally with the remnants of its colonizing role. The Cuban revolution, the U.S. invasion of the Dominican Republic, and the Black Power movement all were pivotal in forcing the conservative Church to begin to look toward change.

The Cuban revolution galvanized hemispheric awareness of the poverty issue and spurred the search for a "developmentalist" model of change which would avoid the need for revolution. The modern Caribbean ecumenical movement came out of the effort to apply such a developmentalist approach to poverty in the Caribbean. Initially these were small, local initiatives, such as the credit union movement started by a nun in Dominica in the 1950s, or the two Barbadian clergymen who addressed the problem of unemployment in the early sixties. Such projects led to an ecumenical dialogue on social issues, resulting in the formation in 1969 of CADEC, Christian Action for Development in the Eastern Caribbean.

Initially funded by Church World Service, the development and disaster relief arm of the National Council of Churches of the USA, CADEC was to become a huge program spanning the English and Dutch Caribbean, with liaison to the French and Spanish islands. It funded grassroots projects in areas such as agriculture, fisheries, small business, and crafts. Despite the positive impact of these projects at the local level, however, progressive church thinkers increasingly questioned the entire developmentalist approach. Out of this first church response to poverty came a new attitude which sought to wrestle with questions of cause, not merely relief.

The Black Power protest which spun through the region at the close of the sixties ended any illusion that the problem of poverty could be solved without first addressing the racial and class structure of Caribbean society. In response to the upheaval, the churches came together for what was to be a turning point: the Ecumenical Consultation on Development, held in Trinidad in 1971. Out of this meeting came a ground-breaking theological piece by the Rev. Idris Hamid, then principal of St. Andrew's Theological College in Trinidad. Entitled "In Search of New Perspectives," the paper critiqued developmentalism and called for the Church to launch a process of internal change:

> The task of the Church is not merely to provide a few more jobs and promote a few projects, essential as these may be. The Church must undertake the more serious task of deep reflection and searching. Within this endeavor, it must engage in the "de-colonialization" of its theology. "Colonialization" took place on at least four levels: political, economic, cultural, and religious. Political independence is merely the ribbon-cutting stage of "de-colonialization," which has not gone as far as the cultural and religious levels where colonialism has done its dirtiest work.[1]

During the Trinidad consultation, the Rt. Rev. Roque Adames from the Dominican Republic introduced the term *concientizacion* (consciousness-raising), coined by the Brazilian educator Paulo Freire. The Roman Catholic Bishop defined the term in this way: "Concientizacion is not only knowledge ... it is recognition of oneself and others and at the same time, because of this, it is a choice, decision and commitment. It is the task of being humanized and humanizing others ... "[2] New voices from other areas of the Caribbean were adding their perspective to the emerging social awareness of the churches.

The context for these developments was a growing international ecumenical movement, led off by the ecumenical and social concerns declarations of Vatican II. This was followed in 1966 by a World Council of Churches conference on church and society, and by a Papal Encyclical on the Development of Peoples in 1967. That year also saw the formation of a joint Vatican/World Council of Churches Committee on Society, Development and Peace (SODEPAX), with a North American Jesuit priest as general secretary and a Trinidadian Presbyterian minister, the Rev. Roy Neehall, as associate general secretary.

Formation of the CCC

In this context, momentum grew toward a Caribbean experiment in ecumenical relations: the joining of forces between the Protestants and Catholics of the region. The mandate for such a body was affirmed at the Trinidad consultation by 260 representatives from 25 denominations spanning 16 territories in the English, Spanish, French and Dutch-speaking Caribbean. Two years later, in 1973, the Caribbean Conference of Churches came into being, with CADEC as its development arm. The CCC called for a regional Christian unity which would transcend the old colonial barriers:

We as Christian people of the Caribbean, separated from each other by barriers of history, language, culture, class and distance, desire, because of our common calling in Christ to join together in a regional fellowship of churches for inspiration, consultation, and cooperative action. We are deeply concerned to promote the human liberation of our people, and are committed to the achievement of social justice and the dignity of man in our society . . . [3]

One sign of the seriousness of this regionalism was that various churches from Cuba were invited to join the CCC. During the 1960s, Cuban Protestant and Catholic leaders had begun to speak out about the biblical and theological lessons of the revolution. By opening itself to this socio-religious process, the CCC reinforced the political opening of the year before, when Jamaica, Barbados, Guyana and Trinidad jointly established diplomatic relations with Cuba.

In the realm of theology, the CCC made an immediate impact through the publication of two anthologies of writings by leading Caribbean theologians, entitled *With Eyes Wide Open* and *Troubling of the Waters*. Edited by Idris Hamid, *Troubling of the Waters* interpreted the Black Power movement as a prophetic call, challenging the Church's complicity with racism and its lack of an incarnational theology. The Rev. Ashley Smith, pastor of the United Church in Jamaica, wrote:

[Falsely preaching] that the Gospel is concerned with man's soul and not with his personality and his rights in the economic and legal situation where he "lives and moves and has his being" . . . has contributed to making the Church a party to the dehumanization of the Black man and also the perpetuation of a situation in which the majority of the people suffer the anaesthetic effects of abject poverty in the midst of growing affluence for a few.[4]

The basic thrust of these writings was to call for the development of a new theology which would be genuinely Caribbean, not an import or imitation. As Idris Hamid argued:

God is really foreign to us. In the religious imagination of our people he is a benign white foreigner—an "expatriate." Even the categories of our religious experience are imports which do not reflect our cultural and native experiences. We experience God as an outsider.[5]

"The foremost task of theology in the Caribbean," wrote the Rev. Hamid, "is to work for the recovery of Caribbean man."[6] This was affirmed by another theologian, Dr. Robert Moore of Guyana, who said:

In order to explore the relationship between God and Caribbean Man, it is necessary that Caribbean Man do more exploration of himself, his environment, and the forces which have given that environment their peculiar structure; in other words, his history.[7]

In keeping with this aim, the CCC complemented its development and theological activities with a monthly newspaper, *Caribbean Contact*. Along with news of the ecumenical movement and reflections by regional religious leaders, *Contact* provided a forum for discussion of social, economic,

political, and cultural developments on a Caribbean-wide basis. It soon became the primary journalistic attempt to tie together the concerns of disparate parts of the region.

Paralleling the CCC's own religious "opening," the 1970s saw the emergence of many small, grassroots church-linked projects dedicated to action for social justice. Sometimes under denominational auspices, these were more often ecumenical or simply the private initiative of activists linked to the Church. The Caribbean Ecumenical Programme, formed in Trinidad in 1976, worked under the direction of Idris Hamid to help people examine their faith in relation to the historical, economic and cultural reality of the Caribbean. In St. Vincent, the Catholic Church set up the Commission for Development of the Peoples to do training and grassroots organizing among Vincentien farmers; while Catholic and Protestant activists independent of the Church organized the Ecumenical Study Group to reflect on social issues in the light of the Gospel message. In the Dominican Republic, the Center for Ecumenical Planning and Action (CEPAE) began in 1969 to work with the Dominican peasantry and base Christian communities on development projects and popular education.

In many cases, these grassroots religious projects overlapped in terms of philosophy and persons with the new political groups emerging during the same era. This was one aspect of a larger process in which activists with religious backgrounds were becoming prominent in regional movements for social change. In Jamaica, for instance, the Jesuit-linked Social Action Centre (SAC, Ltd) helped workers on the sugar estates successfully organize to demand worker-run cooperatives from the Manley government. In the French Antilles, still under colonial rule, Catholic priests and nuns became increasingly involved in the political independence movement. The National Ecumenical Movement of Puerto Rico (PRISA) grew out of an initially modest effort by the Episcopal Church in 1968 to train clergy in a social ministry for the urban San Juan area. It broadened into popular education and organizing among rural communities, workers, youth and Christians, aimed at enabling them to "organize themselves to transform [their] reality and effect their own liberation."[8]

Inevitably, this convergence of religious and secular activism raised hackles in the conservative bastions of the Church. The CCC in the 1970s was not a unified body representing only one religious tendency, nor were all the tendencies within its constituencies equally represented. The CCC leadership basically reflected the thinking of younger, liberal-to-progressive Christians, whereas the Church hierarchies and local Christian Councils were mainly older and more conservative. These two tendencies often found themselves in tension as the decade wore on.

Some of these tensions focused on *Caribbean Contact,* which was steadily gaining recognition as the foremost voice of progressive journalism in the region. *Contact* regularly explored such broad social themes as Caribbean unity, the economic crisis, social change movements, and global issues such as South African apartheid and the north-south dialogue. This made conservative Church leaders highly uneasy to the point of branding *Contact,* privately if not publicly, as "out and out communistic."[9] During the 1970s, these tensions did not erupt into open fights since the Christian Councils in each country tended to go along with the CCC on account of its official status, its large program staff and CADEC's huge financial resources. But there were resentments over the CCC's political positions, theological concepts and bureaucratic privileges (such as staff "junketing" around the Caribbean). These grumblings represented gathering storm clouds which would produce hail and lightning during the 1980s.

The seeds of such divisions were in a sense inherent in the formation of the CCC, with its call not merely to change the social role of the Church, but for the Church itself to change from within. As the CCC's general secretary, the Rev. Roy Neehall, stated at the body's 1973 inaugural assembly:

> In the past the churches have tried to meet the needs of people, but often our efforts have been an inadequate response and have had only a superficial impact. We treated symptoms, yet left the causes untouched. There was an embarrassing gap between the prophetic voice and the practical step. Suggestions for changes in the churches themselves, in approach, method, and priorities, were taken as a threat to their security and privileged status.[10]

Much had changed, but also much had stayed the same. By the end of the decade, concerned Christians were hearing warnings from Dr. Neehall about the gravity of the task before them:

> A massive dose of persuasion will have to be invented in order to have the rich, the powerful and privileged in the churches agree that to support, and even finance, radical social change in the direction of greater justice will be the most Christian and pragmatic way to avoid the violence and alienation that continued resistance to change is sure to create.[11] ∎

Dominican campesinos receiving a course on the importance of peasant organizations from CEPAE, the Center for Ecumenical Planning and Action in the Dominican Republic.

CEPAE

Attempts at Independence: Jamaica and Trinidad

The pressures of growing social unrest led political elites in Jamaica and Trinidad to undertake dramatic policy shifts in the early 1970s. Reacting to the dependency of the Puerto Rican model, both governments moved to sharply increase state control over the economy, leading to Michael Manley's "Democratic Socialism" and Eric Williams' "Third Way."

Jamaica

The height of Jamaica's Black Power movement coincided with the emergence of new leadership within the island's two-party system. Norman Manley, longtime leader of the People's National Party (PNP), died in 1969 leaving his son Michael, a trade union leader, at the head of the party. Michael Manley incorporated Black Power and Rastafarian themes into his campaign, and support for him coalesced among the poorer sectors of society. At the same time, he appealed to much of the middle and upper class which also desired a change. Reflecting the Jamaican people's frustration with the insensitive JLP, Manley and the PNP were elected in 1972 on a platform which promised "power for the people," "land for the landless," and "jobs for the unemployed."

The centerpiece of the new government was an array of programs in health care, housing, education, nutrition, and agricultural cooperatives, giving priority for the first time to the needs of working-class Jamaicans. Externally, Manley declared support for a New International Economic Order to secure fair treatment for Third World producers of raw materials. In this context, Manley asked the bauxite firms to renegotiate their agreements with the government with a view toward better terms for Jamaica. When the companies flatly refused to negotiate, the government imposed a bauxite production levy which tied Jamaica's revenues from mining to the world price of aluminum, bypassing transfer pricing and significantly increasing Jamaica's income from its bauxite resources. This move enjoyed wide support in Jamaica.

In 1974, the Manley government gave ideological form to these actions by announcing a program of "Democratic Socialism." The idea was to substantially increase government intervention in the economy, regulating but not abolishing the private sector, and to transfer key enterprises from foreign to national control. Although foreign investment remained welcome in many areas, Manley attempted to shift the "commanding heights" of the economy to state ownership. This included nationalizing part of the bauxite industry, the telephone company, public transport, Radio Jamaica, and the cement works, among other things. The PNP also strengthened Jamaica's ties with Cuba, receiving Cuban technical assistance in areas such as school construction and modernization of the fishing industry.

Trinidad

The 1970 Black Power protest marked a turning point in Williams' strategy. While responding to the unrest with authoritarian measures, the government simultaneously released its "Perspectives of the New Society" announcing a new economic path for Trinidad. Tacitly acknowledging that past policies had failed, Williams declared that Trinidad henceforth would pursue a "Third Way" which was neither Cuban socialism nor the Puerto Rican model. This would be done by bringing the state into the economy as full and part owner of productive enterprise, and by cultivating a new small business class. By 1972, no new 100% foreign enterprise was allowed in key economic sectors, and existing foreign-owned firms had to take steps to facilitate national participation.[1]

It was, however, OPEC's increase in the price of oil in 1973 which marked the true turning point. Almost overnight, Trinidad's revenues from oil refining multiplied seven-fold, and the country became wealthy enough to carry out initiatives

Michael Manley

Everybody's Magazine

Workers Time

Members of a sugar workers' cooperative on the Frome estate in Jamaica. The cooperative was one of many started by sugar workers under the Manley government in the 1970s, and later dismantled by Edward Seaga's government. Each coop had 150-200 members who leased land from the government and ran the estate collectively.

no other Caribbean government could even dream of. Williams used the windfall to create a huge state sector. Enterprises which the government acquired in full included Shell's oil refining operations, Tate & Lyle's sugar estates, British West Indian Airways, and the telephone and television companies. The government also created new state-owned industries, including iron and steel production, natural gas, cement, and a host of smaller industries. In other areas, the government entered into joint ventures with private capital. By 1980, the government was the dominant partner in the economy, holding assets valued at over US$400 million.[2]

Companies in which government has participation[3]

	1972	1974	1981
Wholly owned by government	4	12	34
Majority ownership	10	11	14
Minority interest	7	9	17
50% ownership	—	—	1
Total	21	32	66

Ironically, Trinidad's extensive nationalizations raised hardly a murmur overseas, in contrast to the clamor of disapproval over Manley's comparatively mild economic reforms. The difference was that whereas Manley paid emotional allegiance to socialism, Williams was clearly pro-capitalist and merely interested in making the system work better. Moreover, the deal was not a bad one for the foreign firms.

With the government of Trinidad an associated partner, substantial advantages accrue to a would-be investor. Primarily these advantages center on the question of risk and uncertainty. A prospective investor, promised the participation of the state in an industrial project, can be reasonably certain that public policy will be favorable to it . . . In addition, state investment reduces the capital outlay required by the multinational firm.[4]

Government participation in a project did not necessarily mean government control. Managerial decisions still tended to be made in the boardrooms of the parent companies abroad.[5] Reflecting on the free enterprise mania which rages in Trinidad to the present, one writer concludes: "Williams' economic strategy has succeeded in strengthening the basis of capitalism in a way that has not been done in any Caribbean society or even in any developing Third World nation."[6] ∎

A Decade of Economic Shocks

The development boom of the 1960s had little impact on a crucial economic problem: dependency vs. self-reliance. The region's economies remained among the most "open" in the world.[1] This meant that they depended to an extraordinary degree on imports and exports, rendering them "open" to the impact of economic forces and decisions located outside the Caribbean and outside their control.

Most Caribbean countries still rely on exports of two or three commodities to bring in the bulk of their foreign exchange. Their value is externally controlled. When the world market price of a commodity such as sugar or bauxite declines, countries dependent on that export reel from the blow. At the same time, much of what is *consumed* in the Caribbean—such as food, machinery, farm tools, clothing and medicines—is imported from outside the region, and Caribbean countries have no control over these prices either. The result is that the import bill often far outstrips foreign exchange earnings from exports—the classic balance-of-payments problem.

Because of this, the boom-and-bust cycles of the international economy have a magnified impact in the Caribbean. The rapid economic expansion of the 1960s forced the industrialized countries to take anti-inflation measures, and by 1970 this had started a trend toward recession. When the OPEC cartel quadrupled the price of oil in 1973, the sudden shock triggered rampant inflation and a series of recessions, each more prolonged than the last. The effect on the Caribbean was devastating. Prices of imports rose steadily, especially for oil, which all but a few Caribbean countries must import. Simultaneously, commodity prices began to fall. With export earnings shrinking and import bills soaring, Caribbean nations sank deeper and deeper into debt.

After the mid-1970s, it became increasingly difficult for developing countries to borrow from the commercial transnational banks. Many Caribbean governments were forced to turn for the first time to the multilateral lending agencies, the International Monetary Fund (IMF) and the World Bank. IMF approval of a country's economy also frequently became necessary in order to secure other loans.

As the Caribbean moved into the 1980s, a rapid-fire barrage of economic shocks jolted the region. Hurricane David ravaged the Eastern Caribbean in August 1979, followed by Hurricane Allen one year later. They caused the virtual destruction of the banana industry in the banana-dependent islands of Dominica, St. Vincent, St. Lucia, and Grenada, as well as in Guadeloupe and Martinique.

No sooner had the region begun to recover from the storms than the effects of world recession struck with full force. By 1981-82, the U.S., Canada, and England were experiencing their worst economic decline since the Great Depression. As world demand for commodities slumped, prices for three Caribbean mainstays—sugar, bananas, and bauxite—collapsed on the world market. By October 1982, the price of raw sugar on the U.S. market had fallen to its lowest level in four years, 6¢ per pound.[3] Bauxite dropped equally severely, while coffee and cocoa (important to Haiti, the Dominican Republic and Grenada) also fell. Tourism declined all around the region as rising air fares and recession in North America and Europe meant that fewer people could afford Caribbean vacations.

Photo One

Wreckage from Hurricane David in Roseau, Dominica.

Bitter Times for Sugar

The Caribbean's dilemma goes beyond the acute crisis of the last few years to encompass the problem of long-term decline in its major economic sectors. Nowhere is this more true than in the sugar industry. The historical cycle of world sugar cane cultivation appears to be coming to an end, according to sugar expert Manuel Moreno Fraginals.[4] Cane sugar is being replaced by beet sugar and by a new sugar substitute, High Fructose Corn Syrup (HFCS), which is used in industrial products like soft drinks. Because of the growing cane surplus, the world price of sugar fell to 4¢ a pound in 1984, equal to about one-quarter the cost of production.[5]

Many former tropical colonies of Spain, England, Holland and France remain locked into economic infrastructures based on growing sugar. They face social dislocation of serious proportions if the cane industry should cease to provide employment for their workforce. For this reason many governments, including those in the Caribbean, subsidize their sugar industries, buying cane from farmers at a fixed price and then reselling it to the transnational sugar brokers at *less* than what was paid to the growers.[6]

Sixty percent of the international sugar market is controlled by four firms: Sucre et Denrees (France), Tate & Lyle (England), F. Mann (England), and Phillips Bros. (U.S.)[7] In the 1970s, the transnationals which owned sugar plantations in the Caribbean began to get out of the unprofitable business of growing cane, and sold out much of their local holdings to Caribbean governments. The companies continued to profit by controlling the marketing, processing and technology. A recent trend has been for the transnationals to come back in on management contracts to run nationally-owned estates, as Tate & Lyle has done in Jamaica. At the same time, the sugar companies also are investing in the development of High Fructose Corn Syrup.

Caribbean countries which depend on sugar include Cuba, Belize, the Dominican Republic, Guyana, St. Kitts-Nevis, Guadeloupe, Barbados, and Jamaica. Cuba, which gets 85% of its export earnings from cane, is also the only country to receive a stable price for its crop, under a long-term barter agreement with the Soviet Union. Those Caribbean countries which sell to the European Economic Community also receive a subsidized price, but EEC policy has shifted toward subsidizing European beet sugar producers at the expense of cane growers.[8]

One partial solution to the sugar crisis is the development of other industries based on cane, such as the manufacture of paper and chemicals from sugar cane byproducts. Cuba has made considerable progress in this area. Such development requires large-scale investment and new marketing structures, something few Caribbean governments are prepared to undertake.

Besides sugar, other Caribbean industries also face troubled futures. They include:

Bauxite. The bauxite industry went into a deep slump when the world recession lowered demand for aluminum, especially in auto manufacture. The aluminum multinationals—Reynolds, Kaiser, Alcan, Alcoa—are also gradually moving

Jamaican cane cutter: An historical cycle coming to a close?

their production out of the Caribbean to Brazil, Australia and Guinea. Reynolds has closed down permanently in Jamaica and Haiti, and Alcoa has suspended mining in the Dominican Republic.

Bananas. The Caribbean banana industry operates under many handicaps. Steep terrain, bad roads for shipping, and vulnerability to hurricanes and disease make Caribbean bananas of less uniform quality and appearance than bananas from Central and South America. Whereas the latter are grown on big plantations by multinationals like United Brands and Standard Fruit, Caribbean banana growers tend to be peasant farmers cultivating small plots of land. Caribbean bananas are not sold in the U.S., which buys all its bananas from Latin America, but instead rely on preferential treatment in the British and French markets.

In recent years, droughts, hurricanes, and disease have hit the banana industries in Jamaica and the Windward Islands, making them unable to fulfil their quotas on the British market. Latin American suppliers have made up the shortfall, thus gaining a growing foothold in the U.K. market.[10]

Boxing bananas for Geest in Grenada.

Tom Barry

Moreover, the low price which Caribbean farmers receive for their fruit acts as a disincentive to production. Prices are set by the Geest Co., a British multinational which purchases and ships all the bananas grown in the Windward Islands, and by United Brands, which markets Jamaican bananas through a British subsidiary. The farmers' income has dropped further with the depreciation of the pound sterling against the dollar (the British pay in pounds, but Caribbean currencies are tied to the U.S. dollar).

The banana industry does not make a profit anywhere in the Caribbean. It is kept alive because it is a crop which grows on mountainous land, which employs people in rural areas, and for which there is a guaranteed market, however low the price.

Oil refining. During most of the 1970s, Trinidad & Tobago's oil-based economy was the only bright spot in the region. Indeed, the Williams government was able to somewhat ease the burden of rising fuel prices for other Caribbean nations by offering them oil on concessional terms. But the bonanza was short-lived. Rising world oil prices spurred the major industrial nations, like the U.S., to develop conservation programs and substitute other energy sources for oil. By the end of the decade, a world oil glut prompted the OPEC countries to sharply curtail their production. At the same time, the oil transnationals began shifting their refining capacity out of the Caribbean to new refineries opening elsewhere. Oil refining and production peaked in Trinidad in 1978, and from then on declined steadily. ∎

ECONOMIC DEPENDENCE OF CARIBBEAN COUNTRIES

Bermuda	tourism, offshore banking
Bahamas	tourism, offshore banking, drug smuggling
Cuba	sugar
Jamaica	bauxite, tourism, sugar
Haiti	coffee, foreign-owned industry
Dominican Republic	tourism, sugar, minerals, coffee
Puerto Rico	foreign-owned industry, U.S. subsidies
U.S. Virgin Islands	tourism, U.S. subsidies
St. Kitts-Nevis	sugar
Antigua	tourism
Guadeloupe	bananas, sugar, tourism, subsidies from France
Dominica	bananas
Martinique	bananas, sugar, subsidies from France
St. Lucia	bananas
St. Vincent	bananas
Barbados	tourism, manufacturing, sugar
Grenada	cocoa, bananas, nutmeg
Trinidad & Tobago	oil refining
Guyana	sugar, bauxite, rice
Suriname	bauxite
French Guiana	subsidies from France, timber, shrimp
Netherlands Antilles	offshore banking, oil refining, tourism
Belize	sugar

NOTES TO PART TWO

Failure of the Puerto Rican Model

1. Ricardo Campos and Frank Bonilla, "Bootstraps and Enterprise Zones: The Underside of Late Capitalism in Puerto Rico and the United States," *Review,* Vol. 4, Spring 1982, p. 559.
2. EPICA, *Puerto Rico: A People Challenging Colonialism* (Washington, DC: EPICA, 1976), p. 59.
3. Dr. Neftali Garcia, "Puerto Rico: Presencia y Efectos de las Companias Transnacionales," paper presented in Washington, DC, May 1983.
4. *Ibid.*
5. Dr. Neftali Garcia, "Puerto Rico: The Multinational Presence," *Multinational Monitor,* February 1980. Based on the work of Industrial Mission, a church-sponsored environmental group in Puerto Rico.
6. Frank Bonilla and Ricardo Campos, "Up by the Bootstraps: Ideologies of Social Levitation," paper presented at Hunter College, New York, August 1984.
7. *San Juan Star,* January 20, 1975.
8. Testimony by Ramon Garcia Santiago, Secretary of Social Services, Commonwealth of Puerto Rico, before Subcommittee on Agricultural Research and General Legislation of the U.S. Senate, November 17, 1975.
9. EPICA, *Jamaica: Caribbean Challenge* (Washington, DC: EPICA, 1979), p. 63.
10. Jay R. Mandle, *Patterns of Caribbean Development: An Interpretive Essay On Economic Change* (New York: Gordon & Breach, 1982), p. 60.
11. *Ibid.,* p. 61.
12. Michael Als, *Is Slavery Again: Some Factors Leading Up to the Introduction of the Industrial Stabilization Act (ISA) 1965, in Trinidad and Tobago* (Trinidad: Cacique Publishers), pp. 11-12.
13. Mandle, p. 60.
14. *Ibid.,* pp. 60-61.
15. Antigua Caribbean Liberation Movement, *Liberation: From the Old Wreckage to the New Society* (St. John's, Antigua).

The Cuban Revolution

1. Eduardo Galeano, *Open Veins of Latin America* (New York: Monthly Review Press, 1973), p. 80.
2. *Ibid.,* p. 86.
3. *Ibid.,* p. 83.
4. Warren Hinkle and William Turner, *The Fish Is Red: The Story of the Secret War Against Castro* (New York: Harper & Row, 1981), p. 290.
5. Eric Williams, *From Columbus to Castro: The History of the Caribbean 1492-1969* (New York: Harper & Row, 1970), pp. 479-480.
6. Fidel Castro, *History Will Absolve Me* (Havana: Guairas Book Institute, 1967), pp. 69-70.
7. Galeano, p. 87.

New Progressive Movement

1. Frank McDonald, "The Commonwealth Caribbean," in Tad Szulc, *The United States and the Caribbean* (New York: Prentice Hall, 1971), p. 147.
2. C.L.R. James, *The Future in the Present* (London: Allison & Busby, 1977), pp. 160-182.
3. *Ibid.,* p. 120.
4. McDonald, p. 153.
5. Adrian M. Moen, "Curacao 1969: Crisis and Change," in Susan Craig, ed., *Contemporary Caribbean: A Sociological Reader* (Trinidad: S. Craig, 1982), Vol. Two, p. 343.
6. EPICA interview with Angel Salsbach, member of Curacao Parliament and a leader of the May Movement, Willemstad, April 1984.
7. Susan Craig, "Background to the 1970 Confrontation in Trinidad and Tobago," in Craig, ed., p. 402.
8. EPICA interview with Rev. Roy Neehall, Trinidad, August 1982.
9. *Ibid.*

Religious Opening in the 1970s

1. Idris Hamid, "In Search of New Perspectives," paper prepared for the Caribbean Ecumenical Consultation for Development, November 1971.
2. *Called to Be—The Official Report of the Caribbean Ecumenical Consultation for Development* (Barbados: CADEC, 1972).
3. Preamble to the Constitution of the Caribbean Conference of Churches.
4. The Rt. Rev. Ashley Smith, "The Religious Significance of Black Power in Caribbean Churches," in Idris Hamid, ed., *Troubling of the Waters* (Trinidad: Idris Hamid, 1973), pp. 87-88.
5. Hamid, "In Search of New Perspectives."
6. Idris Hamid, "Theology and Caribbean Development," in David I. Mitchell, ed., *With Eyes Wide Open* (Barbados: CADEC, 1973), p. 133.
7. Dr. Robert Moore, "The Historical Basis of Theological Reflection," in *Troubling of the Waters,* p. 42.
8. "Inside Puerto Rico 1984: Colonialism and Intervention in the Caribbean and Central America," *PRISA International,* April 1984, p. 19.
9. EPICA interview with Stan Boyd, Gen. Sec. of Dominica Christian Council, August 1982.
10. Dr. Roy G. Neehall, "Christian Witness and Mission in Caribbean Development," in *With Eyes Wide Open,* p. 25.
11. *Caribbean Contact,* February 1980.

Attempts at Independence

1. Raphael Sebastien, "State Sector Development in Trinidad & Tobago 1956-1982," *Tribune* (Trinidad), Vol. 2, #1, June 1982, p. 56.
2. *Ibid.,* p. 62.
3. *Ibid.,* p. 61 and appendix.
4. Mandle, p. 133.
5. Clive Y. Thomas, *Dependence and Transformation: The Economics of the Transition to Socialism* (New York: Monthly Review Press, 1974).
6. Sebastien, p. 77.

Decade of Economic Shocks

1. Inter-American Development Bank, *Economic and Social Progress in Latin America: The External Sector* (IDB, 1982), p. 24 and country profiles. An open economy is one with a high ratio of imports/exports to gross domestic product. Trinidad & Tobago, Barbados, Guyana, and Jamaica are four of the six most open economies in Latin America, according to the IDB.
2. Subcommittee on Inter-American Affairs, 97th Congress, "Security Assistance Proposals for Latin America and the Caribbean," April 21, 1982, p. 72.
3. Caribbean Development Bank, *Annual Report 1982,* p. 30.
4. Manuel Moreno Fraginals, paper presented at Hunter College, New York, August 1984.
5. *Ibid.*
6. "How the International Sugar Economy Works," part 1 of *Sugar and Sugarworkers* (Toronto: GATT-Fly, 1978), p. 5.
7. International Commission for Coordination of Solidarity Among Sugar Workers, "Solidarity Among Sugar Workers" (Toronto, 1983), p. 26.
8. *Ibid.*
9. Central Bank of Barbados, *Annual Report 1982,* p. 15, and Caribbean Development Bank, *Annual Report 1983,* p. 28.
10. Interview with marketing director of Fyffes (British subsidiary of United Brands) in *The Courier,* March-April 1983, p. 88.

PART THREE
Forced Migration
And Caribbean Peoples Abroad

Migration in Caribbean History

Migration is and always has been an integral part of the Caribbean experience. Modern Caribbean societies were born in the voluntary migration of Europeans to the region and the forced migration of the Africans they enslaved. They were made ethnically complex by immigration from India, China, and other parts of the world. The Caribbean's diversity, its outstanding characteristic, is a diversity founded in migrations.

The history of Caribbean migration since emancipation can be divided into four phases.[1] The first, from 1835 until about 1880, was the movement of the newly freed slaves away from the plantations. They moved to the towns to seek work, to the hills to farm, and where there was no vacant land—as in Barbados—they emigrated, going primarily to Trinidad and Guyana where plantation wages were higher.

This pattern was dramatically altered after 1880 by the flood of U.S. investment into the region. Caribbean migration in its second phase became movement "in search of the Yankee dollar." On the Atlantic coast of Central America, West Indians joined the plantation and railroad workforce for the United Fruit Company's banana operations. U.S. investment also caused a sugar boom in Cuba and the Dominican Republic just as the sugar industry in the British West Indies was dying out. Many West Indian workers, especially from Jamaica, migrated to the Spanish-speaking islands to cut cane.

But it was the building of the gigantic Panama Canal which dominated the migration of the time. Panama became a mecca for the unemployed and underemployed all over the Caribbean. West Indian laborers on the canal lived in disease-ridden slums and did hazardous, debilitating work for discriminatory rates of pay. Nonetheless, their remittances were an unprecedented injection of cash into the stagnant agrarian economies of the islands. For the first time, some peasants and workers were able to buy land, learn a trade, or open a shop. This was especially true in Barbados, where "Panama money" finally permitted the formation of a limited smallholder class through land purchases.[2] The memory of Panama as a source of wealth—as well as memories of hardship and discrimination—endures as part of the West Indian popular consciousness today.

The completion of the Canal in 1914 signaled the end of this boom period of migration. In the years before and during the Great Depression, there were few outlets for the swelling Caribbean work force. The only new destinations in this third phase were the oil fields starting up in Venezuela and the Shell refinery in Curacao, and these did not approach the scale of the Panama operation.

Migration to the Colonial "Mother Countries"

In the 19th and early 20th centuries, migration to England, France and Holland was largely limited to the Caribbean middle and upper classes. It was a common practice for such families to send a son off to the "metropole" to finish his education and qualify for a post in the colonial civil service. This elite pattern continued, but was overshadowed by the mass popular emigration in search of employment which began during World War Two.

The war ended the Depression and created a labor shortage in the United States and England, leading to the recruitment of West Indians to take up war-time jobs. After the war ended, however, the United States again limited immigration, and the flow turned toward the colonial "mother countries": British West Indians migrated to Britain, French Antilleans to France, Surinamers to Holland, and Puerto Ricans—nominally U.S. citizens—to the United States. France and Britain gave citizenship to their colonial subjects in 1946 and 1948 respectively, which had the effect of allowing free and unselected emigration to the metropoles.

The floodgates opened; the era of mass emigration had begun. People rushed to escape the stifling Caribbean societies with their rigid class distinctions and lack of opportunities for the working class. Between 1946 and 1960, many Caribbean societies saw their natural population increase severely offset by emigration. Most affected were Puerto Rico; Jamaica; and the smaller sugar-producing islands such as Antigua, St. Kitts and Montserrat.[3]

Everybody was leaving—or at least this was the perception in the islands. Hardly a family could be found which did not have some member overseas. Emigrants departed by the boatload, and steel bands would play at the pier as the ship sailed away. Jamaican poet Louise Bennett recalls the epoch in patois:

Wat a joyful news, Miss Mattie,
I feel like me heart gwine burs'
Jamaica people colonizin
Englan in reverse.

By de hundred, by de t'ousan
From country and from town,
By de ship-load, by de plane-load
Jamaica is Englan boun.

Dem a-pour out o' Jamaica,
Everybody future plan
Is fe get a big-time job
An settle in de mother lan.

What a islan! What a people!
Man an woman, old an young
Jusa pack dem bag an baggage
An tun history upside dung![4]

France and Britain had granted citizenship to their colonial subjects in order to reinforce their empires and, in the case of Britain, to avoid a complete break in the near future when the colonies would become independent.[5] The tidal wave of emigrants was an unforeseen result. West Indians, Africans, East Indians and Pakistanis immigrating into England in the 1950s entered a virtually all-white society which reacted to their arrival with racism and hostility. After 1962, the British government responded to the white public's outcry with a series of restrictive immigration laws, reducing the flow of immigrants to a trickle.

At about the same time, however, Canada and the United States opened their doors, as their economies expanded and low-wage jobs needed to be filled. Until 1962, Canada's immigration laws openly discriminated against non-whites. In that year, the law was changed to stress educational and occupational credentials and West Indians began migrating in large numbers to Canada, primarily to Toronto and Montreal. U.S. immigration also was liberalized in 1965, and today Caribbean emigration is primarily to the United States and Canada.

Inter-island migration meanwhile has continued, with the stronger Caribbean economies drawing from nearby weaker ones. Trinidad draws from the Windward Islands, particularly Grenada. Guadeloupe draws from Dominica; Martinique from St. Lucia; while workers from throughout the Leeward Islands go to the Bahamas and the U.S. Virgin Islands to work in the tourist industry. A special, organized migration is the seasonal flow of Haitians to cut sugar cane in the Dominican Republic, which began in the 1920s while both the Dominican Republic and Haiti were under U.S. occupation. Today, Haitians make up 90% of the cane cutting force in the Dominican sugar industry, the backbone of the Dominican economy.

Within the broad context of migration for economic reasons, there have been several major migratory waves which are primarily political in nature. After the Cuban revolution, as is well known, many upper and middle-class Cubans emigrated to the United States, where they formed a militant exile community centered in Miami. Less publicized was the flight of tens of thousands of people from the Dominican Republic after the United States invaded that country in 1965. Today, the Dominican community in New York City numbers some 800,000. Since the beginning of the 1970s, two new groups of political refugees have arrived on the scene: the Haitians and the Guyanese, fleeing the corrupt and repressive regimes of Jean Claude Duvalier and Forbes Burnham.

The Migration Dream

Maurice Bishop of Grenada, criticizing the colonial educational system, referred to the "visa mentality": the obsessive desire to emigrate which is especially prevalent among educated youth and middle-class professionals. The educational system is important because it traditionally has served to impart foreign values and an orientation away from the Caribbean. For many years, West Indian school children learned the history of Europe, but little about their own past. Although Caribbean history and geography now are taught in the region's schools, the educational process still does not emphasize skills needed to build Caribbean societies. The schools prepare one to emigrate.

Reflecting this lack of relevance, unemployment actually is higher among those who have gone part way through high school (secondary school) than it is for those with less than five years of elementary education.[6] Youth with some secondary schooling tend to reject farming and aspire to white-collar or clerical jobs. Yet those few positions are quickly filled by high school graduates, leaving partly educated youth with three options: farming, unemployment, or emigration.

At the upper end of the educational ladder, emigration promises better working conditions, a higher salary, and possibilities for advancement to those in the professions. Certain fields such as teaching and nursing have seen a steady outflow of qualified persons to permanent residence in the developed countries. Another group which emigrates heavily is writers and artists, who often find, to their chagrin, that they must abandon the very societies which give meaning to their work because of greater receptivity and markets abroad.

Most of those who emigrate, however, are ordinary people confronted with the staggering unemployment in their home countries. In a few places—the tiny island of Carriacou is an example—there is so little economic activity that a majority of adult men historically have emigrated.

England Ah Want to Go!

Two years now ah waiting
Ah get ah letter, me voucher coming—
Man ah felt so glad!
Ah send for two grips in Trinidad,
When ah hear the blows—
Me voucher turned in Barbados.

England ah want to go
Send me voucher
Send me passport
Tell me what to do
Ah can't stay no more in Carriacou.

Man ah felt so bad
So very sad,
Everybody leaving
Imagine how ah feeling.
Who going Canada
Also America
But ah can't understand
Why me voucher won't come this time.

— Grenadian calypsonian The Mighty Scraper, 1970

For most Caribbean societies, money sent back by nationals abroad is an important source of foreign exchange. Remittances from family members working overseas have paid for houses, land and schooling in the Caribbean. The recession which began in 1981, however, diminished the flow of remittances because of unemployment in the U.S., Canada and Britain.

Popular mythology in the Caribbean tends to center on the wealth and opportunities abroad, rather than on the unemployment, racial discrimination, and alienation which Caribbean emigrants often suffer. Emigrants often send back artificially glowing reports, lest dissatisfaction be interpreted as a sign that the emigrant is not "making it" in his new milieu. But on a deeper level, the vast divide between the have and have-not nations virtually ensures a steady flow of people to where conditions are better. In that sense, Caribbean people are only following the path of their own resources and the wealth created by their labor: out of the region to the developed world. ■

Blacks in Britain: A Bitter Trial

In the spring of 1981, the predominantly West Indian neighborhood of Brixton in South London exploded in violent riots which turned the eyes of the world on the bitter, 30-year-old struggle between blacks in Britain and the racist British state. Perhaps more than any other emigrant experience, the saga of British colonial "subjects" in the motherland illustrates the process through which white society creates a black underclass, and the resistance to that pressure which is a continuing part of the Caribbean experience abroad.

Two themes run side by side throughout the history of West Indians in Britain. One is a virulent strain of white racism and neo-fascism which has fueled violence against the black minority. The other is a growing Third World unity across generational and ethnic lines (West Indian, African, and Asian), based on a philosophy which looks beyond the surface of race discrimination to its roots in the system of colonial domination.

British colonial subjects from the Caribbean, Africa, India and Pakistan started coming to the U.K. in large numbers in the 1950s, when Britain was desperate for labor to help with post-war reconstruction. The immigrants filled jobs British workers would not take—the dirtiest, lowest paid, least skilled occupations. But it soon became clear that while their cheap labor was welcome, the immigrants' presence in British society was not. Rampant discrimination in the housing market, particularly in middle-class neighborhoods, forced West Indians to jam together into ghetto apartments. White Britons then pointed to these substandard conditions as evidence of black inferiority, while landlords cited "over-crowding" as a reason not to rent to blacks.

Another form of discrimination was the so-called "color bar," which kept non-whites out of public entertainment spots like pubs, bars and clubs. For the young, working-class men who made up the bulk of the post-war immigrant wave, this was highly provocative and sparked frequent fights between black and white youth.

The presence of a racial minority was a lightning rod for the frustrations and fears of the white working class, at a time when this class could no longer compensate for its own low status by sharing in the illusion of British world supremacy.

> The loss of India and the impending loss of the Caribbean and Africa has spelt the end of empire and the decline of Britain as a great power. All that was left of the colonial enterprise was the ideology of racial superiority; it was something to fall back on . . . [1]

The result was a resurgence of the fascist tendency which had long been an undercurrent of British political life. Societies for "racial preservation" and neo-fascist organizations preaching race hatred began to multiply. Stimulated by racist propaganda put out by these groups and echoed in the press, white youth gangs called "teddy boys" roamed the streets armed with knives and iron pipes, making unprovoked attacks on blacks and Asians. This was called "nigger-hunting" and "Paki-bashing" and was regarded as harmless sport by the police. Finally, in August 1958, an incident in the London district of Nottingham sparked four days of violence in which white mobs ripped through London, attacking blacks and black homes with bricks and gasoline bombs.[2]

The hysteria inflamed by the riots paved the way for the first restrictive immigration legislation, the 1962 Commonwealth Immigration Act. This law sought to "improve" race relations in Britain by limiting the number of non-whites who could enter. Immigration became subject to quotas and controls, institutionalizing racism at the state level.

Polarization in the 1960s

The passage of the Commonwealth Immigration Act deepened the rift between the immigrant community and the larger society. The police became more openly racist and brutal toward blacks. White tenant groups organized to exclude blacks from housing, while black workers found that their demands for fair treatment met with active collaboration between white unions and management. New problems emerged in the area of education, as the first generation of children born in Britain to immigrant parents were entering the schools. Under pressure from white parents, the school system shunted many black children to special schools for the mentally retarded or emotionally disturbed. This threatened to create a generation of miseducated black children who would grow to be adults equipped only for the menial tasks of an underclass.

In the past, immigrants had responded to discrimination by forming their own social institutions: clubs, churches, and mutual associations, such as revolving credit cooperatives

Protesters march past burned-out Ruddock house after fire which killed 13 West Indian schoolchildren. Note banner with portrait of Marcus Garvey, center-left.

Photo: R. MacMillan

based on the Trinidadian *susu*. Barred from the housing market, immigrants pooled their savings to buy property jointly. Afro-Caribbean people (Africans and West Indians) and Asians (primarily Indians and Pakistanis) tended to fight similar battles independently of each other. But as the society became more racist, the quality of resistance began to change.

The fight against the 1962 Commonwealth Immigration Act stimulated a temporary unity between Afro-Caribbean and Asian groups. Now this cooperation was revived and given a political grounding by the rise of the U.S. civil rights movement and the decolonization of various African and Caribbean nations. The visits of prominent black activists to Britain—such as Martin Luther King, Jr. in 1964 and Malcolm X in 1965—spurred the formation of new, militant organizations, notably the Racial Action Adjustment Society (RAAS). RAAS moved quickly to broaden the struggle by supporting an Asian factory workers' strike at the request of the Asian workers.

> RAAS's "nationalism," stemming as it did from the West Indian experience, combined an understanding of how colonialism had divided the Asian and African and Caribbean peoples ("coolie, savage, and slave") with an awareness of how that same colonialism made them one people now: they were all blacks.[3]

A visit by Stokely Carmichael to London in July 1967 helped inspire the formation of the Universal Coloured Peoples' Association (UCPA). UCPA stressed that the struggle for black and Asian rights was fundamentally an anti-capitalist and anti-imperialist struggle, linking racism in Britain to the war in Vietnam, colonialism in Africa, and to the entire system of white domination.

White Britain tried to portray this new consciousness as the machinations of "black power" and communist agitators from abroad. It was, in fact, an indigenous movement with roots in Britain. London in the 1930s and '40s was a major center of the Pan-African movement and the home of intellectuals in the vanguard of the anti-colonial movement: C.L.R. James, George Padmore, Jomo Kenyatta, and Kwame Nkrumah among others.

In 1945, the fifth Pan-African Congress was held in Manchester, England, and vowed to struggle for "the absolute and complete independence of the colonies" and for "the liquidation of colonialism and imperialism." In the same year, Asians, Africans and West Indians in Britain came together for a Subject People's Conference, foreshadowing the multi-ethnic unity reforged twenty years later.

In 1968, the Black People's Alliance was formed as a national coordinating body for over fifty Afro-Caribbean and Asian organizations. Under the BPA's banner, thousands of people marched through the streets to demand the repeal of the Immigration Act. Meanwhile, blacks were organizing at the local level to redress the social deprivation which they and their children had suffered. Militant organizations set up youth centers and schools staffed by black teachers. Black-oriented newspapers, bookstores, counseling centers and other self-help projects proliferated.

Black People's Day of Action, March 1981 in London.

White Britain reacted to this growing unity with a redoubling of racist violence. Hate leaflets circulated, and crosses were burned outside black homes. In 1967, the League of Empire Loyalists, the British National Party, and local groups of the Racial Preservation Society merged to form the National Front, a fascist electoral party. To make matters worse, a Joseph McCarthy-type demagogue emerged, a Member of Parliament named Enoch Powell. Powell inflamed public hysteria with dire warnings of England being overrun by Asian hordes, a theme picked up by the sensation-hungry press much as McCarthy's anticommunist accusations fed the U.S. press in the 1950s. The result of this upsurge of grassroots racism was that the Labour Party—basically hypocritical on race matters from the start—moved further right and passed an overtly racist piece of immigration legislation, the 1968 "Kenyan Asians Act."

Three years later, under a Tory government, Powell's ideas were transformed into policy. The 1971 Immigration Act cleverly managed to terminate black immigration while permitting white immigration by restricting entry to "patrials"—persons with a parent or grandparent born in Britain. In practice this meant whites from Canada, Australia, South Africa and New Zealand. Residency rights were withdrawn from nonpatrial immigrants retroactively, rendering most of the black population suddenly "illegal." Although the retroactive clause was eventually withdrawn, raids to round up black immigrants became common under the Illegal Immigration Intelligence Unit of the police.

The 1970s: Youth in Struggle

The success of Black Power had brought down on its head the wrath of the system. Its leaders were persecuted, its meetings disrupted, its places of work destroyed. But it had gone on gaining momentum and strength: it was not a party, but a movement, gathering to its concerns all the strands of capitalist oppression, gathering to its programme all the problems of oppressed peoples. There was hardly a black in the country that did not identify with it, and through it, to all the non-whites of the world, in one way or another. And as for the British-born youth, who had been schooled in white racism, the movement was the cradle of their consciousness.[4]

By the mid-1970s, a generation of British-born black youth had come of age. They had never seen the lands of their parents' birth and had few connections, emotional or otherwise, with the West Indies, Africa, India or Pakistan. Yet they were not regarded as "British" because they were black. Compounding this identity crisis were the pernicious effects of stereotyping in the school system, and the youths' own alienation from the society since the success ladder via merit and achievement was largely closed to blacks. The need for low-wage labor had receded in the sixties as capital began going abroad to where labor was even cheaper. This meant rising unemployment for black youth, and even calls (led by Powell) for repatriating all immigrants now that their labor was no longer in demand.

In their anger and frustration, some youth turned to petty crime such as shoplifting, mugging, and auto theft. The old conflict between the black and white working class was overshadowed by the increasingly violent clash between blacks and the police. Under antiquated vagrancy laws, blacks were stopped and searched on mere "suspicion" that they might be armed or planning to commit a crime. Entire black neighborhoods were virtually placed under seige by the police and the paramilitary Special Patrol Group.

The stage was set for widespread violence. West Indian and Asian youth groups joined together to strike back, no longer willing to settle for the moderate and largely ineffectual tactics of their parents. Provocations such as marches by the fascist National Front through black communities, under police protection, would no longer be tolerated.

In January 1981, thirteen West Indian children attending a birthday party at a home in New Cross were burned to death in a fire of suspicious origins. Angered by the cursory investigation of the fire, more than 10,000 blacks—parents, youth and children—marched through the heart of London as squadrons of police stood by in riot gear.

The riots erupted one month later. In April, Brixton exploded, followed by the Asian area of Southall in July—and then the rage spread throughout England, to over thirty towns and cities. It was a long journey from Jamaica, Trinidad and Barbados to the flames of Brixton—but one which reveals as much about colonialism as the poverty of the Caribbean islands the emigrants left behind.

Postscript: Thatcher

The Conservative victory which brought Margaret Thatcher to power in 1979 stimulated two contradictory trends. On the one hand, state racism was intensified. In 1981 the government passed a Nationality Act providing that children *born in Britain* would not automatically become British citizens if their parents were not—thus creating a potentially huge group of stateless persons. At the grassroots level, new neo-fascist groups appeared, notably the British Movement. On the other hand, Thatcher's anti-working class policies enabled some whites to begin identifying the enemy as the system, not the blacks. Unemployed, unskilled white youth saw that they too had become marginal. During the 1981 riots, whites in some cities fought side by side with blacks and Asians against the police.

The combined effect of recession and the Nationality Act has meant a dwindling of migration to Britain. Immigration by "nonwhites" in 1983 was the lowest since 1962, the year restrictions were introduced.[5] Moreover, some Caribbean nationals who emigrated in the 1940s and '50s are now returning home because of worsened economic conditions in Britain.

The Caribbean community in Britain is no longer so much an immigrant population, struggling to survive in an alien environment, as it is becoming a permanent and culturally distinct part of British society. The 1980s have seen a flowering of Caribbean culture in Britain related particularly to Jamaican cultural trends such as reggae and "dub" poetry (verse chanted over a drum base). Some of the best new reggae since the death of Bob Marley is coming out of the West Indian community in Britain. Black newspapers, cinema and theater are all flourishing as the West Indian diaspora makes its dynamic imprint on British society. ∎

MIGRATION TO THE NETHERLANDS & FRANCE

Caribbean emigrants to the other colonial centers have faced experiences similar to those of West Indians in Britain. The Dutch and French governments have been generally less willing than the British to condone racist violence. But immigrants still face racial discrimination in the job and housing markets, social isolation and stereotyping of non-white children in the schools. Discrimination in these key areas has sufficed to turn major segments of the immigrant community into a subjugated underclass.

In the five years preceding Suriname's independence from Holland in 1975, thousands of Surinamers seized their last opportunity to migrate to the "mother country." By the time Holland shut its doors to all but dependent kin, there were some 180,000 Surinamers in the Netherlands.[6] They came from all of Suriname's ethnic groups: Creoles of African descent, "Folkcreoles" descended from Suriname's Maroons, as well as Javanese, East Indians, and Chinese. In addition, there are some 40,000 persons from the Netherlands Antilles in Holland.[7] This heterogeneous immigrant population has had many problems being accepted by white Dutch society. "They told us there was no racism in Holland," says a white Dutchman living in the Caribbean, "until the first Negro appeared."[8]

The experience of French Antilleans in France resembles that of Caribbean immigrants in Britain and Holland, but with one major difference: the French government actively promotes emigration from the French "overseas departments" of Guadeloupe, Martinique, and French Guiana. Even after immigrants from other countries were no longer welcome, Antilleans were still encouraged to go to France since emigration is viewed as an escape valve for social unrest in the colonies. Moreover, the French policy of cultural assimilation, aimed at increasing the dependence of its colonies, favors higher education of Antillean youth in France. Despite this assimilationist thrust, France became a center of anti-colonial activity in the 1950s among students from French colonies in the Caribbean and North Africa, who organized in support of the Algerian war of independence. These groups later became the nucleus of an independence movement for the French Caribbean.

The Puerto Rican Experience

Each year, an estimated quarter of a million persons crowd the New York-San Juan air corridor that has been called the "aerial bridge" between the U.S. and Puerto Rico.[1] This restless traffic flows in both directions, from Puerto Rico to the U.S. and back again; says one writer, "Puerto Ricans do not emigrate—they commute."[2] There are currently two million Puerto Ricans living in the United States and three million on the Island. How and why this massive northward exodus occurred can only be understood within the context of U.S. colonialism in Puerto Rico—colonialism based on economic, political, military and cultural ties of which continuous migration is only one part.[3]

No Caribbean society has been so deeply affected by migration as Puerto Rico. But the forces which produced that migration are not the result of special privilege, as official myth would have it. Rather, they are the same forces of economic and cultural imperialism which have dislocated people all over the Caribbean. The process attains extremes in Puerto Rico because of the greater wealth and proximity of the U.S. "metropole"(compared to the European colonizing countries) and its calculated plan to subsume Puerto Ricans into the U.S. labor force.

After being invaded and occupied by the U.S. in 1898, Puerto Rico became a U.S. colony in all but name. The U.S. Supreme Court in 1901 decreed the island to be a "non-incorporated territory which belongs to, but is not part of, the United States." In 1952 Puerto Rico became a "state in free association" with the U.S., a status ambiguously labeled "Commonwealth." But the Supreme Court's ruling was never invalidated, and the colonial reality remained unchanged.

Mass emigration played a central role in United States policy toward Puerto Rico from the beginning. The first colonial governor of the Island, Charles Allen, who administered from 1900-1901, remarked in his annual report that it would be preferable for the poor to emigrate since what Puerto Rico needed was "men with capital."[4] A labor surplus rapidly formed as U.S. sugar companies moved in and acquired lands previously occupied by coffee plantations and peasant farm plots. Many Puerto Ricans who were left unemployed and landless were sent to Hawaii to cut sugar cane, while others migrated to Cuba and the Dominican Republic. In 1917, U.S. citizenship was imposed on Puerto Ricans against their will to facilitate migration and to make them eligible for military conscription.

By the 1930s, Puerto Rico was a stagnant backwater of appalling poverty, of flimsy rural shacks and undernourished people. This suffering fueled a Nationalist movement led by Pedro Albizu Campos, who attempted to link the question of Puerto Rican independence to long-standing socialist currents. The movement was repressed by the U.S. authorities and finally co-opted by a new party, the Populares, who joined with the U.S. after World War Two to promote Operation Bootstrap. Intended to defuse discontent in Puerto Rico, Bootstrap's deeper purpose was to provide labor for the U.S. economy as it entered its postwar period of rapid growth. Under the Bootstrap plan, U.S. firms would set up factories in Puerto Rico employing low-wage labor, while the "surplus" Puerto Rican work force would migrate to New York.

The migration strategy was mapped out jointly by the Puerto Rican island administration and New York City officials. An Advisory Committee on Immigration was formed, and in 1954 Mayor Wagner of New York traveled to Puerto Rico to advertise the availability of factory jobs in his city. U.S. firms were encouraged to recruit labor from the Island. Between 1945 and 1965, over half a million Puerto Ricans emigrated.[5]

On a "parcela," a resettlement area for landless farm workers. Bayamon, Puerto Rico, 1945.

Photo by L. Rosskam, courtesy of Centro de Estudios Puertorriquenos, City University of New York

Street scene in El Barrio: A twin image of poverty and cultural dynamism.

The Promised Land

Puerto Ricans entered the economy of New York and other northeastern cities as laborers in factories and sweat-shops. They were crucial to the urban economy; indeed, the influx of Puerto Rican workers is credited with keeping the garment industry in New York long after other industries had left.[6] While manufacturing jobs initially were plentiful, by the 1960s the factories began to flee the cities for the suburbs, and at the same time, to automate. This produced heavy blue-collar unemployment which forced many Puerto Rican workers into the service sector as waiters, janitors, and so on. Others became agricultural laborers in the fruit orchards along the east coast.

Non-white and non-English speaking, Puerto Ricans became a new underclass, with lower incomes than either U.S. blacks or whites.[7] The average wage for Puerto Rican workers is below that of both black and white workers in every occupational sector.[8] One third of Puerto Ricans in the U.S. live below the poverty line.[9]

El Barrio, the section of Manhattan also known as East Harlem, was one of the first areas of Puerto Rican settlement, and is still the heart of the New York Puerto Rican community. Other areas of concentration were Hell's Kitchen on the west side, and "Loisida" (the lower east side). As time went on, some people were able to move out of these inner city areas to Brooklyn and the Bronx, and outward in widening circles to New Jersey, Connecticut, Massachusetts, Pennsylvania, and Illinois.

Today, the Puerto Rican neighborhoods of New York present a twin image of entrenched poverty and cultural dynamism. Community hearings held in New York in 1983 found that Puerto Ricans live in the city's oldest and most overcrowded housing, yet pay a higher proportion of their income in rent than either black or white residents of the city.[10] As in the case of other poor neighborhoods, red-lining by banks impedes rehabilitation of Puerto Rican areas. More than one-third of the children in the New York City public schools are Puerto Rican, yet the schools do not serve their needs, and more than 75% drop out before finishing high school.[11] Politically, Puerto Ricans in the U.S. are marginalized and fragmented, wielding little power even in the New York City administration.

Despite this experience, the presence of a million Puerto Ricans in New York has left an indelible stamp on the life of the city. They are the dominant element in a larger New York Latin community which also includes Dominicans, Cubans, Panamanians and others. Together these groups have enriched the urban fabric with a vibrant and original culture drawing on Latin American, Afro-Caribbean, and North American roots. This cultural innovation is a continuing two-way process: new arrivals from the region infuse Caribbean elements, which are then blended or transformed in New York and ultimately re-exported to the Caribbean by people returning home. *Salsa,* for example, combines elements of Afro-Caribbean music, Latin American folk, and rock 'n roll. These fused in the crucible of New York's Latin community to form a new genre which has taken its place beside rumba and merengue as popular music of the Spanish-speaking Caribbean.

The last two decades have also seen a cultural blossoming by young Puerto Rican New Yorkers in drama, literature, and the visual arts, tied closely to themes of nationalism and support for Puerto Rican independence. There is an active *independentista* community in New York.

Migration touches the lives of virtually all Puerto Ricans in one way or another. A recent study found that more than 42% of the population living in Puerto Rico has had some type of migratory experience.[12] A basic quality of Puerto Rican migration is its ebb-and-flow character in response to fluctuations in the U.S. economy, of which Puerto Rico is an integral part. When recession hit the U.S. in the 1970s, a period of "reverse migration" occurred in which the number of people returning to Puerto Rico offset the number leaving the Island. Recently, however, emigration has been rising again, as the Reagan administration's budget cuts reduce federal subsidies to Puerto Rico and worsen conditions there.

This continuous movement has vastly complicated the struggle to define and preserve a Puerto Rican nationhood in the face of U.S. cultural domination. It has left many Puerto Ricans bilingual—in some cases more fluent in English than Spanish—and divided between two cultures. Several years ago, for example, the Puerto Rican governor cited the problem of children returning from the U.S. speaking only English as a justification for introducing bilingual instruction into Puerto Rican schools—viewed by many as a step backward toward the days when English was imposed as the colonial language of instruction in Puerto Rico.

Few Puerto Ricans still hold any illusions about life in the United States. It is no longer a dream and a goal to migrate, as it was for some in the 1950s. Migration is now merely one option among others, an individual survival strategy held in reserve for dealing with poverty and unemployment in the colony.   ■

Puerto Rican New Yorkers.

Tony Velez

Brooklyn: West Indian Melting Pot

Nostrand Avenue cuts through the Flatbush section of Brooklyn, the heart of New York City's West Indian community. Lilting Jamaican and Grenadian English mingles with Haitian Creole on the street. Groceries offer coconuts, plantains, yucca root, mangoes, Jamaican meat patties and Trinidadian *roti*. The small businesses which line Nostrand Avenue are West Indian-owned and cater to the needs of the immigrant community. Ever Ready Caribbean Shipping & Moving will ship stateside goods by the box or barrel to families back at home. Alken Group Tours offers chartered flights to the islands for Carnival or Christmas. And at Winston's Caribbean Cuisine, one can nostalgically dine on lobster, cow foot soup, or curry goat.

Brooklyn is a Caribbean capital in its own right, one of the largest in the world. Once home to Eastern European, German and Irish immigrants, the city has become the pole of attraction for many West Indians entering the United States. No one knows exactly how many West Indians live there, but estimates surpass 500,000—several times the size of the average West Indian island.[1] Certain areas like the Flatbush and Crown Heights sections are now 90% West Indian.[2]

Two factors have made the experience of West Indians in the U.S. significantly different from that of West Indians in Britain. First, the proximity of the Caribbean to the United States has meant continuing back-and-forth travel and a constant renewal of cultural and social ties to "home." This in turn has encouraged the persistence of insularity—of Jamaicans feeling distinct from Antiguans who in turn set themselves apart from Trinidadians or Guyanese, and so forth. In Britain, by contrast, the distance from the Caribbean and the difficulty of returning has encouraged the evolution of a pan-Caribbean unity across national lines.[3]

Secondly, West Indians entering the U.S. arrived for the most part in multi-ethnic urban areas in which the presence of black Americans served as a buffer and a natural vehicle for assimilation. This has eased some of the pressures associated with being a racial minority and lessened the potential for violence directed specifically against West Indians. On the other hand, it has also diminished the need for Caribbean people to stand together as a group.

The social life of Caribbean Brooklyn is based on island affiliation, at least for the older generation with vivid memories of home. There are hundreds of social groups: one can attend a dance sponsored by the Dominica Benevolent Society, for example, or a luncheon of the St. Vincent Benefit & Educational Fund, aimed at raising money for charities in the respective islands. The Jamaica Progressive League holds a "Miss Jamaica-USA" pageant every year. While every country has at least one broad-based "national association," there is further fragmentation according to occupation or affinity group. There is the Jamaican Nurses Association, the Jamaican Policemen's Association, and even—reflecting the sheer numbers of Jamaicans in the area—the St. Andrew's Anglican Secondary School Alumni Association in New York. This

Tobago Crusoe, the 1983 Calypso Monarch of Trinidad, performs in a Brooklyn Carnival tent.

Everybody's Magazine

complexity is not surprising in view of the fact that each country has thousands of nationals in the city, and some of the smaller islands, such as Nevis or Anguilla, have more of their nationals in New York than living on the island.

Much of what serves to unify people in the Caribbean also unifies people from the different islands in New York. There are three cricket leagues in the New York City area. Calypso flourishes in Brooklyn, as does steelband; they are popular with New Yorkers from all over the West Indies, not just Trinidad. Rastafarianism has spread among West Indian youth in the U.S. (and Britain) just as it spread from island to island in the region. The largest Caribbean organization in Brooklyn is a Rastafarian group, the Twelve Tribes of Israel.

But it is Carnival—the two-day "bacchanal" of costumed parades, steelband and calypso competitions—which draws together, however briefly, virtually the whole West Indian community of New York. This is true even though Carnival is not indigenous to all the islands. The New York Carnival has become a pan-Caribbean festival celebrating the vibrancy and exuberance of West Indian culture. It is held every year on Labor Day, which has been designated "West Indian-American Day" by the New York state legislature. In terms of sheer numbers, Brooklyn's Carnival exceeds even Port-of-Spain's, although it does not approach the Trinidadian festival in quality or organization.[4]

77

Whatever sense of West Indian identity exists at the cultural level has not, as yet, produced the type of unity which could forge the Caribbean community into a politically potent ethnic block. An underlying concern of Brooklyn's West Indians is their lack of unity and political clout vis-a-vis other groups in Brooklyn, some of whom—like the Hassidic Jews—have made up for their minority status with strong internal organization. In terms of national politics, West Indians in the U.S. have not influenced U.S. policy toward the Caribbean in the way that Polish Americans have influenced policy toward Poland or Jewish Americans policy toward Israel. A few politicians of Caribbean descent have won elective office in the U.S.—former Congresswoman Shirley Chisholm, for example, is of Barbadian and Guyanese parentage. But until recently, they have not attempted to speak for the U.S. Caribbean community.[5]

Many West Indians do not hold U.S. citizenship and therefore do not vote in U.S. elections. They remain oriented to the politics of their home country, and in fact a number of Caribbean political parties maintain overseas branches in New York. But the problem goes deeper, relating to the fragmentation of the community by national group and to a "transient" outlook which discourages West Indians from involving themselves in U.S. politics, no matter how long they live in New York. The traditional West Indian immigrant comes to the U.S. with a specific goal in mind: to make a sum of money by working and saving, and then to return home. Although many end up living abroad permanently, the prevailing ethic remains that of "making it" within the system, and many have done very well.[6] West Indians own homes and small businesses in New York, work in professional as well as blue-collar jobs, and are well represented on the faculties and student bodies of area colleges (particularly the City University of New York).

However, it is becoming less easy for West Indians in the U.S. to ignore either the general situation of blacks in society or the fact that the U.S. government's policies are having a major impact on their home countries. This new consciousness has emerged most clearly among youth, whose interest in U.S. society is greater—they know their future is here—and who tend to assimilate into the Afro-American community, with its strong concerns about racial and economic justice. Many people feel that black Americans and West Indians should join together to put pressure on the system, but this unity has been elusive. Not since Marcus Garvey organized the UNIA in the 1920s have Caribbean and U.S. blacks come together in a single strong organization. The Black United Front which started in Brooklyn in 1967 draws from both groups, but has not developed into a truly mass movement.

There have been recent initiatives toward forming an umbrella organization which would press the interests of the U.S. Caribbean community. The Caribbean Action Lobby, with branches in Washington and New York, reflects the desire of the Caribbean professional and business class for a stronger political voice. Titular leader of this movement is Trinidad-born Congressman Mervyn Dymally (D-Cal.), one of the first U.S. politicians of Caribbean descent to throw his influence behind Caribbean concerns. Previous attempts to create such an umbrella group have fizzled, but the Reagan administration's controversial Caribbean policies and the growing economic crisis in the region are leading to the politicization of larger segments of the Caribbean community in the United States. ■

Local steelband performs in Brooklyn.

Trinidadians in Brooklyn pay tribute to Dr. Eric Williams after his death in 1981.

Cuban Miami: Right-Wing Haven

The story of Miami's transformation from a sleepy Florida resort into a hub of Latin capitalism, counter-revolution and organized crime is intimately bound to the story of Cuban emigration to the United States.

After 1959, thousands of Cubans fled to Miami rather than await the results of Fidel Castro's social revolution. From the beginning, the U.S. government sought to stimulate emigration from Cuba. As part of its anti-Castro strategy, the Kennedy administration encouraged Cubans to migrate to Miami and used federal funds to subsidize the growth of an exile community there. This had the twin purpose of damaging Castro's international image and forcing Cuba to remain permanently militarized—at great expense—because of the exile threat so close at hand.[1] Moreover, the nearby presence of a comparatively affluent exile colony exerted a continuing "pull" factor toward further migration. Drawn initially from the Cuban elite, this migration later became multi-class in character, with the most recent wave (the 1980 Mariel boatlift) drawn mainly from the working class.

Concentrated in Florida, northern New Jersey, and Puerto Rico, the Cuban exiles are one of the most militantly anticommunist and politically reactionary elements in U.S. society today. In addition to waging their own terrorist campaigns, they have served the U.S. government as a right-wing paramilitary strike force and are increasingly important actors in the Reagan administration's political plans, especially in relation to Central America.

After the CIA's failed attempt to overthrow Castro at the Bay of Pigs, the Cuban exiles who made up the mercenary army were ransomed back to the U.S. in exchange for $6 million worth of food and medicine. These Bay of Pigs "veterans" were quickly incorporated into the U.S. national security apparatus. Some were given inducements to join the Special Forces of the U.S. Army, and were assigned to counterinsurgency operations in Vietnam, Cambodia, Laos, the Congo, and Latin America.[2]

Many others, however, remained on the CIA payroll as footsoldiers, agents and informers in the Kennedy Administration's "Cuba Project" of ongoing attacks against Castro. The CIA's Miami station, JM-WAVE, became the largest intelligence station in the world. The Agency kept thousands of anti-Castro exiles bivouaced in cheap rooming houses and rural encampments throughout the southeastern U.S., where they were trained in paramilitary techniques and use of outlawed weaponry: " . . . bullets that explode on impact, silencer-equipped machine guns, home-made explosives, and self-made napalm . . . We were taught demolition techniques, practicing on late-model cars, railroad trucks, and gas storage tanks . . . "[3] CIA-sponsored exile commandos launched repeated attacks on Cuba's shoreline, while the CIA and the Mafia cooperated in at least a dozen attempts on Castro's life.

When the Johnson administration wound down the Secret War against Cuba, it was already too late to dismantle the monster of exile terrorism which had been lavishly

Areito

"*Cuba: To the Martyrs of the Assault Brigade." Monument in Little Havana section of Miami honors fallen members of the Bay of Pigs invasion force.*

financed, armed and trained. In the late sixties, the exiles turned their skills toward other profitable activities such as drug smuggling, gun running, and murder for hire. In addition, they mounted an autonomous terrorist campaign which included bombings of targets such as the Cuban Interest Section in Washington, DC, the Soviet Mission to the U.N., and the Cuban Mission to the U.N. Exile terrorism spun a murderous web linking the Cubans with far-flung segments of the international right, including the South Korean secret police, the Mafia, the Salvadoran death squads, the Somocistas, Jonas Savimbi's UNITA, and various European neo-fascist groups.[4] The exiles cooperated with several Latin intelligence services including DINA, Pinochet's secret police. In 1976, a conspiracy between DINA and an exile group known as the Cuban Nationalist Movement resulted in the bombing murder of Orlando Letelier, who had served as Chilean ambassador to the U.S. under Allende. Letelier was blown up in an exclusive diplomatic neighborhood of Washington, DC, bringing exile terrorism to the very doorstep of the U.S. government.

In addition to the Cuban Nationalist Movement, with branches in Miami and Union City, New Jersey, a myriad of exile groups have surfaced and faded over the years. In June 1976, there was an attempt at unity when exile leaders gathered in the Dominican Republic on an estate owned by the Falconbridge Mining Co. and formed CORU, the "Commando of the Union of Revolutionary Organizations." Four months later, a powerful bomb exploded aboard a Cubana airliner as the plane took off from Barbados, killing all 73 persons aboard including the entire Cuban national fencing team. CORU claimed responsibility, and its leader, Orlando Bosch, was jailed in Venezuela.

Terrorist activities in the U.S. were coordinated until recently by a shadowy umbrella network known as Omega 7, linked to the Cuban Nationalist Movement. In 1980, Havana's U.N. attache Felix Garcia was machine-gunned to death on the streets of New York, and the Cuban ambassador to the U.N., Raul Roa, was targeted in an attempted car-bomb murder. The head of Omega 7 was convicted in 1984 of first-degree murder in connection with Garcia's death and on numerous other counts including conspiracy in over a dozen terrorist bombings.[5]

A primary aim of exile terrorism is to intimidate persons within the Cuban emigré community who do not conform to the anti-Castro ideological model. There is in fact a sizable segment of the emigré population which accepts the permanence of Castro's government and favors establishing dialogue and trade ties. The Cuban-American Committee, formed in 1977, gathered 10,000 Cuban-American signatures on a petition calling for normalized relations between the U.S. and Cuba. Others formed the "Committee of 75," which successfully negotiated with Castro for the release of prisoners and permission for exiles to visit their relatives in Cuba. The Antonio Maceo Brigade, consisting mainly of young Cuban-Americans, is openly sympathetic to the revolution. But the climate of violent intimidation within the exile community means that moderate voices are often silenced. Among the victims of terrorist bombings have been:

- Firms doing business with Cuba, including pharmacies shipping medical supplies.
- Individuals who support dialogue with Cuba, notably the "Committee of 75."
- Travel agents organizing visits to Cuba.
- Consulates and airlines of the Dominican Republic and the Bahamas, Caribbean countries which recognize Cuba.

Ideological control in Miami: Insignia of the Antonio Maceo Brigade defaced by swastika.

- Liberal Cuban expatriate magazines (*Replica* and *Areito*).
- U.S. federal buildings, to protest gestures toward dialogue with Cuba.

In a letter to the *Washington Post,* Manuel Gomez, president of the Cuban-American Committee, wrote:

> . . . At best, to favor a policy of firm dialogue with Cuba is sure to elicit vicious and slanderous attacks in the media; at worst, it can bring death or maiming at the hands of Cuban exile terrorists. I know; the FBI has warned me of threats against my life. Little wonder then that Mr. Evans and Mr. Novak think of Cuban-Americans who favor dialogue with Cuba as a "rare breed." We are not really that rare; it's just that we often have to keep our mouths tightly shut.[6]

Reagan and the Cuban Right

As the Reagan administration consolidates its control in the Caribbean, the Cuban exile right and its primary base, Miami, have taken on an importance far beyond anything they previously held.

Miami in the eighties is a center of counterrevolution. It is a refuge for deposed dictators and Central American oligarchs fleeing revolutionary upheaval. Not only Cubans—who now make up 40% of Miami's population—but also wealthy Salvadorans, Nicaraguans and Jamaicans have sought refuge there for themselves and their capital. In paramilitary camps scattered through the Everglades, Cuban and Nicaraguan exiles train for military assaults on the governments of their homelands. As the likelihood of unseating Castro appears increasingly remote, anti-Castro Cubans have turned much of their attention to newer right-wing causes, particularly the *contra* war against Nicaragua. According to press reports, wealthy Miami Cubans have funded a secret training and supply base in Costa Rica near the Nicaraguan border from which a team of Cuban exiles harasses Sandinista targets.[7]

Miami is also the hub of a huge legal and illegal business empire which stretches its tentacles throughout the Caribbean and Latin America. Numerous multinational corporations have their Latin American headquarters in Miami, and the city hosts the annual conference of Caribbean/Central American Action, a corporate-governmental coalition which helped design Reagan's Caribbean Basin Initiative. Wealthy elites from Latin America and the Caribbean stash their capital in Miami banks or invest in grossly inflated Florida real estate. Miami is a consumer mecca for the middle and upper class of the Caribbean, who fly in for a weekend and return home laden with televisions, Cuisinarts, and video recorders. On the illegal side, Miami is the clearinghouse for a voluminous hard drug trade based on marijuana and cocaine from Colombia and controlled by Cuban exiles. Illegal drug profits are deposited in cooperative Miami banks and form a substantial part of south Florida's economic base."[8]

Rabidly anticommunist, the elite of the exile community are being used to demonstrate "Hispanic" support for Reagan administration policies and to fill positions with Hispanics who are ideologically close to Reagan. Some fifty administration appointments have gone to Cuban-Americans, particularly in sensitive areas touching on hemispheric relations.[9]

For example, the Reagan-appointed U.S. Director on the board of the Inter-American Development Bank is Jose Manuel Casanova, whose father was one of prerevolutionary Cuba's wealthiest sugar tycoons. Other examples include Rita M. Rodriguez, Director of the Export-Import Bank; Manuel J. Justiz, Director of the National Institute of Education; Pedro San Juan, Assistant Secretary for Territorial and International Affairs in the Department of the Interior; Victor Blanco, chairman of the board of the Inter-American Foundation; and Alberto Martinez Piedra, U.S. ambassador to Guatemala.

Cubans are highly visible within the U.S. diplomatic and aid bureaucracies abroad, particularly in the Dominican Republic and Puerto Rico. Agencies such as the Peace Corps, the U.S. Agency for International Development and the U.S. International Communications Agency in these countries are peppered with Cubans. This reflects the role which the Reagan administration has assigned to Cuban emigres as an anticommunist "control" factor in other Latin countries. In the Dominican Republic, for example, Cubans started up an anti-Castro radio station, Radio Clarín, with U.S. government funding. In Puerto Rico, the Cuban exile community numbers some 60,000 and wields extensive influence in the Church, real estate and the media, where many of the top journalists and producers are Cuban.[10] The hand of anti-Castro terrorism has reached Puerto Rico: in April 1979 Carlos Muñiz Varela, a travel agent handling trips to Cuba, was murdered on the street by the Comando Zero, an offshoot of Omega 7.

Under Reagan, the Cuban right is boldly expanding its reach to target the North American left and progressive elements within other Hispanic communities. In May 1983, a North American solidarity group in Miami, LACASA, planned a demonstration to protest the administration's policies in El Salvador, but had to cancel it after death threats from Omega 7. A subsequent press conference called by LACASA was broken up by a mob of exiles as police looked on. Two weeks later, President Reagan visited Miami at the invitation of the Cuban-American National Foundation, a right-wing group of prominent exiles which lobbies on Central American policy. In his speech to hundreds of cheering Cubans, the president referred to the special role that exiles can play in convincing Americans that his Central American policies are correct. Thus encouraged, the exiles stepped up their harassment against critics of Reagan's views. The black city manager of Miami, Howard Gary, was threatened by Cubans and required round-the-clock police protection after

Areito

Carlos Muñiz Varela, slain at age 27 by Cuban exile terrorists in Puerto Rico. He was a founding member of the Antonio Maceo Brigade.

he criticized Reagan in a speech to Miami's black community. Several weeks later, a Socialist Workers Party bookstore in Miami was firebombed, and a film showing by LACASA had to be cancelled because of disruption by the Cuban terrorist group Alpha 66.

All signs point to an expansion in the role of the Cuban right, both domestically and abroad. Cuban emigré political economist Lourdes Arguelles predicts:

Cuban Miami will continue to grow as a major operational base of transnational capital and its Latin American intermediaries and beneficiaries . . . [The Cuban exiles] will strengthen existing ties to neofascist parties and the Moral Majority constituency . . . They will become more deeply involved in these groups' expanding activities against the Left, ethnic minorities, and powerless social groups in the United States.[11] ∎

The Haitian Boat People

In the waters off northern Haiti in June 1984, a U.S. Coast Guard cutter apprehended a small wooden sailboat in which some 70 Haitian men, women and children were attempting to flee to Florida. As agents of the U.S. Immigration and Naturalization Service stepped aboard, the frightened refugees crowded to one side and the boat capsized, sending twelve people to their deaths.[1] It was another "interdiction" under the Haitian Migration Interdiction Operation, aimed at closing off escape routes from the desperate land of U.S.-backed President-for-Life Jean Claude Duvalier.

The first boatload of Haitian refugees beached on the south Florida coast in December 1972. More followed throughout the decade, crammed to the gunnels with the weakened survivors of an 800-mile voyage which sent many to their deaths from hunger, thirst and drowning. Six months after Reagan's inauguration in 1981, the administration launched a "get-tough" policy toward the Haitians. Incoming refugees were incarcerated in federal prison camps located in Miami and Puerto Rico, sometimes for periods of a year or more. At the same time, the Coast Guard began patrolling the waters off northern Haiti under an agreement with the Haitian government, seizing boatloads of refugees and turning them over to the Haitian military.

Meanwhile, another group of refugees entered the United States under quite different circumstances. To the trumpeting of media fanfare, the "freedom flotilla" escorted 130,000 Cubans from the port of Mariel to the U.S. in the spring of 1980. Described by the U.S. government as "political refugees from communism," the Cubans were welcomed and assisted with federal funds for their resettlement. In November 1984, the Reagan administration announced its decision to offer permanent resident status to the Mariel Cubans, with eligibility for U.S. citizenship in 2½ years (half the normal waiting time). The Administration has stated categorically that the same benefits are not available to Haitians.

The 1980 Refugee Act provides that persons fearing persecution in their country have a right to receive political asylum in the United States. Soviet, East European and Chinese defectors—mostly white and anticommunist—have an excellence chance of obtaining asylum, even though they may have lived privileged lives at home. Refugees from Poland, Afghanistan, and six other countries currently enjoy Extended Voluntary Departure, a special status allowing them to remain in the U.S. until "violence" in their home country subsides. But Haitians, fleeing a right-wing government friendly to Washington, are handed over to the custody of the Haitian

Newly arrived Haitians share food donated by residents of a nearby condominium on Miami Beach.

Steve Dozier, *Miami Herald*

military without ever getting a chance to apply for asylum. On March 25, 1985, the U.S. Supreme Court heard a class action suit (*Jean v. Nelson*) on behalf of 2,000 Haitian boat people, arguing that their rights to apply for admission and asylum have been denied. The suit seeks to overturn a ruling by a Georgia court of appeals which found the Haitians to be "excludable aliens" with no constitutional rights to due process in the United States.

Rise of the Duvalier Dynasty

There are now an estimated one million Haitians living outside their native land. This includes approximately 30,000 in the Bahamas (the stopping-off point for many hoping to reach the U.S.); 300,000 in the Dominican Republic; 20,000 in the French Caribbean colonies; 35,000 in Canada, primarily Montreal; and an indeterminate number, probably over 500,000, in the U.S., where they are concentrated in New York and Miami.[2]

To understand why hundreds of thousands of people would risk their lives to flee a country which is not at war, it is necessary to go back to the roots of the repression against the Haitian peasantry. After winning independence from France in its slave revolution, Haiti set up a constitutional government in 1804. But the death of Toussaint L'Ouverture and hostility from the United States and European colonial nations led to the concentration of power in the hands of the Haitian military. Haitian Army officers became landowners, competing with the mulatto elite which controlled commerce.

For the rest of the century the Haitian peasantry struggled against this ruling class, culminating in a wave of peasant rebellions between 1911 and 1915. With North American capital gaining control over Haiti's export trade, the U.S. viewed this grassroots revolution as a threat to its interests; and in 1915, U.S. Marines marched into Haiti. It took them four years to crush the nationalist resistance led by "Haiti's Sandino," Charlemagne Peralte, in a war which cost some 50,000 Haitian peasants their lives. When the U.S. finally withdrew from Haiti in 1934, the Marines left behind a Haitian National Guard trained to suppress the popular classes.

By integrating Haiti more fully into circuits of international commerce, the U.S. occupation served to strengthen the mulatto oligarchy which functioned as a partner of foreign capital. Determined to regain dominance, the black, landowning sectors of the ruling class responded with the "noirist" (pro-black) ideology of Francois Duvalier. "Papa Doc" portrayed his coming to power in 1957 as a victory for the black masses. In fact, it marked the beginning of a reign of terror in which thousands of Haitians were killed, tortured, arbitrarily imprisoned or made to "disappear." This repression was directed against Papa Doc's rivals and against the mulatto elite in general, mostly businessmen, professionals, and members of the urban petty bourgeoisie. Because this class was historically allied with the United States, the U.S. welcomed them as refugees and criticized Papa Doc's repression.[3]

Papa Doc died in 1971 after designating his 19-year-old son Jean Claude ("Baby Doc") as president-for-life. Whereas relations between the U.S. and Papa Doc had been strained, Baby Doc proved willing to open the Haitian economy to U.S. penetration, and Washington embraced his regime as more "liberal" than his father's. U.S. corporations entered Haiti to set up low-wage assembly plants and mechanized plantations, displacing many of the feudal landowners and thousands of peasants from their lands. This sweeping rural dispossession produced the second wave of refugees, the "boat people," consisting primarily of poor peasants. The first group arrived in Florida a year after Jean Claude came to power.

The Casernes Dessalines

Far from liberalizing, Baby Doc has continued his father's repression. The armed militia created by Papa Doc, the National Security Volunteers—commonly known as *tontons macoutes*—are everywhere, functioning as political police and spies for the regime. All political parties not authorized by the presidency are banned, and persons suspected of political activity are regularly arrested and imprisoned without ever seeing an arrest warrant, a lawyer or a court of law. Amnesty International reported in 1984:

Torture and ill-treatment of detainees in Haiti has been regularly reported to Amnesty International since President for life, Jean Claude Duvalier took office in 1971.

Methods of torture described in testimonies received by Amnesty International [since 1980] include beatings on the head or other parts of the body with sticks, obliging detainees to remain standing still for very long periods, and the so-called Parrot's Perch, known in Haiti as the "Jack."

Long-term incommunicado detention, unacknowledged

Portraits of Jean Claude Duvalier and his wife Michelle Bennett in front of the National Palace in Port-au-Prince. The sign behind reads: "Political power will always be exercised for the good of the greatest number with respect to the liberty and dignity of the citizen conscious of his rights and duties toward the national collectivity."

by the authorities for months or years, and sometimes never acknowledged, without access to lawyers, relatives, or doctors, has become the pattern of political detention in Haiti.[4]

Prison conditions in Haiti are among the worst in the world. Most political detainees are interrogated in the Port-au-Prince military barracks, the dreaded Casernes Dessalines. Amnesty International reports:

> Political detainees taken to the Casernes Dessalines are held in damp, dark and dirty cells, either naked or dressed only in their underwear. Detainees leave the cells only once a day, early in the morning, for a shower. There is said to be no furniture at all in the cells, only a dirty mattress and a paint tin which serves as a toilet.
>
> Prisoners are allowed no visits whatsoever and are kept completely isolated. No reading materials or correspondence are permitted and the prisoners do not work. They are not allowed to communicate with each other and if caught doing so are likely to be beaten.[5]

As with Salvadoran refugees, the U.S. State Department denies that refugees deported back to Haiti are subject to persecution despite much evidence to the contrary. Former

tontons macoutes and secret police now living in exile have revealed that anyone who returns to Haiti after unsuccessfully seeking political asylum abroad is regarded as a "kamokin" (traitor) and often arrested, imprisoned and tortured.[6]

The Reagan administration's support for anti-communist dictatorships has encouraged the Haitian government to intensify its repression, causing greater numbers to flee the country. In 1984 the Coast Guard intercepted more than 2,200 Haitian refugees, three times the number in 1983 and more than ten times that in 1982.[7] The Duvalier regime plays a double game with the U.S. over the refugee question. On the one hand, it uses the flow of refugees to get foreign aid, claiming that conditions in Haiti can be improved by giving aid to the regime. At the same time, those close to the National Palace are heavily involved in the lucrative business of smuggling out refugees, an activity reportedly on the increase in recent months. Peasants pay up to $2,000 for a place on a boat, and must often sell their small plot of land to speculators in order to raise the cash. They thus give up everything they have for a chance to flee; but neither this reality nor the high disaster rate for the leaky sailboats on their ocean trip deter the refugees. Alternatives have run out in rural Haiti.

CONTEMPORARY SLAVERY

Each December before the annual sugar harvest, some 19,000 Haitians board trucks for the jolting journey across the border into the Dominican Republic, where they will spend six months cutting cane under a contract between the Haitian and Dominican governments. This legal migrant flow, which supplies labor to the 12 estates of the Dominican State Sugar Council, complements a much larger trade in "illegal" immigrants who provide the major workforce for private landowners such as Gulf + Western. These are smuggled in by an organized network of traffickers (alleged to include members of the Dominican military) who pay for the laborers in Haiti and "resell" them to landowners in the Dominican Republic.[8]

The working conditions of the Haitian cane cutters are often compared to those of the slavery era. During the harvest, it is not uncommon for cane cutters to work 16 hours a day, beginning as early as 4:30 in the morning. The pay is 1 peso and 55 cents per ton cut; the average worker might cut two tons a day, although many manage to cut more. Workers are routinely cheated at the scales when the cut cane is weighed, resulting in the loss of one-quarter to one-third of their earnings. In addition, the contract between the two governments provides for 1 peso to be taken every two weeks from the worker's pay and turned over to the Haitian Embassy for "compulsory savings." The worker never sees this money again.

The workers live in squalid camps called *bateyes* adjacent to the cane fields. Here a family of six or more might share a 12-foot shack, sleeping on a rusty metal bed and cooking on a charcoal stove on the floor. There is no indoor plumbing, and running water and electricity are rare. With income to cover only about half of their daily food needs, cane cutters and their families live near the edge

of starvation, especially in the six-month "dead" season between harvests. A common sight in the bateyes are spindly-legged children sucking sugar cane to stave off hunger.

No unions function in the camps, and the Haitians have no recourse in case of injustices such as cheating at the scales. Those who come in under the governmental contract supposedly are under the protection of the Haitian Embassy in Santo Domingo. But the Haitian government's interest begins and ends with financial gain and the diversion of unemployed workers as an escape valve for social pressures in Haiti.

In addition to the annual laborers, called "congos," some 300,000 Haitians live permanently in the Dominican Republic as an oppressed and scorned minority group. Although many of them have been in the Dominican Republic for two or three generations, they are considered illegal and can be forcibly deported to Haiti at any time. Anti-Haitian racism is an important tool of the Dominican elite for distracting Dominican workers from social struggle. They thus encourage racism against "black" Haitians (even though many Dominicans also are black) and promote the idea that Haitians take away jobs from Dominicans. At the same time, the society encourages Dominicans to shun cane cutting as degrading "Haitian work," so that Haitians can be employed under more exploitative and profitable conditions.

(Right) An elderly Haitian cane cutter.

(Below) A view of the batey at La Romana, adjacent to cane fields owned by Gulf + Western.

Cathy Sunshine

Laurence Simon

NOTES TO PART THREE

Migration in Caribbean History

1. Dawn I. Marshal, "The History of Caribbean Migrations: The Case of the West Indies," *Caribbean Review,* Vol. XI, No. 1, Winter 1982, p. 6.
2. Cecilia A. Karch, "The Growth of the Corporate Economy in Barbados: Class/Race Factors 1890-1977" in Susan Craig, ed., *Contemporary Caribbean: A Sociological Reader* (Trinidad: S. Craig, 1982), Vol. I, pp. 213-238.
3. Ransford W. Palmer, *Caribbean Dependence on the United States Economy* (New York: Praeger, 1979), Chapter 6.
4. Excerpted from "Colonisation in Reverse," in Louise Bennett, *Jamaica Labrish* (Kingston: Sangster's Book Stores, 1966), pp. 179-180.
5. Gary P. Freeman, "Caribbean Migration to Britain and France," *Caribbean Review,* Vol. XI, No. 1, Winter 1982, p. 30.
6. Jack Harewood, "Unemployment and Under-Employment in the Commonwealth Caribbean," in Craig, ed., Vol. I, pp. 143-166.

Blacks in Britain

1. A. Sivanandan, "From Resistance to Rebellion: Asian and Afro-Caribbean Struggles in Britain," *Race & Class,* XXIII, 2/3 (1981-82), p. 116.
2. Alan Stinton, "From Roots to Riots," in Arif Ali, ed., *Third World Impact* (London: Hansib Publishing Ltd., 1982), pp. 10-11.
3. Sivanandan, pp. 126-127.
4. *Ibid.,* p. 135.
5. *Washington Post,* June 1, 1984.
6. Frank Bovenkerk, "Caribbean Migration to the Netherlands," *Caribbean Review,* Vol. XI, No. 1, p. 37.
7. *Antillean Review,* (Curacao), August/Sept. 1983, p. 33.
8. EPICA interview with Alfonso Roman, Puerto Rico, Sept. 1983.

Puerto Rican Experience

1. Manuel Maldonado-Denis, "Puerto Rican Emigration: Proposals for Its Study," in Marlene Dixon and Susanne Jonas, eds., *The New Nomads: From Immigrant Labor to Transnational Working Class* (San Francisco: Synthesis Publications, 1982), p. 24.
2. Gordon K. Lewis, "Migration and Caribbean Consciousness" (Occasional Paper No. 1, Center for Latin American Studies, University of Florida at Gainesville), p. 11.
3. Frank Bonilla and Ricardo Campos, "Imperialist Initiatives and the Puerto Rican Worker: From Foraker to Reagan," in Dixon and Jonas, eds., p. 1.
4. First annual report of Gov. Charles Allen, cited in *Sources for the Study of Puerto Rican Migration* (New York: Center for Puerto Rican Studies, CUNY), pp. 14-15.
5. Bonilla and Campos, p. 8.
6. Clara Rodriguez, "Economic Factors Affecting Puerto Ricans in New York," Craig, ed., p. 64.
7. Based on data from 1980 census.
8. Rodriguez, p. 57.
9. Public Hearings Project, "On the State of the Puerto Rican Community—New York/Tri-State Areas" (May 16, 1983).
10. *Ibid.*
11. *Ibid.*
12. *El Reportero,* May 31, 1983.

Brooklyn

1. Tony Best, "How West Indians Are Doing in USA," *Caribbean Contact,* August 1982.
2. EPICA interview with Dr. Basil Wilson, City University of New York, July 1983.
3. *Ibid.*
4. EPICA interview with Herman Hall, Brooklyn, NY, July 1983.
5. EPICA interview with Dr. Basil Wilson.
6. Best, *op. cit.*

Cuban Miami

1. EPICA interview with Lourdes Arguelles, Washington, DC, August 1983.
2. Lourdes Arguelles, "Cuban Miami: The Roots, Development and Everyday Life of an Emigre Enclave in the U.S. National Security State," in Dixon and Jones, eds., p. 30.
3. Description of training at CIA's demolition training headquarters, where Cubans were trained, by former officer of CIA's Clandestine Services. Cited in Victor Marchetti and J. Marks, *The CIA and the Cult of Intelligence* (New York: Dell, 1974), p. 111.
4. Warren Hinkle and William Turner, *The Fish is Red: The Story of the Secret War Against Castro* (New York: Harper & Row, 1981), p. 317.
5. *Washington Post,* September 23, 1984.
6. *Washington Post,* August 30, 1983.
7. Jack Anderson, "Anti-Castro Cubans Aid Contra Rebels," *Washington Post,* November 20, 1984.
8. Penny Lernoux, "The Miami Connection," *The Nation,* February 18, 1984.
9. EPICA interview with Lourdes Arguelles.
10. EPICA interview with staff of PRISA, National Ecumenical Movement of Puerto Rico, October 1983.
11. Arguelles, "Cuban Miami," p. 41.

Haitian Boat People

1. *Washington Post,* June 8, 1984.
2. Jean-Jacques Honorat, "The Political Economy of the Haitian Refugee Crisis" (Queens Village, NY: Institute of Haitian Studies, 1982), pp. 3-4.
3. Mouvement Haitien de Liberation, "Do You Really Understand the Haitian Refugee Problem?" (White Plains, NY, 1980).
4. Amnesty International, *Torture in the Eighties* (London: Amnesty International, 1984), pp. 162-163.
5. Amnesty International, "Haiti Briefing," March 1985, p. 12.
6. From interviews published in the *Miami Herald* and Fort Meyers *News-Press,* cited in Church World Service, Immigration and Refugee Program, "Haitian Refugees Need Asylum: A Briefing Paper," April 9, 1980.
7. *Miami Herald,* October 29, 1984; *Haiti Observateur,* December 5, 1984.
8. *Caribbean Contact,* May 1985, p. 9.

PART FOUR
Alternative Models of Development
Cuba & Grenada

cky Surles

Introduction

Revolution in Cuba and Grenada has become an emotional subject for North Americans. We are told that Cuba is a "totalitarian dictatorship," where there are no rights or freedoms. The revolutionary government in Grenada is said to have been a "Cuban-style communist dictatorship," and both are blamed for threatening our security by bringing Soviet influence to the doorstep of the United States.

Barred by U.S. law from visiting Cuba and subjected to a 25-year news blackout punctuated by biased and false reports, most North Americans are abjectly ignorant of the Cuban reality. Behind this shield of ignorance and fear, successive U.S. administrations have elevated the campaign for the downfall of Cuban leader Fidel Castro into a bizarre kind of holy war. The Central Intelligence Agency has tried numerous times to assassinate Castro, and has sponsored attacks by anti-Castro exiles on Cuban shores. CIA-organized mercenaries invaded Cuba in 1961 and were defeated by the Cuban people who defended their country. Cuba has suffered a U.S. trade embargo for twenty years, placing enormous and unnatural strains on its economy—but failing utterly to dislodge the Castro government.

In the case of Grenada, the U.S. campaigned to block the country's access to badly-needed international aid and loans. Hostile propaganda emanating from Washington (such as the untrue story that a Soviet naval base was being built in Grenada) scared U.S. visitors away from the island, cutting deeply into revenues from tourism. Twice—in 1981 and 1982—U.S. armed forces practiced a mock invasion of Grenada, and the constant specter of a U.S. attack helped raise blood pressures on the tiny island. In October 1983, a fatal split in the ruling party opened the door to the real invasion and the Grenada revolution was no more.

The U.S. government campaign against Cuba and Grenada not only has threatened their existence; it has largely hidden from view the real accomplishments and meaning of the two revolutions. Cuba is not a perfect society, nor was revolutionary Grenada. Both encountered many problems and made mistakes in the course of social transformation. But they have won respect in the Caribbean and outside the region for their bold attempts to find solutions to the poverty and inequality which resulted from centuries of domination by outside powers.

Both revolutions put the ordinary people—the poor majority—at the center of their process. In Cuba, the primary task was to rectify the gross social inequalities and foreign domination which marked the society during the dictator Batista's rule. Under the revolution, for the first time, a peasant farmer or sugar worker could get good medical care, eat a nutritious diet, live in a house with running water, and send his or her children to school. And for the first time, ordinary Cubans could see the vast and fertile island as belonging to *them* rather than to colonial powers, a corrupt ruling clique, foreign corporations and wealthy tourists.

Grenada's 1979 revolution borrowed a number of ideas and structures from the Cuban experience, primarily in the areas of health, education and defense, where Cuban technicians assisted the Grenadian government. But there were also significant differences between the two. Grenada, for example, did not attempt to rapidly convert its economy to socialism. The bulk of the Grenadian economy remained in private hands, with the goal for the near future a mixed economy comprising a public sector, a private sector and cooperatives. A more important difference was that Grenada's short-lived experiment never approached the stage of consolidation and maturity achieved by the Cuban revolution after 25 years. While the government of Maurice Bishop instituted many successful programs and raised the standard of living dramatically compared to pre-1979 days, it had only begun the task of creating political institutions which could both provide effective leadership and develop meaningful channels for popular participation.

It is difficult for most North Americans to imagine living all one's life illiterate, malnourished and exploited in a society where everything is controlled by a privileged elite. Because we are distanced from this experience, we fail also to appreciate that education, health care, shelter and employment are *rights* that are fundamental to human freedom and dignity. When we talk about the rights that sometimes are abridged by revolutions—such as the right to publish—we must weigh these against the fulfillment of other rights which have been denied to the majority for many years. It is precisely because these rights are so important that the majority of Cubans support Fidel Castro and the majority of Grenadians supported the Bishop government.

Ruling circles in the United States chose long ago to oppose attempts toward social justice in Latin America, throwing U.S. power instead behind the maintenance of elite privilege and foreign domination. For this reason, both Cuba and Grenada had to defy U.S. dictates in order to be free to transform their societies. In the process, they became vocal adherents of "anti-imperialism," adding to American perceptions of a hostile threat. But as anyone who has visited Cuba or revolutionary Grenada can attest, anti-imperialism does not mean ill-will toward the American *people*. Rather, it is an affirmation of the right to engage in social change and to create a model different from the one imposed by colonial and neocolonial powers. These efforts deserve our understanding and support. Far from threatening the security of the hemisphere, they hold out hope of an alternative path to development for the Caribbean which may succeed where previous attempts have consistently failed. ∎

Cuba

The revolutionary movement which overthrew the dictatorship of Fulgencio Batista in December 1958 quickly became a symbol of hope to the poor throughout Latin America. While only a few attempted the same strategies the Cuban revolutionaries had used, all drew the same lesson: that an organized popular movement could sweep away an apparently powerful, well-armed regime. It had been done in Cuba, and that fact altered the political reality of Latin America and long-standing assumptions about the right and ability of the United States to dominate the hemisphere.

The influence which the Cuban revolution has assumed as a symbol and model in the quarter-century of its existence must be understood in the context of Cuba's prerevolutionary conditions. Batista presided over a social order of rural poverty, gross inequality, ignorance, and foreign exploitation—conditions which still plague much of Latin America and the Caribbean. At the same time, the Cuban revolution has been a unique process of trial and error shaped by its own conditions and by the impact of U.S. attacks on Cuba over a period of 26 years.

The Secret War

The revolution meant the expulsion from Cuba of U.S. business and crime interests which, together with Batista's corrupt henchmen, had made Havana the "sin city" of the Caribbean. These elements immediately joined forces with Cuban exiles and the CIA to wage a "secret war" against Castro from U.S. soil. As described in a 1981 study, *The Fish is Red:*

> The Cuba Project was an overreaching program of clandestine warfare, offhanded military adventures, sabotage, and political and economic subversion. It ran the gamut from counterfeiting to biological warfare to assassination. It began in 1959 during the Eisenhower administration, reached its paramilitary heights under the brothers Kennedy, slumbered under Lyndon Johnson, and was reawakened with a vengeance under Richard Nixon. Vestiges remain operational.[1]

Although freedom from U.S. hegemony had long been a Cuban demand, Castro initially sought an accommodation and trade relations with the United States. In April 1959 he visited Washington and met with Vice President Nixon, who had ties with Batista's empire through such individuals as Bebe Rebozo and Howard Hughes.[2] Nixon denounced Castro as a communist and recommended organizing a force of Cuban exiles to overthrow him. The CIA's quick ouster of the Arbenz government in Guatemala just six years earlier was an encouraging precedent, and the CIA began recruiting and training Cuban exiles in the Miami area for the planned invasion.

Meanwhile, relations between Washington and Havana deteriorated rapidly as the revolution began chipping away at the vast U.S. private holdings in Cuba. When the first agrarian reform law of May 1959 affected U.S. investments, Washington responded by slashing Cuba's quota on the U.S. sugar market. Cuba, a monocultural producer, could not survive without a market for its sugar, so Castro turned to the Soviet Union, which offered to buy five million tons over a five-year period. Some of the sugar was paid for with Soviet oil. When the U.S.-owned refineries in Cuba refused to refine the oil, they were nationalized by the Cuban government.[3] Later other North American holdings were nationalized as well.

The CIA's planned invasion of Cuba was an open secret. As signs of the preparations mounted, Cuba mobilized to defend itself. The result of the CIA's profoundly misconceived invasion at *Playa Girón*—the Bay of Pigs—was North American humiliation and a dramatic confirmation of the Castro government's popular support.

> Through the long months of preparation, the American planners and their Cuban exiles had accepted unquestioningly the assumption that Castro ruled by force and fear. Given a clear alternative, they believed, the Cuban masses would unite behind a revolutionary movement aimed at overthrowing Castro. In the tense days of mid-April 1961, Castro proved he had the loyalty of the Cuban people.[4]

The failed Bay of Pigs invasion was merely the opening salvo of what became a prolonged dirty war against Cuba. Most damaging of all was a permanent economic blockade which cut off Cuba's access to goods previously imported from the U.S., including food, medicines, machinery and spare parts. The blockade pushed Cuba to shift the bulk of its trade to the Soviet Union. Politically as well, U.S. hostility made the Soviet Union appear as a needed protector. Castro declared the revolution a Marxist one after the Bay of Pigs invasion.

As Cuba cemented its ties to the socialist world, U.S. propaganda came to focus on the Soviet connection. But the

Fidel Castro meets Vice-President Nixon in 1959.

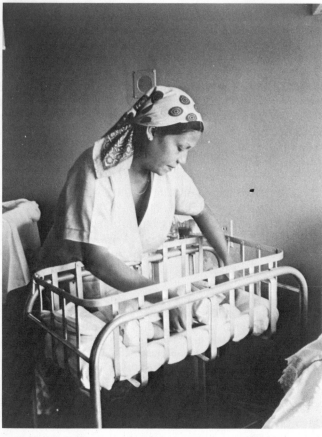

Marcelo Montecino

barefoot and ill-nourished in the countryside, mostly as landless laborers on the sugar estates.

In a country where many adults could not read and where disease and malnutrition were rampant, education and health became urgent priorities of the young revolution. Cuba's innovations in these areas are among the most widely emulated aspects of its development process.

Between 1960 and 1962, Cuba closed most of its secondary schools for a year and sent thousands of students into the countryside, where they worked side by side with the rural population on farms and in factories. At night, they taught their campesino hosts to read and write.

> The number of illiterates was estimated at one million. Primary school teachers, secondary school students, and adults were recruited and grouped into brigades. Each member was supplied with a uniform, hammock, blanket, instruction books, a teaching manual, a Cuban flag, and a paraffin lamp (in the absence of rural electricity) which became the symbol of the campaign.[7]

The success of the literacy drive was highly attractive to other poor countries. New revolutionary states in the late 1960s and '70s such as Angola, Mozambique, Nicaragua and Grenada also undertook national literacy campaigns. Each country designed its program to suit national conditions and priorities, with most opting for a more gradual approach than Cuba's.

Before the revolution, most Cuban high schools were located in Havana and the larger towns, where they served an urban elite. Today, new schools dot the countryside, and education from the elementary through university level is free. By the mid-1960s, most Cubans had attained the equivalent of a third-grade education, and by the mid-1970s, a sixth-grade level was the goal. Today the target is that all Cubans complete a ninth-grade education.[8]

Within the span of a single generation, Cuba has created what is widely regarded as perhaps the best health care system in the Third World. It has done so against formidable odds. In 1959, most Cuban doctors and hospitals were concentrated in Havana. Half the country's 6,000 doctors emigrated in the first two years of the revolution, and the U.S. blockade cut off needed medicines and supplies.

Cuba's response was to construct a totally new health care system based on a decentralized network of polyclinics, extending free medical care to the farthest reaches of the countryside. Along with intensive training of new doctors (16,000 by 1982), the government gave priority to preventive medicine, public sanitation and nutrition. Many of the old *bohíos*—dirt-floored, windowless huts in which most rural Cubans lived—were replaced by new housing. While there is still a housing shortage, most Cuban dwellings now have plumbing and electricity.

real reason for Washington's hostility went deeper. Cuba forced the U.S. to confront the inevitability of revolution in Latin America, implying the eventual break-up of the North American corporate and political empire. Because of these larger implications, Washington's desire to destroy the revolution has scarcely diminished in the last twenty years, despite the futility of efforts thus far. The Reagan administration launched its first term with threats of a naval blockade or a direct military strike at Cuba. As one administration official stated in 1982, "There is a lot more we can do to hurt the Cubans, and we are seriously considering all the options."[5]

Education and Health: Models of Innovation

Among the myths which the United States has used to disparage Cuban accomplishments is the notion that Cuba was not poor and underdeveloped before the revolution. The U.S. State Department, for instance, claims that Cuba's living standards in 1959 "rivalled some West European countries."[6] This deception obscures the basic characteristic of prerevolutionary Cuba—the tremendous inequality in living standards, particularly between Havana and the rural areas. While Havana was a luxury playground for the Cuban and North American elite, the great majority of the population lived

A central aspect of the strategy was the decision to make a nutritionally adequate diet available to all Cubans. Basic foods such as rice, beans, milk, sugar, meat and chicken are heavily subsidized and sold below production costs at prices which have risen only once since 1965.[9] There were food shortages in the early years of the revolution, but the government has steadily expanded food production, especially of proteins such as eggs, milk and fish. Food distribution in Cuba is egalitarian. Every household receives a ration book (*libreta*) which entitles them to buy a certain quantity of staple foods at the rock-bottom subsidized prices. Rationed foods account for only 26¢ of every food dollar spent, however, with the rest of the food supply sold through non-rationed channels at higher prices. The ration system is essentially a safety net which ensures that no one in Cuba goes hungry, even if people do not always get all the variety they want.

The San Francisco-based Institute for Food and Development Policy calls eliminating hunger the "single most unassailable achievement of the Cuban revolution."[10] Cuba ranks second in per capita food consumption in Latin America (after Argentina), according to the Organization of American States.[11] Childhood malnutrition is virtually unknown, and malnutrition-related diarrhea is no longer a significant killer of children in Cuba as it is in most underdeveloped countries.

Cuba's health indicators now bear a closer resemblance to those of Western Europe and the United States than to the rest of the Third World. Infant mortality, which was 70 per 1000 live births in 1960, fell to 15 per 1000 in 1984 (the U.S. rate is 12 per 1000).[12] Life expectancy at birth was 73 in 1981, just short of the U.S. figure of 75, and contrasting dramatically with life expectancy of 62 years in the neighboring Dominican Republic and 54 in Haiti.[13] Cuba's health problems are no longer the infectious diseases of underdevelopment, but the "industrialized" health problems of cancer, heart disease and obesity. Many developing countries have examined Cuba's health care system with interest, and there are over 3,000 Cuban doctors and health technicians giving assistance in 27 countries of the Third World.[14]

Sugar and the Revolution

Despite its impressive accomplishments over the past generation, Cuba has not resolved the problem facing every Caribbean nation: economic dependency. The symptoms are Cuba's continuing reliance on sugar for over 80% of its export earnings; its dependence on Soviet economic support; and its external debt, of which $3.2 billion is owed to Western nations in hard currency.

Cuban economic planners have vacillated over the years in terms of their attitude toward the country's historical monoculture. In the early years of the revolution, Cuba attempted to diversify away from sugar into food and other non-sugar crops. But by 1963, mounting balance-of-payments problems prompted a return to emphasis on sugar, which was seen as a way to generate foreign exchange to invest in agricultural diversification and industry. The 1965-70 "Sugar Plan" called for a harvest of 10 million tons of sugar in 1970. That effort failed, although the country did produce a record 8.5 million tons in that year. The all-out attempt to reach the ten-million-ton goal, however, diverted investment, labor and

High school students work on a farm as part of a work study program. The Cubans consider it important to link physical and intellectual labor.

resources from other sectors of the economy, so that Cuba's overall production fell sharply in 1971.

Within two years, Cuba's debt to the Soviet Union had risen significantly, and the two countries decided to renegotiate their economic relationship. One result was that Cuba joined the Eastern European Economic Community (COMECON) in 1972. This deepening integration somewhat decreased Cuba's attractiveness as a developmental model to its Caribbean neighbors, who tend to see Cuba as little closer to the goal of self-reliance than other countries in the region. On the other hand, aspects of the Soviet relationship with Cuba contrast favorably with the terms on which other industrialized nations deal with their clients. In particular, the stable, long-term agreement under which the Soviet Union buys Cuban sugar is envied by other sugar-producing nations, who are at the mercy of the unstable and declining world sugar market. The Soviet Union also sells Cuba oil at a subsidized price. Most of these exchanges are in the form of barter, making the $4 billion per year estimate of Soviet aid a somewhat arbitrary figure.[15]

Although Cuba is still dependent on sugar—and remains the world's largest sugar exporter—the industry has been significantly modernized under the revolution. Sixty percent of the cane is cut by machine, and the machines are made in Cuba. In contrast to colonial days, when those laboring in the cane fields were the most exploited members of society, Cuban sugar workers receive preferential wages, special benefits and many other incentives.[16]

Reforms in the 1970s

The failure of the ten-million-ton harvest spurred a far-reaching set of policy changes aimed at increasing productivity and popular participation. Early revolutionary initiatives such as the land reform had been highly effective in combatting inequality and rural poverty, but less effective in expanding total production. Cuban leaders also realized that bureaucratic over-centralization and the policy of paying all workers equally—regardless of their output—had somewhat stifled popular enthusiasm. Absenteeism in the work force had become a nagging problem.[17]

Accordingly, the new decade of the 1970s was launched with a call to "institutionalize" the revolution. Mechanisms were put in place to subject major legislation to public discussion before promulgation. For example, the Cuban Workers Confederation helped draft laws which revitalized the trade unions and introduced material incentives into the workplace.[18]

In 1976, under a new constitution, the country instituted a system known as *Poder Popular* (People's Power). This allows Cubans to elect delegates to a National Assembly with legislative powers. Poder Popular marked an important departure in the long-term democratization of the system, but up to now it has been a mixed success. Decision-making on local affairs is relatively decentralized, carried out by local "Committees for the Defense of the Revolution" and by municipal and provincial sub-assemblies of Poder Popular. At the top, the National Assembly makes some decisions on the

running of the country; but the major direction of national and international policy still rests in the hands of the party's Central Committee. In an analysis entitled *Cuba en los 80* (Cuba in the '80s), a sympathetic Cuban-American observer comments:

> Poder Popular supposedly constitutes the highest level of state power in Cuba. Nonetheless, just as the ministries have shown a certain resistance to giving autonomy . . . to state [productive] enterprises, so too has the state apparatus been somewhat reluctant to submit to the supervision of Poder Popular.[19]

The Cuban government also experimented with new economic structures. Profitability criteria were introduced for state-run farms to make them more efficient. In 1975, an official decision was made to encourage agricultural cooperatives, previously frowned upon as a form of private ownership. Small farmers—who comprise virtually the only private sector left in Cuba—are offered incentives such as new housing to join their holdings into producer coops, although nobody is forced to join. The cooperatives soon proved to be better organized, more efficient and more economical than the large state farms.[20]

Other economic initiatives were not so successful, notably the introduction of private farmers' markets where peasants could sell their surplus produce at unregulated prices. This "dash of capitalism" turned out to be fraught with problems

The National Assembly.

Courtesy of *Areito*

(such as price gouging and abuse of the system by shrewd middlemen).[21]

Cuba's ties to the socialist bloc have not entirely insulated it from the negative world economic trends which have spread disaster through the Caribbean. The drop in world sugar prices in 1982 sharply reduced Cuba's income from the one-third of its crop which is sold for hard currency on the open market. Although only about 15-20% of Cuba's trade is with non-socialist states (primarily Canada, Japan, France and Spain), inflationary prices for imports from the capitalist world and high interest rates on loans have cost Cuba money. As a result, Cuba had to reschedule part of its hard-currency debt to Western governments and banks—a process the Reagan administration has tried hard to obstruct.

Other problems have been internal, including agricultural failures due to weather, and—according to Cuban officials—inadequate economic planning.[22] Recently Cuba has had difficulty fulfilling its export quotas to the Soviet Union because of the need to divert goods to the hard-currency market. Cuban planners assert that the revolution has accomplished its primary social goals and that now the need is to expand and diversify production and trade. Cuba already exports tobacco, nickel, citrus and seafood in addition to sugar. The government plans new investment in steel, nickel refining, textiles, nuclear power, and electronics, and has declared its openness to foreign investment in joint ventures.

A Revolution in Values

In the face of these difficulties, the continuing internal dynamism of the revolution has perplexed some observers. It stems in part from that legendary empathy between the Cuban people and Fidel Castro, which Che Guevara early in the revolution characterized as "almost intuitive."[23] The average Cuban still regards Fidel as a hero, twenty-five years after the victory in the hills of the Sierra Maestra. This feeling prevails even among the generation of young Cubans who have no first-hand memory of the Batista regime or the struggle against it. The reason is that the revolutionary process is bigger than Castro himself and is rooted in a set of values and goals widely shared by the Cuban people.

Cuba is unquestionably one of the most egalitarian societies in the world. There are income differences, but they do not approach the gap between the rich and poor in most countries. In particular, the revolution has equalized social services and amenities available to city and rural dwellers, erasing the traditional backwardness of the countryside. Racism also has been virtually eliminated: black, white and mulatto Cubans live and work side by side with little apparent concern about color distinctions.

The campaign to create a racially harmonious society has been more successful than the effort to eradicate *machismo,* the traditional Latin American ethic of male dominance. Women's rights are protected by a progressive Family Code, but such laws can only go so far in regulating what happens in the home. Women are well represented at lower and middle levels of government and trade unions, but top Cuban officials are still nearly all male. Linked to machismo is a bias against homosexuals, who have suffered discrimination and persecution—one of Cuba's most controversial policies.

As a result of their own experience, Cubans wholeheartedly support the principle of the Third World's right to revolution and of their own obligation to assist in whatever way possible. While this principle has remained constant, enshrined in Cuban ideology as "internationalism," Havana's actual policies are more pragmatic and have varied according to changing circumstances over the years.

The early 1960s saw unrealistic attempts to promote the Cuban style of insurgency to other Latin American revolutionaries. Led by the Argentinian doctor Che Guevara, efforts to employ the Cuban *foco* model of armed struggle by small bands based in the mountains proved ill-suited to conditions in other countries. The CIA soon developed techniques aimed at destroying this type of insurgency, leading to the murder of Che in Bolivia in 1968 and to the ultimate abandonment of the foco model.

By the 1970s, the Cuban government had adopted a more cautious stance toward revolution in Latin America. Since 1975, Cuba's major military involvement has been in Africa. In that year, Cuba sent troops in response to Angolan requests for help in repelling U.S./South African intervention which was aimed at destroying the new government of the MPLA (Popular Movement for the Liberation of Mozambique). Cuba subsequently sent troops to support the Haile Mengistu regime in Ethiopia as well.

In recent years, Cuba has been extremely cautious about aiding revolutionary movements in active struggle. The Cuban leadership increasingly has stressed its position that revolution can only result from a country's internal process and cannot be "exported."[24] Allegations of Cuban military aid to leftist parties in the Caribbean are false. However, Havana does give ideological and organizational support to the Caribbean left, hosting conventions of progressive party leaders and advising on the creation of broad opposition coalitions.

Cuba gives civilian aid generously to both socialist and non-socialist Third World countries. This aid is given most enthusiastically to revolutionary states: when the call went out for 2,000 volunteers to aid in the Nicaraguan literacy campaign, more than 57,000 young Cubans applied.[25] Cuba also sent engineers and 600 construction workers to help Grenada build its new international airport. But aid is not limited to progressive governments. For example, Cuba offers scholarships each year to various Caribbean governments to award to their nationals for training in fields such as medicine, agronomy and engineering.

Cuba does not advocate that every new progressive government attempt to replicate its experience. In their relations with the Manley government in Jamaica and with the Nicaraguan Sandinistas, the Cuban leadership advised against the adoption of certain policies which Cuba itself had followed a decade earlier. One reason is the recognition that internal conditions in other countries now differ significantly from those of Cuba in the sixties, and that there is no reason to repeat mistakes the Cubans now acknowledge. Equally im-

In Revolution Square, Havana. Portraits show Che Guevara, left, and Camilo Cienfuegos, another hero of Batista's overthrow.

portant is a realistic view of international power relationships. The Soviet Union, Havana is well aware, is unwilling to take on the economic burden of supporting new revolutionary states, and is far from eager to challenge the U.S. militarily in the western hemisphere. This makes U.S. hostility to revolution a reality from which there is little escape, at least for countries in Central America and the Caribbean. Havana therefore counseled the Nicaraguans to avoid antagonizing Washington and to try to keep the U.S. as a trading partner.[26]

The level at which Cuba remains a compelling model is that of values, especially those of social justice and Latin American self-determination. Recently President Castro issued calls for Latin America's staggering debt to be cancelled as "unpayable," thus giving bold expression to sentiments felt throughout the debt-crippled continent. The revolution commands respect even from adversaries on the basis of its sheer survival power: Cuba has ridden out not only its internal development problems, but also a quarter-century of active hostility from its powerful northern neighbor. The ability of the Cuban revolution to survive for a generation without betraying its internal principles and direction has given hope to many other struggling peoples that radical change is possible and can endure.

If Cuba had become such an overwhelming priority in our emotions, it was because we were bearing witness to a miracle that had happened here. This miracle, described simply, was the conquest of fear. The revolution had exorcised the demon of fear.

It is my view that a major part of the respect and moral authority which Cuba would later exercise throughout this hemisphere has to do with this unique triumph. It is also the major source of that extraordinary rage and fury which United States governments experience at the mere sound of the word, "Cuba."

Today, the same furies exist; but the same truth prevails. To say Cuba is to say: "I am not afraid."

— George Lamming[28]

THE REVOLUTION AND THE CHURCH

The abrupt shift of the Cuban Church to an attitude of open antagonism toward the revolution reflected the Cuban religious community's middle-class, pro-Western and individualistic philosophy. The churches had welcomed the overthrow of Batista, but were totally unprepared for life in a revolutionary society. Their shift to a counterrevolutionary position occurred between September 8, 1960, when the government forbade a Catholic pilgrimage for Our Lady of Charity, and May 1, 1961, when Castro announced that Cuba was a socialist republic. On that same date, the government nationalized all private schools. These actions triggered a massive flight of Cuban religious leaders to "freedom in exile," especially by Catholics and Methodists, 80% of whose clergy and religious left Cuba.

The next five years were hard for those who chose to remain. A number of clergy were arrested and held in indoctrination camps for three years, although none were physically tortured. Most difficult for the Church was the loss of all its privileges as an elite social institution. While this offended the middle class, many other Cubans were not particularly disturbed since the Catholic and Protestant churches traditionally had weak links to the Cuban popular classes, especially in the countryside.

Little was heard from the churches during this quiet period from 1962-67, but internally, theological reflection was taking place which allowed some Protestant clergy to begin coming to terms with the changed social reality in Cuba. In the fall of 1968, North American clergy made their first contacts with the Cuban churches, while clergy there began to communicate their experiences to the U.S. For the Catholic Church, the turning point was the Medellin Conference of Catholic bishops in December 1968, which gave hierarchical approval to the involvement of Catholics in social change. On April 10, 1969, the Catholic bishops of Cuba issued a pastoral letter in which they called for the lifting of the U.S. trade embargo and for cooperation in the project of "national development."

Thus the formerly inward-looking, parochially oriented Church gradually became a "servant" church—beginning to serve the people and the community—even though many of its members remained unenthusiastic about the revolution. Some Cuban church leaders affirm the goals and accomplishments of the revolution but reject Marxist ideology; while others accept Marxism as the source of a social transformation in keeping with Christian values. The Rev. Dr. Adolfo Ham, chairman of the Cuban Ecumenical Council, told representatives of the Caribbean Conference of Churches in September 1983:

We are not a martyred or suppressed church but we have lost all the privileges and comforts of churches who were part of and responsible for the establishment.

Naturally, some people think it is impossible for the Churches to fulfill their mission unless they have a privileged place in society. But we have learned the hard lesson that only when the Church is a servant—when the Church can be fully identified with the needs and spirit of the people, is when she can be the Church.

We do not think either that the Cuban experience has to be repeated, but one thing we can demonstrate to you: it is possible for a small and underdeveloped country to challenge a great empire and begin a revolution which can guarantee full human dignity and development for all the people.[27]

Grenada

"No examination of the Grenada revolution of 1979-83 should end on a pessimistic note. For there is much to be proud about," writes Caribbean historian Gordon K. Lewis.[1] Grenada's revolution ended in October 1983, and any analysis of its four-and-a-half year lifespan must consider the now-apparent contradictions which led to discord within the ruling party and opened the door to U.S. invasion [see Part V, Chapter 6]. But to focus exclusively on these negatives would be a profound mistake. For the Grenada revolution was, on balance—and at the *popular* level—overwhelmingly positive; and the possibilities it raised have changed the face of the Caribbean forever.

The roster of achievements of the People's Revolutionary Government (PRG) is familiar to many in the Caribbean and throughout the world. Rational and creative economic policies, an egalitarian restructuring of education and health care, and a broad-based spirit of voluntarism were the hallmarks of revolutionary Grenada. To understand what these advances meant for the people of the Caribbean, it is necessary to view them in the context of the entrenched neocolonial social and economic structures in the region. Grenada went farther than any other English-speaking Caribbean society toward identifying these obstacles to development and creating new structures to replace them.

The Economic Program

Judged in conventional economic terms, the revolution was shaping up as a success. The government pursued a mixed economy embracing the traditional private sector plus an expanded public sector and a newly-created cooperative sector. This expanded activity caused unemployment to fall sharply from 49% before the revolution to 14% in 1983, according to Grenadian government figures.

The International Monetary Fund put Grenada's growth over this period at an average of 3% per year.[2] This compared favorably with growth rates in the rest of the Caribbean and Latin America, where many countries were experiencing negative or zero growth. Moreover, it came despite formidable obstacles: low prices for Grenada's export crops, weather disasters, and hostile U.S. propaganda which scared tourists away from the island. The world price of cocoa, Grenada's leading export, fell from $1.90 per pound in 1979 to $1.05 in 1983. The price of nutmeg dropped by almost 50%, while banana exports were severely affected by bad weather and the declining value of the British pound.[3]

In the face of these problems, the PRG's excellent financial management and lack of corruption helped the economy stay afloat. Its policies were praised by the World Bank in a 1982 memorandum which stated:

The government which came to power in 1979 inherited a deteriorating economy, and is now addressing the task of rehabilitation and of laying better foundations for growth

within the framework of a mixed economy . . . Government objectives are centered on the critical development issues and touch on the country's most promising development areas.[4]

Despite the invective heaped upon Grenada for allegedly going "communist," the PRG's economic strategy was distinguished by its gradualism. The New Jewel Movement considered itself a "socialist-oriented" party, meaning that while socialism was the ultimate goal, the government's actual policies were pragmatic and did not envision any sudden transformation. The private sector continued to dominate, accounting for 60% of production.[5] Grenada's private sector, however, consists mainly of peasant farmers and fishermen, who clearly benefitted from the revolution's programs. Whereas in the past they could rarely get credit for lack of collateral, the PRG established two state-owned banks which made loans to small producers, enabling them to expand or diversify their production. A Marketing and National Import Board purchased fruits and vegetables from the farmers and sold them throughout the island. This marketing assistance encouraged the farmers to diversify and helped lessen the country's dependence on imported food. The IMF reported in 1983 that an improvement in domestic food supplies had helped to keep inflation down in Grenada.[6]

Student at the Mirabeau agricultural school.

Bruce Paton

Members of the cabinet (standing, l-r): Prime Minister Maurice Bishop, Deputy Prime Minister Bernard Coard, Minister of Agriculture George Louison, and Minister of Housing Norris Bain.

When the PRG took over in 1979, it nationalized only a few hotels and nightclubs which had been Eric Gairy's personal property and which had become notorious as disguised brothels. Otherwise, the structure of ownership in the country remained much as it had been. In 1981, the government finally implemented a mild land reform law calling for the compulsory lease of unused tracts over 100 acres. Considering the wastage associated with idle land on a small island, this was not an unexpected act and was not openly resisted by landowners.

The major economic change under the PRG was the creation of a state sector which came to encompass about 30% of the economy. Consisting of some 23 enterprises, this sector operated mainly in areas of natural monopolies (i.e. the utilities) and where the private sector had failed to invest. Examples of the latter included an Agro-Industry Plant which made juices and jellies from locally grown fruits, and a Fish Processing Plant which produced dried salted fish (a West Indian dietary staple) from locally caught fish. Other state-owned enterprises included a sugar factory, several hotels, and a number of state farms. Most of these enterprises lost money in the first years of the revolution. They were important, however, because they opened up new areas of production using local resources—a departure from the neocolonial dependency economics of the Caribbean.

The reason for having the state take these initiatives rather than the private sector is that the indigenous business class, in Grenada as in the rest of the Caribbean, generally has been reluctant to invest in production. They are merchants, who buy goods from abroad and resell them at a profit. The PRG placed some curbs on this sector by increasing taxes on imports and by giving the state a monopoly to import certain basic goods such as rice, sugar, flour and fertilizer. Although these measures angered some businessmen, the commercial sector benefitted from the overall growth of the economy, and most realized healthy profits during the revolution.[7]

Despite its innovations, Grenada remained tied to its traditional exports of cocoa, nutmeg, and bananas. This meant that the economy was still vulnerable to declining commodity prices and weather disasters, both of which hit Grenada hard from 1979 to 1983. The PRG's strategy for coping with these problems was also a traditional one: to expand tourism as a source of foreign exchange. To do so required, first and foremost, a modern airport, the *sine qua non* of Caribbean tourism. Every serious analyst of the Grenadian economy, from the IMF to the Caribbean Development Bank to the Grenadian Chamber of Commerce, agreed that the island's rickety old airfield, Pearls, held back the growth of tourism. Only the Reagan administration continued to insist that the new airport was "too big" for Grenada's economic needs and must therefore be intended as a military base.

For Grenadians, the construction of the new airport became a symbol of Grenada's entry into the modern world and its determined bid for self-reliance. Ironically—in light of Washington's attempts to block its construction—the airport was a pet project of the Grenadian business class, which appreciated its potential value to the private sector of merchants and hoteliers. Grenadians of all classes bought "airport bonds" and held neighborhood fundraising events to raise money for the airport's completion.

The People: "Heart and Center"

Maurice Bishop, prime minister of Grenada during the revolution, described the Grenadian people as being "always at the center and heart and focus of all our activities."[8] The revolution's populism was at once its greatest strength and its

Primary school children: Education was upgraded under the PRG.

Bruce Paton

area of deepest contradictions.

There is no question but that the revolution improved life for the majority of the island's people. Among its most successful programs were free education through the high school level; free high-quality medical and dental care; hot school lunches and distribution of milk to mothers and infants; a revolving loan fund to help poor families repair their houses; and a voluntary literacy program which enabled illiterate adults to learn to read and write.

The Bishop government's programs, however, went beyond simple welfarism to attack the elitist social structures in Caribbean society. To take one example, education—fundamental to a people's ability to participate in government—has been treated with pointed neglect by many post-colonial Caribbean leaders. This was certainly true of Gairy, whose educational philosophy could be summed up in a few words: Keep them ignorant to rule them better.

There were two types of education in pre-1979 Grenada. The children of the peasantry received a few years of schooling in deteriorating rural schools, often without bathrooms, desks or even chairs. Teachers were untrained and many had not gone beyond eighth or ninth grade themselves. Since high school enrollment was extremely limited, and most poor families could not afford to pay tuition and purchase books and uniforms, most secondary school pupils came from the small middle and upper classes. Higher education was viewed as leading to one goal: emigration from the Caribbean to "become somebody" in England, Canada or the U.S.

This colonial concept of education was systematically refuted by the Bishop government. Soon after the revolution, the PRG created a Centre for Popular Education which undertook a broad literacy and adult education program. Under the slogan "Each One Teach One," volunteer tutors helped hundreds of mostly rural Grenadians to achieve a functional literacy for the first time in their lives. While up to 1979 the state had built only one high school in Grenada, the PRG opened three in the space of four years and abolished high school entrance fees. Government assistance subsidized school books and uniforms for poor families, further breaking down class barriers to education. A new experiment, the National In-Service Teacher Education Program, upgraded the skills of Grenadian teachers and was viewed as a potential model by other Caribbean educators.

In addition to these major programs, Grenada was abuzz with small discussion groups, skills training seminars, and cultural workshops aimed at developing the talents of the Grenadian people. One observer wrote, "The impression given was that the whole island was one large school constantly engaged in transforming the colonial mentality and the spirit of dependency."[9]

In health, a similarly anti-elitist process took place, drawing on the assistance and experience of the Cubans. Before the revolution, good medical treatment had been a privilege reserved for people who lived in St. George's and could afford to pay private doctors. The poor went to a dirty, understaffed public hospital with inadequate equipment and medicines and sometimes even no bed sheets; while people in the rural areas frequently had no access to health care at all. With help from Cuban health planners, the PRG restructured Grenada's health care system from top to bottom. While preserving the option of private care, the government expanded free health care to the entire country through a network of rural clinics. Cuban volunteer doctors nearly doubled the number of physicians in the country, and seven dental clinics were established (compared to one before 1979). The PRG also sought help from abroad, primarily Europe, to refurbish the main hospital and add specialized new facilities such as an Opthalmic Clinic.

"Perhaps the most celebrated aspect of the Grenadian revolution was the impulse which it gave to the self-organization of the society at large," writes the Latin American Bureau in their post-invasion analysis.[10] After languishing for two decades under Gairy's autocratic rule, Grenadians eagerly embraced the chance to organize at the grassroots level after 1979.

In the first several years, efforts toward creating a "popular democracy" of grassroots decision-making appeared to be making steady progress. Trade union membership reached 80% under a mandatory union recognition law, one of a very few such progressive laws in the Caribbean. Membership swelled in the National Women's Organization (NWO) and the National Youth Organization (NYO), which mobilized their members to take part in the revolution's programs. The unions, the NWO and the NYO elected delegates from among their members to attend national conferences which then made recommendations to the government on policy issues.

In 1982, the decentralization of power went a step further with the formation of zonal councils and parish councils. This fulfilled a part of the New Jewel Movement's original 1973 manifesto, which had called for the creation of "popular assemblies" placing decision-making power directly in people's hands. To a certain extent this goal was realized. At the monthly meetings of the grassroots councils, Grenadians debated local, national, and international issues in a format somewhat like that of a New England town meeting. Most major legislation underwent critique by these councils and by the NWO, the NYO and the trade unions. In this experimental process, the mass organizations would discuss proposed legislation and send back recommendations to the government, which would take their suggestions into account before passing the law in final form. The national budgets for both 1982 and 1983 went through this procedure.

This was an entirely new process in Grenada and in fact one without precedent in the Caribbean. Its relative success was due partly to the fact that Grenada is a micro-society of 110,000 people, making it possible to experiment with new structures which would be impractical in a larger country.

In retrospect, however, it is apparent that the system of popular democracy was in some ways a deception. Not all of the leadership was equally committed to making the system work, and the grassroots organs were only marginally plugged in to the real power structure. While Grenadians turned out in large numbers for the meetings of the parish and zonal councils, these meetings were often top-heavy with speeches by government officials. Debate was lively on a variety of topics, yet actual policy decisions were still being made by the NJM's Central Committee, whose membership was not even known to a majority of Grenadians.

Maurice Bishop is considered by many to have been strongly committed to making popular democracy work. Don Rojas, Bishop's press secretary, reflects:

It was certainly Maurice's hope that this system of councils at the local level, village level, and parish level would become institutionalized as organs of people's power. It was our hope to have it become part of the ultimate legal framework of the revolution as part of the new people's constitution we were preparing.

Organizationally there were still weaknesses in the organs of popular democracy such as the zonal and parish councils. Weaknesses not so much in terms of the willingness of people to participate in these organs, but more in the way they were structured. For example, in some cases there would be meetings without agendas. In some cases there would be meetings that were not chaired.

The people's reaction was, "Why should we come to this meeting, sit here, and do a lot of rambling? We can identify the problems in our community. Let's look for the solution in a structured way."

Looking at it in hindsight, the process of decentralizing power inside the community was moving faster than the process of decentralizing power inside the party itself.[11]

Yet the final lesson of Grenada is still a positive one. The Grenadian people showed themselves ready to take on the challenge of creating new democratic forms and economic structures to replace dictatorship and stagnation. By the time U.S. pressures and internal conflicts caused the PRG to "implode," enough positive changes had taken place to confirm the potential of Grenada's alternative development model. The impact of this achievement should outlast the tragedy of the revolution's finale and point the way to other Caribbean peoples seeking change.

One Caribbean churchman had this to say:

One can understand why the Grenada revolution upset the dominant classes, the privileged minorities and the leaders of the establishment in the region. Here, for the first time, the poor and powerless masses were being given pride of place. Their needs, problems and aspirations became the raison d'etre, the central focus of policymaking, economic activity and social legislation.

Now, Caribbean governments and centers of power will find it harder to say to the masses that their hopes are but idle dreams . . . [12]

HIGHLIGHTS OF U.S. DESTABILIZATION CAMPAIGN AGAINST GRENADA

1979   After Bishop government takes power, U.S. turns down Grenada's request for development aid and assistance to build new airport; Washington warns Grenada not to have relations with Cuba.

U.S. State Department advises travel agents that Grenada is "unsafe" to visit; tourism falls sharply.

1980   U.S. attempts to block hurricane relief aid to Grenada from the Organization of American States.

U.S. offers hurricane relief aid to regional banana marketing agency, WINBAN, on condition that Grenada be excluded from assistance.

1981   U.S. attempts to block International Monetary Fund loan to Grenada.

U.S. offers $4 million aid package to the Caribbean Development Bank on condition that none of the aid go to Grenada. The CDB rejects the aid.

U.S. pressures Western European nations not to give aid toward building Grenada's new airport.

Senate Intelligence Committee of U.S. Congress rejects CIA plan for a covert destabilization operation against the Bishop government.

Caribbean newspapers, influenced by Washington, condemn the PRG in simultaneous editorials published on Sept. 27.

U.S. stages "Ocean Venture '81," massive naval exercises which include a mock invasion of Grenada.

1982   U.S. stages "Ocean Venture '82," again including mock invasion of Grenada, and adding a simulated "rescue" of Americans as part of invasion scenario.

U.S. begins sale of military equipment to Grenada's Eastern Caribbean neighbors and increases spending on military training, especially for Barbados.

1983   President Reagan denounces Grenada as a threat to the United States in March "Star Wars" speech, describing new airport as a Soviet military base.

Reagan refuses to meet with Prime Minister Bishop during his visit to Washington.

U.S. Army Rangers practice airport seizure at a remote site in Washington state from September 23 to October 2.

U.S. invades Grenada on October 25, 1983.

NOTES TO PART FOUR

Cuba

1. Warren Hinkle and William Turner, *The Fish Is Red: The Story of the Secret War Against Castro* (New York: Harper & Row, 1981), p. 13.
2. *Ibid.*, pp. 282-290.
3. Eric Williams, *From Columbus to Castro: The History of the Caribbean 1492-1969* (New York: Harper & Row, 1970), pp. 480-483.
4. Lester D. Langley, *The United States and the Caribbean 1900-1970* (Athens: University of Georgia Press, 1980), p. 225.
5. *Business Week,* Sept. 20, 1983, p. 61.
6. U.S. Department of State, "The United States and Cuba," address by Kenneth N. Skoug Jr., Director of Office of Cuban Affairs, Dec. 17, 1984.
7. Williams, p. 487.
8. Jean-Pierre Beauvais, "Achievements and Contradictions of the Cuban Workers' State," in Fitzroy Ambursley and Robin Cohen, eds., *Crisis in the Caribbean* (New York: Monthly Review Press, 1983), pp. 52-53.
9. Medea, Benjamin, Joseph Collins and Michael Scott, *No Free Lunch: Food and Revolution in Cuba Today* (San Francisco: Institute for Food and Development Policy, 1984), ch. 3.
10. *Ibid.,* p. 101.
11. Ibid., p. 85.
12. UNICEF, *The State of the World's Children 1984,* p. 115; and Cuban government statements, *Washington Post,* Feb. 3, 1985, p. 1.
13. UNICEF, p. 119.
14. Government of Cuba, "Health for All: 25 Years of Cuban Experience" (Havana: July 1983), p. 24.
15. Kirby Jones, remarks delivered at Howard University, Washington, DC, Oct. 25, 1984.
16. Benjamin et al., p. 173.
17. Frank T. Fitzgerald, "The Direction of Cuban Socialism: A Critique of the Sovietization Thesis," in Susan Craig, ed., *Contemporary Caribbean* (Trinidad: S. Craig, 1982), Vol. II, p. 264.
18. Marifeli Perez-Stable, "Cuba en los 80," *Areito,* Vol. IX, No. 36 (1984), p. 92.
19. *Ibid.,* p. 94.
20. Benjamin et al., pp. 177-178.
21. *Ibid.,* Ch. 5.
22. *Washington Post,* Feb. 4, 1985, p. 1.
23. Che Guevara, *Socialism and Man in Cuba,* cited in Lee Lockwood, *Castro's Cuba, Cuba's Fidel* (New York: Vintage, 1969), p. 149.
24. *Washington Post,* Feb. 3, 1985, p. 1.
25. Gil Green, *Cuba at 25* (New York: International Publishers, 1983), p. 100.
26. *Washington Post,* Nov. 9, 1980, p. 1.
27. *Caribbean Contact,* Nov. 1983.
28. *Caribbean Contact,* June 1984.

Grenada

1. *Caribbean Contact,* July 1984.
2. International Monetary Fund, staff report, EBS/83/164, Aug. 9, 1984, p. 3.
3. [Interim] Government of Grenada and Caribbean Development Bank, "Economic Memorandum on Grenada," Vol. I (1984), pp. 10-14.
4. World Bank, "Economic Memorandum on Grenada," Report No. 3825-GRD, Aug. 4, 1982, p. i.
5. [Interim] Government of Grenada and Caribbean Development Bank, "Economic Memorandum on Grenada, Vol. I," p. 9.
6. International Monetary Fund, p. 3.
7. Latin America Bureau, *Grenada: Whose Freedom?* (London: Latin America Bureau 1984), p. 37.
8. Maurice Bishop, speech at Hunter College, New York City, June 5, 1983.
9. Dr. Roy Neehall, "Significance of the Grenada Revolution for the People of the Caribbean," speech at Howard University, Washington, DC, October 25, 1984.
10. Latin America Bureau, p. 37.
11. Interview with Don Rojas, *Intercontinental Press,* December 26, 1983.
12. Dr. Roy Neehall, "Significance of the Grenada Revolution for the People of the Caribbean."

PART FIVE

U.S. in the Caribbean
Imperial Strategies of Control

Vicky Surles

A Pattern of Military Interventions

In the 19th and early 20th century, the concept of the western hemisphere as a U.S. empire rested on the presumption of the Caribbean as an "American lake." This metaphor has since been replaced with terms like "front yard," "back yard," or, in the words of the U.S. State Department, "our third border."[1] While the terminology has changed, the concept of the Caribbean as a U.S. appendage rather than a group of sovereign nations has scarcely altered.

Methods of maintaining imperial control over the region, however, have shifted with time. The era of gunboat diplomacy from 1898 through the 1930s established a pattern of U.S. military invasion and occupation, which President Theodore Roosevelt called "the Big Stick."

After World War Two, the focus shifted to non-military methods of control. The Central Intelligence Agency was created in 1947, and under the new banner of Cold War anticommunism, worked through the Caribbean labor movement and the media to subvert elected governments. These methods were first used to oust the government of Jacobo Arbenz in Guatemala when his program of land reform threatened the interests of the United Fruit Company. A decade later, the CIA used the newly-created American Institute for Free Labor Development (AIFLD) to depose the progressive government of Cheddi Jagan in Guyana.

Despite these new strategies, the option of invasion was never discarded. It was held in reserve and resurrected in 1961 against Cuba at the infamous Bay of Pigs. The invasion stained the image of the United States throughout Latin America and the world, casting the U.S. as a bullying brutalizer of small nations while earning the Cubans respect for their spirited national defense. Carried out by Cuban exile mercenaries organized by the CIA, the botched invasion also pointed up the difficulty of overthrowing a popular government without the use of U.S. troops.

In 1961, the Dominican dictator Trujillo was assassinated, an act sanctioned by the CIA which saw the continuation of dictatorship as paving the way for another Cuban-style revolution. But with Trujillo out of the way, things did not go as Washington had expected. Dominicans elected Juan Bosch, who implemented land reform and wage reform under a new constitution. In September 1963, Bosch was ousted by a right-wing military coup which abolished the constitution and discarded most of his reforms.

Led by disgruntled junior officers and members of Bosch's party, rebellion broke out on the streets of Santo Domingo on April 24, 1965, demanding a return to constitutionalist rule. The Johnson administration first asserted that American lives were in danger and called the intervention a rescue mission. Almost immediately, however, the president shifted to the rationale of a communist threat, calling for "armed intervention which goes beyond mere protection of Americans" to "prevent another Cuba."[2]

The Dominican invasion was the prototype for the so-called multinational intervention, in which the U.S. is joined

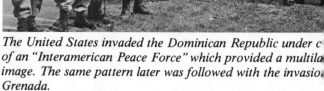

The United States invaded the Dominican Republic under c of an "Interamerican Peace Force" which provided a multila image. The same pattern later was followed with the invasio Grenada.

by token forces from conservative regional allies. Troops fo an "Interamerican Peace Force" were supplied by the right wing governments of Honduras and Brazil, the latter installe in a U.S.-sponsored coup just a year earlier. The 22,000 U.S Marines were well into their occupation of Santo Doming before the supporting Latin troops were brought in. Neverthe less, Washington used their presence to claim that its invasio was actually a multilateral action under the auspices of th Organization of American States.

The period from 1965 through the end of the 1970s was a hiatus in terms of U.S. military intervention in the Caribbean The U.S. was bogged down in Vietnam through 1975

Dominican troops carry out repression in Santo Domingo following U.S. invasion in 1965.

afterwards, the "Vietnam syndrome" dampened enthusiasm for military adventurism for several years. During this time, however, U.S. meddling in the hemisphere was not abandoned. Economic warfare emerged as a weapon and was used to fatally weaken the governments of Salvador Allende in Chile and Michael Manley in Jamaica. In this context, the International Monetary Fund played a central role in reversing progressive change by imposing economic policies on countries to which it made loans.

The last year of the Carter administration saw a growing militarization of U.S. strategy in the Caribbean and elsewhere. The groundwork for the Reagan administration's strategy was laid in the summer and fall of 1979, when Carter began a military build-up in the Caribbean and Central America in response to revolutions in Nicaragua and Grenada. This marked the beginning of a swing back to force as a method of preventing revolution in the region, a process which came full circle with the invasion of Grenada.

The Grenada episode found its main precedent and model in the invasion of the Dominican Republic 18 years earlier. As in 1965, Washington first called the invasion a "rescue mission"

to protect American lives, then quickly shifted to an anti-communist rationale. Also following the Dominican model was the use of allied troops in the region to lend the image of a multinational force. Leaflets dropped on Grenada by U.S. helicopters read: "PEOPLE OF GRENADA: YOUR CARIBBEAN NEIGHBORS WITH U.S. SUPPORT HAVE COME TO GRENADA TO RESTORE DEMOCRACY AND INSURE YOUR SAFETY."

The following sections examine some of the methods which the United States has used to exert influence and control in the Caribbean. Through the media, through the labor movement, through loans and economic aid, U.S influence has been pervasive. Since the Grenada revolution in 1979, Washington has used all of these methods to polarize the region ideologically and court allies for the eventual strike against Grenada. This action, when it came, took many North Americans by surprise. In the Caribbean, however, it was expected, confirming that the U.S. has not abandoned its long-standing practice of military intervention in its "backyard." ∎

IMF and the Banks

"When the IMF says they deal only in money and not in politics," remarked Rep. Tom Harkin to Congress on February 22, 1982, "I would suggest that there is nothing in this world more political than money, how it is loaned, and under what conditions it is loaned." In the Caribbean, the multilateral lending agencies and private transnational banks have played an important role in shaping and controlling economic development. This influence takes place in three ways:
- Who gets loans and when: the "political" use of multilateral lending to support or penalize particular governments;
- "Conditionality" on IMF loans which negatively affects the economy of the recipient country;
- Private bank lending, which provides support for international capitalism rather than self-reliant development.

Politicized Lending

Contrary to the image of the multilaterals as not dominated by any one country, the United States actually wields considerable (though not exclusive) influence in their lending decisions. In the Inter-American Development Bank (IDB), the U.S. controls 35% of the voting power and virtually holds free rein.[1] In the International Monetary Fund and the World Bank, where the U.S. holds 19% and 22% of the votes respectively, the United States' influence goes beyond its actual voting share.[2] While it is not always easy for the U.S. to sway other members to its wishes, it frequently manages to do so, often disguising political motives with artfully constructed economic and technical arguments.[3]

Within the U.S. government, power over participation in the multilaterals is closely held by the Executive Branch acting through the Treasury. Thus the banks often end up supporting White House policy objectives. A classic example was the cut-off of World Bank and IDB loans and the denial of an IMF stand-by agreement to the socialist Allende government in Chile, following President Nixon's order to "make the economy scream." Shortly after a U.S.-backed coup replaced Allende with the Pinochet dictatorship, the IMF awarded a $373 million loan to the new government. More recently, the Reagan administration has waged a battle within the IMF, the IDB, and the World Bank to channel huge loans to the governments of El Salvador and Guatemala while freezing aid to Nicaragua. This campaign has been largely successful.[4]

After Edward Seaga defeated the pro-socialist Manley government in the Jamaican election of 1980, President Reagan vowed to make Jamaica a free enterprise model for the Caribbean. Thus no one was surprised when, in addition to generous U.S. bilateral aid, World Bank and IDB loans, Jamaica received a US$650 million aid package from the IMF. Moreover, the IMF was initially lenient when the Seaga administration failed to meet agreed-upon economic targets, adding weight to regional complaints about the "pampering" of Jamaica.[5]

According to a 1983 study which the Congressional Research Service attempted to suppress, the Reagan administration had a "hit list" of five countries which it attempted to prevent from securing multilateral aid. Three of the five were Caribbean Basin countries: Cuba, Nicaragua, and Grenada.[6]

> According to an extremely reliable executive branch source, then-Secretary of State Alexander Haig emphatically stated in a meeting of high-ranking State Department officials in 1981 that "not a penny" of indirect, international assistance was to be provided to Grenada. Shortly thereafter, the Treasury provided the U.S. Executive Director to the IMF with objections to the drawing proposed for Grenada . . . objections which focused on the construction of an airport by Grenada as the primary cause of Grenada's economic difficulties.[7]

The result of this pressure was that the IMF reduced its proposal for a three-year loan to Grenada to one year, and one-third of the amount proposed.

While blocking aid to revolutionary governments, the Reagan administration has resisted Congressional attempts to require the U.S. to vote against loans to apartheid South Africa, arguing that this would "politicize" the IMF. Largely on account of U.S. pressure, the IMF approved a $1.1 billion loan to South Africa in November 1982.

IMF as Destabilizer: The Case of Jamaica

The International Monetary Fund was set up by the United States and Britain to help the war-torn countries of Europe cover their balance-of-payments shortfalls. The purpose was to ensure that countries continued to participate in and did not drop out of or hinder the international system of capitalist trade, a goal which continued when the IMF turned to making loans to the Third World. Many Third World economists feel that there is an inherent contradiction between this purpose and the attempt by former colonies to achieve economic independence, since the IMF helps perpetuate the same trade structures which underlay colonialism and underlie neocolonialism today.

The IMF makes loans on condition that the recipient follow a strict program to rectify supposedly faulty economic policies. This "structural adjustment" generally entails a rigid austerity program designed to depress consumption and increase exports and private foreign investment. Typical elements of the IMF prescription include:
- Major cuts in government spending. This means deep cutbacks in social programs, and lay-offs or firings of public sector workers.
- Wage restraint or freeze.
- Currency devaluation to make imports more expensive for the country's people and exports cheaper for foreign buyers.
- Removal of price controls and government subsidies on goods and services.
- Restrictions on government involvement in productive enterprise. Attempts to denationalize parts of the public

Now let's see you get up and move.

sector are sometimes included.

The brunt of such a program falls squarely on the backs of the working class. The cost of living rises sharply while wages fail to keep up, and unemployment rises because of public sector layoffs. Public services like hospitals, schools, public transportation and utilities must fire staff and decrease the quality of their services.

The relationship between the IMF and Jamaica in the 1970s is an example of how the economic strings on IMF lending can affect the course of social change in the Caribbean. The Manley government was driven to the IMF after rising oil prices, declining bauxite markets and a "capital strike" by investors and bankers reacting to democratic socialism brought Jamaica's foreign reserves to zero at the end of 1976.[8] Manley initially avoided turning to the Fund, stating that "We are the masters in our house and in our house there shall be no other master but ourselves."[9] But worsening conditions finally forced him to negotiate a loan agreement in July 1977.

This initial agreement came without too many harsh conditions. However, after Jamaica failed the IMF's "performance tests" in December, the agreement was suspended and a new one negotiated in May 1978, bringing with it a severe hardening of the IMF's conditions. The Fund wanted not just the usual austerity measures, but a complete overturn of the Manley government's economic program.[10] Changes imposed by the IMF included a 30% currency devaluation, J$180 million in new taxes, the lifting of price controls to guarantee a 20% profit margin to the private sector, and reduction in real wages of approximately 25%.[11]

These measures were an economic bombshell for Jamaica. Prices skyrocketed 39% in the twelve months following the loan agreement, and social services deteriorated. The falling standard of living sparked strikes and unrest among workers and the middle class, and many people left the country. The government nevertheless carried out the IMF prescription dutifully. It returned to a strategy of export-led growth, yet the economy failed to recover: expected new investments did not materialize, nor did commercial banks resume making loans to Jamaica. In December 1979, Jamaica once again failed the performance tests.

Rising hardship and the government's loss of "moral authority" before the IMF shattered the consensus behind Manley's party, the PNP.[12] By surrendering to the Fund, the Manley government reversed and discredited its own program of social reforms. Democratic socialism had been a promise to improve conditions for the poor, but the IMF austerity delivered the exact opposite. By the time Manley made the belated decision to break with the Fund, the damage had been done, contributing to the crumbling of the PNP's class alliance and its resounding defeat in the 1980 election.

The case of Jamaica is a striking one because the IMF's economic measures conflicted head-on with everything the Manley government stood for, effectively reversing an attempt at social change. But the negative impact of IMF austerity is feared even by governments with more conservative economic policies. Trade unions and popular organizations generally oppose involvement with the Fund, and governments often avoid the IMF for as long as possible because of the political consequences of imposing further "austerity" on an already hard-pressed people. But falling commodity prices and rising interest rates on indebtedness have left many Caribbean countries with little choice but to accept the Fund's conditions.

The Transnational Banks

The private transnational banks originated in the late 19th century and expanded in the 1960s and '70s when many corporations based in the industrialized nations moved abroad.[13] This new global economy required banking services, so U.S., European, Canadian, and Japanese banks acquired overseas branches and subsidiaries to service the transnational corporations. Given their roots in this relationship, it is not surprising that the transnational banks' impact in the Caribbean has been to encourage international capitalism rather than self-reliant development.

Canadian, British, and U.S. banks dominate banking throughout the Caribbean, except in Cuba. The leaders are Barclays (U.K.), Royal Bank of Canada, Chase Manhattan (U.S.), Citibank (U.S.), Canadian Imperial Bank of Commerce, and the Bank of Nova Scotia (Canada).[14] Caribbean countries have relatively few banks of their own, so transnationals provide many local banking services involving deposits, loans, and currency exchange. While they thus take in deposits from the whole population, they tend to lend the money out to a select group of often foreign borrowers. Like all banks, they favor short-term, high interest loans with little risk. This means lending to local branches of multinational corporations; to businessmen involved in the profitable import-export business; and to upper-income consumers buying luxury goods.[15]

On the other hand, the banks hardly ever lend to farmers or fishermen, whose only collateral would be their entire livelihood, i.e., land or a fishing boat. Nor do the banks make many loans for agriculture or local manufacturing, which they perceive as high-risk.

These lending patterns are not politically neutral. They are biased in favor of the old neocolonial habits of import-export dependence. The banks' reluctance to finance indigenous production (for example in agriculture and agro-industry) and their eagerness to loan to foreign enterprise perpetuates the strategy of industrialization by invitation. And by lending local capital to foreign corporations which repatriate their profits, the banks help to channel the Caribbean's wealth out of the region. ∎

Transnational banks line the "Golden Mile" in downtown San Juan, Puerto Rico.

The American Institute for Free Labor Development

In a region where politics and trade unionism have been closely linked for the last fifty years, it is natural that the labor movement would be a target of U.S. penetration. The primary instrument of this penetration is AIFLD, the American Institute for Free Labor Development. AIFLD, however, must be understood as operating within a regional system of linkages through which the United States has tried—with considerable success—to align the Caribbean labor movement to the U.S. and hinder the growth of progressive unions favoring social change.

The AFL and Business Unionism

Unlike most of the world's trade unions, the American Federation of Labor (AFL) was built on the idea that labor's advance would come through cooperation—not confrontation—with employers. This so-called "business unionism" reflected the AFL leadership's belief that expanded corporate profits would mean higher wages for workers. It led to an unofficial business/labor/government pact in which the AFL supported capitalism and the U.S. government's foreign policy in exchange for gains for organized labor.[1]

As early as 1901, the AFL began organizing in Latin America to oppose "revolutionary unionism," which sought gains for workers through class-based political action. Instead, the AFL sought to build up unions which would cooperate with American corporate expansion abroad.[2] The concept of a business/labor pact, however, was an alien one to most Latin and Caribbean workers. George C. Lodge, Assistant Secretary of Labor for International Affairs from 1958-1960, wrote that because Latin Americans are faced with . . .

> the threat of military dictatorship from the right and the continuing exploitative oligarchy of rich landowners and businessmen, the class struggle is very much alive in Latin American society . . . mutuality of interest between management and labor is not an easy concept for the Latin American laborer.[3]

Faced with the popularity of militant, anti-capitalist unions, the AFL resorted to infiltrating and disrupting the Latin labor movement in order to set up parallel or "dual" unions which could be more easily manipulated. In the late 1940s, as the U.S. entered the Cold War, the AFL's activities were stepped up and recast as part of a "world fight against Communism." Under its Latin American representative Serafino Romualdi—a former operative of the wartime Office of Special Services, the precursor of the CIA—the AFL collaborated with the CIA to set up dual unions in various Latin American countries.[4]

A key part of this postwar drive was the splitting of the world trade union movement and the creation of an anticommunist labor network under U.S. control. The World Federation of Trade Unions (WFTU) had been created in 1945, incorporating nearly every major labor union in the world. The AFL, however, refused to join the WFTU because it included Soviet unions; and in 1949, the AFL leadership successfully pressured the Congress of Industrial Organizations (CIO) to expel its progressive unions and withdraw from the WFTU. The AFL, the CIO, and the U.S. State Department then created a parallel body, the International Confederation of Free Trade Unions (ICFTU). Wooed with AFL and Marshall Plan funds, many British and European unions switched their allegiance from the WFTU to the anticommunist ICFTU.

In 1950, Romualdi's Latin American organizing finally bore fruit when the AFL set up a pan-American union confederation called ORIT. Although nominally the Latin American branch of the ICFTU, ORIT was controlled by the AFL through Romualdi. ORIT's impact soon became clear with its role in the overthrow of the elected government of Jacobo Arbenz in Guatemala in 1954. While the coup was planned, financed, and directed by the CIA and the State Department, the AFL led an anti-Arbenz propaganda campaign and supplied the overthrow force with members of a dual union created by Romualdi and ORIT.[5] After the overthrow, the U.S.-backed dictator Castillo Armas dissolved the country's major unions and jailed 5,000-8,000 people, the majority of them trade unionists.[6]

Destruction of Caribbean Labor Unity After World War Two

After the West Indian strikes of the 1930s, the emerging Caribbean labor movement initially took a militant anticolonial stance. In 1945, the union leaders met in Barbados and founded the Caribbean Labour Congress (CLC), a regional trade union grouping. The years 1945-48 were a period of great enthusiasm within the CLC. Plans were made for a West Indies Federation with a strong central government which could implement economic planning on a regional basis.

The splitting of the world trade union movement soon intruded upon this labor unity. Caribbean unions, most of which had affiliated with the WFTU when it was formed, came under pressure from the U.S. and Britain to defect to the ICFTU. The debate was framed in threatening ideological terms, portraying the WFTU as under "totalitarian domination" and the ICFTU as representing "free trade unions." British support for the ICFTU influenced the president of the CLC, Sir Grantley Adams, who also headed the Barbados Workers Union. Although Adams supported Caribbean self-government, he was a fundamentally neocolonial politician and was close to the Labour Party which had just come to power in Britain. His Jamaican counterpart was Norman Manley, who although more of a serious nationalist, also feared a leftist challenge from within the labor movement.

Adams and Manley became instruments of the ICFTU's takeover of Caribbean labor.[7] From his position as CLC president, Grantley Adams pushed for the expulsion of the remaining WFTU-affiliated unions from the CLC. Unable to get majority support for this move, "Adams came to a firm and irrevocable decision. The Caribbean Labour Congress must be dissolved."[8] He engineered the withdrawal of major unions, including his own Barbados Workers Union.

Meanwhile, Norman Manley and the right wing of his People's National Party moved to destroy the progressive elements within the Jamaican labor movement. The key figure was Richard Hart, secretary of the CLC. Hart was one of the famous "four H's"* who were the leading leftists in the PNP and also controlled the PNP-linked Trade Union Congress (TUC). In March 1952, Manley forced the four H's out of the party and unleashed an anticommunist smear campaign to destroy their popularity among Kingston's workers. Finally, a new union was created out of thin air to supplant the TUC: the National Workers Union (NWU), later headed by Norman Manley's son, Michael.[9]

This divisive process spelled the end of the Caribbean Labour Congress. The unions withdrawing from the CLC, plus Manley's NWU, joined a newly-organized Caribbean division of ORIT called CADORIT. CADORIT was headquartered in Barbados with Frank Walcott, second-ranking official of the Barbados Workers Union, as its chairman. The real power over CADORIT, however, belonged to Romualdi and the AFL.[10]

The final step in the dismantling of the radical labor bloc was the intervention to unseat Cheddi Jagan's government in Guyana. Jagan was a popular, Marxist labor leader who together with Richard Hart led the fight to keep the CLC from being taken over by the ICFTU. ORIT and Romualdi had been active in Guyana since 1951, opposing Jagan's militant union and supporting the union favored by the Bookers sugar company.[11] After Jagan was elected premier in 1953, the British stepped in and deposed his government, claiming "communist subversion."

Thus by 1954, the Caribbean labor movement had been largely incorporated into an emerging U.S.-controlled labor

*Richard Hart, Ken Hill, Frank Hill, and Arthur Henry.

network. This process was consolidated in 1960 with the creation of a new regional body to replace the CLC. Reflecting the AFL's use of confusing nomenclature for its dual unions, the new organization was called the Caribbean Congress of Labour (CCL). The CCL received 50% of its funding from ORIT/ICFTU, and was swiftly perceived in the Caribbean as "a political organization rather than a workers' organization."[12]

Impact of AIFLD

The success of the Cuban revolution in 1959 worried the U.S. that ORIT was not strong enough to stave off revolution in Latin America. To provide a more direct vehicle for anticommunist organizing, the American Institute for Free Labor Development (AIFLD) was formed in 1961 as a "tripartite venture" between government (the Kennedy administration); labor (the AFL-CIO under George Meany); and big business. In addition, there was a silent fourth partner in the venture: the CIA, which had put "several years of study and planning" into a new program of anticommunist labor organizing.[13]

The creation of AIFLD gave institutional form to the old labor/business/government alliance. Ninety-five percent of AIFLD's funding comes from the U.S. government through the Agency for International Development (USAID). Until 1981, AIFLD's Board of Directors was dominated by representatives of U.S. multinationals operating in Latin America, including W.R. Grace, the Rockefeller empire, Anaconda Copper, Pan American Airlines, and others.

The core of AIFLD's program is its training of Latin American and Caribbean labor leaders in regional extension courses and at AIFLD's center in the United States (formerly in Front Royal, Virginia and currently at the George Meany Center for Labor Studies outside Washington, DC). The sessions are billed as training in techniques of effective labor organizing and collective bargaining. From the trainees who graduate from the U.S. center, individuals are selected to pursue "internships" under which they return to their country as union organizers on an AIFLD salary.

The real purpose and impact of AIFLD's training has been revealed over the years by sources ranging from AIFLD graduates to Congressional committees and the press. J. William Fulbright of the Senate Foreign Relations Committee charged in 1969 that the AIFLD curriculum was primarily political in nature, and that "for trade unionists to be brought to this country to be given training in political and social structures at an institution conducted by AIFLD is a little unusual."[14] In fact, AIFLD's training is essentially ideological indoctrination. Courses bear names like "Democratic Theory" and "Totalitarian Ideologies," and even courses ostensibly dealing with organizing techniques emphasize anticommunist themes. As one Grenadian unionist remembered his AIFLD training in 1977:

In the opening orientation we saw clearly that these people were very, very anticommunist. The courses were oriented to getting you to hate communists, to see communists as a group of people trying to create chaos in the world.[15]

AIFLD instructor teaching course in Spanish on "Open and Closed Societies."

AIFLD's training programs became an arena for the recruitment of agents to work within the Latin and Caribbean labor movement. According to labor historian Ronald Radosh, the AIFLD "interns" . . .

> function as a corps of salaried anti-Communist activists, ready to do the bidding of the Department of State. They work primarily to impose AFL-CIO-style unionism upon Latin American workers, and to destroy existing unions outside of the conservative orbit.[16]

By 1966, there were charges in the press and within the labor movement that AIFLD was involved with the CIA.[17] According to former CIA officer Philip Agee, Serafino Romualdi, who served as executive director of AIFLD from 1962 to 1966, was by then a top official in the CIA's Latin American division. During that period, graduates of AIFLD's training were involved in several CIA-sponsored coups and disruptions in Latin America and the Caribbean. William C. Doherty, then AIFLD Social Projects Director, proudly boasted of AIFLD's role in the 1964 overthrow of the Goulart regime in Brazil.[18]

In the Caribbean, AIFLD played a major role in destabilizing Cheddi Jagan's government after he was reelected in 1961. Agents, including 11 Guyanese graduates of AIFLD training, entered Guyana as "labor representatives" and worked with the AFL-supported union to organize a general strike. As was later revealed by the *London Times,* the CIA also sent strike funds into Guyana channeled through the international affairs department of the American Federation of State, County and Municipal Employees (AFSCME).[19] The result of this organizing was a wave of racial violence and an 80-day general strike that effectively brought down the Jagan government.

In the Dominican Republic, the AFL-CIO entered the country after the election of the popular Juan Bosch government. Although Bosch had overwhelming labor support and gave unprecedented freedom to the country's trade unions, the AFL-CIO went to work against the new government, targeting the newly-formed FOUPSA union. When attempts to control FOUPSA failed, a dual union was created and called Bloque FOUPSA Libre ("Free FOUPSA"). Later known as CON-ATRAL, the union received funding from AIFLD and ORIT and was run by a group of right-wing Cuban exiles who were brought into AIFLD and ORIT positions after 1959. Alone among Dominican unions, CONATRAL supported the military coup against Bosch, refused to participate in the constitutionalist uprising, and supported the U.S. Marine invasion in 1965. The main AFL-CIO operative in the Dominican Republic was Andrew McLellan, who replaced Romualdi as AIFLD director in 1967.

AIFLD in the Caribbean Today

As a result of more than 20 years of organizing and training, AIFLD now has a core of Caribbean unions which are tied to the U.S. through their leadership. On the surface, AIFLD training promotes labor economism: that is, the concept that unions should stick to negotiations over wages and benefits and not become involved in more substantive economic and political issues. On a deeper level, however, the training pushes unions to undertake a reactionary political role.

Unions whose leaders have been trained by AIFLD are generally more supportive of conservative governments than are non-AIFLD unions. In Trinidad & Tobago, an extreme example, unions are divided between the pro-government Labour Congress and the anti-government Council of Progressive Trades Unions. The former have AIFLD ties, while the latter do not. Certain types of unions are frequently penetrated by AIFLD. Communications, electrical, and transport workers (especially dockworkers) are commonly targeted because of their strategic importance to island economies.

AIFLD's Caribbean programs are carried out primarily through the Caribbean Congress of Labour, which includes ORIT affiliates in 14 countries of the English-speaking Caribbean plus Suriname, Curaçao and St. Maartin. (Since 1981, AIFLD has also worked with unions in the French Antilles through a French union called Force Ouvrière.) Funded by both AIFLD and the ICFTU, the CCL is like a club of U.S.-approved unions which progressive unions cannot join. Among the incentives offered to unions in this U.S. camp are the training programs, most of which take place at three regional centers: the Barbados Labour College, the Trade Union Education Institute in Jamaica, and the Guyana Industrial Training Center in Guyana. Since 1962, AIFLD has trained 21,331 trade unionists from the English-speaking Caribbean and 31,768 from the Dominican Republic in in-country seminars.[20] Trade unionists who are deemed promising are then invited to the U.S. center for the advanced training, offered to at least 20 Caribbean unionists each year. These all-expense paid sessions and the paid "internships" for selected graduates are the biggest incentives for cooperative labor leaders.

AIFLD'S CARIBBEAN COURSE

The 1983-84 program of courses at AIFLD's George Meany Center in Washington, DC offered one course specifically geared toward the Caribbean. The course description reveals the ideological nature of AIFLD instruction:

The Role of Organized Labor in Developing Democracy (Caribbean)

The course covers the origins and purposes of trade unionism within the framework of a **democratic society.** Particular emphasis will be given to an analysis of **democratic theory,** the **nature of dictatorships,** and the **impact of ideologies** on labor activities, principally in the field of **labor and human rights.** The course will also cover the role of the labor movement in promoting **pluralistic political and economic systems** on the national level, the **difference between democratic labor and other labor forces,** and the role of labor in economic development and other activities being undertaken in the Caribbean. Finally, the course analyzes the current situation of the labor movement in the Caribbean and its institutional role in the **political progress** of the nation.

(Emphasis added.)

AIFLD also offers material incentives to unions, primarily housing for workers. However, these benefits are—as AIFLD states—only for members of "free democratic trade unions,"[21] i.e., for unions aligned with or created by AIFLD. In the Caribbean, such housing has been built in Barbados, Guyana, and the Dominican Republic, reflecting AIFLD's ties with the Barbados Workers Union, the Guyana Trades Union Council, and the National Confederation of Dominican Workers. Recently, AIFLD constructed or renovated union headquarters for CCL affiliates in five Eastern Caribbean islands. The unions received gleaming new "labor community centers" including office space, a meeting hall, medical clinics, and so forth, adding to the prestige and predominance of AIFLD-linked unions.

At the same time, AIFLD seeks to break or bypass progressive unions and to force dissenters out of AIFLD unions. For example, while the leadership of the powerful Barbados Workers Union (BWU) is central to the AIFLD/CCL network, several years ago two minor BWU officials were active in Monali, a small leftist party in Barbados. Within a two-month period, the BWU received visits from William Doherty, AIFLD's executive director; Milan Bish, then U.S. ambassador to the Eastern Caribbean; Richard Luce, a British minister; and Hugh Shearer, foreign minister of the Seaga government, all urging the ouster of "Marxist" elements from the union.[22]

In 1982, a leftist labor lawyer named Bobby Clarke formed a new union in Barbados known as BIGWU (Barbados Industrial and General Workers Union). BIGWU's membership grew rapidly, reflecting its activist orientation and workers' frustration with the more traditional and bureaucratic Barbados Workers Union. To counter this threat, the employers, the BWU hierarchy, the Barbados government, and the U.S. Embassy launched a red-baiting attack on Clarke and his union. When BIGWU workers at three factories went on strike they were fired, then rehired with a raise on condition they renounced BIGWU. This effectively broke the union.[23]

Similarly, AIFLD has tried to undermine the Caribbean Union of Teachers (CUT), a regional confederation which came under new progressive leadership in 1979. CUT reflects the growing role of white-collar unions, especially teachers' unions, as a progressive political force in the region. When attempts to co-opt the organization failed, AIFLD branded the CUT executive "communist" and sought to woo member unions away with the aim of setting up a parallel body.[24]

As in the past, AIFLD continues to collaborate with other U.S. agencies to discredit and destabilize regimes which the U.S. opposes. It has put freed Cuban political prisoners and anti-Sandinista leaders on tour through the United States. In Suriname, the extent of AIFLD involvement is not fully known, but it appears to have played a major role in efforts to unseat the Bouterse government. The country's largest union, the Moederbond, has conducted harassment strikes, while its AIFLD-trained leader, Cyril Daal, publicly called for Bouterse's overthrow. Daal was among 15 Surinamers killed by the government during a coup attempt in 1982.

AIFLD played a political role in Grenada during the years of the revolution, although the extent of its involvement is still unknown. At the time of the 1979 revolution, AIFLD had longstanding ties to the Seamen and Waterfront Workers Union (SWWU) and also had trained the leadership of several other Grenadian unions. Within a few months after the revolution, these unions began to figure in a pattern of labor disturbances aimed at harassing the new government. The main instigators were officials of the SWWU and the electrical workers—including one on the AIFLD payroll since 1973—who called strikes on flimsy pretexts and without support of the rank and file. Because of the revolution's wide support, these disruptive attempts failed, and eventually the AIFLD-trained leaders were replaced in several unions by rank-and-file vote. The SWWU, however, maintained its close ties to AIFLD through its general secretary Eric Pierre, and was the one union consistently to oppose the Bishop government.

Whether AIFLD had anything to do with the splits which

destroyed the New Jewel Movement is unknown. It is a matter of record, however, that in early October 1983, the AFL-CIO adopted a resolution condemning "the dictatorship of Maurice Bishop in Grenada."[25] After the U.S. invasion which came several weeks later, AIFLD opened an office in St. George's and assumed a central role in the Reagan administration's ideological campaign to win Grenadians over to anticommunism. [see Part VII, Ch. 3.]

Challenges to AIFLD and the CCL

Hard economic times in the Caribbean have brought the contradictions within AIFLD to the fore. On the one hand, AIFLD's preaching of economism raises expectations of higher wages and tough union negotiation. On the other hand, its closeness to the U.S. government and corporate interests puts pressure on unions to accept anti-worker and anti-union measures favoring foreign investors. This has put CCL/AIFLD unions into a difficult position and has brought them under pressure from their rank and file to break with the U.S. position on certain major issues.

This is the case, for example, in regards to the policy of wage restraint, which is an integral part of the Reagan/IMF economic strategies. Despite clauses in the Caribbean Basin Initiative referring to the rights of trade unions, the reality is that attracting foreign investment relies on keeping wages low. The current emphasis on this model has led many Caribbean governments to attempt to limit wage increases or even impose a wage freeze. AIFLD-linked unions tend to be more compliant with such policies: in St. Lucia, for example, union leaders with AIFLD training went along with the Compton

AIFLD director William C. Doherty with freed Cuban political prisoner Huber Matos.

AIFLD

government's Tripartite Commission to study wage restraint even though the plan was unpopular with workers and the largest union in the country opposed it. But economic pressures are so severe that union leaders cannot easily back such policies, and the Caribbean Congress of Labour therefore has come out officially against a wage freeze.

Moreover, workers know that U.S. investors in the Caribbean have resisted dealing with unions and have often connived with governments to secure non-union shops. Thus even such "establishment" unions as the Barbados Workers Union—whose general secretary, Frank Walcott, headed the CCL until 1980—have publicly aired their reservations about the CBI. These criticisms from the BWU and other unions set off an intense lobbying offensive by U.S. officials, who toured the Caribbean attempting to persuade unions to back the CBI. The CCL has found itself in an uncomfortable middle position. On the one hand it is under pressure from its member unions to defend worker protections. But it is also under attack from employers and governments for supposedly placing the interests of a unionized "elite" above those of the unorganized majority—who, it is implied, will be grateful for jobs even on exploitative terms.

A similar rank-and-file challenge developed around the Emergency Powers Bills introduced by various island governments in the early 1980s. Designed to shore up government control in case of social unrest, these repressive statutes contain clauses abrogating the rights of unions to strike when the government declares an "emergency." The bills met public and worker opposition everywhere, forcing pro-government AIFLD unions to respond to these popular pressures.

In St. Vincent, for example, the largest union, the Commercial Technical and Allied Workers Union (CTAWU), was formed by AIFLD as a dual union in 1962 and was close to the government of Milton Cato.[26] CTAWU's general secretary, Burns Bonadie, served as general secretary of the CCL from 1980-1983, during which time he wielded extensive influence at the regional level as de facto front man for AIFLD. He is also Milton Cato's nephew. Yet when the Cato government tried to pass an Emergency Powers Bill in 1981, the vehemence of rank-and-file opposition left Bonadie no choice, and the CTAWU led a coalition which successfully demonstrated for the bill's repeal.

Caribbean trade unionists are well aware that AIFLD and by extension, the CCL, are funded by the U.S. government and multinationals and that "he who pays the piper calls the tune."[27] The result is the growing alienation of a significant portion of the labor movement, as well as pressures within the CCL toward greater independence. An example of this was the position which the CCL took on the Grenada invasion, expressing its "deep concern" and calling for the early withdrawal of U.S. troops. Although the original proposal was for a stronger condemnation, even the version finally passed was a significant gesture for a traditionally U.S.-controlled organization. These rank-and-file challenges to the labor establishment mean that AIFLD may be seeing its influence wane as unions increasingly confront the implications of U.S. labor policy. ∎

The Media

Within the U.S. media's global reach, the Caribbean is an especially fertile ground for influence through newspapers, television, radio, and film. This is true first of all because much of the Caribbean speaks English, and until recently was under British control. In his book *The Media Are American,* Jeremy Tunstall describes Britain as the "linchpin" of the worldwide spread of the U.S. media. Britain's ascendency as the first media power made English the language of mass communications, and collaboration between the U.S. and British media paved the way for U.S. penetration of the Commonwealth, or British Empire, market.[1] Secondly, both the Caribbean and Latin America are subject to special controls operating to ensure U.S. hegemony in the hemisphere. In media, as in the labor movement, the United States began serious efforts to gain control during the First World War and consolidated that control at the end of World War Two.

The Major Dailies: Voice of the Bourgeoisie

The major media is privately owned in most of the larger Caribbean territories, including Jamaica, Trinidad, Barbados, the Dominican Republic, Puerto Rico, and the French and Dutch Antilles. Newspapers and radio stations operate in competition and without formal government restrictions, leading the U.S. to deem the media "free" in these countries.

In reality, however, each country is dominated by one to four daily newspapers owned by wealthy families or commercial conglomerates. While other newspapers are not illegal, they are overshadowed by the establishment papers and operate under financial and sometimes political pressures. Jamaica's only daily paper is the conservative *Daily Gleaner* (along with its evening edition, *The Star*). It is published by the Gleaner Company, which is controlled by members of the island's elite "21 families." The company's board of directors is headed by the powerful Ashenheim family which also holds interests in cement, steel, sugar, insurance, real estate, tourism, and manufacturing. The more liberal *Daily News,* acquired by the Manley government in 1979, was closed down by Seaga in April 1983. Seaga also purged the state-owned JBC television network of progressive journalists shortly after he came to power.

Besides the *Gleaner,* the other influential dailies in the English-speaking Caribbean are the Barbados *Advocate* and *Nation* and the Trinidad *Guardian* and *Express.* The latter are both owned by Trinidadian conglomerates, the *Express* by the Neal & Massy group and the *Guardian* by the McEnearney/Alstons group. These conglomerates are the largest and most diversified indigenous capitalist groups in the Caribbean. McEnearney/Alstons also owns the Barbados *Advocate,* formerly a member of the U.S.-based Thomson chain.

Shopping center in San Juan, Puerto Rico.

Cathy Sunshine

112

In the Dominican Republic, the prominent *Listin Diario* and *Ultima Hora* are both owned by the Pellerano family, part of the wealthy Dominican elite. *Hoy* and *El Nacional* belong to a Spanish millionaire businessman whose holdings also include one of the local television stations. *El Caribe,* although smaller in circulation, is even more right-wing and is linked to Trujillista interests. Only *El Nuevo Diario,* where the journalists own 33% of the shares, is progressive, and it has come under nearly fatal pressures from rising costs linked to the IMF's austerity plan.

The press in those territories which are still colonies is dominated, predictably, by metropolitan interests. The main newspaper in Guadeloupe and Martinique, *France-Antilles,* is part of a French newspaper chain owned by the conservative media tycoon Robert Hersant. Although other newspapers and magazines circulate in the French islands, *France-Antilles* is the only daily and is an important link in the French system of ideological control. The paper views the world from the vantage point of Paris; news of Guadeloupe and Martinique is relegated to pages entitled "In the Department," emphasizing the subordinate link to France.

In much the same way, Puerto Rico's three major dailies reflect and promote the colonial relationship with the United States. *El Mundo* is owned by Puerto Rican magnate Argentina Hills, who controls a local media empire that also includes Radio El Mundo and Telemundo Inc. She is married to Lee Hills, former head of the U.S.-based Knight-Ridder newspaper chain. *El Nuevo Día* is owned by the wealthy Ferré family, founders of the New Progressive Party which favors U.S. statehood for Puerto Rico. The English-language *San Juan Star* is owned by the U.S.-based Scripps-Howard newspaper chain. All three subtly reinforce the message that Puerto Rico is a part of the United States, especially the *Star* which is the voice of the U.S. business community on the island.

The major Caribbean dailies are generally conservative in their editorial slant, although dissenting viewpoints appear in columns and letters to the editor. They support capitalism and middle-class consumerism; they are anticommunist; and they rarely challenge the principle of U.S. hegemony in the region or the world. All the major papers supported the U.S. invasion of Grenada, even in Trinidad where the government opposed it; in fact the Trinidad *Express* and *Guardian* led the attack on the Chambers government for refusing to join the U.S.-led force.

The papers also serve as a direct vehicle for information generated in the U.S. Like most Third World papers, Caribbean newspapers get most of their international news in the form of dispatches from the major wire services—the Associated Press (AP) and United Press International (UPI) based in the U.S., and the British Reuters. Stories and photos used from the wires result in an Anglo-American slant to interpretation of world news. Papers like the *Gleaner* and the *San Juan Star* also frequently reprint articles and editorials from U.S. papers.

The Caribbean has its own wire service, CANA, which is linked to Reuters and supplies the region with Caribbean news. Other than CANA, the only region-wide news medium is

Caribbean Contact, a monthly newspaper published by the Caribbean Conference of Churches. *Contact* is largely independent of the establishment media structure and analyzes regional developments from a progressive, ecumenical Christian perspective.

The media picture looks different in the smaller islands such as Antigua, Dominica, and St. Lucia. These countries do not have daily papers, but only one or more weeklies, with the leading one usually owned by the government. Government also generally controls radio and television in the smaller islands. Opposition political parties usually publish their own newsletters since they are often denied access to the government-controlled media, especially around election time.

In Antigua, for instance, one of the two weekly papers is owned by the government and the other by the ruling Antigua Labour Party. Of the two radio stations, one is the government station and the other is privately owned by the family of Prime Minister Vere C. Bird. The island's television station is government-owned, and the cable T.V. franchise is held by the prime minister's son, Vere Bird Jr. Swimming against this formidable tide is *Outlet,* the weekly paper of the Antigua Caribbean Liberation Movement. The editor of *Outlet* has been arrested, its offices raided and the paper hit with libel suits in an endless campaign of government harassment.

The Impact of Television

Television brings images of the world to the Caribbean. More precisely, it brings images of the United States. Some 75% of television programming in the English-speaking Caribbean originates outside the region, primarily in North America and Britain.[2] As elsewhere in the Third World, stations have large stretches of broadcast time to fill, but limited capability to produce programs locally. The result is a steady diet of *Dallas, Love Boat, Hawaii Five-O,* and other Hollywood fare.

Outlet

Young Cuban dancers practice on outskirts of Havana.

Marcelo Montecino

In Barbados, nine of the ten most popular television programs are U.S. in origin. (The eighth most popular program is the nightly news, produced locally.) "Days of Our Lives" and "Dallas" are common topics of conversation in Barbados.[3]

The U.S.-based Cable News Network (CNN) produces a "Headline News" broadcast which is the only international news carried by a number of stations in the Eastern Caribbean. CNN's slogan is "Around the World—Around the Clock." It is, however, heavily slanted toward the United States, with little coverage of other countries and virtually nothing on the Third World save the random earthquake or coup. CNN is a subtle but persuasive vehicle of U.S. cultural bias. For example, the *lead* story one night in May 1984 was the opening of the New Orleans World's Fair. The following night it was the fact that five people won the New York state lottery. Neither of these are important world events, but they reinforce an image of the U.S. as a fairyland where life is affluent and exciting. This is matched by a pejorative slant toward news about the socialist countries.

The appearance of new communications technologies has greatly speeded and intensified this process of cultural invasion. Satellite dishes for Direct Broadcast Satellite reception have proliferated in the yards of affluent households in Kingston and Port-of-Spain. Video cassette recorders and cable television are the new status symbols for the middle class; Barbados, for example, has 33 video rental parlors, where materials ranging from comedies to pornography can be rented at low rates. Three new U.S. cable channels recently came to Puerto Rico, all broadcasting in English (including the Disney channel and the Playboy channel).

By displacing and devaluing what is indigenous, the media onslaught threatens to paralyze the development of authentic Caribbean cultures. The "top 40" has largely crowded Jamaican reggae and Trinidad calypso off the airwaves. Likewise, while Caribbean dance and drama struggle to develop, Michael Jackson and break-dancing sweep down from the U.S. and become fads among Caribbean youth.

Thus some observers of the Caribbean media scene speak of the "very real possibility that unique, autonomous Caribbean cultures will never fully develop." This has deep implications for the future of the region:

> . . . Because the health of such cultures is vital to true development, this region, perhaps more than others, needs to build and authenticate its identity before it can successfully move to tasks of social and economic change.[4]

Cuba: Island of Resistance

The main exception to the regional media picture is, of course, Cuba. Cuba has virtually ignored the U.S.-made news and entertainment which innundate the region, choosing instead to orient its arts and media toward support for the revolution and celebration of what is genuinely Cuban.

By the 1950s, radio and television controlled by North American capital were already well established in Cuba. After the revolution, the government took over this infrastructure and redirected it toward the development of Cuban and Latin American culture. Programming on Cuba's two television channels includes news, arts and educational programs, movies (Cuban-made and foreign, including U.S.), animated cartoons (from the U.S. and Eastern Europe), and sports. Absent are the made-in-Hollywood series which fill air time elsewhere, and Cuban television is free of the emphasis on violence which marks U.S. prime time.

Radio stations play primarily Cuban music in its full range of forms, from the traditional *trova* (ballads) to the *nueva trova* (new song movement), *son* (an Afro-Cuban hybrid), *rumba,* and experimental music by Cuban musicians. Other Latin American music is also popular, and American jazz and classical are played. Cuban radio does not play the "Top 40," but Cubans can tune into Miami radio and television stations, a number of which broadcast in Spanish.

Cuban music, drama, dance and film are subsidized by the state through the Instituto Superior de Arte and the Instituto Cubano de Cine. Soviet-style "socialist realism" is not promoted in Cuba. Rather, Cuban artists are free-wheeling in their style and frequently pioneer new forms of expression, although one cannot agitate against the revolution ("Inside the revolution, everything; outside the revolution, nothing" was Castro's most famous statement on the arts).

The Cuban press is state-controlled, with *Granma,* the communist party organ, as the main daily newspaper. *Granma's* news coverage is based on reports from Cuba's two wire services, the domestic Agencia Informacion Nacional and the international Prensa Latina; and from a wide range of other sources including Agence France Press, EFE (Spain), TASS (the Soviet Union), CANA, and many Third World wire services. Other Cuban publications include newspapers for youth, workers, and the military, and newsmagazines, including the popular avant-garde *Opina.*

The Cuban press is generally self-censoring and reflects official policy. This may be undergoing gradual change: a politburo directive in 1984 underscored the right of the press to aggressively seek information and to criticize, although this means criticism of specific problems, not broad principles of the revolution. The intent is to strengthen the system by exposing problems so they can be solved, and to make the Cuban media less tame and more informative.

While the U.S. denounces the Cuban press as not free, it is respected in Latin America and elsewhere as an alternative voice outside the U.S.-controlled media structure. Prensa Latina has numerous subscribers outside Cuba and maintains correspondents in nearly every major world capital except Washington. (The Washington correspondent, a Canadian, was expelled by the Reagan administration in 1984.)

U.S. Influence and the IAPA Connection

Largely through the efforts of Nelson Rockefeller, Coordinator of Inter-American Affairs from 1940-45, the U.S. gained almost total control over news flowing into Latin America during the Second World War.[5] After the war, steps were taken to institutionalize U.S. media operations to serve the aims of the Cold War.

> The Americans became the senior partners in an Anglo-American governmental media alliance which turned from anti-Nazi to anticommunist propaganda . . . The overt agency was the United States Information Agency. The covert media operations of the United States government were carried on primarily by the Central Intelligence Agency.[6]

The CIA's media empire included well-known fronts like Radio Free Europe and Radio Liberty, and several wire services which the CIA set up or controlled (Agencia Orbe Latinoamericana, Forum World Features, and LATIN).[7] The Agency also became involved with commercial and professional journalists. In 1967, it was disclosed that the American Newspaper Guild was among the professional organizations to which the CIA had channeled funds for overseas activities.[8]

The meeting point for these various strands was the Inter American Press Association (IAPA), over which the CIA gained substantial influence in 1950.

> The Inter American Press Association, with its own wire service reaching some 1000 newspapers, is the hub of the entire Latin American media operation. Its past presidents and board members read almost like a roster of key CIA agents in the Latin American media.[9]

IAPA is a membership organization of some 1,200 newspapers in the U.S., Latin America, and the Caribbean. It is based in Miami, where reactionary exiles play a key role in the organization through *Diario de las Américas* and the *Miami Herald,* both newspapers with strong ties to the right-wing Cuban exile community. The current president of IAPA is Horacio Aguirre, a Nicaraguan exile and founder of *Diario de las Américas.* Another important member is past president Argentina Hills, whose husband used to head the chain which owns the *Miami Herald.*[10]

In contrast to the situation in labor, where AIFLD must contend with the basic antipathy of unions toward a worker/capitalist alliance, IAPA represents a natural marriage of interests between Cold War ideologues and upper-class newspaper owners. Journalists, who tend to be more liberal, have been excluded from IAPA since its reorganization in 1950. As A.J. Liebling aptly wrote, freedom of the press belongs to the man who owns one. Defending press freedom is IAPA's self-assigned task, and it has used this campaign as a weapon against progressive governments, directed initially against Cuba in the 1960s.

In 1975, the Senate Select Committee on Intelligence (known as the Church Committee) revealed that the CIA had used IAPA to attack the Allende government in Chile in the period leading up to the 1973 coup. It did so through the conservative newspaper *El Mercurio,* which already had CIA collaborators on its executive staff. In 1969 these agents were elevated to the Board of Directors of IAPA, and the paper began showing signs of a CIA takeover. It became sensationalist in content, and used subtle psychological techniques to arouse anti-government feelings in Chileans. At the same time, IAPA claimed that press freedom was under attack by Allende, and awarded *El Mercurio* its "Freedom of the Press" award in 1972, all helping to prepare the way for the right-wing military coup.[11]

According to Fred Landis, a consultant to the Church Committee, the Jamaica *Gleaner* underwent a similar metamorphosis in the period leading up to the 1980 election which ousted the Manley government.[12] Oliver Clarke, managing director and chairman of the *Gleaner,* was added to the IAPA Board of Directors in 1976, and from then on anti-Manley themes in the *Gleaner* escalated sharply. Given the *Gleaner's* ties to the Jamaican elite and the open preference of this class for Seaga, the newspaper was by nature rather hostile to Manley and the PNP. As the election approached, however, the *Gleaner* began to resemble *El Mercurio* in its use of sensationalism and subliminal persuasion. Techniques included a focus on lurid violence, portrayal of economic chaos, and the fanning of fears about a Cuban takeover.[13] Just as it had in Chile, IAPA cried loudly that press freedom in Jamaica was under attack. The *Gleaner* received the Maria Moors Cabot prize for "defending freedom of the press," an award in which IAPA is influential. The newspaper's campaign against Manley is credited with playing a significant role in the PNP's electoral defeat.

Regional Media vs. Grenada

It was against this background of the destabilization of pro-socialist governments in Chile and Jamaica that the People's Revolutionary Government of Grenada (PRG) made the decision to close the bi-weekly *Torchlight* newspaper in October 1979. It is not at all clear that the *Torchlight* was directly influenced by the U.S. at this early stage. The paper was, however, of the same genre as the Jamaica, Trinidad, and Barbados dailies—in fact the publishers of the Trinidad *Express* held 20% of the shares in the *Torchlight*—and like them it was the voice of the local bourgeoisie. The *Torchlight* therefore welcomed the overthrow of Gairy, but expected a prompt return to traditional capitalist democracy, and became increasingly critical of the PRG.

The *Torchlight's* closure set off a spiraling confrontation

NO PRESS FREEDOM IN HAITI

In the Caribbean's harshest dictatorship, there is no freedom of the press. A 1969 "Anti-Communist Law" provides that anyone who criticizes the government can be convicted of being a communist and sentenced to death. A more recent censorship law, enacted under President Jean Claude Duvalier, makes it an imprisonable offense for journalists to "offend the Chief of State or the First Lady of the Republic."

After a slight liberalization in the late 1970s, during which an independent press began to form, the Haitian government cracked down days after the election of Ronald Reagan in November 1980. Dozens of journalists were jailed or exiled, and all newspapers and radio stations independent of the government were closed down.

In the spring of 1984, the Duvalier regime again relaxed press censorship in response to international pressure to improve human rights. Two weekly magazines started to publish, and on May 14, U.S. Secretary of State Shultz certified to Congress that Haiti was making progress in moving toward democracy. On May 18, the Haitian security forces seized and closed both magazines and jailed their editors, beating one so severely that he required hospitalization.

---

between the PRG and the regional media, organized in the 27-member Caribbean Publishers and Broadcasters Association (CPBA). After closing the *Torchlight,* the PRG announced that no new newspapers would be allowed to publish until a media policy could be formulated, and it closed a Catholic church paper after one issue in February 1980. The following December, the *Gleaner, Advocate, Nation, Guardian,* and *Express* jointly filed a complaint against the PRG with the Organization of American States' human rights arm, centering on the lack of elections and threats to press freedom. Several months later, a new newspaper appeared in Grenada calling itself the *Grenadian Voice.* The PRG again closed the paper after one issue, citing what it termed convincing evidence that the paper—owned by prominent Grenadian lawyers and businessmen, including the former managing director of the *Torchlight*—was linked to the CIA through the U.S. Embassy in Barbados. The editor of the *Grenadian Voice* was Leslie Pierre, whose brother Eric Pierre was AIFLD's main operative in the Grenadian labor movement.

The confrontation hardened over the summer as the regional media stepped up its negative coverage of Grenada.[14] While the Reagan administration courted Caribbean journalists (CPBA members gathered in Washington in June for a conference sponsored by large corporations and the U.S. International Communication Agency)[15] the PRG stiffened its position, moving its media system into closer cooperation with the Prague-based International Organization of Journalists. On September 27, 1981, member newspapers of the CPBA—

RADIO WHO?

On May 20, 1985, the Reagan administration began its controversial radio broadcasts to "tell the Cuban people what is happening in Cuba." While the Cuban government reacted angrily by suspending a 1984 immigration accord with the U.S., early reports suggested that the Cuban people generally shrugged off Washington's ideological offensive as a laughing stock.

Dubbed "soft-sell propaganda" by the *Washington Post,* Radio Martí operates under the auspices of the Voice of America (VOA) but is more aggressive than VOA in criticizing Soviet and Cuban policies. Although the station purports to inform Cubans about their country, it has no correspondents inside Cuba, and relies on editorials and commentaries to denounce the Cuban system. The soft-sell consists of music, sports and *novelas* (soap operas) designed to attract listeners. The station's studios are in Washington, the transmitters in Florida, and the broadcasters generally come from the anti-Castro exile community.

"If you ask my opinion, I would say it is right out of the '50s," one Cuban woman remarked to U.S. journalists in Havana. "All these people still have the ideology and the outlook of the 1950s. It sounds as if the programs were taped 25 years ago."

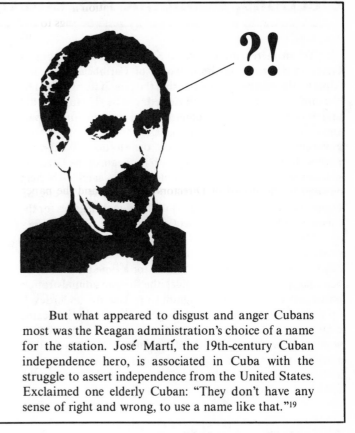

But what appeared to disgust and anger Cubans most was the Reagan administration's choice of a name for the station. José Martí, the 19th-century Cuban independence hero, is associated in Cuba with the struggle to assert independence from the United States. Exclaimed one elderly Cuban: "They don't have any sense of right and wrong, to use a name like that."[19]

---

with the exception of the Barbados *Nation*—simultaneously ran identical editorials condemning the PRG. The editorials were inserted by the publishers without consulting journalists, and the move was decried by journalists' organizations in both Trinidad and Jamaica. In October 1982, IAPA also passed a resolution condemning the PRG.

The media campaign against Grenada was thus distinguished by its regional nature, tending to blur the U.S. connection although the CPBA has direct links to IAPA.[16] This regional aspect was the result of the PRG's decision to close down provocative newspapers instead of tolerating them as Allende and Manley had done. By removing the natural local agent—the *Torchlight*—this forced the regional media to take on the instrumental role in any IAPA destabilization campaign. But it also made the PRG's restrictions on the press a fact, in contrast to Chile and Jamaica where press freedom was never actually in danger. This incurred the enmity of the regional press barons quite independently of any encouragement from the U.S.

The forces arrayed against the PRG placed it in a no-win situation. If it allowed critical papers to publish, the chances were good that they would be used to help destabilize the revolution. By closing them down, however, the PRG marred its regional and international image and damaged relations with the Grenadian middle class. But the greatest cost was to Grenada's own political process, since the state-controlled media failed to provide a platform for debate within the

revolution. So tame was the press that no hint of the conflicts within the New Jewel Movement leaked to the Grenadian public before October 1983, contributing to the explosiveness of the clash when it finally came.

Postscript

The U.S. government still views the media as an effective vehicle for propaganda and covert activities, despite greater awareness of these linkages at home and abroad. In 1979, the Newspaper Guild (formerly the American Newspaper Guild) was slated to receive $100,000 from the government through AIFLD to restart its Latin American organizing, which had been terminated in 1967. The Guild's membership of 35,000 professional journalists voted to refuse the money because of AIFLD's CIA ties.[17]

More recently, IAPA was pegged to play a role in Project Democracy, the Reagan administration's global propaganda plan. In Congressional hearings, the director of the U.S. Information Agency (USIA), Charles Wick, admitted that USIA planned to channel $50,000 to IAPA through a conduit, since IAPA's charter forbids accepting government funds.[18] And in 1982, the year the U.S.-funded "contra" war against Nicaragua was officially launched, IAPA awarded a prize to the editor of *La Prensa,* voice of the anti-Sandinista bourgeoisie, for its "unswerving opposition to efforts of totalitarian regimes" to limit freedom of the press. ∎

Elections, Economic Aid, and the Caribbean Basin Initiative

To an increasing extent, U.S. influence has become a factor in determining the outcome of Caribbean elections. Most Caribbean people assume that the candidate preferred by Washington is the one who, if elected, will be able to bring aid and investment into the country. Washington for its part encourages this idea, promising assistance to conservative governments and warning against the election of left-wing parties. In 1979-82—coinciding with the years of the Grenada revolution—the United States used these tactics to help conservative leaders win elections in Jamaica, St. Vincent, St. Lucia and Dominica, helping to mold regional alliances for the eventual military move against Grenada.

More than any overt U.S. involvement in the electoral process, it was the expectation of U.S. aid which brought results. These expectations centered for a time on the Caribbean Basin Initiative (CBI), which the Reagan administration portrayed as a bold new program to reverse the underdevelopment of the region. But early hopes soon ebbed as it became clear that the highly politicized CBI promised more than it would deliver. Facing popular demands they could not satisfy and economic problems they could not solve, the U.S. "allies" in the region welcomed the political diversion provided by the 1983 invasion of Grenada.

Jamaica: Riding Reagan's Coattails

The alliance between Ronald Reagan and Edward Seaga began well before their respective elections in the fall of 1980. While still in opposition under the PNP government of Michael Manley, Seaga's Jamaica Labour Party (JLP) began building ties with right-wing political and business groups in the U.S. which formed the core of Reagan's support.[1] With the U.S. electorate moving to the right and Reagan's victory a near certainty, Seaga appeared ideologically in step with this rising right-wing tide.

The victory of the JLP on October 30, 1980 was also, perhaps foremost, a repudiation of the PNP by the Jamaican people.[2] Manley's capitulation to the IMF, the suffering wrought by the Fund's austerity program, and the PNP's final, belated break with the Fund painted a picture of political weakness and economic chaos. The so-called "capital strike," in which international bankers and investors showed their displeasure with the PNP by shutting off funds, left the society vulnerable to Seaga's promises that he could bring loans and investment into Jamaica again. The U.S. strategy for helping the JLP to power was therefore to nurture the impression that a Seaga victory would unlock a flood of aid, trade and investment which would restore Jamaica to prosperity.

As early as 1979, elements within the Carter administration were maneuvering to build ties between Seaga and the international financial establishment.[3] Seaga began negotiating with IMF officials in June 1980, an extraordinary act since he was an opposition party leader, not a member of the administration, and the Jamaican government had just broken

off relations with the Fund.[4] The JLP's manifesto published a few months later outlined how much aid they expected to receive from the IMF and World Bank and the form in which it would come.

Seaga's close relations with U.S. bankers and multilateral lenders convinced many Jamaicans that the JLP would be able to make good on its campaign promise to "Make money jingle in your pocket." The pro-JLP *Daily Gleaner* frequently headlined large sums of money which it said would be available to a Seaga administration. In addition, most of the U.S. press, especially *Time* and *Newsweek,* was heavily biased against Manley and in favor of Seaga, influencing not only U.S. public opinion but also a significant readership abroad.[5] Seaga's campaign was run by the New York public relations firm of Ann Sabo Associates.

The JLP's promises initially came true as both the International Monetary Fund and the World Bank announced large loans to the new government in the spring of 1981. U.S. bilateral aid flooded the Jamaican treasury, and delegations of U.S. technicians and consultants arrived to engineer the expected economic recovery.

Prime Minister Seaga of Jamaica flanked by President Reagan and Vice-President Bush during a White House visit.

The Eastern Caribbean: Reversing the "Leftist Tide"

The overthrow of Eric Gairy by Grenada's New Jewel Movement in March 1979 was the dramatic opener to a period which saw the people of several Eastern Caribbean islands reject entrenched conservative governments. On May 29, 1979, a broad popular uprising in Dominica forced the resignation of the corrupt Patrick John government and its replacement by an interim government headed by O.J. Seraphin. In July, St. Lucians voted out the United Workers Party of John Compton after 15 years in office; it was replaced by the St. Lucia Labour Party headed by Allan Louisy as prime minister and the charismatic, liberal George Odlum as foreign minister. Meanwhile, three opposition parties in St. Vincent and the Grenadines finally managed to coalesce as the United People's Movement, shaping up as a leftist challenge to the government of Milton Cato in the approaching Vincentian elections.

Dominica under Seraphin, St. Lucia under Louisy and Odlum, and Bishop's Grenada then moved to strengthen their mutual ties in the summer of 1979 by holding a mini-summit in St. George's which produced a declaration of cooperation and "unity." The move had strong popular support on the three islands. In this context, Grenada and St. Lucia announced that they would not participate in the regional "coast guard" being pushed by the Carter administration, because of its disguised purpose as a device to crush internal unrest. St. Lucia's unexpected withdrawal forced the coast guard plan to be temporarily shelved.

This series of developments was seen by Washington as an ominous leftward swing in the Eastern Caribbean, confirming dire predictions about the "model effect" of Grenada's revolution. Yet by May 1982—three years later—the liberal administrations in Dominica and St. Lucia were out of power, St. Vincent's UPM had been trounced at the polls, and conservative, pro-U.S. regimes were firmly in the driver's seat in all three islands.

What happened must be understood at two levels. On the one hand, the liberal/progressive forces were weak and divided, and quickly became discredited through internal squabbles and corruption. On the other hand, the summer and fall of 1979 saw a shift by the Carter administration toward a hard-line policy in the Caribbean; so that by January 1980 *Latin America Regional Reports* could write of a "new confidence by Washington that after months of political work, it has now turned, or at least stemmed, the rising left-wing tide in the sensitive Eastern Caribbean."[6]

The turning point came in September 1979 with the Carter administration's sudden and opportune "discovery" of a Soviet combat brigade in Cuba. Although the White House later admitted that these were the same Soviet trainers who had been in Cuba for 17 years, it used the flap to announce new measures to contain the supposed Cuban threat. Foremost was the creation of a permanent "Caribbean Task Force" based in Key West, Florida, as a quick-strike military force in the region. The carrot accompanying this military stick, Carter announced, would be an increase in economic aid to U.S. allies in the region to meet "human needs."[7]

The first fruits of this new policy came in December with the reelection of Cato's St. Vincent Labour Party (SVLP) and the defeat of the United People's Movement (UPM). Some observers in St. Vincent believe Cato had direct help from Washington. What is certain is that Cato ran a very anti-communist campaign: government sound trucks patrolled the capital at 4 a.m., booming "Do not let the communists take over in St. Vincent! If you vote UPM, you vote for communism! If you have two sheep, they'll take one! If you have one sheep, they'll cut it in half!"[8] Moreover, Cato made shrewd political use of the aid which came into St. Vincent after the eruption of the island's Soufriere volcano the preceding April. Some of this aid was distributed as electoral bribes, but the larger effect was to suggest that Cato was Washington's preferred candidate:

> Cato made much of the international support that his government commanded and of the "special relationship" St. Vincent maintained with its "friends" in the region, particularly Trinidad and Barbados (two countries that helped in relief work and that were approached for help with rehabilitation loans). Cato also identified St. Vincent's "special friends" as Canada, the United States, and Great Britain. Their relief efforts, which included dramatic air lifts of some refugees and regular visits by ships, were presented as signs of tangible support which the SVLP was able to tap when in need. There was also the threat that less aid would be forthcoming should St. Vincent take the path of Grenada, a revolutionary trajectory with which the UPM was labeled.[9]

It was also at this time that the "Barbados connection" between Washington and the other Eastern Caribbean islands emerged. Two days after Cato's election, the Adams government sent Barbadian soldiers to help the Vincentian police squelch a minor uprising in one of the Grenadines, Union Island. This act heralded the role of Barbados as "regional policeman" and U.S. surrogate, as Adams announced he would send Barbadian troops to assist any government which might request them.

In Dominica, meanwhile, the interim government which replaced Patrick John had failed to lead any serious process of change, instead becoming enmeshed in scandals of its own. Dominica had been badly hit by Hurricane David in August 1979, and in January 1980, the U.S. and Britain used hurricane aid as a lever to pressure Seraphin into ousting two progressive ministers from his cabinet (Atherton Martin and Rosie Douglas).[10] Against this backdrop of government weakness and vacillation, the "Freedom Party" of Eugenia Charles, a conservative lawyer, promised strong leadership. Charles also emphasized that her ideological kinship to the incoming Reagan forces would mean economic aid and investment from the U.S. She was elected in a landslide victory in July 1980.

Finally, the St. Lucia Labour Party (SLP) of Louisy and Odlum tore itself apart in a bitter public fracas, paving the way for Compton's return to power in May 1982. The dispute was triggered by Louisy's refusal to honor an earlier agreement to hand over the leadership to Odlum. In part this reflected the unrealistic ambitions of the Odlum faction given its tenuous hold on the party machinery. It is also clear, however, that

Louisy had the support of the U.S. and England, which correctly attributed St. Lucia's earlier accommodation with Grenada and withdrawal from the coast guard to Odlum's influence.

The uproar created by the Louisy-Odlum split plunged the party into disarray. Louisy was replaced by a third SLP politician, Winston Cenac, while Odlum broke off to form the Progressive Labour Party (PLP). The Cenac administration soon became embroiled in conflict-of-interest scandals, and by January 1982, people were demonstrating in the streets of Castries for Cenac's resignation. Just as violence seemed imminent, a compromise was negotiated and an interim government formed under the PLP deputy leader Michael Pilgrim.

Although the PLP really had no clear ideology, its liberal tendencies displeased Washington. When President Reagan visited Barbados in the spring of 1982, the White House pointedly did not invite Pilgrim to the meeting between Reagan and all the other Eastern Caribbean heads of state, citing the upcoming elections in St. Lucia as the reason. The implication was that a PLP government, if elected, would not have the cooperation of the United States and might even be cut out of the Caribbean Basin Initiative. Washington's choice was obviously Compton, who ran a campaign based on promises that U.S. aid and investment would pour into St. Lucia if he were elected. In May, a tired and disgusted electorate returned Compton's UWP to power, the same party they had thrown out of office three years earlier over its anti-worker policies.

Compton's election was trumpeted by the Reagan administration as a decisive choice in favor of "free enterprise" forces by yet another Caribbean country. Immediately after the election, the U.S. rushed a special task force to St. Lucia to discuss "economic recovery and development" for the island. Yet the promise of a massive rescue effort soon faded as no new economic aid arrived.

Raised Hopes and Empty Promises: The Caribbean Basin Initiative

Reagan's boosterism of Jamaica and his emphasis on capitalist development for the Caribbean convinced many people that he planned to offer the region significant economic aid. Soon after Reagan's election, Jamaican prime minister Seaga and Barbadian prime minister Adams approached the U.S. president with their idea for a Caribbean "mini-Marshall plan," to be patterned on U.S. assistance to Europe after World War Two. In the spring of 1982, the Reagan administration announced it was sending Congress a comprehensive package of aid, trade, and investment incentives called the Caribbean Basin Initiative (CBI).

The administration made clear from the start that the CBI's real purpose was counterinsurgency. The very concept of the Caribbean "basin" was a Reaganite invention, allowing the administration to annex Central America and its guerrilla insurgencies to the traditional Caribbean and disguise additional funding for the U.S. war in El Salvador as "Caribbean

aid." In his February 24, 1982 speech launching the CBI, Reagan passed fluidly from a discussion of economic recovery to a dramatic anticommunist polemic:

> A new kind of colonialism stalks the world today and threatens our independence. It is brutal and totalitarian. It is not of our hemisphere but it threatens our hemisphere and has established footholds on American soil . . .
>
> The dark future is foreshadowed by the poverty and repression of Castro's Cuba, the tightening grip of the totalitarian left in Grenada and Nicaragua, and the expansion of Soviet-backed, Cuban-managed support for violent revolution in Central America.
>
> Nowhere in its whole sordid history have the promises of communism been redeemed . . .[11]

Behind this rhetoric was the troublesome knowledge that in much of the Caribbean and Central America, the promises of *capitalism* had not been redeemed. The Reagan administration saw its task as one of making capitalism work for the Caribbean, thereby dampening interest in alternative models; while at the same time working to discredit and destroy popular movements. In this respect the CBI resembled the Alliance for Progress, launched by the Kennedy administration in the early 1960s to prevent "another Cuba." The Alliance for Progress, however, approached its economic goals through development aid, while the CBI focused almost exclusively on private sector support.

The CBI's main planks as originally proposed were:
- Duty-free entry to the U.S. market for Caribbean-made products (minimum added value 25%) for a period of 12 years, except textiles, footwear, sugar, and rum;
- A 10% tax credit for U.S. businesses which invest in the Caribbean;
- A supplemental aid appropriation of $350 million for fiscal year 1982, to be divided among certain countries of the Reagan administration's choosing.

Announcement of the CBI caused initial excitement in the Caribbean. But as the bill's slow passage through the U.S. Congress allowed time for reflection, it became apparent that there was less to the CBI than met the eye. The duty-free provisions were of little import since 87% of all Caribbean exports already enter the U.S. duty-free under the Generalized System of Preferences. Moreover, for the smaller islands which lack the basic infrastructure required by industrial investors, they were nearly irrelevant. "If you have nothing to trade, the most liberal trade concessions are of no value to you," complained a Dominican trade union leader close to the Charles government.[12] Nothing in the CBI addressed the crucial problem of low and unstable prices for commodities like sugar, bananas, and bauxite—the chief cause of balance-of-payments problems in the region.

Both the duty-free provisions and the tax incentives were aimed primarily at U.S. corporations seeking to set up branch plants in the Caribbean. This was not surprising in light of the fact that the CBI was designed by Caribbean/Central American Action (C/CAA), a corporate-governmental group established in 1980 with financial support from multinational corporations operating in the region (including Alcoa, Gulf &

Western, Chase Manhattan Bank, Inter-Continental Hotels, Tesoro Petroleum, United Brands, and others.[13]) The concept underlying the CBI was, in fact, a recycled version of the Puerto Rican model, based on inviting foreign-owned industry to exploit cheap Caribbean labor. This provoked opposition to the CBI on the part of U.S. labor unions—which feared more runaway factories—as well as from domestic industries fearing competition from imports. Facing Congressional opposition, the administration dropped the investor tax credits, while the duty-free provisions languished in Congress until the summer of 1983.

The only part to be passed immediately by Congress, the supplemental aid, came to be seen as purely political in its motivations. In the first place, $350 million was a drop in the bucket compared to the region's $4 billion per year balance-of-payments deficit. A report produced for CARICOM asserted that the region needed $580 million in emergency aid for 1982 alone, and another $4.7 billion in external financing from 1982-86.[14]

Moreover, the distribution of the $350 million reflected Washington's political designs, not the realities of need. Initially, over one-third of the total ($128 million) was earmarked for El Salvador. This was later reduced to $75 million by Congress. Other big recipients were strategic Central American countries—Costa Rica ($70 million), Honduras ($35 million), and Guatemala ($10 million); and U.S. clients in the Caribbean—Jamaica ($50 million), the Dominican Republic ($41 million), and Haiti ($10 million). By contrast, the extremely underdeveloped Eastern Caribbean was to divide $20 million among *all of its countries*—a cold-water bath for Cato, Compton, Charles, and all the others who had promised their electorates a U.S. bail-out.

A final controversial element was the bilateral nature of the assistance. The White House reserved the right to decide who would be included in the CBI and who wouldn't; and predictably, Cuba, Grenada, and Nicaragua were excluded. All the CARICOM governments except Seaga's voiced their objection to this principle of exclusion.[15]

By 1983, what had been trumpeted as a Marshall Plan for the region no longer aroused many hopes. The one-time grant of $350 million had disappeared into the region's yawning deficit cavern with hardly a trace. Although a scaled-down version of the trade incentives was finally passed in August 1983, only 5.9% of U.S. imports from the Caribbean entered under the CBI's duty-free provisions in the first eight months of 1984.[16] When pressed on the question of Caribbean aid, Reagan continued to talk about export industry, private investment, and the CBI. But the small islands still lacked the most basic infrastructure such as roads, telecommunications and electricity that foreign investors looked for. Instead of economic aid to build infrastructure, the U.S. increased its *military* aid to the Caribbean, sending military equipment for the first time in 1982 to the tiny Eastern Caribbean islands.

The victors in the conservative "sweep" were left high and dry, facing popular expectations they could not fulfill. They had staked their political viability on a close relationship with Washington, but could do little to gain more attention other than echo Reagan's claims about a Cuban and Grenadian threat to the region. Increasingly, Grenada *was* seen as a threat, because its rising prosperity and employment contrasted embarrassingly with conditions in neighboring countries. The "threat" was that Grenada's revolution would be seen as a positive model, since more conventional models had failed.

This, then, was the situation in the fall of 1983. Dissatisfaction in the islands was palpable and growing, and the popularity of the conservative prime ministers ebbing fast. So it is not surprising that when the opportunity appeared in October 1983 to join the U.S.-led invasion of Grenada—incurring the gratitude of Washington as well as removing the troublesome Grenadian example from their ranks—the leaders jumped on board. The invasion was a last chance to solidify the patron-client bond with affluent Washington. As Eugenia Charles bluntly exclaimed, "It is going to mean more aid for us. I think America must recognize that we will require it."[17] The invasion bandwagon was the culmination of a process which began as early as 1979, as U.S. incentives and pressures helped surround Grenada with conservative, U.S.-aligned states. ■

The Grenada Invasion: Return to the "Big Stick"

The return to a predominantly militaristic strategy in the Caribbean began under the Carter administration in the fall of 1979, after a series of events (revolutions in Iran, Nicaragua and Grenada, and the Soviet invasion of Afghanistan) brought Carter under pressure to discard his human-rights approach to the Third World.[1] This shift in direction helped propel the Reagan administration into office, committed from the start to a foreign policy based on force. The militarization of the Caribbean accelerated swiftly after Reagan took office in January 1981.

With pressure against Cuba, Grenada, and Nicaragua the cornerstone of its policy, the administration systematically laid the basis for military intervention in the region. In December 1981, amid official talk of a naval blockade of Cuba, Reagan upgraded Carter's Caribbean Task Force at Key West to a Caribbean Command. This brought the whole Caribbean "basin" (the Caribbean Sea, the Gulf of Mexico, and portions of the Pacific bordering on Central America) under a unified military command for the first time.[2] It was headed by Rear Admiral Robert P. McKenzie, former commander of the Caribbean Task Force.

An important part of the new militarism was the frequent staging of naval "exercises" or war games in the region. These served two purposes: to intimidate countries considered enemies—Cuba, Nicaragua, and Grenada—and to serve as dress rehearsals for actual intervention.

From August to October 1981, Operation Ocean Venture '81 dramatically foreshadowed the invasion of Grenada which was to take place two years later. The largest peacetime maneuver by Western forces since World War Two, Ocean Venture '81 involved 120,000 troops, 240 warships and 1,000 aircraft from the United States and thirteen western nations. The Caribbean phase of the four-part maneuvers was commanded by Rear Admiral McKenzie and followed a fictional war-game scenario. A hypothetical island in the Eastern Caribbean dubbed "Amber," which has engaged in "anti-democratic revolutionary activities," seizes American hostages. After negotiations with Amber break down, U.S. forces mount an amphibious and air attack on the island to rescue the hostages. Afterwards, according to the scenario, U.S. troops stay on Amber Island until an election can be held and a regime installed which is "favorable to the way of life we espouse."[3]

This hypothetical hostage rescue mission, as the State Department called it, was rehearsed on the U.S.-controlled

U.S. Army Rangers guard captured Grenadians and Cubans on first day of the Grenada invasion.

Department of Defense

island of Vieques, part of Puerto Rico. Everyone in the Caribbean understood "Amber" to refer to Grenada, which resembles Vieques in size and terrain. The mock invasion of Vieques matched the later real invasion of Grenada in many details, including a pre-dawn drop of 300 paratroopers, an amphibious landing of Marines, and intervention of an Army contingent. Units of the 75th Ranger Division which later invaded Grenada took part in the Vieques maneuver.

Ocean Venture '81 was the first of what became an almost continuous series of U.S. military maneuvers in the region's waters. The following spring, Ocean Venture '82 again simulated the invasion of a hostile island. This time, Navy families from the U.S. base at Guantanamo were "evacuated" to the aircraft carrier Guam in a further elaboration of the hostage rescue scenario.

A second major aspect of the Reagan strategy was the militarization of various Caribbean countries and their integration into regional alliances under U.S. control. This had three interrelated elements:

- The "Caribbeanization" of Puerto Rico, stressing Puerto Rico's Caribbean identity in order to facilitate its role as a U.S. surrogate in the region;
- The emergence of Jamaica and Barbados as U.S. surrogates in the English-speaking Caribbean;
- Militarization of the small islands of the Eastern Caribbean, culminating in the formation of a five-nation "regional defense force" to surround and isolate Grenada.

Caribbeanization of Puerto Rico. "In the last two years, the government of Puerto Rico has discovered the Caribbean," wrote militarism expert Jorge Rodriguez Beruff in 1982. "The delay in making this discovery should not be too surprising in a country that until a short time ago was geographically located—for advertising purposes—somewhere in the Atlantic Ocean, near the Eastern Seaboard of the United States, and in some cases just off the island of Manhattan."[4]

The official myth that Puerto Rico is part of the U.S., used to attract industry and disguise the island's colonial status, has given way to a rediscovery of Puerto Rico's Caribbean identity. This new emphasis permits Washington to increase its military involvement in the Caribbean without appearing to be an imperial power.

In March 1981, the Puerto Rican governor, Carlos Romero Barcelo, traveled to Panama for a briefing on the political and military situation in the Caribbean from officials of the U.S. Southern Command. He was accompanied by the commander of the Puerto Rican National Guard and the Chief of Civil Defense. Later, Romero met with Secretary of State Alexander Haig to discuss Puerto Rico's "leadership" role in the administration's Caribbean plan.[5]

Long a military bastion for the United States in the Caribbean, Puerto Rico is home to the Roosevelt Roads Naval Station, the largest U.S. naval base in the hemisphere. In preparation for Puerto Rico's expanded military role, the administration undertook a large-scale expansion of Roosevelt Roads. It also reopened the Ramey Air Force Base, closed for over ten years, and reactivated an underground Navy communications network in the nearby town of Aguada. A powerful military communications tower was moved from Panama to Puerto Rico for use in communicating with U.S. nuclear submarines.

Besides its physical location in the Caribbean, Puerto Rico possesses another attribute of interest to the administration—a Spanish-speaking army, the Puerto Rican National Guard (PRNG). Considered one of the most "efficient" of the U.S. national guards, the PRNG has increased in size from 7,000 in the early 1970s to 11,000 in 1980.[6] From 1980-81, federal spending on the PRNG jumped from $3.6 million to $5.4 million, reflecting the Reagan administration's plans to use the Guard for external intervention in the region.[7] The PRNG participated alongside regular U.S. and NATO forces in Ocean Venture '81 and '82, and in January 1983, units of the PRNG were sent to Honduras to take part in the Big Pine military maneuvers on the Nicaraguan border. Puerto Ricans also have increasingly served the U.S. as elite troops and advisors in Central America, and recruitment of Puerto Ricans for the regular U.S. armed forces has risen sharply.[8]

Surrogate role of Barbados and Jamaica. One task of the Puerto Rican National Guard is to train soldiers from other Caribbean countries. Members of the Barbados Defense Force (BDF), the Jamaica Defense Force (JDF), and the army of the Dominican Republic were trained in Puerto Rico in 1980, 1982 and 1983, receiving U.S.-sponsored military training behind a facade of intra-Caribbean cooperation.[9]

Jamaica and Barbados have emerged as U.S. partners in the region for several reasons. The Jamaican security forces have a history of collaboration with the U.S., and the Jamaica Defense Force is the largest army in the Commonwealth Caribbean. Additionally, Jamaica is a leader in setting political trends in the English-speaking Caribbean, and the rise of Seaga made the island available to the Reagan administration for the kingpin role in its regional strategy.

Barbados emerged as the U.S. ally in the Eastern Caribbean partly by inclination—it has a pro-British, pro-American political culture—and partly by default. Washington initially turned to the Tom Adams government after the prime minister of Trinidad, Eric Williams, rebuffed U.S. overtures aimed at enlisting Trinidad's cooperation in the U.S. campaign against Manley in Jamaica.[10] Later, Adams' personal hostility toward the Grenada revolution together with Barbados' proximity to Grenada made Barbados the obvious choice for an active anti-Grenada role.

Since Reagan took office, the United States has been building up and financing both the Jamaican and Barbadian defense forces. U.S. military aid to Jamaica went from zero during the Manley administration to over $4 million in 1984 to train and equip the 5,000-man JDF.[11] Barbados first received U.S. military assistance in 1981, and in 1982 received $2 million in military equipment and training for the BDF. State Department presentations to Congress in that year stated bluntly that Barbados " . . . has supported U.S. global and regional interests," and justified expansion of the Barbados Defense Force "in light of continuing Cuban support for the radical government in Grenada."[12]

Member of U.S. 82nd Airborne instructs Caribbean soldiers who provided token multinational presence in the Grenada invasion. Countries which joined the invasion signed a U.S.-backed regional defense pact in 1982.

Formation of the Regional Defense Force. Along with U.S. military aid to Barbados and Jamaica came, for the first time, military allocations for the mini-states of the Eastern Caribbean. Initially this meant small sums (about $60,000 per island) for military training. Less important than the quantity of aid, however, was the link being established between the U.S. and the police forces of the small islands, paving the way for their integration into a regional military alliance.

This occurred in the fall of 1982. Since entering office, the Reagan administration had been building ties to conservative leaders in Barbados, St. Vincent, St. Lucia, Dominica and Antigua; and in October 1982, this marriage of convenience took on a military aspect with the formation of a Security and Military Cooperation Pact among the five islands. It was the Caribbean "coast guard" which the U.S. had long sought, presented in terms of its usefulness for controlling smuggling and illegal immigration, search and rescue, and pollution control.[13] The force was headquartered in Barbados and financed through specially allocated U.S. military aid ($3 million in 1984).[14]

The regional leaders' real interest in the "coast guard" was accidentally revealed when Prime Minister Vere Bird of Antigua announced that the force would hinder revolutionaries from taking power in the islands. For the Reagan admini-

stration, the regional pact had an additional purpose: to surround Grenada with a U.S.-controlled military alliance of conservative states.

There was a fourth aspect of the Reagan administration's preparations for military action against Grenada, and that was the preparation of U.S. public opinion. The constant talk of hostages was one aspect of this, playing on U.S. fears and anger after the Iranian hostage experience. Another was heightened anti-Cuba propaganda, such as a State Department "White Paper" which made unsubstantiated charges that Cuba was arming and training left-wing parties all over the Caribbean. In March 1983, Reagan delivered his famous "Star Wars" speech in which he declared that Grenada was a threat to U.S. national security. Displaying aerial spy photographs of the airport under construction at Point Salines—which, as Maurice Bishop later pointed out, could just as well have been taken with an instamatic camera at the totally unrestricted site—the President described the new airport as a sophisticated military installation. The allegations came a month after the *Washington Post* published details of a covert destabilization plan which the CIA had prepared against Grenada in the summer of 1981. The plan was said to have been scrapped because of objections from the Senate Intelligence Committee.[15]

Prime Minister Eugenia Charles of Dominica meets with President Reagan, Secretary of State George Shultz and national security advisor Robert McFarlane in the White House on the morning of the invasion. Charles extended the invitation to the U.S. to invade, ostensibly on behalf of the Organization of Eastern Caribbean States.

White House photo

The Grenada Invasion

All these political and military preparations fell into place in the pre-dawn hours of Tuesday, October 25, 1983, after internal developments in Grenada provided the U.S. with its long-sought opportunity to invade. Tragically, it was a split within Grenada's ruling party and the death of Prime Minister Maurice Bishop which caused the revolution to collapse and opened the door to the U.S. attack.

Divisions and tensions had been mounting within the New Jewel Movement since the summer of 1982, although this was unknown to all but a few persons outside the party's inner circle. The context was one of intense pressures on the Grenadian leadership—caused by U.S. hostility, by popular expectations in the face of economic constraints, and by a severe shortage of trained, experienced people to carry out government programs. In this pressure-cooker situation, in which top-level party and government leaders were over-worked and frequently exhausted or ill, both the efficiency of the ruling party and its rapport with the Grenadian people began to suffer. This led to growing friction and arguments over who was to blame, with criticism often framed in ideological rather than personal terms [see Part VII, Ch. 1].

In September 1983, a majority of the New Jewel Movement's Central Committee decided to institute joint leadership of the party between Prime Minister Bishop and Deputy Prime Minister Bernard Coard, a decision subsequently ratified by the NJM's 60-odd full members. This decision was to be kept secret from the Grenadian people because of their attachment to Bishop, who had always been sole party leader. Bishop initially accepted the idea, but subsequently asked for the matter to be reopened. This angered the party's Central Committee, a majority of whose members supported Coard. In the tense days between October 8 and October 15, Bishop was accused of spreading a rumor that Coard planned to kill him, an accusation Bishop denied. Finally, on October 13, the NJM Central Committee had the prime minister put under house arrest.

Bishop's arrest was the first time ordinary Grenadians knew there were any problems within the party. They reacted with fury: pro-Bishop demonstrations snowballed, and party members met with angry rejection when they tried to convince the people that Bishop was at fault. On Wednesday, October 19, a large crowd moved up to Bishop's house and freed him and education minister Jacqueline Creft. Chanting, "We get we leader," the crowd carried the two to Fort Rupert, an army administrative post, while Coard and his supporters gathered at Fort Frederick on the opposite side of town. Soon afterward, three armored cars and a truckload of soldiers rolled up to Fort Rupert and fired on the crowd. As people fled the scene in panic, soldiers led Bishop, Creft, ministers Unison Whiteman and Norris Bain, and labor leaders Fitzroy Bain and Vincent Noel into the inner courtyard of the fort and shot them.

That night, General Hudson Austin announced the formation of the Revolutionary Military Council (RMC), a sixteen-man governing junta, and imposed a round-the-clock, shoot-on-sight curfew affecting the whole island.

The first conversations regarding possible military action in Grenada to which the U.S. State Department admits took place between Washington officials and Caribbean leaders on October 15, four days before the killings occurred in Grenada. However, unnamed "top Jamaican government officials" later told the *Washington Post* that the Reagan administration had "for several months" been urging Caribbean states to isolate Grenada and to consider military action against the island.[16] The Army Ranger battalion which parachuted into the Grenada airport on October 25 had in fact practiced the maneuver more than a month earlier, from September 23 to

October 2, at a remote municipal airport in eastern Washington state. The manager of the site says the military sought to avoid publicity about the exercise, which resembled the later invasion in many details.[17]

On Friday, October 21, the prime ministers of Antigua & Barbuda, Dominica, St. Lucia, St. Vincent and the Grenadines, St. Kitts-Nevis and Montserrat gathered in Barbados to decide what to do about the Grenada situation. They were joined at their meeting by Prime Minister Adams of Barbados and by a high-ranking U.S. official, Deputy Secretary of State for Inter-American Affairs Charles Gillespie. Out of that meeting came the "urgent invitation" for the United States to intervene militarily in Grenada. The invitation was offered on behalf of the Organization of Eastern Caribbean States (OECS), even though that body's charter called for unanimous decisions and one OECS member—Grenada—was neither present nor consulted. Later, Jamaican prime minister Edward Seaga arrived to take part in the invasion planning.

Five of the inviting countries plus Barbados and Jamaica sent token contingents of troops or policemen to accompany the U.S. invasion force. (Montserrat, a British colony, did not send forces.) The largest contingent consisted of soldiers from the Jamaica Defense Force, followed by a unit from the Barbados Defense Force.

Puerto Rico and Barbados provided the primary bases for launching the invasion. The Ranger battalion which led the assault was transported to Roosevelt Roads naval base in Puerto Rico several days in advance. In the pre-dawn hours of October 25, according to a Navy newsletter, Roosevelt Roads was "swinging into action to support the front line forces" going into Grenada, including the "largest group of C-130's

U.S. Major captures a souvenir.

Barbados *Nation*

[troop transport planes] ever brought together at the same time since Danang."[18]

Meanwhile, the Caribbean soldiers and policemen assembled in Barbados, which made its Grantley Adams International Airport available as the staging site for the assault. The U.S. Embassy in Bridgetown served as political command center, overseeing the evacuation of the U.S. medical students from Grenada, coordination between the invading nations, and press relations (which consisted of keeping the press away from Grenada while dispensing the Pentagon and White House version of events).

Perhaps no other political/military event in recent history has been such a masterpiece of deception as the Grenada invasion. By barring the press from the island for the first two days, the White House and the Pentagon achieved total control over information dispensed by the media during the crucial period when public opinion was being formed. Much of this information later turned out to be false, as the *New York Times* detailed in an article entitled "In Wake of Invasion, Much Official Misinformation by U.S. Comes to Light."[19]

Pentagon spokesmen denied up to the last minute that an invasion was underway, saying on the night of October 24 that they knew of no plans for U.S. military action in Grenada.[20] This statement arrived on American breakfast tables the morning of the 25th, as 1,900 Marines and Rangers were bearing down on the island in helicopters and parachutes. Admiral Wesley McDonald, commander of the U.S. Atlantic forces, stated at a news conference that there were at least 1,100 Cubans in Grenada, all "well-trained professional soldiers." Subsequently the State Department admitted that only 784 Cubans—the number given by the Cuban government—were in Grenada, and that the majority were ordinary workers.

The administration insisted that the invasion had not resulted in any known civilian casualties, a position it maintained through October 30. Only after reporters discovered a bombed-out mental hospital strewn with the bodies of patients did the Pentagon admit that a Navy plane had "inadvertently" bombed the hospital on October 25, the first day of the assault.[21]

The official deception went beyond specific falsehoods, however, to embrace the entire rationalization for the invasion and the context in which it was presented to the American people. The administration's first justification for the action was that it was a "rescue mission" to save American students at the St. George's University medical school in Grenada from the threat of being taken hostage. This was a deliberate attempt to play to the strong emotions which even a potential hostage seizure was guaranteed to arouse in the United States. In reality, there was no evident hostage threat and no reason that the students could not have been evacuated peacefully. After the takeover by Coard's military junta, school officials were already in discussion with General Austin regarding protection of the students and arrangements for their departure. On Saturday, October 22, two counselors from the U.S. Embassy in Bridgetown visited Grenada, talked with school officials and with Austin and concluded that there was no immediate danger to the students. Deputy Secretary of State Kenneth

U.S. med students: were they ever in danger?

Department of Defense

Dam later testified to Congress that the State Department had no information that any Americans were either harmed or threatened after the coup took place.[22]

But the White House did not want the students evacuated peacefully; it wanted an invasion. The U.S. ambassador based in Barbados, Milan Bish, telephoned officials of the medical school in New York, seeking a statement of concern for the students and a request for U.S. intervention. The officials declined. While Canada and Britain were arranging charter evacuation flights for their nationals, the U.S. government was making no attempt to evacuate Americans, but was instead deep in planning for the military attack. The White House statement that Grenada's airport was "closed" on Monday, the day before the invasion, was a lie. Four charter planes flew in and departed on that day, carrying out foreign nationals.[23]

While the Reagan administration was talking about the safety of the students, the leaders of Barbados, Jamaica, and the small islands presented the issue in terms of the need to rescue Grenada from the clutches of the Revolutionary Military Council (RMC). The brief reign of the RMC was indeed a bitter experience for Grenadians. After the army's slaughter of Maurice Bishop and five other leaders, the 24-hour, shoot-on-sight curfew angered and frightened the population. Something clearly had to be done, but it is not clear that invasion was the necessary action. The larger community of English-speaking Caribbean nations—CARICOM—had already drawn up plans for a non-violent resolution of the crisis. Meeting in Trinidad on Saturday October 22 and Sunday October 23, the emergency CARICOM summit decided to apply sanctions which would force the RMC to the negotiating table, aimed at an immediate return to civilian government and early elections. These sanctions included Grenada's suspension from CARICOM and all CARICOM trade arrangements. Additionally, no new currency issues would be made to the regime by the East Caribbean Central Bank; and all air and sea links with Grenada would be cut. Foreign nationals would be evacuated peacefully and a CARICOM peace-keeping force deployed on the island.[24]

Only if these sanctions failed to work would the use of force be considered. Prime Minister Chambers of Trinidad asserted in his speech to the Trinidad Parliament that . . .

> . . . force, be it regional or extra regional, should not be the first resort in respect of a sister CARICOM state.[25]

There was every reason to believe that the RMC would have responded to these pressures. The Central Committee members had erred fatally in their takeover, both by assuming that they could strong-arm Grenadians into accepting the change, and by assuming Cuba would support them. Confronting a hostile population, with no external support whatsoever, the RMC was in a quite untenable position by five days after Bishop's death.

The CARICOM plan was never given a chance to work. By Friday, before the U.S. had even lined up its "urgent invitation" from Caribbean allies, the flotilla of U.S. warships had been diverted from Lebanon and was steaming toward Grenada. As Errol Barrow, leader of the Barbadian opposition, later wrote:

> . . . Reagan's mind was made up; like a sheriff whose posse was ready to mount, some of them on donkeys, he rode into town with guns ablaze looking for an enemy.[26]

Guns ablaze and looking for an enemy.

White House photo

127

Within hours after the attack, questions were being raised about the validity of the administration's stories. Statements by officials of the medical school raised doubt about the danger to the students, while an examination of the so-called "invitation from the Organization of Eastern Caribbean States" revealed it to be a legal fiction. Under pressure to justify the use of U.S. troops in combat, President Reagan deftly turned to a new theme in his televised address of Thursday, October 27. Grenada was "a Soviet-Cuban colony being readied to export terrorism and undermine democracy . . . We got there just in time," intoned the president.

Like the hostage story, this was highly successful from a public relations point of view. However, it relied on fantasy—what the *New York Times* called "misleading factual allegations to bolster President Reagan's unproven assertion that the invasion was necessary to prevent a Cuban military takeover."[27] Nothing in any of the documents made public by the administration supported its claim that a terrorist training base existed or that Cubans planned to take over Grenada. The weapons found in Grenada—mostly antiquated small arms and ammunition—belonged to the civilian militia, and were intended for defense of the island against the long-expected U.S. attack.

All of this and more gradually entered public and congressional debate. That debate, however, was largely preempted by the administration's public opinion coup. Faced with overwhelming public support for the invasion in the U.S., Congressional liberals retreated rather than take an unpopular position.

The real reasons for the invasion had nothing to do with the students' safety or with an altruistic response to a call for help. Rather, the decision reflected the Reagan administration's need to win a victory—however small—after a four year campaign to "roll back communism" which had produced only U.S. frustration in its main arena, Central America. Grenada was an easy target, both because of its miniature size and because the death of Bishop destroyed the will of most Grenadians to resist. At a deeper level, the U.S. public's support for the invasion revealed the fears and insecurities of a population which had never come to terms with the limits of U.S. hegemony or with the growing anti-imperialist consensus in the Third World. As a vocal critic of U.S. imperialism, Grenada came to be seen as a symbol of this Third World defiance, stimulating North American desires for revenge. As Vice Admiral Joseph Metcalf III proclaimed with satisfaction when it was over, "We blew them away."[28]

At the peak of the occupation, there were over 6,000 U.S. troops in Grenada. This was one for every 18½ Grenadians, or the equivalent of a 14 million man army occupying the United States. Most of these troops came home in December 1983, leaving behind several hundred U.S. military police, the 400-man Caribbean Peace Force, and a psychological warfare team whose job was to whip up anticommunist and pro-American sentiments among Grenadians. The troops' withdrawal marked the opening of a new stage in U.S.-Caribbean relations. Temporarily at least, Washington had turned the tide forcefully against the regional left and in favor of U.S. neocolonial control. Afterward, the administration took steps to consolidate that control so that radical change couldn't happen again. ∎

Graffiti in U.S. soldiers' barracks in Grenada.

Corinne Johnson

BRIEF CHRONOLOGY OF THE INVASION

September 1982	Deputy Prime Minister Bernard Coard resigns from the New Jewel Movement's Central Committee, citing dissatisfaction with the workings of the party under Maurice Bishop's leadership.
September 1983	Central Committee meets to discuss low morale of the party and "crisis" in the revolution. Proposal to divide leadership of the party between Bishop and Coard is approved by a majority and accepted in principle by Bishop. Bishop leaves for a trip abroad.
October 8-12	Bishop returns and announces he has reconsidered on joint leadership question. He is accused of spreading a rumor that Coard plans to assassinate him.
October 13	Central Committee places Bishop under house arrest.
October 13-18	Attempts to mediate between Bishop and Coard supporters within the party fail. Popular demonstrations escalate demanding Bishop's release.
Wednesday, October 19	A large crowd frees Bishop and Jacqueline Creft from house arrest and carries them to Fort Rupert.
	Some time later, armored personnel carriers roll up to the fort and fire on the crowd. Army officers take Bishop, Creft, Unison Whiteman, Norris Bain, Fitzroy Bain and Vincent Noel into the fort and execute them.
	"Revolutionary Military Council" announces its control and decrees a round-the-clock, shoot-on-sight curfew.
Thursday, October 20	U.S. naval task force headed for Lebanon is diverted to Grenada.
Friday, October 21	Leaders from Barbados, Antigua, Dominica, St. Lucia, and St. Vincent meet with Reagan administration officials in Bridgetown, Barbados and issue invitation to the U.S. to militarily intervene in Grenada.
Saturday-Sunday, October 22-23	Emergency CARICOM summit meets in Trinidad and decides on diplomatic and trade sanctions against RMC. Summit is not informed of invasion plan.
Monday, October 24	Curfew is lifted in Grenada. Airport opens and four chartered planes evacuate foreign nationals.
	U.S. troops begin arriving in Barbados. Pentagon spokesmen say they know of no plans for U.S. military action in Grenada.
Tuesday, October 25	U.S. invades Grenada massively, encountering resistance from members of Grenadian army. Popular militia, demoralized by Bishop's death, does not fight. U.S. concentrates heaviest attack on Cuban workers at construction site of new airport. Some 48 Cubans are killed and the remainder captured and interrogated by U.S. intelligence.
November	U.S. mounts sweeping intelligence operation in Grenada to identify supporters of Bishop government. Hundreds of Grenadians are interrogated about their political beliefs; most are released but some 50 are detained in prison without charge. Homes are searched by U.S. troops looking for "Cubans and leftists." U.S. psychological operations teams from Fort Bragg, NC mount anti-communist propaganda campaign.
November 15	"Interim government" of Grenadians is named to run island temporarily. U.S. and Caribbean troops remain until April 1985 as occupation force and to train new Grenadian military and police.

NOTES TO PART FIVE

A Pattern of Military Interventions

1. U.S. Department of State, "Congressional Presentation: Security Assistance," FY 1984.
2. President Lyndon Johnson, televised address, May 2, 1965.

IMF and Banks

1. Center for International Policy, "Central America: The Financial War" (Washington, DC: C.I.P., March 1983).

2. *Ibid.;* also, Lars Schoultz, *Human Rights and United States Policy Toward Latin America* (Princeton: Princeton University Press, 1981), Chapter 7.
3. Caleb Rossiter, "Would an Anti-Apartheid Amendment 'Politicize' the IMF?" (Washington, DC: Center for International Policy, May 4, 1983).
4. Center for International Policy, "Central America: The Financial War."
5. *Latin America Regional Reports - Caribbean,* March 31, 1983.
6. "U.S. Charged with Bias in IMF Votes," *Wall Street Journal,* May 18, 1983. The WSJ obtained the original version of the suppressed study, which was done by Cornell University professor Caleb Rossiter for the Congressional Research Service. A modified summary was later released by Rossiter as a Center for International Policy publication (footnote 3).

7. Rossiter, p. 4.
8. Norman Girvan, Richard Bernal, and Wesley Hughes, "The IMF and the Third World: The Case of Jamaica 1974-80," *Development Dialogue* (1980), p. 113.
9. Prime Minister Manley, Speech to the Nation, January 5, 1977.
10. Girvan et al., pp. 125-127.
11. *Ibid.,* pp. 125-126.
12. *Ibid.,* p. 154.
13. United Nations Centre on Transnational Corporations, *Transnational Banks: Operations, Strategies, and their Effects in Developing Countries* (New York: United Nations, 1981), pp. 22-23.
14. Maurice Odle, *Multinational Banks and Underdevelopment* (New York: Pergamon Press, 1981), p. 55.
15. Hilbourne Watson, "Transnational Banks and Crisis in the Capitalist World Economy: Impacts on the Caribbean" (Paper presented at Symposium on the Impact of Transnational Corporations on the Caribbean, Universidad Nacional Autonomo de Mexico, May 18-20, 1983).

AIFLD

1. Ronald Radosh, *American Labor and United States Foreign Policy* (New York: Random House, 1969), chapter 1.
2. *Ibid.,* p. 350.
3. *Ibid.,* p. 372.
4. George Morris, *CIA and American Labor: The Subversion of the AFL-CIO's Foreign Policy* (New York: International Publishers, 1967), pp. 63-66.
5. Radosh, p. 388.
6. Morris, p. 83. Information reported by an official of the CIO who visited Guatemala two weeks after the coup.
7. Richard Hart, "Trade Unionism in the English-speaking Caribbean: The Formative Years and the Caribbean Labour Congress," in Susan Craig, ed., *Contemporary Caribbean* (Trinidad: S. Craig, 1982), Vol. II, pp. 89-91.
8. F.A. Hoyos, *Grantley Adams and the Social Revolution* (London: Macmillan, 1974), p. 178.
9. Hart, pp. 71-84.
10. Serafino Romualdi, *Presidents and Peons: Recollections of a Labor Ambassador in Latin America* (New York: Funk & Wagnalls, 1967), p. 343.
11. Radosh, pp. 393-405.
12. Jamaica *Daily Gleaner,* September 8, 1963, cited in Jeffrey Harrod, *Trade Union Foreign Policy: A Study of British and American Trade Union Activities in Jamaica* (London: Macmillan, 1972), p. 295.
13. Philip Agee, *Inside the Company: CIA Diary* (New York: Stonehill Publishing Co., 1975), p. 243.
14. Hearing, Senate Committee on Foreign Relations, August 1, 1969, p. 55.
15. EPICA interview with former official of Seaman and Waterfront Workers Union, Grenada, September 1981.
16. Radosh, p. 422.
17. The issue gained wide publicity when Victor Reuther, International Affairs Director of the United Auto Workers, accused AIFLD of working with the CIA.
18. William C. Doherty Jr., radio broadcast, July 1964.
19. Radosh, pp. 400-404.
20. AIFLD, Annual Progress Report for 1983.
21. *Ibid.*
22. EPICA interview with Monali, August 1982.
23. EPICA interview with Ronald Clarke, Caribbean Union of Teachers, May 1984.
24. *Ibid.*
25. *AIFLD Report,* September-October 1983.
26. Ralph E. Gonsalves, "The Trade Union Movement in St. Vincent and the Grenadines" (mimeographed paper, April 1983).
27. EPICA interview with George Walters, Antigua Workers Union, September 1982.

The Media

1. Jeremy Tunstall, *The Media Are American: Anglo-American Media in the World* (New York: Columbia University Press, 1977), chapter 5.
2. Hugh Cholmondeley, UNESCO Caribbean Representative, "Media's Changing Sights," *Caricom Perspective,* May-June 1984.
3. Stewart M. Hoover, "Report of the Special Study Committee on Emerging Communication Technologies in National Development" (INTERMEDIA, 475 Riverside Dr., New York, NY), p. 32.
4. *Ibid.,* pp. 4, 25.
5. Tunstall, p. 140.
6. *Ibid.,* pp. 225-226.
7. Fred Landis, "The CIA and the Media: IAPA and the Jamaica Daily Gleaner" *Covert Action Information Bulletin,* No. 7 (December 1979-January 1980), pp. 10-11.
8. *New York Times,* February 18, 1967.
9. Landis, "The CIA and the Media," p. 11.
10. *The Daily Gleaner,* April 13, 1984, p. 3.
11. Fred Landis, "CIA Media Operations in Chile, Jamaica and Nicaragua," *Covert Action Information Bulletin,* No. 16 (December 1981).
12. *Ibid.*

13. Fred Landis, "Psychological Warfare in the Media: The Case of Jamaica" (Press Association of Jamaica, 1980).
14. Ramesh Deosaran, "Government vs. the Pen," *Caribbean Contact,* March 1984. A survey of coverage of Grenada in the Trinidad *Express* and *Guardian* from March 14, 1979 to October 19, 1983 found that, of the 288 stories which could be judged favorable or unfavorable to the PRG, 79% were unfavorable.
15. "Towards an Understanding of the Caribbean: A Report of the Proceedings and Recommendations of the Seminar for Caribbean Publishers and Broadcasters" conducted by the Caribbeana Council, Washington, DC, June 22-24, 1981.
16. Deosaran, p. 9.
17. *Guild Forum,* October 31, 1978.
18. *Washington Post,* March 3, 1983.
19. Quotations from *Washington Post,* June 3, 1985.

Elections, Economic Aid and CBI

1. George Beckford and Michael Witter, *Small Garden . . . Bitter Weed: Struggle and Change in Jamaica* (London: Zed Press, 1980), p. 137.
2. *Ibid.,* p. 126.
3. EPICA interview with a Jamaican economist, September 1983.
4. Fitzroy Ambursley, "Jamaica: From Michael Manley to Edward Seaga," in F. Ambursley and Robin Cohen, eds., *Crisis in the Caribbean* (New York: Monthly Review Press, 1983), p. 93.
5. Jack Johnson-Hill, "Unheard Voices: Jamaica's Struggle and the Multinational Media" (unpublished paper, 1981).
6. *Latin America Regional Reports - Caribbean,* January 18, 1980, p. 1.
7. *Washington Post,* September 28, 1980, p. 1.
8. EPICA interview with St. Vincent Union of Teachers, August 1982.
9. Philip Nanton, "The Changing Patterns of State Control in St. Vincent and the Grenadines," in Ambursley and Cohen, p. 239.
10. *Latin America Regional Reports - Caribbean,* January 18, 1980, p. 1.
11. President Ronald Reagan, address before the Organization of American States, February 24, 1982.
12. EPICA interview with Charles Savarin, Dominica Civil Service Association, August 1982.
13. Washington Office on Latin America, "Economic Aspects of the Caribbean Basin Initiative."
14. *Caribbean Contact,* May 1982, p. 1.
15. CARICOM foreign ministers endorsed the principle of non-exclusion of any state from the CBI at their conference in Belize in April 1982.
16. U.S. Commerce Department statistics.
17. *Washington Post,* December 17, 1983, p. A27.

The Grenada Invasion

1. Jorge Rodriguez Beruff, "Militarization and the Caribbean Basin Initiative," *Puerto Rico Libre!* Vol. VI, No. 4, p. 4.
2. *Washington Post,* November 24, 1981.
3. Rear Admiral Robert P. McKenzie, press conference, August 9, 1981, Vieques, Puerto Rico.
4. Rodriguez Beruff, p. 3.
5. *Ibid.,* p. 3.
6. Governor of Puerto Rico, 1982 Budget, cited in *Intercambio* (Caribbean Project for Justice and Peace, Rio Piedras, P.R.), No. 4, April 1983, p. 17.
7. Budget of Puerto Rico figures, cited in *Ibid.,* p. 17.
8. *San Juan Star,* February 8, 1982.
9. *Intercambio,* No. 4, April 1983, p. 18.
10. EPICA interview with Dr. James Millette, University of the West Indies, Trinidad, August 1982.
11. U.S. State Department, "Congressional Presentation: Security Assistance," FY 1982.
12. *Ibid.,* FY 1984.
13. "Congressional Presentation: Security Assistance," FY 1982.
14. *Ibid.,* FY 1984.
15. *Washington Post,* February 27, 1983.
16. *Washington Post,* October 27, 1983.
17. Pacific News Service report, *Cleveland Plain Dealer,* November 3, 1983.
18. *El Navegante,* Vol. 8, No. 12, December 1983.
19. *New York Times,* November 6, 1983, p. 20.
20. *Washington Post,* October 25, 1983.
21. *New York Times,* November 6, 1983.
22. Testimony November 2, 1983 to the House Foreign Affairs Committee, cited in W. Frick Curry, "Grenada: Force as a First Resort" (Washington, DC: Center for International Policy, January 1984).
23. *New York Times,* November 6, 1983.
24. Speech by Trinidad Prime Minister George Chambers to Trinidad Parliament, October 26, 1983.
25. *Ibid.*
26. *Caribbean Review,* Fall 1983, p. 4.
27. *New York Times,* November 6, 1983.
28. *Washington Post,* November 6, 1983, p. 1.

Introduction

The Caribbean entered the eighties in a state of growing crisis. North Americans, preoccupied with their own declining affluence, scarcely noticed that some 25% of the Caribbean work force was unemployed; that declining commodity prices had pushed several countries to the brink of bankruptcy; or that even "model" economies like that of Barbados were beginning an ominous decline. But for Caribbean governments, the perilous economic state of the region became the overwhelming concern. And in the poor villages and barrios of the region, talk turned increasingly to the question of survival.

The decline allowed employers to go on the offensive and reverse labor gains of the 1970s. A number of transnational corporations, facing slack markets in oil, bauxite and sugar or simply reorganizing their global operations, prepared to pull out of the region. They used the threat of their departure to extract concessions from governments and labor unions, including reduced corporate taxation, layoffs and dismissals, give-backs of benefits, and wages which lag behind the rising cost of living.

Most seriously, the crisis forced a number of countries to turn to the International Monetary Fund for loans, submitting their economies to the IMF's harsh prescription. Massive layoffs, frozen wages and spiraling prices for food and fuel have made survival increasingly tenuous for the poor majority in these countries. The explosion of riots in the Dominican Republic and Jamaica in 1984 and 1985 signalled the start of long-feared social protest against this deepening impoverish-ment.

In those territories still under colonial rule, the economic situation has set back attempts to build a strong pro-independence movement. Puerto Rico, the French Antilles and the Netherlands Antilles all receive colonial subsidies which have partially buffered the impact of recession. This has allowed opponents of independence to argue that the loss of subsidies would leave the colonies "as poor as the rest of the Caribbean."

For the independent countries of the region, the crisis has stimulated two contradictory trends. On the one hand, it has reinforced neocolonial dependency by renewing the emphasis on securing aid and support from outside the region—the economic (or military!) "rescue mission." This has opened the door wider to U.S. domination, allowing Washington to impose its economic and ideological models as a condition for aid. At the same time, however, the crisis is laying the basis for future change by demonstrating the failure of the U.S. and IMF-imposed models. Sectors of the poor and working population are now highly politicized in some countries, injecting a new dynamism into the scene even as the organized left struggles through its most difficult period in years. The outcome of these conflicting trends is far from decided; all that can be said with certainty is that poverty and repression are bound to increase before a solution to the region's suffering is found. ∎

INDEPENDENT COUNTRIES: EASTERN CARIBBEAN

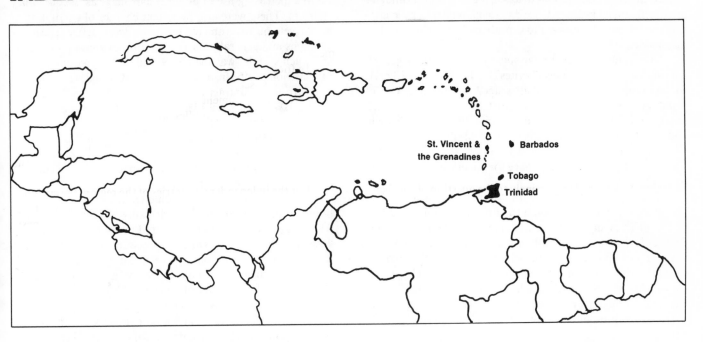

St. Vincent & the Grenadines

Barbados

Tobago
Trinidad

Trinidad & Tobago: "Capitalism Gone Mad"

At the southern tip of the Windward Island chain, nine miles off the coast of Venezuela, lies the twin-island nation of Trinidad & Tobago. Like Jamaica, Trinidad is an economic and political leader in the English-speaking Caribbean. It is a place where trends are made and broken—as in 1962, when the withdrawal of both Trinidad and Jamaica from the West Indies Federation spelled the end of the federal venture. Since the 1970s, Trinidad & Tobago's oil-based economy has been the wealthiest in the region, making the country's 1.2 million people the major market for intra-regional trade. The end of the oil "boom" in 1982 has not only spelled disaster for Trinidad, therefore, but has been a negative blow to its CARICOM trading partners as well.

The history of Trinidad & Tobago has left it with an ethnic and cultural mix unique within the English-speaking Caribbean. Originally a Spanish colony, Trinidad gave haven to several thousand French royalists fleeing Guadeloupe, Martinique and Haiti during the French revolution. By the 1790s, Trinidad had changed from a "backward Amerindian colony governed by Spain into a Spanish colony run by Frenchmen and worked by African slaves."[1] Britain conquered Trinidad in 1797 and took possession of it under the Treaty of Paris in 1814. In 1889 the neighboring British island of Tobago was annexed to Trinidad.

After the emancipation of the slaves, the British brought in hundreds of thousands of indentured laborers from India to work on Trinidad's sugar estates. The East Indians became the backbone of the country's agricultural peasantry, while the freed slaves moved away from the estates to form an incipient urban working class. In 1857, oil was discovered in southern Trinidad, and U.S.-based oil companies arrived in the early 20th century. Oil accounted for almost 60% of Trinidad and Tobago's exports by 1935, the rest consisting mainly of sugar and cocoa. The growth of the oil sector set Trinidad apart from most of the Caribbean islands, where the peasantry predominated and the working class was small. It meant that the Trinidadian masses were split very early into industrial and agrarian sectors, broadly corresponding to the racial split between blacks (in the oil industry and urban areas) and East Indians (in the rural sugar-growing areas). Tobago, however, remained almost entirely black.

A second major factor which shaped the country's history was the construction of the U.S. naval base at Chaguaramas during World War Two. With "Yankee dollars" pouring into the economy, many people left their homes to seek work on and around the base, further enlarging the working class and superimposing North American influences on the already complex Trinidadian cultural scene.

The presence of the base also influenced the anti-colonial nationalist movement which flowered after the war. Led by black intellectuals, it was embodied in the People's National Movement (PNM) of Dr. Eric Williams, a scholar educated at Oxford in England and later in the United States. Williams welcomed foreign investment, which he saw as a basis for industrializing Trinidad, but rejected colonial and neocolonial political control. On April 22, 1960, the PNM led a march through Port-of-Spain demanding that the U.S. give Chaguaramas back to Trinidad to become the capital site for the

West Indies Federation. This struggle, together with Trinidad's relative financial independence due to oil, rendered its leadership comparatively resistant to capture by U.S. influence after independence in 1962.

"The center of West Indian society as a culture *sui generis* is Trinidad and not Jamaica," writes Gordon K. Lewis.[2] This is so, he argues, because Trinidad escaped the stifling effects of prolonged unbroken British rule. Instead, its culture is a rich amalgam of African, East Indian, Spanish, French, British, and North American influences. In addition, the division within the ruling class between British Protestants and French Catholics allowed breathing space for a working-class culture to develop.

Trinidad is best known for the pre-Lenten festival of Carnival, which draws on both the French Catholic tradition of Mardi Gras and the black emancipation celebration called Canboulay. Trinidadian culture is flavored by the irreverent wit and *picong* (exchange of personal insults) of the calypsonians, who perform their new compositions each year at Carnival time [see Part VII, Ch. 4]. In much the same vein, electoral campaigns are marked by ribald mud-slinging and personal rivalries, often at the expense of substantive political issues.

The Boom

Over the past decade Trinidad and Tobago has experienced a different kind of carnival: a national spending spree which began after OPEC raised the world price of oil and bloated the Trinidad economy with windfall profits. Construction, commerce, and real estate speculation boomed as oil dollars were spent on luxuries or channeled into projects like the glossy Riverside Plaza and the US$100 million Caroni racetrack complex (complete with 700 air-conditioned stables for the horses). Suddenly it was a seller's market for labor power. Real wages rose steadily, while unemployment fell from 17% to 11% in ten years. The high demand for labor and the use of jobs as political patronage caused a relaxation of workplace discipline (some public workers signed off at 10 a.m.!) as well as escalating corruption.

Oil money transformed the face of Trinidad. Port-of-Spain streets are lined with Kentucky Fried Chicken outlets and dozens of imitators, traffic jams clog the narrow streets, rock music blares from radios, while blue jeans sell for TT$80 a pair in the capital's many import emporiums. Easy credit made it possible for many working families to buy color televisions, refrigerators, washing machines, air conditioners, even late model cars and video cassette recorders.

Eric Williams, who ruled uninterrupted from 1956 until his death in 1981, once said that in Trinidad & Tobago "Money is not the problem." He never said what the problem was, but the chaos and corruption in the society reached shocking proportions by the time of his death. Telephones, electricity, and running water functioned sporadically, reflecting an infrastructure overwhelmed by the boom and a civil service described by one of the country's top economists as "horrendously inefficient, badly organized, and at top levels . . . backward and incompetent."[3] This resulted in part from the

PNM's increasing use of political patronage as the oil money rolled in. There were also persistent charges of corruption at high levels of government, but these were deftly fielded by Williams and generally shrugged off by a cynical population. One such scandal was the DC-9 deal, in which a high public official took a bribe from the McDonnell Douglas corporation in return for a contract to sell aircraft to Trinidad's national airline, BWIA. In April 1983, the corruption issue again blew open when Johnny O'Halloran, a former minister in the Williams government and a close confidante of Williams, was accused in court of taking a US$1.4 million kickback from a U.S. financier in exchange for the main construction contract on the Caroni racetrack project.[5]

Trinidadians enjoyed the unfettered consumerism of the boom, which came to be jokingly called the *fete* (party). But while many profited, others suffered in the mad scramble to keep up with rising prices and the pressures of a society in rapid flux. As multimillion dollar projects bid up the price of land and building materials, housing became scarce and unaffordable, driving the economically marginal into squatters' settlements on vacant land. Many people, while better off materially than before, wondered what would happen when the bubble burst. The Mighty Sparrow expressed some of these anxieties in his 1983 calypso "Capitalism Gone Mad":

You have to be a millionaire
Or some kind of petty bourgeoisie
Anytime you living here in this country
You have to be a sculduggery
Making your money illicitly
To live like somebody in this country
It's outrageous and insane
The crazy prices here in Port of Spain . . .
Where you ever hear a television costs seven thousand dollars?
Quarter million dollars for a piece of land
A pair of sneakers two hundred dollars
Eighty to ninety thousand dollars for motor cars
At last here in Trinidad we see capitalism gone mad . . .

The Crash

"The fete is over," announced newly-elected PNM Prime Minister George Chambers in 1982, "and the country must go back to work."[6] Trinidad & Tobago's oil boom peaked in 1978, and by 1983 the crash was a reality. As the world price of oil declined, the U.S. multinationals—Texaco, Amoco, and Tesoro—virtually ceased exploration for new Trinidadian crude. At the same time, the companies steadily cut back on processing in their aging Trinidad refineries in favor of new refineries in the Middle East and the United States.

Initially Trinidad refused to accept that the boom was really over. Export revenues fell 18% in the first half of 1982, but spending on imports leapt ahead by 23.4%.[7] By 1984, however, few people entertained any illusions about the country's predicament.

Trinidad & Tobago's standard of living, subsidized for nearly a decade by windfall oil prices, is now seriously threatened. Its foreign reserves have been halved in barely two years; in the same period it moved from a balance of payments surplus to a deficit of over TT$2 billion; the oil industry is struggling to hold production levels at two-thirds of the 1979 figures, and refining has virtually collapsed; government revenue from oil fell by a quarter in 1983 alone.[8]

The crash has been a rude come-down for the working class as thousands of jobs have been lost with the oil companies and their subcontractors. Employers have taken advantage of the widespread fear of job loss to weaken unions and make demands, focusing on "higher productivity"—meaning cutbacks in numbers of employees—and lower wages. Some employers have implemented new technologies permanently reducing their need for labor, while all have pushed for wage restraint and give-backs of benefits previously won by unions. There have even been attempts to deregister certain unions as bargaining agents by employers acting through the government's Industrial Court.

To conserve foreign exchange, the Chambers government has raised personal income taxes and removed many subsidies, allowing prices of food, fuel, transport and utilities to rise. This has eroded the economic position not only of workers but also of many small entrepreneurs and others in the middle and lower-middle class. From the unions' point of view, the major question is that of who assumes the burden of sacrifice in a time of economic contraction. They argue that workers are being made to bear the brunt of the slowdown, while the profits of the multinationals and large conglomerates (like Trinidad's Neal & Massy and McEnearney-Alstons) hold steady. The Oilfields Workers Trade Union (OWTU), the most powerful union in the country, comments:

> All these measures adversely affect working people. None of them affect the very rich or the businessmen since increased costs can always be passed on to the consumer.
> . . . Not only are the burdens being placed on the backs of the working people while the rich get richer, but the underlying structure of the neocolonial economy remains unaltered.[9]

Indeed, a striking aspect of Trinidad's experience is the failure to transform the economy during the decade-long boom. It was basically an "import boom": productivity in non-oil sectors rose hardly at all, and in agriculture it declined, leaving the country with a TT$900 million yearly food import bill. The oil revenues were not used to diversify the economy away from its dependence on oil. Before his death, Williams

Oilfields Workers Trade Union leads May Day march through Port-of-Spain. Tubal Uriah Butler, with white beard, waves from truck.

OWTU

did attempt to lay the basis for such a shift by creating a new sector of natural gas-fueled heavy industries clustered at the Point Lisas industrial estate. But these industries—iron, steel, ammonia, urea, and methanol—faced depressed world markets, and thus far have been a net drain on the treasury.

The government failed from early on to deal decisively with the multinationals. Despite repeated calls for nationalization of the country's oil resources—something the OWTU has advocated since 1937—such moves came only after the companies' profits declined and they opted out. Over the past few years, the government has attempted to keep the companies in Trinidad by lowering taxes on their production and granting many other concessions. This has decreased government revenues by millions of dollars but in the end had no impact on the multinationals' plans. In 1985, Texaco completed its withdrawal by selling its huge but rundown Pointe-a-Pierre refinery to the Trinidad government.

That year as well, the government announced that the money-losing Iron and Steel Company of Trinidad and Tobago (ISCOTT) would be leased to a joint venture company in which 40% of the shares are held by the California-based Bechtel Corporation and another U.S. firm. The move reflects a new, more accommodating approach to foreign investors—and heralds a probable growing involvement of U.S. capital in the Trinidad economy.

Challenge to the PNM

The ruling party is taking much of the blame for the economic crisis, and this, together with the death of Eric Williams, has rendered the People's National Movement politically vulnerable for the first time in a generation.

Brilliant, arrogant and eccentric, Dr. Williams totally dominated the politics of Trinidad & Tobago during the 25 years of his rule.

> . . . Williams as ideologue, statesman and politician almost singlehandedly ran the whole show, towering over everyone else. He cultivated this situation by weeding out from his party anything and anybody who appeared to be a threat to his supremacy . . . [10]

The People's National Movement stayed solidly in power through a formidable race-based party machinery and a fragmented opposition. The only serious challenge to its hegemony arose after the Black Power protest of 1970, when oil and sugar workers from both ethnic groups formed the United Labour Front in 1975. But the ULF split after two years, becoming predominantly Indian, and there has been no further success at creating a racially unified labor-based party.

The lack of a united opposition and entrenched PNM predominance was sufficient to get the party reelected under Chambers after Williams' death in 1981. But in July 1984, the ULF and several smaller opposition parties came together in a coalition called the National Alliance for Reconstruction (NAR). Although this hodgepodge of anti-PNM elements lacked political clarity, the economic crisis and PNM corruption lent automatic legitimacy to a unified opposition bid.

Shortly thereafter, the NAR won an unexpected victory in local elections in Trinidad—and suddenly a credible threat to the PNM had emerged.

One member of the NAR was the Democratic Action Congress (DAC), based in Tobago. It controls the Tobago House of Assembly and also Tobago's two seats in the Trinidad & Tobago Parliament, and symbolizes the long-standing autonomist sentiments of many Tobagonians. The PNM has long smoldered over Tobago's autonomist challenge, and in November 1984, the ruling party decided to make an all-out bid to regain control of the House of Assembly in Tobago's local elections. The entire PNM machinery swung into action. Prime Minister Chambers staked his personal prestige on the outcome, even taking up official residence in Tobago for the duration of the campaign. ("We will bury him in Tobago," proclaimed the DAC leader in typical picong style.) In the end, the PNM suffered a humiliating defeat as the DAC—supported by the National Alliance for Reconstruction—swept 11 of the 12 seats.

As the countdown begins to the 1986 national elections, Trinidad & Tobago finds itself in political limbo. After two successive rebuffs to the PNM, the mystique and authority with which Williams invested the party has worn thin. Possibilities for patronage have declined now that oil money no longer lubricates the economy, and the party is ridden with factionalism. But the defeat in Tobago does not mean that smashing the PNM in its Trinidad heartland will be easy. While riding a wave of popularity, the NAR (now renamed the National Alliance of Trinidad & Tobago) is far from a stable or ideologically unified force. It is a marriage of convenience between unlikely partners, including the Tobagonian DAC, the Indian-based ULF, the small Tapia House Movement, and the right-wing, business-oriented Organization for National Reconstruction (ONR). The ONR, led by the authoritarian Karl Hudson-Philips, is viewed with mistrust by many in Trinidad & Tobago, and fear of the ONR was a key factor in returning the PNM to power after Williams' death.

The failure of the opposition to define an alternative to the PNM program reflects, in turn, persistent divisions within the trade unions and the working class. Recently there have been renewed attempts to bring about trade union unity, including cooperative activities between the opposing labor camps leading up to a joint May Day celebration in 1983. But in 1984, separate celebrations were again held by each faction amid bitterness and recriminations.

Trinidad has an array of small left parties whose ideological fragmentation and sectarianism has precluded the emergence of a unified progressive force. The National Joint Action Committee (NJAC) has contested elections since 1980, but its emphasis on cultural issues has failed to sustain the dynamism of its leadership role in the 1970 uprising. The strongest progressive force in the country, the Oilfields Workers Trade Union, is not a party, and is struggling to maintain its clout in the face of declining economic leverage. If the PNM falls in '86, it will reflect not the positive challenge of new ideas, but the disgruntled popular rejection of a ruling party which failed to find alternatives to the impending crisis when it still had a chance. ∎

St. Vincent & the Grenadines: Small Island Woes

To understand what the Grenada revolution meant to the people of the Caribbean, one should begin by traveling northward up Windward and Leeward chain. In these tiny, underdeveloped island nations—St. Vincent, St. Lucia, Dominica, Antigua and the rest—one finds many of the problems, minus the deranged Gairy, of prerevolutionary Grenada. And in the contrast between these countries and Grenada during the revolution, one sees not only where Grenadians came from, but how far they had to go to break with the past and build something new.

On St. Vincent's rugged volcanic slopes, 114,000 people eke out a living growing the island's two export crops: bananas and arrowroot (a starchy tuber). Like Grenada's bananas, cocoa and nutmeg, these crops face depressed world markets, especially in recessionary times. Most of the foreign exchange from exports goes to pay for imported food. St. Vincent's mountainous terrain is traversed by broken roads little better than tracks, and much of the island lacks running water and electricity.

There are other, deeper similarities between St. Vincent and pre-1979 Grenada. Grenada was led to independence by Eric Gairy, who dominated Grenadian politics for 28 years. His Vincentian counterpart was Milton Cato, who was elected in 1967 and governed St. Vincent for 15 of the next 17 years. Both are members of the generation of Caribbean leaders who rose through the labor movement but soon settled into a neglectful and repressive rule. The hallmark of such governments has been stagnation. Little is done at the top to develop the country because of disinterest, corruption, and lack of resources. And little can be done at the bottom, because people are subtly discouraged from acting together to improve their situation. To a Gairy or a Cato, any grassroots organization, even on purely local issues, presents a potential challenge to their rule.

The dependency syndrome is entrenched in St. Vincent. People have always assumed that they will be taken care of—initially by England, and more recently by the United States. They accept that most decisions which affect them lie

Abandoned village stands covered with ash after eruption of St. Vincent's Soufriere volcano in 1979.

Barbados *Nation*

outside their hands and usually outside the island. Toward their own political process, many Vincentians have long been alienated and cynical. Elections are seen as a change from "a few men to a few men" within the context of the same corrupt system.

Agriculture: No Respect

> Agriculture is the major earner of foreign currency to St. Vincent and the Grenadines. It also takes care of employment for more than 50% of the working population especially in rural areas yet agriculture in St. Vincent and the Grenadines is never treated with respect.[1]

This complaint from *The Farmer* newsletter reflects a problem found throughout the Caribbean. Countries which depend on agriculture remain mired in low productivity, technical backwardness, and monoculture. Governments proclaim agriculture to be the "backbone" of the economy, yet no one really supports the peasant farmer. In St. Vincent, for example, banks made only 6.8% of their loans to the agricultural sector in 1981.[2] It is much easier to get a loan to buy a car than to get one to buy land.

Bananas account for over 60% of St. Vincent's agricultural earnings. The sole buyer is Geest, the British multinational which markets Windward island bananas in the U.K. Farmers have no choice but to accept Geest's prices, which fluctuate depending on demand in Britain and on Geest's charges for a variety of services. The major problem in recent years has been the declining value of the British pound against the strong U.S. dollar. While Geest's prices are quoted in pounds sterling, the Eastern Caribbean currency used in St. Vincent is pegged in value to the U.S. dollar. The exchange rate disadvantage means less real income for St. Vincent and its farmers.

The arrowroot industry, for its part, is on the verge of collapse. Arrowroot starch is used in food processing and for certain industrial uses such as coating computer paper. It is not a high-demand product, and it faces competition from cheaper substitutes. Vincentian farmers also grow food, mainly the traditional Windward island root crops like yams and tannia, which grow well on steep land. Internal marketing for these crops, however, is rudimentary—produce grown on one side of the island is not usually sold on the other side, so that all buyers and sellers must travel to Kingstown, on the southern tip of the island.

Most Vincentian farmers are smallholders, cultivating plots of less than five acres. The 1972 agricultural census—the last taken—showed 88.6% of farms accounting for only 23.5% of arable land, while 0.3% of the farms controlled 53.8% of the total.[3] Since then, the Vincentian government has responded to the land hunger of the peasants by acquiring a number of large private estates and leasing them in small subdivisions. Besides providing the opportunity for patronage to party supporters, this fragmentation encourages the farmers to continue to function as isolated individuals on uneconomically small holdings. Farming cooperatives, which could raise productivity on St. Vincent's marginal soils, have not been encouraged by the government.

Another problem affecting land tenure is foreign ownership, especially in the Grenadines. These small islets which stretch south from St. Vincent are known as vacation spots for the rich and famous, many of whom own or lease portions of land. The island of Mustique is leased to the Mustique Company and sub-leased by celebrities including Mick Jagger and Princess Margaret (Mustique made headlines when British Prince Andrew vacationed there with his friend Koo Stark). Palm Island is controlled by a Texas businessman, John Caldwell, and foreigners also own land on Bequia and Canouan.

The traditionally unorganized character of the Vincentian peasantry has begun to change slowly in recent years. A first turning point was the eruption of Soufriere, the cloud-shrouded volcano which bathed much of the island in deadly ash on April 13, 1979. Many farmers lost their land, reconstruction aid did not come or was used as bribes by the government, and the whole experience forced some people to begin questioning the wisdom of passively depending on the powers that be. After the disaster, farmers from the devastated northwest part of the island organized themselves in anticipation of receiving aid from the St. Vincent Christian Council. The aid never came, but the farmers persisted with their organization, and the North Leeward Farmers Movement was born. Working with progressive elements of the Catholic Church, the group sought loans, markets and assistance on a collective basis for its members.[4] A year later, the National Farmers Union was formed to fight against "years of neglect, against a stigma of inferiority, and against the separateness of farming communities." Both groups represent efforts to breach the individualism of the peasantry and improve their bargaining position with respect to the outside forces which control their livelihood.

The Pico Affair

The traditional response to agricultural backwardness in the Caribbean is not to develop agriculture, but to invite in foreign industry in hopes that factories will provide jobs for those displaced from the rural sector. The concept underlying this strategy is "jobs at any price." The price exacted by foreign investors is two-fold: low wages and passive unions, or no unions at all.

Minimum wage in St. Vincent and the Grenadines is US$5.00 per day for men and $3.85 per day for women.[5] Women make up the majority of the work force in the handful of electronics and garment firms operating outside Kingstown. Like many Caribbean countries, St. Vincent promises investors a "cooperative" industrial climate,[6] and there is no compulsory trade union law.

In St. Vincent, moreover, the head of the largest union is Burns Bonadie of the Commercial Technical and Allied Workers Union (CTAWU), who is close to the St. Vincent Labour Party of his uncle, Milton Cato. At the time of the Pico affair, the Cato government was in power and Bonadie was parliamentary secretary in the Ministry of Trade and Agriculture. He also was linked to the United States through the American Institute for Free Labor Development, serving as

Milton Cato, ousted in 1984.

head of the Caribbean Congress of Labour until 1983 [see Part V, Ch. 3].

In February 1984, a dispute broke out between the CTAWU and Pico Ltd., a New York-based electronics firm assembling cable TV parts in St. Vincent. It centered on the firing of a CTAWU shopsteward, Louise Glasgow, who was subsequently judged by the Labour Commissioner to have been unfairly dismissed. Pico refused to reinstate her and instead closed the plant, locking out 136 employees and demanding as a condition for reopening that the union no longer represent the workers. Company officials actually left the island, leaving matters in the hands of their lawyer who was also a parliamentary senator of the Labour party.

Three weeks later, a "settlement" was reached in a meeting between Pico, CTAWU officials, and Prime Minister Cato, and the company reopened its doors. Under the terms of the settlement, Pico agreed to rehire 90% of the locked-out employees in return for a "cooling off" period of several months in which union activity would be replaced with negotiation by an internal grievance committee.

The ink was hardly dry on the Cato-Pico agreement when it became clear that the company had pulled off a masterful stroke of union-busting. Instead of rehiring 90% of the workers—a provision which in itself would have permitted the exclusion of union activists—Pico selected some 60 workers of whom less than 40% were union members.[7] Within a week of their employment, pressures were brought to bear on the latter group, and the CTAWU received a batch of nearly identical letters from the workers saying they no longer wanted the union to represent them. With the union out, the "grievance committee" set up by Pico looked suspiciously like a precursor to a company union.

As Vincentians reflected on what had happened, their anger rose. Everyone knew that wages paid by Pico had risen because of the presence of CTAWU at the plant; yet the company had been able to bust the union simply by threatening to leave the island. Since foreign investors use only imported materials and do not pass technical skills on to nationals, St. Vincent probably could not have continued to operate the plant if the company pulled out. The incident therefore aroused emotions of anti-Americanism unusual for St. Vincent, with Pico seen as typical of U.S. corporations which exploit cheap Caribbean labor and refuse to respect unions. "Is this what we are going to get from the Caribbean Basin Initiative?" demanded one local paper.[8]

The second major impact was to raise doubts about the CTAWU leadership, its links to the ruling party and to the United States. People felt that Bonadie had given in too easily and saw this as reflecting his closeness to the Cato regime, which in turn had proved willing to sell out the workers' interests to a U.S. corporation. At a deeper level, therefore, people began to perceive the contradictions of a situation in which the company, the union, and the government were all directly or indirectly tied to the United States.

Exit Cato

In July 1984, in a surprising upset, Vincentians threw out the Labour Party which had dominated the island's politics for so many years. Corruption, economic stagnation and repression were the issues which brought 80% of the electorate to the polls to deliver a stinging rebuke to Cato, one of the senior politicians in the region.

The victor was James F. "Son" Mitchell, the main opposition politician who earlier served as premier in a coalition government from 1972-74. He is from Bequia, with his political base in the Grenadines. Currently riding a wave of popularity, Mitchell is a liberal reformer who believes that social and economic problems are serious and must be tackled by working within the existing system. He has emphasized land reform, including tighter controls on foreign ownership of land. At the same time, the pro-business Mitchell does not favor state investment in productive enterprise, but says government's role is to provide infrastructure for the private sector.[9]

Despite the in-between nature of Mitchell's proposed reforms, his victory over Cato was significant. It showed that the mechanisms through which the neocolonial generation of leadership has held onto power are seriously eroded, and indeed the Labour Party has largely faded from the scene with Cato's defeat and subsequent retirement from politics. The defeat was especially telling since Cato had called the election early, expecting to catch the opposition unprepared. "Cato felt very secure," said one Vincentian observer. "He didn't understand the mood of the people for change."[10] ■

Barbados: Hard Times on a "Model" Island

When British settlers first arrived in Barbados some 350 years ago, they found the flat, uninhabited island "better agreeing with the temper of the English Nacion" than its mountainous, Carib-dominated neighbors.[1] With its gently rolling terrain, Barbados was ideal for colonial sugar plantations. Britain claimed Barbados in 1605 and did not leave until independence in 1966, making it the one British Caribbean possession never held by any other colonial power.

The consummate plantation society, Barbados was so valuable to the British that they concentrated on its development, building roads and public services far superior to those on neighboring islands. Socially, Barbados developed as an ultra-conservative, anglophile society, dominated by a white planter-merchant elite with cultural roots in Victorian England. For the black majority, however, life was physically circumscribed by the omnipresent cane fields and socially defined by a rigid system of class and color distinctions. After emancipation, the outlet for many was emigration.

Barbados' special relationship with Britain has been partly supplanted, in the 1980s, by a special friendship with Britain's neocolonial replacement: the United States. The U.S. State Department proclaims that "as the most developed nation in the Eastern Caribbean, Barbados serves as a model for the entire region."[2] Indeed, the country boasts nearly universal literacy, superior social services, and a history of strong trade unionism and non-repressive government. The Barbadian economy is doing somewhat better than others in the region. But the experience of the early eighties, when the U.S. recession dragged Barbados down with it, illustrates the perennial vulnerability of dependent Caribbean economies. Economic recovery in the U.S. and Canada eventually restored positive growth to Barbados; but this growth remained largely based on the country's ties outside the region, with all the risks and constraints that implies.

"Tourism is Vital"

Unlike Jamaica or Trinidad, Barbados had no bauxite or oil to which it could turn to offset the decline of sugar in the 20th century. Tourism became its boom industry of the sixties, trading on the island's special "English" atmosphere and image of social tranquility. The west and southwest coasts became a manicured stage set of pastel hotels, shops and "vacation villas" into which the Caribbean reality rarely intruded. As elsewhere, the tourists bought not local products but foreign imports: English crystal and bone china, Scotch tweeds and European perfumes, palm-tree ashtrays manufactured in Taiwan, food jetted in from the United States. With tourism the country's biggest source of foreign exchange, it became crucial for Barbadians to welcome the pale outsiders descending on the island every winter, and to suppress any resentment over playing the servile roles of waiter and chauffeur. Government advertising on Bridgetown buses warns Bajans: "Tourism is vital. Play your part. Make a friend for Barbados today."

The tourist industry continued to expand rapidly through the 1970s, but in the 1980s the U.S. recession applied the brakes. Tourist arrivals fell by 5% in 1981 and by 17% in 1982, combining with low sugar prices and the closure of some U.S.-owned factories to drag the entire economy into negative growth for the first time in two decades.[3]

Economic pressures brought suppressed class and racial tensions closer to the surface. Compared to countries like the Bahamas or the U.S. Virgin Islands, where high-volume tourism has produced explosive strains, Barbados prides itself on its placid social relations. But it is still a quietly stratified society, where until recently skin color was firmly linked to social class. Today, the once all-powerful mercantile elite is visibly symbolized by the row of large department stores they own along Bridgetown's Broad Street. Over the past two decades these families have branched out into manufacturing and tourism, often in partnerships with U.S. investors. So while several large hotels are owned by foreign multinationals—such as the prestigious Sam Lord's Castle, owned by the Marriott Corporation—many of the small and medium-sized businesses in the tourist sector are owned by white, near-white and brown-skinned Barbadians.

This leaves the bottom ranks of society to hustle for the tourist dollar, from taxi drivers and tour guides to vendors peddling coral jewelry along the beaches and even "beach boys" offering sex to tourists in search of exoticism. In 1982, controversy flared when the chairman of the Barbados Tourist Board, Jack Dear, a wealthy man with close ties to the oligarchy, criticized the jewelry vendors for harassing tourists and suggested that their presence on the beaches be curbed. Although targeted specifically at the vendors, his statement touched a sensitive nerve among working-class youth in general, who interpreted it as an attempt to bar them from the beaches and make them second-class citizens in their own country. The upsurge of indignation was expressed in a calypso called "Jack":

Jack don't want me to bathe on my beach
Jack tell dem to kick me out ah reach
Jack tell dem I will nevah mek de grade
Jack tell dem: strengthen security, build barricade . . .

Dat can't happen here in dis country
I want Jack to know dat the beach belong to we
Dat can't happen here over my dead body
Tell big guts Jack dat the beach belong to we.

The establishment tried to portray "Jack" as a provocative racial protest which would threaten the tourist industry. It was, in fact, a more profound critique, in which the reserving of beaches for the exclusive use of tourists became a symbol for the selling out of the Caribbean birthright to foreigners. "Jack" was popular not only in Barbados but throughout the English-speaking Caribbean, reflecting submerged anger over the need to pander to tourists and the frustration of those marginalized from economic power.

Offshore Paradise

Even before the recession, it was clear that sugar and tourism alone could not sustain Barbados. For one thing, both are seasonal, and the long summer period of idleness strikes both industries together. The strategy Barbados has chosen for the future is a typically Caribbean one: to become an "international business center" where foreign banks, insurance companies and manufacturers can take advantage of low taxes and labor costs.

Although Barbados has an established garment industry, the island is basically priced out of the assembly market by cheaper wage havens like Haiti. It sees its future instead in high-technology industries which pay higher wages and require more skills. Barbados already has some ten U.S.-owned electronics firms, including TRW, Corcom, Aerotron, and Micro Data. Intel, the largest, manufactures micro-processors and computer chips with a work force of over 1,000. In addition, Barbados is the beneficiary of a new trend in runaway firms: offshore office work. Advanced satellite technology now enables large U.S. firms to ship tasks such as data entry and word processing overseas, where they can pay one-fifth the wages office workers earn in the U.S. American Airlines, for example, has moved its entire ticket-processing operation from Tulsa, Oklahoma to Barbados, where it pays Barbadian workers US$2.50 an hour.[4]

It is no accident that Barbados attracts these firms. The manager of Intel's Barbados plant explained to *Business Week* that while his plant has to pay higher wages than Intel's other branch plants in Malaysia and the Philippines, the company chose Barbados as a "politically stable site to cover its exposure in other parts of the world."[5] In exchange for its higher wage scale, Barbados offers investors a haven from social protest and the assurance of a close alliance with the United States.

This bargain was effectively sealed in October 1983, when the government of Prime Minister Tom Adams capped three and a half years of allegiance to the Reagan administration by offering Barbados as the base for the U.S. invasion of neighboring Grenada. While Adams had his own political dispute with the Grenada revolution, his role in the invasion

Tourist and vendor on a Barbados beach.

also had economic implications, given Barbados' dependence on the confidence of U.S. investors. As *Business Week* put it, "Grenada hasn't hurt."[6]

This prediction was seemingly confirmed when, immediately following the invasion, the U.S.-owned St. George's University medical school left its campus in Grenada and set up temporarily in Barbados. It soon began negotiating with the Adams government for permission to establish a permanent campus. As the oldest of the U.S.-owned medical schools which dot the Caribbean, St. George's considers itself the respectable elite of an industry tainted by its profit-making status and an image of low standards (most students at the offshore schools have failed to gain admission to medical schools in the United States). But for Barbados, it was one more welcome source of income. "We have a policy of promoting Barbados as a center for offshore business activity and the medical school is an offshore activity that comes highly recommended," said a government minister.[7]

Thus the Adams government was stunned when a storm of controversy erupted over the siting of the U.S. school. The Barbados Association of Medical Practitioners argued that the influx of foreign students would crowd local teaching hospitals and jeopardize standards at the highly-regarded University of the West Indies medical school. At the popular level, there was an outcry when the school brought in 15 corpses to Barbados—for use in anatomy classes—apparently without permission or monitoring by the Barbadian government. This not only offended the conservative religious values of many Barbadians, but suggested that the American school regarded itself as above local law and unaccountable to the Barbadian authorities. The school thus became both symbol and scapegoat for the country's dependence on foreign interests, and suggested, to some, an excessive subservience on the part of the Adams government toward the United States. "The medical school is a manifestation of a deeper selling out of sovereignty by the government," proclaimed opposition politician Branford Taitt.[8]

In spite of a 2.9% economic growth rate in 1984, there were troubling reminders that the economic crisis hovered just offshore. Joblessness that year rose to 18.3%, its highest level in a decade.[9] The Barbados Workers Union lost one-sixth of its members between 1981 and 1984 due to layoffs and job losses.[10]

The unexpected death of Prime Minister Tom Adams on March 11, 1985 left behind a nation more uncertain of its path than ever before. Under Adams' successor, former Deputy Prime Minister Bernard St. John, the course remained set for growth as an offshore center based on high-tech industries and tourism. But the success of this model clearly would depend upon outside forces: the strength of the U.S. economy, the viability of the electronics market, the confidence of U.S. investors, and—ultimately—on Barbados' image as a close U.S. ally. For many Barbadians, the tentative recovery could not erase fears about the future nor the impact of unemployment in the present. And for a few, there was the beginning of cautious new doubt about the course Adams had charted for the country and the lengths to which the Washington alliance might require Barbados to go. ∎

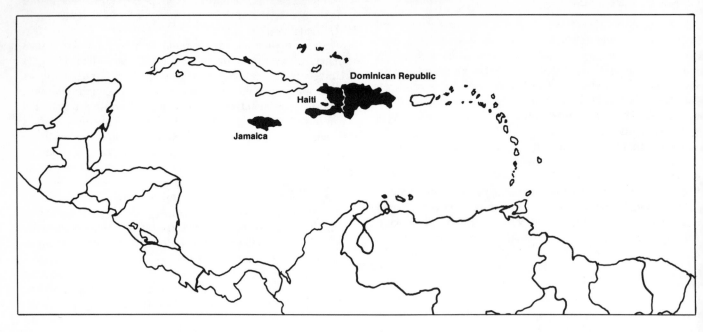

The Dominican Republic: Society Without Solutions

For the troubled Dominican Republic, the free and fair election which brought Juan Bosch's Dominican Revolutionary Party (PRD) to power in 1963 appeared to open a new era of democratic rule after 31 years under the brutal dictator Trujillo. But for the Trujillista loyalists, the Dominican military and oligarchy, the conservative Catholic hierarchy, and U.S. business, Bosch's moves toward constitutional and land reform were seen as no less than a revolutionary takeover. Bosch was overthrown by a military coup on September 25, 1963, after only seven months in office.

Two years later, his supporters took to the streets in the famous April 1965 insurrection, "la guerra de abril." Although the uprising was broad-based and demanded a return to constitutional rule, for the United States it was too threateningly close in time and geography to the Cuban revolution. Using the trumped-up charge of a communist threat, President Lyndon Johnson ordered 22,000 U.S. Marines to invade the country, leaving 3,000 Dominicans dead on the streets of Santo Domingo. Dead also was any genuine democracy for the next twelve years.

Whether or not the election held in 1966 was technically without coercion, the atmosphere of the time was anything but free. Stunned by the firepower of the Marine invasion, bowed by poverty and fearful for the future, tens of thousands of PRD supporters and others fled into exile in New York City. Those Dominicans who remained on the island filed to the polls in shock to elect the candidate chosen by the U.S.: Joaquin Balaguer, former right-hand man of Trujillo, symbolizing to many a return to the "peace" of Trujillo's time. The mood of

ambivalence and cynicism over the return to foreign dependence was reflected in T-shirts worn around Santo Domingo that summer which read: "*Vete Yanqui y Llevame Contigo*" (Get Out Yankee and Take Me With You).

Balaguer collaborated with the U.S. government to smash the remaining Dominican popular forces. U.S. military and police trainers were sent in to reorganize the Dominican security forces and link them to their U.S. counterparts. The streets of Santo Domingo and other cities became the scene of bloody repression against youth and other suspected dissidents; Dominican jails were full of political prisoners, while the government continually harassed trade unions and other popular organizations. Only in exile in New York City did Dominicans experience anything close to freedom of speech and association.

The Trujillo economy, although personally dominated by the dictator's family and cronies, had been basically nationalistic in nature. Balaguer, by contrast, ushered in a period of foreign corporate takeovers in all the important sectors of the economy. One of his first acts as president was to invite in the U.S. multinational Gulf + Western, which took over the South Puerto Rico Sugar Corporation and went on to build a sprawling Dominican empire including sugar holdings, cattle raising for export, and luxury tourism. President Johnson promised G + W that if another April rebellion should occur, Washington would again intervene to protect U.S. interests. The U.S. also made loans and grants to finance construction of an infrastructure for foreign investors, including roads, electricity, water and housing, primarily in the area around Santo

Domingo. Several "free zones" were established where foreign-owned industries could set up under tax exemptions and non-union conditions.

The foreign corporations had virtually free rein to exploit Dominican workers. Gulf + Western, for example, was able to maintain artificially low wages for its sugar cane cutters and millhands by crushing the main union in La Romana, the Sindicato Unido. In July 1966, a right-wing Cuban exile named Teobaldo Rosell was put in charge of the La Romana operation. He mounted a vicious union-busting campaign without protest from the Dominican government:

> The Union's property and bank account were seized, its meetings were regularly broken up, and a new spy system was introduced into the mill and fields. But the union continued to fight, led by its leader Guido Gil. On January 16, 1967, Gil disappeared from La Romana; his body has never been recovered.[1]

Because of high world sugar prices and the influx of U.S. aid, Balaguer's strategy initially produced impressive economic growth. The foreign exchange earned by the government, however, was spent primarily on imports to raise the quality of life for the upper and middle class, mainly in Santo Domingo. By contrast, small farmers and independent tobacco growers could not market their produce, and much peasant land was taken over by large and medium-sized landowners producing for the export market. As a result, the country's import bill for foodstuffs alone soared to nearly $200 million a year.[2]

Furthermore, to satisfy the greed of military and business interests frustrated by their exclusion from profit-making during the Trujillo era, Balaguer permitted rising corruption. Dozens of those newly in power became millionaires through bribes and kickbacks, while in the slums and rural areas, workers and peasants languished.

This unrelieved impoverishment combined with constant repression was eventually to produce Balaguer's downfall. Campaigning on a platform of opposition to human rights abuses, Francisco Peña Gómez reunified the PRD into a strong opposition party in both Santo Domingo and New York. The PRD emerged as the unexpected winner in the 1978 national elections, prompting Balaguer to attempt a military takeover to prevent the PRD's return to power. But the Dominican ruling class and the Carter administration, fearing a repeat of the 1965 uprising, stepped in and forced recognition of the democratic vote.

Popular Forces Reemerge

The PRD had gone through internal convulsions during the Balaguer years. Juan Bosch, its founder, had split from his popular spokesman Peña Gómez and founded the Dominican Liberation Party (PLD). Within the PRD itself, new leadership emerged in the person of Antonio Guzmán, representing the interests of medium-sized landowners, and Jacobo Majluta, favored by upcoming middle-class business entrepreneurs. Neither Guzmán, who became president, nor Majluta as vice-president had links to or really believed in the Dominican workers and peasants, the rank-and-file of the PRD's constituency. As a multi-class party, the PRD was still based on an anti-Trujillo, anti-Balaguer philosophy which lacked economic and political clarity, and was thus unable to build a creative economic alternative to the Balaguer model.

The PRD victory in 1978 gave rise, however, to an important social development: an *apertura,* or political opening which allowed new freedom for labor and peasant organizing. The next four years saw a tremendous growth in political consciousness among the poor. The General Workers Confederation (CGT) emerged as the largest and most pro-

Children gaze in a store window on downtown Santo Domingo street. Foreign exchange was spent on imports for the middle class while sugar revenues fell.

Tom Barry

Members of the Independent Peasant Movement (MCI).

CEPAE

gressive labor network in the country; Guzmán attempted to create a parallel PRD labor organization, but this failed miserably, while the CGT was winning labor demands with relative ease. Even more importantly, the peasantry was on the move, organizing a democratic grassroots body called the Independent Peasant Movement (MCI). This raised political consciousness in the countryside while fighting for fundamental peasants' rights.

On the other hand, the economy entered a period of crisis marked by spiraling corruption and indebtedness. The crisis had begun during Balaguer's last years when the world price of sugar fell steeply while petroleum prices rose. During a conference on the Caribbean held in Miami in 1979, Vice-President Majluta admitted that the cost of petroleum products imported into the Dominican Republic equalled the revenues from sugar, the mainstay of the economy. Without altering Balaguer's strategy of reliance on foreign investment, Guzman was forced to borrow more and more money, including twenty loans from Citibank, Chase Manhattan, and the Bank of America, and 65 major loans from USAID, the Inter-American Development Bank and the International Monetary Fund. By the end of the first trimester of 1979, the external debt had reached $1.3 billion, taking the country to the edge of bankruptcy.[3]

To compensate, Guzmán froze government salaries and subsidies, increased public utility and gasoline prices, fired employees of state-owned industries and made it increasingly difficult to import machinery and spare parts. The result was a public transport drivers' strike to which the government responded by sending in the military to make mass arrests. In the countryside, popular resistance took the form of land occupations (*recuperaciones de tierras*) by the campesinos, many of whom were only trying to recover lands from which they had been forcibly displaced. This also met with government repression and thousands of arrests. "The Dominican rural areas are a volcano that could erupt at any moment," warned the Bishop of Santiago;[4] while the MCI affirmed that "We will demand our right to the land even if running all the risks entailed should cost us our lives."[5]

Juan Bosch.

El Nuevo Diario

To make matters worse, Hurricane David struck the Dominican Republic in August 1979, causing more than a billion dollars' worth of damage. The government was blamed for corrupt mishandling of the post-hurricane aid which came in, although it was military officers and businessmen who made huge profits while little aid trickled down to those most affected by the disaster. The economic crisis became so severe, and resentment against the PRD so deep, that in 1980 the party withdrew its support from its own president in office, switching its loyalty to Peña Gómez and Salvador Jorge Blanco.

The popular forces continued to expand during Guzmán's last two years. Local parishes and grassroots Christian communities (*comunidades de base*) began supporting the demands of slum-dwellers and poor peasants to such a degree that Guzman ordered a number of foreign Catholic clergy and religious expelled, politicizing many in the Church. Dominican women meanwhile were organizing in the rural areas under the name *Amas de Casa* (Housewives' Club), which in time gave birth to the National Federation of Campesina Women, associated with the MCI.

Paradoxically, while these grassroots sectors pressed their demands against the government, they still saw the PRD as their best hope for maintaining a politically open society which allowed such organizing. This fact, combined with the PRD's renunciation of Guzmán and Majluta in 1980—isolating the party from the unpopularity of those leaders—allowed the PRD to win again in the presidential elections of 1982. Salvador Jorge Blanco became president, while Peña Gómez became mayor of Santo Domingo. But the PRD's victory could not rescue it from the economic chaos of the Guzmán years. By 1982, the International Monetary Fund was demanding direct supervision of the Dominican economy because of the country's $2 billion foreign debt. It was in this context that Jorge Blanco concluded secret agreements with the IMF in Washington, DC before he even assumed the presidency.

Revolt Against the IMF

If you can't swim
And you are pushed to the depths
A sad end awaits you
No one will save you from the bottom [del Fondo].

They speak of tightening the belt
But on someone else's stomach.
That is, on our stomachs
In order to keep theirs full.

This crisis they have created
Is not our fault
We are not the ones called upon
To pay for the broken plates.

In this blind alley
There is but one exit
To fight for the poor
Against those above.

— Dominican popular song, 1984

When Jorge Blanco's agreement with the IMF became public in November 1982, the Dominican Congress was furious that it had been bypassed in the most important national decision made since 1965. After the pact was formally signed in January 1983, the government began to implement

Salvador Jorge Blanco.

El Nuevo Diario

measures required by the Fund: closing down government-run hotels and industries, breaking strikes, and most importantly, freezing wages while increasing prices on basic food and fuel. The result was galloping inflation and the daily devaluation of the Dominican peso. Since such devaluation was prohibited by the constitution, a network of exchange houses called *casas de cambio* was set up independent of the banks.

The skyrocketing cost of living shook the society. Even middle-class businessmen felt the pressure as they were unable to get foreign exchange to import products and parts from abroad. But the real tragedy took place in the rural villages and poor urban barrios, where survival became more tenuous every day. As one taxi driver complained:

> The main problem is that bandit IMF. The prices of almost everything have gone up in the past two or three months. Two months ago I bought tires for this car for 100 pesos. Now the same tires cost 330 pesos. I used to be able to pay 40 pesos for a decent pair of shoes. Now it's 90 or even 100. It's a scandal.[6]

By January 1984 it was time for Jorge Blanco to sign the second phase of the IMF accord, bringing with it a second round of even harsher austerity measures. By now the IMF was an infamous household word throughout the Dominican Republic. The main trade union federations in the country jointly called for the government to break with the Fund. Street protests increased, including a march by 30,000 workers through Santo Domingo and another through the city of Santiago. In mid-March, Peña Gómez broke with the government, rejecting any alliance with either the Jorge Blanco or Majluta factions of the PRD.

Facing heavy domestic pressures to resist the IMF, Jorge Blanco was also under pressure from the Reagan administration to conclude the accord. When the Dominican president confided his fears that further austerity measures would set off social unrest, President Reagan bluntly replied that U.S. assistance to the Dominican Republic was contingent on submitting the country's economy to the discipline of the Fund: "Once an agreement [with the IMF] has been reached, I assure you that aid from the United States government will be rapidly disbursed."[7] During an official visit to Washington at the beginning of April, President Jorge Blanco announced the signing of the accord.

No sooner had the measures taken effect than new hardship came crashing down on poor households throughout the country. The prices of bread, milk, cooking oil, sugar and medicines rose sharply, some tripling their previous prices. On April 23, rioting broke out in the city of Santo Domingo and elsewhere in the country: cars were set afire, store windows smashed, and burning tires piled in the streets, while mobs of poor people threw stones at the police. The government responded by unleashing the military to quell the disturbance. By the end of the three-day uprising, the police and military had killed over 70 persons, wounded another 200, and made more than 4,000 arrests.[8]

Jorge Blanco charged that the violence was the fruit of a conspiracy against the government, accusing both Balaguer's Reformist Party and the smaller Dominican Leftist Front

Protesters in town of Bayaguana set flaming barricades in street.

(Right) Woman protests police brutality: A people destined for more hardship and repression?

(FID). In fact, the riots were a spontaneous popular revolt whose intensity caught all political parties in the country more or less by surprise. The president was casual about his decision to use violence against the protesters, saying that "the responsibility belongs with those who began the disorders, the looting and the burning. [The shootings were] very reasonable because of the chaotic situation."[9]

The poor saw things differently, however. Pedro de León, secretary general of the MCI, said on April 28:

> Given the just protest of the people, expressed massively throughout the country against the unjust measures taken by the government after concluding its negotiations with the IMF, one would not expect anything other than this popular revolt.[10]

The remainder of 1984 saw the rift widen between the government and the people. Neither Jorge Blanco nor even Peña Gómez could muster a show of public support, while high-level corruption within the military exploded onto the front pages of the press. The government kept up the repression throughout the year, staging periodic sweeps in which leftist and labor leaders were picked up and detained. While urban resistance was still disorganized, the MCI was emerging as an independent but unified national organization.

In January 1985, the government announced a new round of austerity measures, driving food and fuel prices up by an average of 50%. In the days before the January 28 announcement, the police and military moved into the poor barrios of Santo Domingo to guard against a second violent protest. The new price increases triggered a series of local strikes around the country culminating in a 24-hour, non-violent general strike affecting 90% of the economy. The government met the work stoppages with continuous repression, and the number of detentions reached into the thousands.[11]

An obvious question raised by the Dominican crisis is whether the PRD can possibly survive the 1986 elections. Equally uncertain, however, is whether either Bosch or Balaguer can replace the PRD, although Balaguer is sometimes described as the "real beneficiary" of the recent discontent. Neither of the two major opposition parties has offered a concrete alternative for restructuring the Dominican economy, now fully in the hands of the IMF. And for many Dominicans, at least in middle and upper class circles, the memory of the 1965 invasion remains as a subliminal warning that the U.S. probably would not allow the Dominican Republic to choose a truly progressive path.

Nor is there an obvious right-wing solution. Even if the military were to install another puppet government like that of Balaguer in 1966, there would be no economic boom this time around, given the low price of sugar and the world recession. At the same time, popular forces in the Dominican Republic are now well organized and highly politicized. Under these circumstances, the country appears to be a society without solutions: a nation where the poor majority are destined for more hardship and repression. ∎

146

El Nuevo Diario

*Police arrest protester.
Thousands of poor people,
trade unionists and left
leaders have been arrested
and detained since 1984.*

El Nuevo Diario

Haiti: The Region's Shame

Flying into the Haitian capital of Port-au-Prince, one gazes down upon what appears to be a vast waterfront landfill, a sprawling garbage heap through which figures mysteriously move. It is Cité Simone, a shantytown named in honor of the former Haitian President's wife, where the poorest of the urban poor crowd together amid foraging animals and open sewers. Each year the shacks of Cité Simone swell with new arrivals in flight from the starvation and desolation of the countryside. The poorest country in the western hemisphere, Haiti is the shame of the Caribbean, a nation of squalor, ignorance, and despair.

Presiding over this misery is the government of President-for-Life Jean Claude Duvalier, who heads a Haitian oligarchy of some 200 wealthy families.

These families are millionaires in dollars. They raise deluxe automobiles (Mercedes, Volvo, BMW) like cattle in the backyards of their air-conditioned villas in the fashionable suburbs of Port-au-Prince. They hold unidentified bank accounts in the U.S. where their profits and commissions are directly deposited in order to avoid local taxation. They own

Woman sells peanuts on Port-au-Prince street.

real estate in Florida and California. They have private aircraft and beaches, which allow them to play with drug smuggling and other quick-money businesses. They identify themselves as *la haute société,* the high society of Port-au-Prince. They are the living outcome of the process that has been ironically and cynically labeled Haiti's development for the past eleven years...[1]

The Haitian socio-economic system can be described as a kind of internal colonialism in which the wealth created by the peasantry is systematically drained off into the hands of an urban elite. The 1.5 million peasants who grow coffee receive one-third of the revenues from coffee exports. Meanwhile, another one-third goes as profits to a mercantile clique consisting of some 800 middlemen and 25 large exporters, most of whom are Haitian mulattos, foreign whites, Syrians, Lebanese and Jews. The middlemen, agents of the urban merchants, also sell supplies and make loans to the peasants. The peasants are thus in ever-increasing debt to the merchants and must sell their coffee at whatever price is offered.[2]

A small group of large landowners, primarily elite black families, control the country's best irrigated flatlands. Much of this prime land is left lying idle, while the peasants have been forced farther and farther up the mountainsides onto land worn to rock by overcultivation and erosion. From this barren soil, rural families coax corn, yams and beans for their survival. Although productivity is low, peasants often resist attempts by international aid agencies to improve the lands they farm. Once value has been added through road construction or irrigation, the urban landowners often decide to repossess their land and evict the peasants. A rural Haitian saying warns: *Bon te pa pou abitan*—good lands are not left to peasants.[3]

Baseball, Haitian Style

While one sector of the urban bourgeoisie controls coffee exports, a competing sector is linked more closely to the foreign capital which penetrated the Haitian economy after Jean Claude Duvalier assumed the presidency [see Part III, Ch. 6]. Many members of the mulatto elite exiled to the U.S. under Francois Duvalier have now returned to become subcontractors and managers for the 200 U.S.-owned firms clustered in and around Port-au-Prince.

For these runaway firms, Haiti offers rock-bottom wages (a minimum wage of $3.00 a day is not usually enforced), no trade unions, and "political stability" under the iron-fisted Duvalier regime. The list of U.S. corporations which profit from this arrangement includes many familiar names: electronics firms like TRW, Phillips, Motorola, Sylvania and Allied Control; garment firms like Levi Strauss and Mac-Gregor; as well as firms making toys, cosmetics, sporting goods and other export items. Haiti is the world's largest producer of baseballs, with every major U.S. sporting goods firm—Rawlings, Wilson, Spalding, and the rest—ensconced outside the capital paying women $3.00 to stitch baseballs all day.

Recently, the Coleco Company moved its entire production of Cabbage Patch dolls from Atlanta to Haiti.

U.S. involvement in Haiti goes far beyond the relatively limited impact of the assembly factories. U.S. aid props up much of the economy; it comes both from governmental sources (primarily from the U.S. Agency for International Development, USAID) and from private agencies like CARE. USAID virtually controls many of the country's technical institutions, and external financing is used for most government expenditures.[4] Haiti receives more foreign economic aid per capita than any country in the world, and the United States is the largest single source of aid to Haiti.

Foreign aid to Haiti has been a windfall of wealth for official and unofficial embezzlement and theft. All revenues passing through official hands are systematically looted by the Duvalier clique, and the family has amassed a personal fortune estimated at $1 billion in foreign bank accounts and European villas and yachts. In December 1980, $20 million of a $22 million IMF credit vanished two days after it arrived in Haiti. A confidential U.S. State Department cable reported that "Unfortunately, instead of being applied to relieve the foreign exchange shortage, the funds were almost immediately siphoned off by the presidency."[5]

While the U.S. is the major supplier of economic aid to Haiti, the primary source of military aid is Israel. Brought into Haiti by the U.S. in the late 1960s to do agricultural projects, Israel is now extensively involved in military, counterinsurgency and intelligence training as well as sale of military hardware. Standard issue for the *tontons macoutes,* Duvalier's paramilitary squad, is the Israeli Uzi submachine gun.

Sophisticated repression over the 29 years of Duvalier family dictatorship has left the Haitian opposition fragmented and feeble. Haiti is a police state: most opponents of the government are dead, exiled or in jail, and no grassroots organization of any sort is permitted to emerge. Censorship of the media and an illiteracy rate of approximately 70% help keep the Haitian masses isolated and ignorant of events beyond their immediate horizons. The U.S. supports this order on the basis of the Duvalier government's professed anti-communism—just a few miles across the water from Cuba—and on its obeisance to U.S. regional control. The Haitian government knows its value to Washington and does not hesitate to play the "communist card" when concerns are raised about human rights. As Haiti's foreign minister told Secretary of State Alexander Haig in 1981: "Only America can save Haiti from Moscow."[6]

The Liberalization Game

The Duvalier government's policy is a tightrope walk between the repression necessary to stay in power and the appearance of liberalization necessary to obtain foreign aid. The degree of repression in Haiti fluctuates according to whichever goal is primary at a given moment. This in turn depends on the international political environment and above all on the political climate in Washington.

In 1977-80, pressures from the Carter administration produced a brief democratic "springtime" in Haiti. Two non-

Patrick Ahern

Children of Cité Simone: What future for them?

governmental political parties were allowed to form, the Christian Democratic Party of Sylvio Claude and the Social Christian Party of Grégoire Eugène. Other nascent organizations included independent trade unions, intellectual and cultural organizations, and an independent press. On November 28, 1980, twenty-four days after the election of Ronald Reagan, the Duvalier security forces staged a crackdown which brought the democratic opening to an abrupt end. Over 200 people were arrested, including human rights activists, trade union organizers, journalists, doctors, lawyers, and development workers—described as "national and international Communist agitators" in a statement by the Chief of Police. A number were exiled after undergoing interrogation and torture.

Concerned about the appearance of U.S. support for an internationally condemned dictatorship, the U.S. Congress has required the State Department to certify each year that Haiti is making "progress" in improving human rights. These pressures prompted the Haitian government to relax press censorship in early 1984 and to hold legislative elections on February 12, a few months before Congressional certification was due. The "elections," however, were a sham:

Political parties which opposed Duvalier's government

were not allowed to participate. The only three candidates who were considered even mildly independent of the Duvalier regime were prevented from running.

Sylvio Claude, president of the Haitian Christian Democratic Party, was jailed to prevent his participation. While in prison he was severely beaten. Grégoire Eugène was prevented from returning to Haiti to participate in the elections, after having been jailed and forcibly exiled in 1980. The only mildly independent candidate who began a campaign, Serge Beaulieu, had his party headquarters ransacked and spent election day in hiding. Two of his staff were detained without explanation.[7]

The elections were followed by a highly-publicized series of letters from President Duvalier to the heads of the Haitian police, armed forces, militia and the justice minister, ordering them to respect the legal rights of detainees and to refrain from using torture. This unprecedented move was cited by the U.S. State Department when it certified on May 14, 1984 that Haiti was making progress toward improving human rights. Almost simultaneously, however, the National Palace published a decree warning the nation that all unauthorized political parties and newspapers remained illegal.

The government's tantalizing gestures of reform raised hopes among the Haitian people for an easing of terror from the security forces. These hopes soon were dashed. Arrests

Dignity amidst poverty.

Patrick Ahern

without warrants and detentions without charge continued as if the letters had never been written.[8] On May 21, police in the town of Gonaives beat a pregnant woman, and suddenly Haiti exploded as it had not in a quarter-century of dictatorial rule. Rioting spread from town to town in the impoverished north, beginning as a protest against police brutality but quickly escalating to a brash political challenge to Duvalier's rule. Crowds crying *"Aba la faim! Aba la misere! Aba Duvaye!"*— Down with hunger! Down with misery! Down with Duvalier!— attacked the CARE warehouses and started mass distribution of food. By the time counterinsurgency and army troops had quelled the riots, at least 30 people lay dead.

> *The game is: a few months of liberalization, a few months of repression. When international pressure is very strong upon the government, they make a few [gestures of] liberalization.*
>
> *But the government knows it is impossible to really liberalize the regime because the regime depends on repression. Otherwise, the population is so hungry it would explode.*
>
> *The opposition is general in Haiti now. The government is still in power only by the repression.*
>
> — Opposition politician Grégoire Eugène[9]

The Church Speaks Out

In the politically deadened atmosphere which followed the crackdown of November 1980, the Church began to grow in importance as a catalyst for change. To begin with, churches were virtually the only place where the peasantry could participate in any form of social organization. Sunday services emerged as a forum for communication which filled a crucial need in the absence of literacy and the right to assemble. At the same time, many Catholic and Protestant priests and lay workers were active in their communities, providing social services and working toward empowerment of the peasants on issues which affect them. The government responded with surveillance and harassment of religious workers and public warnings to the Church to stay out of politics.

In December 1982, the government arrested Catholic lay worker Gerard Duclerville, associated with the Church's Radio Cacique. During the 42 days of Duclerville's imprisonment, during which he was severely beaten, the bishops of Haiti issued a pastoral letter proclaiming that "the Church of Haiti is living now in a situation of challenge" and affirming that "Where a man is humiliated and tortured, it is the whole of humanity who is humiliated and tortured."[10] The letter was signed by all the Haitian bishops including the Archbishop, François Wolf Ligonde, related to Duvalier's wife and long considered close to the regime.

Two months later, Pope John Paul II visited Haiti and publicly rebuked the government for "the injustice, the excessive inequality, the degradation of the quality of life, the misery, the hunger, the fear of many people" in Haiti. The Pope approved the human rights initiative of the Haitian Church, saying "I have come to encourage this awakening, this leap, this movement of the Church for the good of the whole country."[11]

In November 1984, immediately following Reagan's reelection to a second term, a new wave of arrests swept Haiti. This time, the churches and their development institutions were the primary targets. The government announced that it had uncovered "a plot of Marxist-Leninist inspiration against the security of the State," and named the Diocesan Institute for the Education of Adults, a literacy project of the Holy Cross order, as involved. Amid the daily arrests and mounting red-baiting of the Church, the Haitian bishops issued a pastoral letter on November 13 proclaiming that . . .

> . . . In the name of love which links all the members of the Body of Christ, and in our pastoral responsibility, we have decided to intervene before the responsible authorities to obtain respect for fundamental rights such as individual freedom, the physical and moral integrity of every citizen, and the tranquility and peace of the household.

When the pastoral letter was read to a congregation in the Cathedral of Cap Haitien, the Prefect—the local government representative—interrupted the service to criticize the bishops' message. Several weeks later, a similar incident occurred at the beginning of a Mass in the town of Dessalines; and in the town of Milot, on the day of the town's patron saint, two armed *tontons macoutes* posted themselves on either side of the altar until the closing prayer.[12] Religious leaders viewed these government intrusions into the sanctity of the Church as a sacrilege and a breach of the freedom to worship. As 1985 wore on, Haiti found itself in the midst of a deepening confrontation between Church and State.

The Church's decision to speak out has given new courage to other popular sectors. Two Church initiatives, the "Global Plan" of the Conference of Haitian Religious and a "Charter for Human Promotion" drafted by the Haitian bishops, call for economic justice, human dignity and political participation—heady ideals which have provided substance for a new public dialogue on the possibility of change.

Equally important in creating the present atmosphere of uncertainty are deepening divisions within the Duvalier government and the bourgeoisie as a whole. These center on competition between the "old guard" loyal to Francois Duvalier—sometimes referred to as *les dinosaures*—and the rising class of technocrats and businessmen linked to U.S. economic interests, who have gained the upper hand since the younger Duvalier came to power. In policy terms, this translates into a dispute over the validity of the USAID-imposed economic strategy which favors sectors linked to U.S. capital. The bourgeoisie is united, however, on one point: that the Duvalier regime is economically and politically bankrupt. The real competition is between the various forces seeking to forge an alternative to the crumbling regime. Jean Claude Duvalier himself lacks a personal power base; with his limited experience outside the plush confines of the National Palace, he is little more than a pawn in the power struggles between his family members and associates.

While passivity and fear have long ruled Haiti, the activism of the Church and the cracks within the power structure have opened the door to a popular challenge. "The Haitian masses have always been outside political power," says a Haitian exile who heads the Washington Office on Haiti. "The question now is how long the regime can hold on."[13] ∎

LETTER FROM THE HAITIAN PEOPLE

We have decided to write this letter because we feel defenseless and unprotected, without support and without security before the civil and military authorities of this country . . . For some time now we have been in a desperate situation. Every day the government proclaims, on radio and television, in the newspapers and in meetings, that we have rights, but every time that we demand them, we are answered with beatings and prison.

. . . It appears that the constitution only applies to a minority; only they have the right to meet. If by chance, two or three persons of the town meet together, they are suspected of subversion and mistreated. This is the way the voice of the poor and miserable is silenced. The army appears with weapons to disperse the participants in even the smallest public demonstration.

. . . Even in holy places, in a country that calls itself Christian, we are forbidden to complain. They commit the sacrilege of insulting priests in their parishes, accusing them of being responsible for our misery.

. . . We do not ask for money nor do we demand contributions of food and used clothing; that is humiliating. We only demand that which money cannot provide: freedom, equality, democracy, justice for everyone, work, access to the land, and the means with which to cultivate the land.

With all our strength, we ask this for those whose rights have been violated, for those who have been arrested without warrant; for those who have been imprisoned without a hearing; for those who are tortured, be they sentenced or innocent; and for those who are innocent, that they be released without delay.

. . . We who sign this letter live in all parts of the country, in every geographic department. We decided to publish this letter with two thousand signatures, but we continue to receive new additions. We ask all who agree with this letter to immediately send your signatures of unity and solidarity.

Excerpts from an open letter published in **CRIE,** *Regional Center for Ecumenical Information, Mexico, on November 21, 1984.*

Jamaica: Reaganomics in the Caribbean

Jamaica lies at the center of the Caribbean like the hub of a great wheel. Around it sweep Cuba and the Bahamas to the north, the island archipelago to the east, the continental rim to the south, and the Central American isthmus to the west. Jamaica also is central to the political drama being played out in the Caribbean. It is the keystone of U.S. strategy in the region, and increasingly, the arena in which the failure of that strategy is being revealed.

Reagan's Capitalist Showcase

Edward Seaga's Jamaica Labour Party (JLP) defeated Michael Manley's People's National Party (PNP) on October 30, 1980, just four days before the electoral victory of Seaga's ideological soulmate Ronald Reagan. Early in his first term, President Reagan announced that Jamaica would become the model for the Caribbean. Under the supervision of the U.S. Agency for International Development and the International Monetary Fund, Seaga was to restructure the island's economy to reflect the Reagan ideology. This meant removing government restraints on the private sector and going all out to attract foreign investment which would produce for export. In this way, Reagan said, the "magic of the marketplace" would show Jamaica and the rest of the Caribbean the path to development.

While cloaked in rhetoric about a return to democracy, this strategy was actually a continuation of the long-standing U.S. effort to construct a capitalist model for the region. Like previous efforts, its fundamental purpose was to undermine socialism's appeal. Administration strategists hoped that by pumping enough aid dollars into Jamaica, an attractive scale model of Third World capitalism could be made to function and would serve to negate the revolutionary models of Cuba, Nicaragua, and Grenada. So confident was the administration

Edward Seaga.

of success that it spoke of Jamaica as key not only to U.S. policy in the Caribbean, but also Central America. Said Reagan: "Free-enterprise Jamaica, not Marxist Cuba, should serve as a model for Central America in the struggle to overcome poverty and move towards democracy."[1]

To make the miracle happen, the United States and multilateral lenders poured capital into Jamaica. U.S. bilateral aid jumped from US$14 million in Manley's last year to over $200 million in Seaga's first two years.[2] The IMF immediately came through with $698 million in loans for the new government, and the World Bank lent $133 million. Seaga, in fact, borrowed more money in his first two years than Jamaica had in the entire previous decade.

The Reagan administration granted Jamaica many other special favors, such as purchasing $67 million worth of Jamaican bauxite to add to the U.S. stockpile. Former Chase Manhattan Bank chairman David Rockefeller helped set up a "U.S. Business Committee on Jamaica," including representatives of such corporate giants as Eastern Airlines, Gulf + Western, Hilton International, Exxon and Alcoa, to advise the Seaga government on attracting foreign investment. Other advice came from an army of consultants on contract to USAID who trooped through Kingston's posh Pegasus Hotel. Transforming Jamaica's economy became a pet project of the U.S. government which, as one U.S. official put it, could "not afford to have it fail."[3]

In return, Seaga became Reagan's primary ally in the Caribbean. Within weeks of his election, he expelled the Cuban ambassador to Jamaica and announced that his government would be part of a Washington-directed alliance fighting "Marxist adventures" in the region. Seaga moved quickly to sweep out radicals including members of the PNP's left wing and the communist Workers Party of Jamaica (WPJ) from posts in government agencies, the press, and the University of the West Indies. The worker-run sugar cooperatives and other progressive experiments of the Manley era were dismantled. At the same time, the JLP government reinforced the Jamaican military and police with U.S. equipment and training.

Impact of the IMF

Of most far-reaching importance for Jamaica, Seaga took a series of steps mandated by the International Monetary Fund and the World Bank as conditions for their loans. This "structural adjustment," as it was called, was supposed to reorient Jamaica's economy toward producing manufactured goods for export. It was in fact the old Puerto Rican model, although since nearby Puerto Rico was obviously depressed, Seaga preferred to make comparisons to Far Eastern countries like South Korea and Singapore.

The basic planks of the program included:
- Scrapping import restrictions which the Manley government had used to enforce a rational allocation of scarce

Women's protest march in 1980.

Struggle

foreign exchange. The theory was that by saturating the local market with imports, Jamaican manufacturers would be forced to become "more competitive" and to produce for export rather than the domestic market. This fit well with Seaga's own agenda which included promoting consumption of imported luxuries in order to pay his political debt to the middle and upper class.

- Currency devaluations to cheapen the price of labor for foreign investors and make Jamaican exports cheaper for foreign buyers. Although devaluation was implicit in the IMF program, Seaga avoided it for as long as possible because of its negative political impact.
- Lifting price controls on basic foods and abolishing rent-control ceilings.
- Removing budget subsidies from public services such as light and water, allowing their prices to rise.
- Reducing public sector spending by firing or laying off thousands of government employees.
- Divesting government-owned enterprises such as hotels, and bringing in foreign managers for others, such as the sugar industry.

Initially the results seemed promising. Buoyed by foreign aid and loans, the economy resumed positive growth of 2% in 1981 after seven years of negative growth. A total of 116 new investment projects worth US$243 million were reported in 1981 and 1982.[4] There was an atmosphere of jubilation among the country's middle and upper classes, who snatched up expensive consumer goods such as video games which filled store shelves after imports were deregulated. Late-model Toyotas and Hondas jammed Kingston's gritty streets as affluent Jamaicans launched a buying spree to make up for the material privation of the Manley years.

From about mid-1982, however, a stream of negative signs began to appear. With the exception of Control Data, no large corporations and none of those on the U.S.-Jamaica Business Committee were among the investors putting money into Jamaica. Most who did were small businessmen who expected to raise their project financing in Jamaica. Growth remained barely positive in 1982, at one-fifth of 1%.[5] Yet by December of that year Seaga had borrowed US$1.086 billion—an ominously mounting foreign debt.

The backdrop was a sharp decline in production, led by the crucial bauxite sector. The source of 70% of Jamaica's foreign exchange, bauxite was hit after 1980 by world recession and the aluminum multinationals' gradual shift out of the Caribbean. Jamaica had produced 11.9 million tons of raw bauxite in 1980, but this dropped to 7.7 million tons by 1983.[6]

Seaga's decision to open Jamaica to imports wreaked havoc with the country's domestic agricultural production. Farmers suffered losses from the sudden inflows of cheap foreign onions, potatoes, red beans and vegetables. Domestic agriculture declined 18% in 1982, and for thousands of peasant farmers in the hills and villages of Jamaica, times had "never been so bad."[7]

Imports also displaced local manufactures, especially shoes and clothing. Manufacturers had to compete with importers for foreign exchange on the black market; and one by one the smaller Jamaican businesses began to close their

153

doors or scale down their operations, laying off workers. In a workforce of approximately one million, the number of persons listed as unemployed rose from 261,000 in October 1981 to 292,000 a year later.

Meanwhile, the voracious consumerism of the middle and upper class was eating up the country's foreign exchange. Affluent Jamaicans spent more than $100 million scarce U.S. dollars to import 14,000 new cars in 1982.[8] With export earnings shrinking, this extravagent spending nearly tripled Jamaica's trade deficit in two years, from US$213 million at the end of 1980 to $614 million at the end of 1982.[9]

The IMF initially had been lenient with Seaga. But by early 1983, the economy was so bad that the Fund could no longer pass Jamaica on the twice-yearly performance tests required to keep the loan installments flowing. After failing the March 1983 test, Seaga requested a waiver. It came with a new set of harsh conditions that dramatically worsened conditions in the country. The government was required to restrict imports, not only of consumer goods but also of raw materials and spare parts needed for production. There were new layoffs of public sector workers. Worst of all for the poor, many basic goods were placed on a "parallel market" which meant they had to be purchased with devalued currency. This sent prices spiraling for such necessities as gasoline, bus fares, medicines, school books, farm tools, and soap. Jamaicans called it "the paralyzed market."

Food prices began a relentless rise, pushing staple foods of the poor—rice, beans, chicken backs, canned corned beef and canned milk—out of reach of working-class families. Dr. Carl Stone, a prominent political analyst, wrote in the *Daily Gleaner:*

Shopper in a Kingston market: Relentlessly rising food prices.

The IMF boys, of course, are out to slash the excess consumption of luxuries. But the big spenders and big earners are not the people who are most affected by these drastic reductions in purchasing power. They will continue driving BMWs long after the Jamaican dollar gets down to 20¢ U.S. But will the working class be able to live and will the bulk of those who are classified as middle-class survive?

How do these jokers in the IMF expect the country to motivate people to produce when they can't buy food, pay electricity bills, pay their rent, buy clothes and school books for their children, or even afford to drink a few beers?[10]

The Grenada Diversion

The Seaga government was losing popularity more swiftly than any government in Jamaica's history. By late 1983, with another IMF test failed and a new round of draconian measures imminent, polls showed public opinion swinging strongly back to Manley and the PNP. This was an unprecedented reversal in a country where two-term administrations have long been the norm. The failure of the JLP to restore prosperity, plus its obvious disregard for the suffering of the poor, painted memories of Manley in a more positive light. This was true even though the PNP was keeping a very low profile and indeed had moved substantially to the right, abandoning its progressive stance of 1980-81.

Seaga responded to the growing discontent by attempting to distract the Jamaican public. Jamaica's 21st anniversary of independence was celebrated in August 1983 with great fanfare, including visits from Queen Elizabeth and Vice-President Bush. A much-ballyhooed competition was launched to redesign the country's coat of arms. But the ultimate diversion came in October 1983, when Jamaica played a starring role in the invasion of Grenada. Bombarded with propaganda, the Jamaican people were swept up in a wave of anticommunist hysteria which temporarily arrested the JLP's decline in popularity. Seaga seized the moment to announce the devaluation of the Jamaican dollar by 43% (to US32¢). Before the devaluation's impact on prices could be felt, the prime minister announced a snap election and won a new five-year mandate.

Although he won the election, Seaga took his gamble one step too far. Because the JLP called the elections on an outdated voters' list—violating an earlier promise—and because the timing was extremely disadvantageous for the PNP, the PNP boycotted the election, allowing the JLP to win every Parliamentary seat. For the first time in its history, Jamaica had a de facto one-party government. Critics spoke of a constitutional crisis, while people on the streets began to talk about a "one-party dictatorship," and public disapproval all but neutralized the JLP's gains from its role in the Grenada affair.

Since the election, the economy has continued its downward slide. In early 1984, Reynolds Metals stunned the country when it announced it was closing down its operations and leaving Jamaica. Alcoa followed suit in early 1985, prompting the government to take over the plant to prevent its complete shut down. While the decline continues in bauxite, little new

WHAT THE IMF HAS DONE TO PRICES

	BEFORE IMF			IMF YEARS					
	1975	1976	1977	1978	1979	1980	1981	1983	1985
RICE (1 lb.)	29¢	29¢	29¢	41¢	50¢	59¢	75¢	75¢	$1.75
FLOUR (1 lb.)	14¢	16¢	17¢	22¢	30¢	36¢	45¢	45¢	$1.10
CONDENSED MILK (1 tin)	30¢	30¢	30¢	47¢	67¢	77¢	86¢	$1.12	$2.12
CORNED BEEF (1 tin)	78¢	78¢	78¢	$1.00	$1.93	$2.75	$3.00	$4.15	$6.60

Prices in Jamaican currency.

investment has arrived to bolster the manufacturing sector. As elsewhere in the Caribbean, fuel is costly, services unreliable, and wages, as low as they are in Jamaica, are still lower in places like Haiti, South Korea and the Philippines. Perhaps most important, investors have held back for political reasons, waiting to see if the Seaga regime would be "stable" with no threat of a return to the pro-socialist Manley era.

The only truly buoyant sectors of the economy are tourism and the ganja (marijuana) trade. Tourism is the one industry which depends above all on Jamaica's political relationship with the United States, as was illustrated by the successful U.S. attempt to cut off tourism when Manley was in power. Since 1980 it has recovered strongly, responding to currency devaluations and pro-Seaga publicity. Ganja is Jamaica's largest agricultural export, although the revenues it earns are "invisible," i.e., not counted in the national budget. But the flowering weed which grows lushly in the Jamaican hills is all that is presently keeping many rural families from destitution.

Seaga has continued efforts to involve foreign capital in the economy. United Brands has been invited to plant more than 2,000 acres of bananas under a joint venture agreement. Japanese and Israeli investors are at the heart of Agro-21, Seaga's touted program to grow vegetables for the U.S. market. The former owner of some of Jamaica's largest sugar plantations, Tate & Lyle, has been invited to take over the three largest sugar estates under a ten-year management contract with the government.

This "recolonizing" of the economy is putting highly-paid foreign managers into top positions throughout the country. Tate & Lyle received over J$7 million in fees and expenses for the first year. The foreign head of Agro-21 receives nearly J$1 million. Comparable salaries are paid to expatriate managers in the Bank of Jamaica, the Jamaica Information Service, and elsewhere in the public sector, despite the availability of qualified Jamaicans.[11] "The Seaga government has no nationalist instinct whatsoever," says an activist who worked closely with the disbanded sugar cooperatives. "It is a straight puppet of the foreign transnationals and the U.S. government."[12]

"Seaga Has Destroyed Poor People Living"

Desperation and anger dominated the scene as 1984 drew to a close. A new IMF agreement signed the previous June caused the layoff of 6,000 public sector workers, with rumors of another 5,000 to go. The Jamaican dollar stood at J$4.96 to US$1 by year's end and was still falling. While an employed worker might earn J$60 a week, one chicken costs J$12, a liter of cooking oil J$9 and a dozen eggs J$7. As one Jamaican worker wrote to the WPJ newspaper *Struggle,* "Seaga has destroyed poor people living."

Throughout 1984 street protests rippled around the country, but they were spontaneous and unorganized, focusing mostly on local issues. By the beginning of the new year, Jamaican commentators were publicly remarking on the fact that there had been no large-scale protest. In part this reflected the refusal of the PNP leadership to take to the streets for fear of alienating the middle class. Defections from the JLP had been massive at all levels, but the PNP maintained what many of its rank-and-file saw as perplexing inaction.

But when on January 14, 1985, the government announced an increase in gasoline prices from J$8.99 to J$10.99 a gallon—dreaded harbinger of a new wave of inflation—the people were no longer willing to wait for the party leadership. In the pre-dawn hours of January 15, people in the poor neighborhoods of Kingston and in towns and villages around the island began barricading the roads with flaming piles of tires and debris, until by mid-morning all major roads in Jamaica were blocked and dark, acrid smoke billowed up from the streets. PNP, WPJ, and even many JLP supporters took part, with women and youth prominently involved. Schools and most Kingston businesses closed, and public transport was paralyzed for two days while the protest raged. Prime Minister Seaga was informed of the disturbance while at an official breakfast in honor of Martin Luther King Jr., sponsored by the U.S. Information Agency and the Jamaican-American Society, at which an award for "outstanding humanitarianism" was being presented to the president of the Coca Cola company. The prime minister downplayed the riots, calling them a "letting off of steam." But he knew, as all Jamaicans knew, that the long period of quiescence had come to a close.

The Jamaican Warning

As Seaga's second term wears on, Jamaica is entangled in contradictions at three levels: within Jamaican society, between Jamaica and the United States, and between reality and illusion in U.S. Caribbean policy.

Inside Jamaica, the main conflict is between the poor majority and the elite which wields economic control. Within that context, however, there are divisions within each class. The IMF program has hurt a sector of the elite, those who produce for the domestic market. They are angry at Seaga, although still pro-capitalist in ideology. The middle class likewise has become disillusioned since their initial burst of consumer spending has been curbed. And within Seaga's own party, pressure has emerged from some who feel that the snap election and one-party Parliament violated the sanctity and stability of the two-party system.

The popular majority is divided, as always, by political tribalism and the violence it spawns. Deadly clashes are again increasing between gangs supporting the JLP and PNP, each armed with high-powered weaponry shipped in from Miami. In 1981 the government created the "Special Operations Squad" as a special police unit to deal with violent crime. Dubbed the "Eradication Squad" by Jamaicans, it is responsible for much of the mounting police brutality and killings of which opposition party supporters are disproportionately the victims. In addition, there has been an alarming increase in ordinary crime, including some particularly gruesome episodes, testifying to a society under great strain. The *Daily Gleaner* newspaper counted 57 persons shot, stabbed or lynched in the first 49 days of 1985. Twenty-nine of them had been killed by the police.[14]

Politically, there is no apparent outlet for the growing frustration with the JLP. The PNP has failed to propose any concrete economic alternative to Seaga and the IMF; most Jamaicans believe that Manley *wants* to help the poor, but it is not clear what he would do differently this time to avoid being driven back into the grasp of the IMF. D.K. Duncan, formerly minister of mobilization in the Manley government and representing the left wing of the PNP, comments:

> My view on the PNP's real economic policy is that it's a watered down, more humane version of Seaga's economic policy. [The PNP] has returned to what it was originally, a party of reform and not a party that transforms . . . trying to please every single class. A Social Democratic party capable of mild reforms which definitely cannot meet the aspirations of the people.[15]

The underlying dilemma for Jamaicans is that while Seaga's government has brought only suffering, there is no point in voting him out if not to vote in favor of some positive alternative to his model. Yet the PNP's democratic socialism has been tried and failed; and most people tacitly assume that the United States would promptly destabilize a new Manley

Jamaican worker at rally demanding an end to IMF program.

government if it attempted a serious socialist transformation. Because of this, the PNP has rallied only half-hearted support behind its vocal call for "elections now." Paradoxically, this is so even though the polls show a dramatic swing in public opinion back to the PNP such that the party would easily beat Seaga if an immediate election were held.

While the PNP's popular support has risen sharply at the expense of the JLP, the small Workers Party of Jamaica has also strengthened its position by attracting disaffected supporters from both mainstream parties. The WPJ does offer a real alternative in that it identifies outright with the workers, farmers and unemployed, with none of the PNP's ambivalent desire to "please every class." It is, however, still very small, and is a third party in a country where two-party tribalism has deep roots; it was just beginning to build a grassroots base when the Grenada invasion occurred. The red-baiting which followed the invasion damaged the WPJ severely, especially in light of the party's public backing for the Coard faction in the New Jewel Movement's internal dispute. This unpopular stand reinforced the party's image of ideological rigidity and pro-Moscow alignment and made the job of winning public trust more difficult than before. In spite of this, recent polls show the WPJ's "approval" rating up from 5% to 10% of the electorate, a strong showing for a leftist party in almost any context and one which reflects the growing disenchantment with the alternatives offered by the JLP and the PNP.

THE WIZARD AT WORK

Mr. Prime Minister! People can't pay rent or buy food! What are you going to do about the situation?

I will deal with it by exposing a Cuban plot to hide wanted criminals.

Mr. Prime Minister! We want work. Unemployment is now over 300,000. What are you going to do about the situation?

I will deal with it by exposing a Grenadian plot to invade the Caribbean.

MR. PRIME MINISTER! THE JAMAICAN DOLLAR IS NOW ALMOST WORTHLESS AND THE COUNTRY IS BANK-RUPT! What are you going to do about the situation?

Relax! I Will deal with it by exposing a KGB plot to kill one of our diplomats, a WPJ plot to send troops to Grenada and a PNP plot to sabotage the economy

Let's face it — they don't call me the "financial wizard" for nothing......

From the WPJ newspaper, Struggle.

Meanwhile, the honeymoon between Jamaica and the United States appears to have come to an end. Reagan no longer talks about Jamaica as a miracle; Washington is anxious to divert attention elsewhere, and can do little more to bail out Seaga in any case. Seaga in turn feels that the U.S. has ditched Jamaica in favor of Grenada, the new showcase. Finally, the ganja trade is an issue of growing contention. The United States wants to stop it; Seaga can only lose by undercutting the last pillar of support of the Jamaican peasantry.

The most far-reaching contradiction of all is between the desperate conditions in the Caribbean and the Reagan administration's blind attempt to apply ideological solutions to the problem. Three billion dollars in debt and on the brink of a social explosion, Jamaica is dramatic proof that Reaganomics and the IMF are not the salvation for the region's economies. The "miracle" has turned into a lesson in despair and a warning for the entire Caribbean. ∎

INDEPENDENT COUNTRIES: GUYANA

Guyana

Guyana: Pseudo-Socialism and Starvation

Guyana is a country with vast reserves of natural wealth. Larger than the rest of the English-speaking Caribbean put together, it sprawls across 83,000 square miles on the South American coast, rich with bauxite, manganese, diamonds, gold, timber, sugar, and rice. Yet this nation of barely 700,000 people is slowly starving.[1] This astounding fact is just one aspect of life under the bizarre dictatorship of Forbes Burnham, president of the "Cooperative Republic" of Guyana.

Burnham is notorious in the Caribbean for using a socialist smokescreen to obscure what is actually a repressive, authoritarian state. His government takes a progressive position on most regional and international issues: it supports Nicaragua, for example, opposed the invasion of Grenada, has warm relations with Cuba, and speaks out strongly against apartheid. Yet the internal reality is one of an elitist ruling party which shows no signs of moving in the direction of a true socialist transformation. This has confused critics and allowed Burnham to "play both sides." Guyana has received aid from sources as diverse as Cuba, China, Bulgaria, the International Monetary Fund, the World Bank, and the United States.

It is no accident that Burnham chose pseudo-socialism as a guise for consolidating his party's power. In the period leading up to independence, Guyana was the one British Caribbean colony which attempted to cast off the political and economic structures of colonialism. The late Guyanese historian Walter Rodney wrote:

> More so than any other English-speaking people, Guyanese were exposed to a serious discussion of socialism prior to independence. Nationalization, the equalization of the distri-bution of wealth, firm support for revolutionary governments and movements were all policies which advanced sections of the Guyanese working people understood and accepted . . .[2]

When Guyanese first went to the polls under universal suffrage in 1953, they elected the People's Progressive Party (PPP), which campaigned on a platform of workers' rights and national control over Guyana's wealth. The PPP was led by a popular, Marxist labor leader named Cheddi Jagan—of East Indian descent—with a British-educated black lawyer, Forbes Burnham, as party chairman. The movement behind the PPP thus united the two main sectors of the Guyanese working class: the rural Indo-Guyanese descended from indentured laborers, and the urban Afro-Guyanese descended from slaves.

Jagan's government introduced many pro-worker reforms such as workman's compensation, paid vacations, and social security. The United States, at the height of the Cold War, proclaimed this a Communist government in the making and pressured the British to act. When Jagan had been in office just 133 days, British troops landed in Georgetown, the capital, and suspended the Guyanese constitution. The loss of office widened latent splits within the PPP; and encouraged by the British, Burnham broke away from the party, taking many black voters with him. Jagan nevertheless was reelected in 1957 and again in 1961, each time in free and fair elections.

With the tacit approval of the colonial authorities, Burnham's newly-formed People's National Congress (PNC) together with the Catholic Church and a smaller right-wing party, the United Front, waged a campaign of racial violence and political agitation against the PPP. Meanwhile, the

Central Intelligence Agency and the American Institute for Free Labor Development (AIFLD) organized an 80-day general strike in the spring of 1963 which fatally weakened the Jagan government [see Part V, Ch. 3]. In national elections held the following year under a new system designed by the British, Burnham's PNC and the United Front combined to form a Parliamentary majority and capture control of the government. Two years later, Guyana received independence from Britain.

Ironically—since Jagan had been ousted because of his socialist ideas—1970 saw the sudden conversion of Burnham to "socialism" after a brief and unsuccessful flirtation with the Puerto Rican model. He began by purchasing the two foreign bauxite companies, DEMBA of Canada (a subsidiary of Alcan) and Reynolds of the U.S. By 1976 all major economic sectors had come under state control, including the sugar industry, long controlled by the British multinational Bookers McConnell Ltd. This new thrust was an attempt to co-opt the socialist opposition led by the PPP, and also responded to pressures on the PNC from the ruling party's own left wing. In addition to these political motivations, the nationalized industries provided Burnham's party with an economic base to use in consolidating its power.

Emergence of Dictatorship

"The Burnham dictatorship crept up upon the Guyanese people like a thief in the night," wrote Walter Rodney.[3] After taking full control of the government in fraudulent 1968 elections, Burnham proceeded gradually to establish the basis for permanent PNC rule. The pillars of party control include:

- The armed forces. To supplement the Guyana Defense Force (the army), Burnham created the Guyana National Service and the Guyana People's Militia, which serve as the military arm of the ruling party. They are used to intimidate political opposition and also provide employment to a large number of Afro-Guyanese, reinforcing the racial basis of Burnham's support. Today, 1 out of every 35 Guyanese belongs to a military or paramilitary group.[4]

  In addition, private vigilante squads are used to violently disrupt strikes and opposition meetings and attack political opponents. The predominant one is the so-called House of Israel, headed by a black fugitive from the U.S. who calls himself Rabbi Washington.[5] The cult has boasted of its military training and functions as a private army for the PNC. Burnham has a history of taking in fugitives and cults from abroad who then become bulwarks of PNC support. It is in this context that he invited the California cult leader Jim Jones to set up his "People's Temple" commune deep in the Guyana hinterland, in a rural area traditionally dominated by Jagan's PPP and also the object of a territorial claim by Venezuela.

- "Paramountcy of the Party." Under this 1975 doctrine, the government is considered merely an "executive arm" of the ruling party. The PNC is supposed to be "paramount" over all state functions, including the police, the army, the schools and the courts.

- Direct control of state sector workers. With some 80% of the Guyanese economy under state control, workers fired for political reasons have virtually nowhere to turn. Public sector workers are forced to attend PNC rallies, giving the illusion of mass support for the regime.

- Control of the Trades Union Council (TUC). From the 1960s until recently, Burnham used the TUC as an instrument of party control. This was done by consistently rigging trade union elections in order to stack union executives with PNC supporters. PNC-dominated unions, some fictitious, others with inflated memberships, were given a disproportionate share of the delegates to the TUC, enabling Burnham to retain control of the TUC Executive Committee. This control was successfully challenged in September 1984 by a movement of seven independent unions.

- Fraudulent elections. National elections since 1968, as well as the 1978 Referendum on the Constitution have all been clearly rigged. In 1973, the Army intervened and seized the ballot boxes when an early count seemed headed against Burnham. Burnham rewrote the Constitution over massive popular opposition in 1978 to give himself virtually limitless power. The 1980 national elections, the most recent to renew Burnham's rule, were denounced as a "clumsily managed and blatant fraud" by a team of international observers.[6] A new general election is legally due by March 1986.

- Control of the media. Beginning in 1973, the state gradually acquired all the major media including the only daily paper, the *Chronicle*, and both radio stations. There is no T.V.

Guyanese soldiers seizing ballot boxes in 1973 election.

What remains of an independent press has been curbed through a combination of government libel suits, violence, and the blocking of access to newsprint and ink. Three opposition party newspapers have been reduced to one-page mimeographed sheets; while the *Catholic Standard,* weekly newspaper of the Catholic Church, has been hit with five libel suits. A *Catholic Standard* photographer, Jesuit priest Fr. Bernard Darke, was murdered in broad daylight by House of Israel thugs in 1979.

War on Wheat

Since the mid-1970s the Guyanese economy has been in deep crisis. Mismanagement of state sector enterprises, repressive labor relations, and—to a lesser extent—unfavorable world conditions have caused the perilous decline of the three main sectors of rice, sugar and bauxite. In 1970 Guyana produced 369,000 tons of sugar, but by 1984 this had fallen to 241,851 tons. Dried bauxite production was 2.3 million tons in 1970; in 1983 it was less than 800,000 tons, although there was some recovery in 1984.[7] Only the fact that Guyana produces a special grade of bauxite in high demand and that there is a regional market for Guyana's rice has saved the economy from total collapse.

The impact of the crisis is felt everywhere. Electrical blackouts blanket Georgetown in darkness. Water and sewer systems have broken down in many areas, and obtaining potable drinking water is a severe problem throughout the country. There is not even running water at the Georgetown Hospital, which Guyanese doctors have pronounced a "death trap" due to the filthy conditions, overcrowding and lack of basic drugs and supplies.[8]

In 1982, Burnham announced that the economic crisis would be addressed by substituting local products for imports in order to conserve foreign exchange. Superficially rational, the policy was actually madness in light of the failure of Guyana's own production. To carry out the scheme, the government banned the importation of hundreds of items, including wheat and milk—basic elements in the Guyanese diet—and counseled people to consume rice, praised as a "revolutionary food." It is now a crime in Guyana to import or possess flour, bread, or any other food made from wheat. Police make armed raids on bakeries, extorting protection money from bakers and seizing "illegal" baked goods. The government has even refused gifts of wheat from abroad intended for the nutrition of school children.

By 1984, the list of items in shortage or available only on the black market included wheat flour, bread, milk, tea, margarine, salt, onions, cheese, cooking oil, split peas, cooking gas, soap, toilet paper, matches, tires, batteries, and light bulbs. On the black market, cheese costs G$30 a pound, chicken G$15 a pound, and a 5 lb. tin of powdered milk commands up to G$120 (US$1 = G$4.25).

With the standard wage for the majority of Guyanese workers at G$15.10 per day—recently raised from $12.55—working-class families cannot afford the black market prices. As a result, white rice and starchy root crops like cassava have become the basic diet. Most Guyanese children now suffer some degree of malnutrition, and infant mortality has sky-rocketed. In 1983, the Georgetown Hospital admitted 141 persons suffering from beri-beri (thiamine deficiency disease) linked to a diet of white rice.[9]

Like his political allegiances, Burnham's economic policies have vacillated in a confusing fashion. In 1978 he cooperated willingly with the International Monetary Fund, imposing huge layoffs and cuts in social services to comply with the conditions of an IMF loan. The government also entered into further negotiations with the IMF reportedly centering on the privatization of much of the state sector. In 1983, however, Burnham began vocally rejecting the Fund's conditions, and in 1985 the IMF suspended Guyana's eligibility for new loans. Despite this public rejection of the IMF, basic elements of Burnham's policy are in keeping with IMF theory, such as the devaluation of the Guyanese currency and the low wage levels. The government also has been inviting foreign multinationals back into the country on management contracts, such as the one being worked out with Reynolds and Alcan to run the bauxite industry.

Cracks in the Monolith

There are signs in 1985 that the foundations of the ruling party's dictatorship may be beginning to crack, although the factors mitigating against an early end to PNC control should not be underestimated.

While the two major parties, the PPP and the PNC, still receive most of their support on a racial basis—from East Indians and blacks respectively—race has gradually been declining as a factor in Guyanese politics. This is linked in part to the emergence of the Working People's Alliance (WPA), a small third party. Formed in the early 1970s by dissident elements drawn from the PNC and from African and Indian grassroots groups, the WPA has carried out multi-racial organizing against the Burnham regime.

The WPA's impact has been closely tied to the life and death of Dr. Walter Rodney, best-known member of the party's leadership and beloved by the Guyanese people. On June 13, 1980, a member of the Guyana Defense Force assassinated Rodney by placing a disguised bomb into his hands. Defying official intimidation, forty thousand Guyanese marched twelve miles through the rain behind the young leader's body as the funeral procession wound through Georgetown.

The threat which Burnham feared in Rodney came from what he symbolized and encouraged: a unified Guyanese people taking power back into their own hands. This potential did not die with Rodney, although the WPA has not recovered its earlier momentum since Rodney's death.

It is in the labor arena where the greatest strides have been taken toward healing the deep divisions, racial and otherwise, in the body politic. From 1979 onward, a block of four independent unions, led by the two Indian sugar-workers' unions, fought for workers' rights within the PNC-controlled Trades Union Congress. The primarily black unions in the bauxite sector had long been a PNC stronghold; but after 1980, protracted strikes occurred in the bauxite mines as the workers increasingly found they could not survive or support their families under the prevailing conditions. When the bauxite workers struck for basic foodstuffs in 1983, they were joined by the sugar workers in sympathy strikes. Afterwards, the bauxite unions joined the independent union movement, meaning that workers from the two major productive sectors and the two racial groups were uniting on the basis of their common class interests.

In September 1984, at the Annual Delegates Conference of the TUC, workers voting by secret ballot swept away Burnham operatives from the TUC leadership. This historic move occurred with the help of a silent revolt within the PNC-controlled unions, as many of their rank-and-file secretly cast their votes for independent candidates. The shattering of Burnham's control over the TUC was hailed as a possible harbinger of his eventual loss of control over the society—just as Jagan fell from power in the early sixties after losing control of the TUC.

Another sector in quiet conflict with the PNC is the Guyanese Church. The churches have not opposed the regime directly, although the *Catholic Standard* has been sharply

critical. Rather, they have attempted to play a mediating role between various factions of the society and to relieve suffering by bringing in donated food from abroad—both initiatives sternly rebuffed by Burnham. In early 1985, the Guyana Council of Churches enraged the regime by publishing a paper called "The Role of the Churches in the Search for a Solution to the National Crisis," which without naming the PNC referred in abstract terms to social injustice, "corruption, fraud and violence." When the Guyana Council of Churches attempted to hold its annual meeting shortly afterward, the building was surrounded and barricaded by thugs under the supervision of government officials and the House of Israel.[10]

A further problem for the PNC is the amount of international attention being given to the upcoming elections and the vocal demands both inside and outside Guyana for an election free of fraud. A mission composed of international human rights groups was barred by the Guyana government from entering the country to investigate electoral practices, but it conducted hearings in Trinidad and released an unfavorable report [see sidebar].

Despite these mounting challenges, the most serious in

President Forbes Burnham reviews troops of the Guyana Defense Force.

Guyana Ministry of Information

Burnham's nearly twenty years of rule, the peculiar configuration of Guyanese party politics and the wily president's own ability to maneuver constitute obstacles to any attempt to dislodge the PNC. Burnham has launched a call for "constructive dialogue" with Jagan's PPP (after having rejected unity calls by the PPP for years) in an apparent effort to outwit his opponents with a show of unity behind the government. At the same time he has responded with more repression, attempting to push through a bill which would expand state powers to detain individuals. In an aggressive move to counter church criticism, Burnham has created a "Guyana Council of Religious" linked to the ruling party and headed by the Rabbi Washington.

Probably the most serious obstacle to change is the continuing absence of any creative linkage between the two main opposition parties. The PPP, numerically the far stronger of the two, is an orthodox Marxist-Leninist party which approves of the PNC's anti-imperialism and apparently still sees in the ruling party some hope for an eventual socialist transformation. The WPA, on the other hand, maintains that opposition to the Burnham dictatorship should come "without ideological preconditions," and it has been willing to work with anti-communist opposition forces like the Catholic Church. The WPA argues that Guyana cannot undertake a socialist transformation until the working people have taken control democratically, and for this reason the party has placed great emphasis on the need for clean elections. The relationship between the two parties has become increasingly hostile. The PPP leadership accuses the WPA of lacking a class analysis and of collaborating with right-wing Guyanese elements and even with the CIA; while the WPA condemns the PPP for its willingness to collaborate with the Burnham dictatorship (referring to the PPP's calls for a "united front" government) and for participating in the regime's fraudulent elections.

The situation in Guyana has received little press outside the Caribbean. Inside the region it is being very carefully watched as a crisis situation where significant change of some sort *must* occur soon. One Guyanese commentator writes:

> Today, "socialism," like cooperativism—the instrument that was to give meaning to the PNC's socialist creed—earns very poor ratings in Guyana and provokes many negative responses, largely the result of PNC politics and management of the economy over the past 20 years.
>
> Yet, there are influential voices within the society that still feel that it is in Guyana where the possibilities for "socialist transformation," based on *democratic principles,* remain the strongest among states of the 13-member Caribbean Community.[11] ∎

FINDINGS OF THE ELECTION MISSION

In May 1985, at the request of fourteen civic, religious and political organizations in Guyana, the British Parliamentary Human Rights Group and the New York-based Americas Watch carried out a joint mission to assess political freedom in Guyana in the context of the upcoming elections. Barred by the Burnham government from entering Guyana, the delegation heard evidence in Trinidad from prominent Guyanese representing a cross-section of the political spectrum. Some excerpts from their report:

"...In the course of our discussions, we were struck by a key feature of the Guyanese situation: the ruling party maintains a stranglehold on all aspects of society. It is their total control over the civil service, the military, the economy, the judicial system, the media, and the educational system which has allowed the PNC to maintain itself in power without resorting to a great deal of overt repression. [The regime has] managed to silence to a large extent internal opposition through a combination of intimidation and the selective use of force.

... To the extent that freedom of assembly exists in Guyana, it applies only to the PNC's supporters. Although the campaign for this year's election has not begun in earnest, there are disturbing signs that the experience of past elections with regard to free assembly will be repeated ...

The PNC government's total control over Guyanese society extends also to every aspect of the electoral process, from the means of communicating with the electorate to the actual machinery of the election itself...
Unless this year's election is administered by all the parties or by a completely non-partisan body, another fraudulent election is highly likely. We left Port-of-Spain profoundly pessimistic about the future of democracy in Guyana under the present regime."

Interim Report of the Joint Mission to Investigate Political Freedom in Guyana, May 1985.

Editor's postscript: On August 6, 1985, Forbes Burnham died at age 62 following throat surgery at Georgetown Hospital in the Guyanese capital. He was succeeded by Desmond Hoyte as president and PNC party leader and Hamilton Greene as vice-president and prime minister. Both are considered hard-line advocates of PNC "paramountcy," and President Hoyte's comment on the 1986 election was ominous: "The PNC must win." Despite these suggestions that the upcoming election will be rigged as usual by the ruling party, it is too early to tell what the long-term impact of Burnham's death on the Guyanese political scene will be.

THE LAST COLONIES' DILEMMA

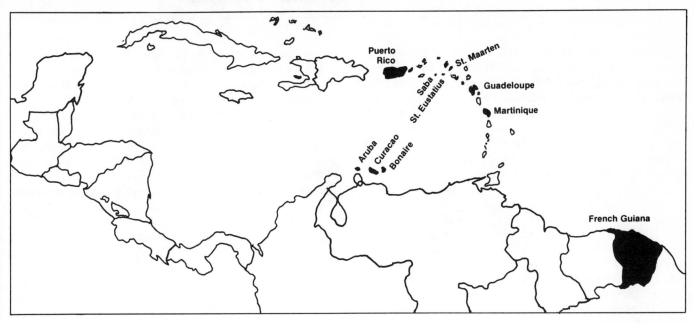

While most of the region wrestles with the problems of neocolonialism and imperialism, the question for several Caribbean territories is even more basic. They are still colonies, aberrations in the 1980s when most of the Caribbean has achieved political independence. In each case, the question of whether or not to press for independence is a dilemma filled with contradictions, conflicting desires and fears about the future. Underlying the confusion is the fundamental question: What kind of independence to struggle for?

Britain, France, Holland and the United States all maintain colonies or trust territories in the Caribbean. Britain's present colonies (or "dependent territories") include Bermuda, Montserrat, the British Virgin Islands, the Cayman Islands, the Turks & Caicos, and Anguilla. With the exception of Bermuda—historically a part of the Caribbean although located in the Atlantic—the British dependencies consist of tiny micro-islands which would have extreme difficulty surviving on their own. Although they are internally self-governing, all have made it clear that they do not want to be separated from Britain.

The French territories consist of Guadeloupe and Martinique, islands in the Windward chain; and French Guiana (Guyane), a larger territory on the South American mainland. Technically, they are not colonies but overseas departments of France. France also controls the tiny island of St. Barthélemy and half of St. Martin (the other half is controlled by Holland).

Since Suriname became independent in 1975, the remaining Dutch colony in the Caribbean is a six-island federation known as the Netherlands Antilles. It is officially an autonomous nation within the Kingdom of the Netherlands. The three larger islands, sometimes called the ABC islands, are Aruba, Bonaire and Curaçao, located just off the coast of Venezuela. The others are the much smaller islands of St. Eustatius, Saba and St. Maarten, located in the Leeward island chain. (They are known, however, as the Dutch Windwards because they lie to the east or windward side of the ABC islands.)

The largest island in the Caribbean still under colonial domination belongs not to a European power, but to the United States. Officially, Puerto Rico is a "commonwealth in free association" with the U.S., a status it acquired in 1952. It has a non-voting representative in the U.S. Congress. But the reality is inescapably a colonial one. The Decolonization Committee of the United Nations has repeatedly declared Puerto Rico to be a colony and called for self-determination for the island. And while they disagree on the goal—independence, statehood, or continued Commonwealth status—all three major political parties in Puerto Rico agree that the island is effectively a colony now.

Finally, the U.S. Virgin Islands are an "unincorporated territory" of the United States, like Guam and American Samoa. Consisting of St. Thomas, St. Croix, and St. John, they are internally self-governing but are subject to most U.S. laws. Like Puerto Rico, the Virgin Islands have only non-voting representation in the U.S. Congress. ∎

The French Antilles: "You Will Remain French"

Arriving in Guadeloupe from the English-speaking Caribbean, one has the sensation of entering a world apart. Highways and high-rise apartments appear on the outskirts of Pointe-à-Pitre, which resembles a medium-sized city in France. In the countryside, small farmers live not in shacks but in pastel houses filled with imported French furniture. People are aware that Guadeloupe is located in the Caribbean, but places like Trinidad and Jamaica are considered alien and remote. The center of the Guadeloupean universe is France.

The superimposition of French consumer culture on a Caribbean island has produced bizarre contrasts. Store shelves overflow with Parisian clothing and housewares, while fresh meats, fruits, and vegetables are flown in daily from France. Racks display magazines with names like *Belle Maison* (House Beautiful) and *La Voiture Individuelle* (The Personal Automobile). Guadeloupeans—the majority of whom are of African descent—speak not of France but of *la métropole,* to which many travel frequently. It is easier to telephone across the Atlantic Ocean to the metropole than it is to call Dominica, 30 miles away.

Yet Guadeloupe, along with its sister island Martinique, is linked to the rest of the Caribbean through its history and people. In the 18th and 19th centuries, while Britain's Caribbean colonies grew sugar for Britain, the French Antilles produced sugar, tobacco, coffee and cocoa for France. In both cases, the wealth was produced by an enslaved African labor force on large estates owned by European planters. In the 20th century, however, the paths of the English and French colonies divided. While Britain's colonies moved toward political independence, France "decolonized" her Caribbean possessions in the opposite manner—by making them part of France. In 1946, Guadeloupe, Martinique, French Guiana, and the island of Réunion in the Indian Ocean became French "overseas departments," or *départements d'outre-mer.*

Living on Welfare

Departmentalization, as it was called, deepened France's cultural, economic, and political hold over the islands. French culture was promoted as *la culture officielle,* and everything indigenous was de-emphasized and rejected. A special office called BUMIDOM was set up to help Antilleans emigrate, easing unemployment in the colonies while filling low-wage jobs in France. The movement of mostly young, unskilled Guadeloupeans to France became a huge transfer of people on the order of some 3,000 per year. At the same time, many white metropolitan Frenchmen arrived in Guadeloupe and Martinique to take highly-paid professional and civil service posts.

When France joined the European Economic Community in 1958, Antillean sugar, produced on antiquated, labor-intensive plantations, came into competition with cheaper European beet sugar. France responded by systematically cutting back production in its Caribbean departments, and by 1980 all but three of Guadeloupe's 28 sugar factories had closed. This meant idleness for many sugar factory workers, cane cutters, and small cane farmers.

The powerful plantocracy, known as *békés* in Martinique and *blanc-pays* in Guadeloupe, meanwhile transferred much of its capital out of sugar and into commerce. Thousands of acres of their lands lie idle and overgrown in the rural areas. Other land has been taken over by French multinationals, such as the Compagnie Fruitière, which controls banana and pineapple production in several former French colonies in Africa. The company arrived in Guadeloupe in 1978 and began buying up cane lands to plant bananas. As small cane farmers lost their lands to this process, they were forced to become wage laborers on the banana plantations.

Guadeloupe's economy, like that of Martinique and French Guiana, functions on the basis of French subsidies for the purchase of French goods. The revenues from banana and sugar exports pay for only about 16% of what Guadeloupe consumes.[1] The standard of living is kept artificially high by an array of *allocations* or payments from France including various forms of welfare, unemployment compensation, and the lucrative "40%," a salary bonus paid to civil servants in the overseas departments.

But there has been a price to pay for this artificial affluence. If the benefits of French colonialism are obvious and material, the drawbacks are largely in the intangible realm: idleness, cultural alienation, and a depressing welfare mentality which saps the energy and self-respect of the Guadeloupean people. Unemployment is around 30%, and underemployment even higher. While emigration has provided an escape valve, it is a far from satisfactory solution. It robs the society of its youngest and strongest members, while Antilleans working at low-wage jobs in France learn few valuable skills. And contrary to the myth of the metropole as a paradise where Antilleans enjoy equal rights with other French citizens, the black immigrant's experience in France is more likely to be one of unemployment and racial discrimination.

As these realities become better known, more Guadeloupean youth have resisted pressures to emigrate. But the best positions at home are filled by metropolitan French, while many unskilled jobs are taken by Haitian and Dominican immigrants whom employers hire illegally in order to pay less than the minimum wage. The only ways out, for many Guadeloupeans, remain emigration or welfare.

While Guadeloupe's agriculture is becoming less important to France, the colony is becoming steadily more important as a base for French influence in Latin America and the Caribbean. The concept of the Antilles as a "window" on the Americas grew out of French president Charles de Gaulle's determination to restore the grandeur of imperial France after the Second World War. Under this plan, Guadeloupe was to become a depot for French exports destined for Latin American markets. Today, the so-called "industrial zone" at the port of Pointe-à-Pitre is actually a series of warehouses for the storage and transshipment of merchandise.

Guadeloupe is the center of the French military presence in the Americas. The *forces de l'ordre* on the island total some 5,000 men, including police, a national guard, French army troops, and the *forces spéciales,* a French strike force for overseas intervention. France is presently constructing several large camps in Guadeloupe for the storage of heavy military equipment.[2] In addition, the Antilles serve as a foothold for the expansion of French political and cultural influence in the Caribbean, directed particularly toward the other Creole-speaking countries of Haiti, Dominica, and St. Lucia.

Because of the strategic value of the French Antilles—plus the desire to maintain the vestiges of empire, however small—France is determined to hold on to its Caribbean departments. Subsidies are a price Paris willingly pays to keep the colonies loyal and ensure that pro-independence sentiments never take root beyond a minority of the population. But in the 1980s, recession in France brought a leveling-off of subsidies and higher taxation of Antilleans, triggering more open grumbling about the terms of the colonial relationship. And in 1984, the explosion of the Kanak independence movement in the Pacific island of New Caledonia has drastically changed the terms of the independence debate.

The Patriotic Movement

General Charles de Gaulle, the father of modern French imperialism, condescendingly referred to the French Antilles as "mere specks of dust on the map."[3] He liked to admonish Antilleans that they had no national traditions other than those France had given them: "You are French, you have always been French, and you will remain French."

Today, the French argument for continuing colonialism still invokes the Gaullist myth that Antilleans are "black Frenchmen" whose love for *la mère patrie*—the mother country—should equal that felt by any metropolitan French-man. This view is shared by the right wing in Guadeloupe and Martinique, consisting primarily of white descendants of the old plantocracy, as well as metropolitan French living in the Antilles. An editorial in the rightist magazine *Guadeloupe 2000* states:

> What we must constantly emphasize is that we are French, for reasons of language, culture, and history, for better or for worse . . . One doesn't choose his country, the land of his forefathers, any more than one chooses his father and mother. One is born French by an accident of birth.[4]

It is true that a majority of French Antilleans presently vote in favor of continued ties to France. But the reasons for most have little to do with any sentimental attachment to French culture. Trapped in an economy based on French subsidies and welfare, most Guadeloupeans, Martiniquans, and Guyanais cannot imagine how they would survive if the umbilical cord were cut. The right wing capitalizes on these fears by threatening that an independent Guadeloupe or Martinique would become "like Haiti" or "like Dominica"—poor independent countries which were once French colonies.

Nonetheless, the question of colonialism versus independence is more complicated and goes deeper than the seemingly clear-cut case to be made for economic interests. At stake are intangible values of national identity, self-respect, and links to other Caribbean and Third World peoples. The Antilles have strong historical connections to the anti-colonial and Pan-African tradition. The mayor of Fort-de-France, the capital of Martinique, is Aimé Césaire, who originated the concept of negritude in the 1930s. Martinique is also the birthplace of Frantz Fanon, who became a world spokesman for national liberation movements through his writings in *The Wretched of the Earth* and *Black Skin, White Masks*.

"Young person don't leave your country. No to BUMIDOM!"

The contemporary independence movement had its birth among young Antilleans studying in France in the 1950s and 1960s. There they were exposed to the ongoing struggles against French colonialism in Algeria and Tunisia, and some were drafted into the French army and sent to fight against the African liberation movements. This experience, plus the racism which many Antilleans encountered in France, led to a realization that France was not the benevolent "motherland" but a racist colonial power which would set one colonized people against another to preserve its empire. In 1963, GONG, an association of Guadeloupean nationals in France, began to push the idea of an Antillean independence struggle. GONG came under heavy repression by de Gaulle, foreshadowing the violent response of the French state to the independence movement.

The movement began to develop a popular base in Guadeloupe in the 1970s with the formation of the Union of Agricultural Workers (UTA). Up to then, all unions in Guadeloupe had been affiliates of unions in France. In 1970, after months of clandestine organizing among sugar cane cutters and small farmers, the UTA was formed and won a battle for recognition which pitted the peasants against the combined forces of the French government, the plantocracy, and the French-based unions.

The following years were a period of growing peasant militancy, with numerous strikes over wages and other demands. These demands received support from middle-class sectors including students, teachers, professionals, youth, and grassroots Christians, many of whom joined in collective cane cutting to symbolize their solidarity with the peasants. Gradually, the UTA developed a political analysis which identified French colonialism as the root problem and linked material demands for workers to political demands for Guadeloupe.[5]

The UTA became the model for a set of new unions in health, education, construction, and other industries, incorporated into a pro-independence federation, the General Union of Guadeloupean Workers. In addition, the movement contains a strong grassroots Christian element. The catalyst for this was a strike in the cane fields in 1975 in which a Catholic priest, Fr. Chérubin Céleste, staged a hunger strike to protest the employers' use of Haitian workers as strikebreakers. He was supported by other Christian groups including Working-Class Christian Youth and the Rural Movement of Christian Youth, both structurally within the Catholic Church but frowned upon by the hierarchy for being "too political." Another pro-independence group, Christians for the Liberation of Guadeloupe, consists of grassroots Christians outside the Church.

Labor, peasants, youth and Christians still constitute the base of the patriotic movement, as the pro-independence forces call themselves. This base is non-violent, a fact not fully understood outside the Antilles since political bombings are often the only news reported about the French islands. The wing of the movement responsible for the bombings consists of a relatively small number of individuals who have resurfaced over the years under various names. Their attacks are targeted against symbols of the French state and large French capitalist interests, and are defended as "violent struggle" in the tradition

of the Algerian revolution. But in contrast to the situation in Algeria, a majority of the population in the French Antilles clearly rejects the use of violence. So while a minority argues that attacks on the state are necessary to keep the colonial issue visible—and the movement as a whole rallies around those arrested for such attacks—the majority of independence activists believe that bombings alienate the public and hinder the development of a mass-based movement.

La Société Bloquée

Pro-independence intellectuals refer to Guadeloupe as *une société bloquée,* a "blocked society," in which the standard of living is maintained by subsidies while true development is frustrated. A priest within the movement sums up:

> The Guadeloupean is not his own person. Under the present system, we don't really exist; we exist only in relation to France.
> At the economic level French control has been a failure. Our economy is based exclusively on the needs of France. All the real potential of our country, especially in agriculture, has been ignored. Importing French social laws and economic structures doesn't work for us. For example, when France raises the minimum wage at home, it goes up here too, which we can't afford to do. The result is layoffs and worse unemployment.
> Independence would undoubtedly create hardship, but it's hard already, especially for the young people. They run after unattainable material success. As a society, we are torn by internal conflict and alienated by what is our own.
> We haven't yet explored our own possibilities. We assume someone else will solve our problems. Haitians and Dominicans are poor, but they are creators. We create nothing.[6]

The political wing of the independence movement is the Popular Union for the Liberation of Guadeloupe (UPLG), a semi-clandestine group. Its platform emphasizes three major themes. One is the revalorization of Antillean culture, especially the indigenous *kréyòl* (Creole) language. Officially suppressed since departmentalization in 1946, the language seems to express the heart of the Antillean identity which is separate from that of France. It is used as a political symbol by the independence movement, which has made headway in forcing the establishment to accord the popular language a place of respect. Also making a comeback is *gwoka,* an indigenous music based on African drum rhythms.

Secondly, the movement stresses the identity of Guadeloupe, Martinique and French Guiana as *Caribbean* countries. Domination by France has largely cut off Antilleans from contact with other Afro-Caribbean peoples whose history they share. Even highly educated Martiniquans and Guadeloupeans are often uninformed about events in the English, Spanish and Dutch-speaking Caribbean. "We know everything that happens in France, and close ourselves to what happens in the rest of the Caribbean," says the leader of a Christian group.[7]

It is in the economic sphere that the independence movement both makes its strongest case and encounters the greatest contradictions. The movement's primary goal is to reestablish production in the Antilles, weaning them from

"Negroes back to Africa—Long live the French in Guadeloupe." Racist graffiti on Pointe-à-Pitre walls expresses right-wing sentiment.

(Right) Collective farming on occupied land in the Guadeloupe countryside.

Ja Ka Ta

dependence on France. Among other things, the UPLG calls for:

- saving the sugar industry to provide employment
- support to small and medium banana farmers
- diversification of agriculture, including food production and livestock raising
- development of fishing, agro-industry and crafts development of new industries such as those based on sugar cane byproducts
- land policy favoring production, not speculation developing trade ties with other Caribbean countries.[8]

Independence activists identify French control as the reason why these things haven't been done, and assert that independence would make them possible. The problem with this theory is that external economic control has persisted in nearly all the politically *independent* countries of the Caribbean. Indeed, the prescription for self-reliance offered by the Antillean independence movement is similar to economic reforms advocated by other Caribbean progressive groups. For the rest of the Caribbean, political independence has not led to economic independence; would it be different for the French Antilles?

Rendering this question even more difficult is the fact that the pro-independence groups do not agree on what kind of independence they are struggling for. Some feel that economic independence must be linked to socialism, while others are vague about the political forms which might emerge. To confuse matters further, the official Socialist and Communist parties in the Antilles do not advocate immediate independence, but call for "autonomy," or self-government without independence.

Impact of New Caledonia

Shock waves from the Kanak movement for independence from France in New Caledonia have reverberated forcefully through the French Caribbean. Against the backdrop of economic decline in the Antilles, New Caledonia has been the catalyst for the latent pro-independence sympathies of the Antillean population, particularly in Guadeloupe. The independence debate has now entered the mainstream of political life. This popularization of an idea long rejected by the majority is ringing alarm bells in Paris and among right-wing circles in the overseas departments. The French newspaper *Le Monde* reported in early 1985:

> A mental tilt has begun, defying objective interests. Little by little the idea of independence is ceasing to be a taboo discussed only by a few nationalist students, nostalgic readers of Frantz Fanon. The idea is spreading, finding its way into political speeches and the regional Assembly, intruding into social conflicts, and even more insidiously, into casual conversation.[9]

After years of semi-clandestinity, the UPLG is now playing an increasingly open and dynamic role. "It is everywhere, this 'patriotic camp'!" exclaimed *Le Monde*. "At strikes, in the sugar cane fields, and in the streets . . . "[10] With the island air charged by the momentum of the Kanak struggle, 1984 was a year of intense and frequent conflicts in Guadeloupean society. Strikes broke out in all sectors, including the port, airlines, hospitals, and the sugar industry, with economic and political demands increasingly intertwined.

The newspaper added that the "principal danger of explosion" appeared to be in the rural areas. The countryside has been an arena of conflict since the late 1970s, when groups of landless farmers, underpaid wage workers, and the unemployed began taking over idle land for collective farming. In some cases, the peasant "occupiers" had worked the plot for years and were simply resisting eviction when the land was sold. In one such case, at Bonne Mère, people lay down in front of bulldozers sent to clear their huts from land being sold to the Compagnie Fruitière.[11]

Despite intimidation, including interventions by the *forces de l'ordre,* the occupations continued. They became in the process an important vehicle for political consciousness, symbolizing the rejection of idleness and dependency, the determination to reclaim the land for production, and the potential of unified militant action. In May 1984, ten thousand people gathered on a farm at St. Rose to collectively cultivate land recovered from large landowners. By early 1985 *Le Monde* reported that some 1,500 hectares in the countryside had come under direct control of pro-independence unions.[12]

Inevitably, there has been a mounting confrontation with the state. The violent fringe of the movement, newly reincarnated as the Revolutionary Caribbean Alliance, stepped up its campaign of bombings in 1983 and 1984. This included for the first time coordinated, simultaneous attacks in Guadeloupe, Martinique and French Guiana. The authorities responded by making some twenty arrests and putting Luc Reinette, presumed leader of the armed faction, behind bars once again. At the same time, violence against the independence movement also has increased, both from the state and from private militias at the service of right-wing béké and corporate interests.

The establishment line is that New Caledonia and the French Caribbean have "nothing in common." But for the UPLG, primary pole of the anti-colonial movement in the French Antilles, the success of the Kanaks in forcing the French to negotiate is an inspiration and a sign that "France is now forced to begin a final era of decolonization" of its remaining colonies.[13] The UPLG has sent representatives to New Caledonia and has declared solidarity with the Kanak people. On April 6-7, 1985, independence activists from all the French overseas departments and territories gathered in Guadeloupe for a conference aimed at coordinating struggles and reinforcing unity against French colonialism.

Winning over the so-called "belly vote" based on economic security is nonetheless not an easy or immediate prospect. The disastrous decline of the Caribbean's independent economies is an added disincentive, forcing many French Antilleans to conclude that colonialism is preferable to a bankrupt independence. The French for their part are unlikely to give up willingly. But the seeds of change have been planted, history presses forward, and Antilleans of all political persuasions are carefully watching the New Caledonia crisis to see what the outcome will be. ∎

GUIANA: FRENCH FOOTHOLD IN LATIN AMERICA

One writer called it the "forgotten colony"—"underpopulated, underexploited . . . [but] never abandoned."[1] French Guiana, known in French as Guyane, is the last remaining colony on the South American continent and the largest Caribbean territory still under colonial domination.

Actually Guiana has never been forgotten, at least not by the French. It has always served a specific purpose, although that purpose has changed over the centuries. After France lost its North American colonies in the 1700s, it opened Guiana to settlement in order to establish a new stronghold in the Americas. Thousands of Frenchmen died in the ill-conceived attempt to settle Guiana's dense jungle, giving the country the nickname of the "Green Hell."[2] In 1852 a prison was constructed at Devil's Island, and Guiana became a notorious graveyard for French prisoners.

Today, the French interest in Guiana focuses on the Kourou Space Center, the European equivalent of Cape Canaveral located on Guiana's coast. The European Space Agency launched the Ariane Rocket from Kourou in 1979 and has since fired 10 shots. The tenth shot in August 1984 launched two telecommunications satellites, one European and one French, representing the European consortium's bid to become a major player in the commercial space race.[3]

The space center is a European enclave with little direct impact on the economy of Guiana. The colony's economic base rests almost entirely on administrative payments and subsidies from France. It has shrimp and timber resources, but neither are fully exploited. Since the population is small (less than 75,000), France clearly feels that keeping the space center is worth the price of subsidizing and maintaining the country.

For these reasons, independence is a remote prospect for French Guiana. There is one small independence group, *Fo Nou Libéré la Guyane* (Creole for "we must liberate Guyane") and there have been scattered bombings coordinated with those in Guadeloupe and Martinique. But the problem of economic dependence is even more acute here than in the French Antilles, due to Guiana's small population and lack of a productive base. This is compounded by its geographic isolation from the Caribbean and by the unusual ethnic diversity of its population. Instead of a nearly homogeneous black population which can look to its African heritage for a sense of nationhood, French Guiana includes Creoles (blacks), six different Amerindian groups, and an array of smaller immigrant groups including Chinese, Javanese, Brazilians, Haitians and Hmong people from Laos.[4] In addition to the other factors mitigating against independence, none of these latter groups are likely to be enthusiastic about an independence movement which is dominated politically by one group, the Creoles.

The Netherlands Antilles: Reluctant Independence

Independence is a serious topic for the Netherlands Antilles in the eighties. Unlike France, Holland wants to rid itself of its colonies—the sooner the better. Reluctantly facing the prospect of eventual separation from Holland, and beset by economic problems stemming from the decline of the oil sector, the Netherlands Antilles are mired in confusion about what they want and when they want it.

The question of independence for the Netherlands Antilles cannot be separated from the question of Aruba's decision to secede from the six-island federation which also includes Curaçao, Bonaire, St. Maarten, St. Eustatius, and Saba. Aruba's controversial separatist movement reflects both its long-standing resentment against domination by Curaçao and a history of separate development which makes all the Antilles unlikely partners in a federation. This separateness dates back to pre-Columbian times, when the Arawak Indians living on Curaçao, Aruba and Bonaire were prevented by difficult ocean currents from traveling between the islands. Instead, lines of commerce and communication developed between each island and the Venezuelan mainland, a pattern which persists today.

The Dutch occupied Curaçao in 1634 as a base for wars against the Spanish, and took over Aruba and Bonaire two years later so that the Spanish could not counterattack from those islands.[2] The largest of the Dutch possessions, Curaçao became the base from which Holland controlled commerce in the Caribbean during its "Golden Age." From their colonial beginnings, therefore, Aruba and Bonaire were viewed as adjuncts to Curaçao and have been administratively subordinated to it.[3]

In addition to this historic tension, the Netherlands Antilles have been deprived of a sense of nationhood by differing histories and geographic distance. Curaçao was once a slave market from which the Dutch supplied other colonies. Its population therefore is largely of African descent, into which subsequent immigration has introduced diverse elements including persons of Dutch, Jewish, and Portuguese origin. Aruba, by contrast, was basically an Amerindian society until well into the 19th century.[4] The Arawak descendants intermarried with Venezuelan immigrants to produce a mestizo population which has always had its own identity. The Dutch Windwards, for their part, lie 600 miles to the north of the ABC islands. Their orientation is not toward Venezuela but toward neighboring islands and the United States. The Windwards speak English, not Papiamento which is spoken in the ABC islands.

When the Netherlands Antilles became a "nation" within the Kingdom of the Netherlands in 1954, they were reorganized into four autonomous units at Aruba's request. Today, each of the four—Curaçao, Aruba, Bonaire, and the Windwards—has its own local government. But the Central government which

"Independence? And how?" The Curaçao Federation of Workers, the largest labor federation on the island, held a conference in 1979 to discuss concerns about independence.

administers the federation and the liaison with Holland is dominated by Curaçao, due to Curaçao's larger population. This has been a continuing source of Aruban resentment.

Led by the charismatic Betico Croes, the Aruban separatist movement brought all parties to a "Round Table Conference" in 1983 to hammer out the islands' future relationship. As a result, Aruba will get *status aparte* on January 1, 1986, separating it from the other five islands but maintaining an individual link to Holland. After ten years of this separate status, Aruba will gain complete independence.

Soon after the Round Table conference, doubts and bitterness began to emerge. Curaçao, Bonaire and the Windwards have always opposed Aruba's separatist aspirations. They face a fundamental contradiction: the recognition of Aruba's right to self-determination versus the desire for strength through unity, which in the Caribbean has always meant inter-island federations. In addition to their fear of fragmentation, the "Antilles of the Five" question the financial consequences of breaking up the federation. Curaçao in particular fears that under the new agreement Holland will be able to shift onto it much of the burden of supporting the weaker islands. Using this as a rallying point, the Curaçao trade unions launched a vehement campaign to reverse the Round Table decisions, calling on Aruba to "stop the nonsense!"[5]

The Multinationals Pull Out

Hanging over the discussion is the larger unknown: the economic future of the Netherlands Antilles. The region-wide decline in the oil industry has undercut the prosperity of the two larger islands, Aruba and Curaçao, whose giant oil refineries have long been the basis of their economies.

Royal Dutch Shell began scaling down its Curaçao operations several years ago, demanding concessions in return for a promise to keep the refinery operating. Workers at the Curaçao refinery voted overwhelmingly in April 1984 to accept a substantial pay cut after bitter and protracted negotiations with the company. Although the island establishment feared social unrest harkening back to the 1969 riots, there was neither protest nor a strike—because Shell held the trump card:

> Mr. Wilson, Shell's manager . . . declared that his orders from London were quite clear. Either the union agrees to the proposed pay cuts and other economizing measures, in which case Shell will continue its construction plans for the next five years, or the Shell company will leave the island within three or four years.[6]

Despite the union's compliance with Shell's demands, the company announced a little over a year later that it would close the Curaçao refinery on October 1, 1985. The Shell pullout followed a similar move by Exxon, which closed its Aruba refinery in March 1985. With the departure of the oil companies, the Netherlands Antilles are seeing an entire period of their history come to a sudden end.

This rising economic insecurity in what is still one of the more affluent consumer societies in the Caribbean has left Curaçaolenes even more nervous than before about the prospect of future independence from Holland. The other sectors of the economy are not doing well either. Tourism has suffered from the devaluation of the Venezuelan bolivar (many tourists to Curaçao are Venezuelans and Colombians on shopping trips), while offshore banking and services, the largest economic sector, is threatened by the probable loss of a tax treaty with the United States. Given this situation, Curaçao is loath to lose Dutch economic aid, and at least 80% of Curaçaolenes say they do not favor independence. A number of unions have taken a stand in favor of eventual independence, but stress that there must be careful planning to make it economically viable.[7]

It is generally assumed that Holland's economic interests in the Netherlands Antilles would remain untouched by political independence. Holland passes enormous sums of money through Curaçao, which serves as the primary base for Dutch capitalism in the western hemisphere. Dutch multinationals such as Phillips, Unilever and KLM have extensive investments in Latin American countries, especially Chile. The suspicion is that Holland wants to shed its financial burden while continuing to use the Netherlands Antilles as a base, leading some people to grumble about a "cheap way out for the Dutch."[8]

The Dutch presence is only a day-to-day reality for Antilleans in limited terms. Dutch influence is concentrated in the structures of government, the educational system, the legal system, and the banks. Holland never made much effort to culturally assimilate its colonies, however, and Dutch is less and less used as a spoken language in the Antilles.[9] In terms of cultural imperialism, Venezuela is perceived as more of a threat than Holland, and U.S. influence through the mass media is growing rapidly.

This means that while many Antilleans express a desire to define a national identity more clearly, the Dutch presence is not seen as the primary obstacle to that process. Rather, the islands' own histories have made them multilingual melting pots unsure of their own identities, much less that of the federation. "There is no nationhood," says a Curaçao teacher.[10] Throughout Caribbean history, the divisions between island and island and between the English, Spanish, French and Dutch domains have separated peoples who share historic and cultural roots. The case of the Netherlands Antilles reveals the reverse side of this process: how the economic, political and military designs of colonialism have forced diverse peoples into artificial groupings, and left them with the task of forging a nation in the post-colonial era. ∎

Puerto Rico: U.S. Colony in the Caribbean

The history of Puerto Rico in this century has been dominated by a tug-of-war between two powerful forces. On one side is the United States, the world's greatest economic and military power, determined to hold on to its base in the Caribbean. On the other side is the Puerto Rican people, their nationhood deeply rooted in history and expressed in recurrent struggles for independence over a period of more than 100 years.

Visible support for independence in Puerto Rican society is presently small. That is, no more than 6-7% of the electorate votes for the Puerto Rican Independence Party (PIP) or the Puerto Rican Socialist Party (PSP) in current elections. This fact must be placed in historical perspective, however, since support for independence has always ebbed and flowed according to certain short-term conditions, including economic fluctuations and the level of political repression. In general, pro-independence sentiment rises in times of economic hardship, and subsides in times of affluence. The backdrop is one of pervasive ideological control through the educational system, the media, and the Church.

The Puerto Rican independence movement today has its base among labor unions, students and intellectuals, and progressive religious and ecumenical groups. They invite North Americans to join them in a decolonizing process for Puerto Rico, one which must begin with an understanding of the nation's history and of how that nationhood has been denied by U.S. control.

The Puerto Rican independence movement has its roots in the 19th century struggle for independence from Spain. On September 23, 1868, this erupted in the *Grito de Lares* (Cry of Lares) led by Puerto Rican patriot Ramón Emeterio Betances, proclaiming the First Republic of Puerto Rico. Although it was quickly crushed by the Spanish militia, the Lares rebellion signaled that independence for the Puerto Rican nation was not far off.

This was not to be. On July 25, 1898, at the conclusion of the Spanish-American War, U.S. troops invaded Puerto Rico and claimed it as "compensation" for wartime expenses. The Foraker Act of 1900 institutionalized U.S. military and political control over the Island, and in 1917, the Jones Act imposed U.S. citizenship on Puerto Ricans, making them eligible for the draft a month before the United States entered World War I. The leading spokesperson for opposition to this U.S. takeover was José de Diego, president of the Puerto Rican Chamber of Deputies.

Although it granted some internal self-government to the Island, the United States continued to exercise complete power over Puerto Rico's laws, currency, customs, immigration, postal service, defense, trade, and foreign relations. English was imposed as the language of instruction in Puerto Rican schools, even though the students and indeed most of the teachers could not speak it. Another assimilating force was the work of the Protestant mission churches, which entered Puerto Rico to evangelize and promote an Americanized, middle-class way of life.

In the 1930s, the economic impact of the Depression fueled a dynamic nationalist movement against U.S. domination. The pro-independence Liberal Party represented nearly half the electorate, while the radical Nationalist Party engaged in direct anti-colonial struggle under the leadership of Pedro Albizu Campos. The Nationalists were violently repressed by the police, culminating in Albizu's imprisonment in 1936 and the Ponce Massacre of 1937, when police opened fire on a Nationalist protest march.

The imprisonment of Albizu decapitated the Nationalist Party and opened the way for new forces to co-opt the movement. In 1938, the radical wing of the Liberal Party broke off to form the Popular Democratic Party ("*los Populares*") under Luis Muñoz Marín. Elected to head the Island's Senate in 1940, Muñoz proceeded to "defer" the status issue while bringing about popular reforms such as a minimum wage law. In 1948, together with U.S. authorities, Muñoz launched

Schoolchild reads from an English-language primer in a Puerto Rican classroom around 1950.

Operation Bootstrap, the industrialization program which tied Puerto Rico's economy to U.S. capital investment and encouraged Puerto Ricans to migrate to the United States [see Part III, Ch. 2].

To facilitate this U.S. economic penetration, Muñoz pushed for a political accommodation with the colonial power. This came in the form of Law 600, which laid the legal basis for the Free Associated State or "Commonwealth" status which was to follow in 1952. Law 600 triggered a violent protest in October 1950 known as the Nationalist Insurrection. The military was called out, over three thousand protesters were arrested, and "when the Free Associated State was established in 1952, the jails were full of Puerto Rican patriots . . . "[1] Although there were some changes (for instance, Spanish was reinstated in the schools) Commonwealth was merely a guise for the continuing reality of colonialism.

Rapid economic growth marked the early years of Bootstrap, giving rise to a new consumerism linked to dependence on the United States. At the same time, hundreds of thousands of Puerto Ricans responded to economic pressures by migrating to New York. Both factors worked to blunt the independence movement for the next two decades, during which time the Populares governed uninterrupted.

In the late 1960s the independence movement took on new life, transforming itself into a pro-socialist movement rooted in student and labor sectors. It emphasized opposition to the U.S. military presence on the Island, and especially to the drafting of Puerto Ricans into the U.S. Army during the Vietnam War. When a plebescite on the status issue was held in 1967, the *independentista* parties called for a boycott, and one-third of the electorate stayed away from the polls.

At the other end of the political spectrum, a pro-statehood position emerged modeled on Hawaii's and Alaska's incorporation into the United States. Linked to wealthy sectors of Puerto Rican society led by the Ferré family, the statehood push resulted in the formation of the New Progressive Party (NPP) in 1967. The NPP candidate, Carlos Romero Barceló, was elected governor in 1976 and narrowly reelected in 1980 in an election tainted with fraud.

Romero's election did not mean that statehood became a reality, since Puerto Rico's political status is determined in Washington, not San Juan. Nor could any Puerto Rican administration, even a pro-statehood one, arrive at such a decision lightly. The prospect of statehood (or "annexation" as critics term it) is highly controversial, due in large part to the new taxes it would impose on Puerto Ricans.

Romero did, however, forge a policy of cultural assimilation and military collaboration with the United States. For example, bilingual English-Spanish programs were introduced into Puerto Rican schools. Romero also attempted to dismantle the Puerto Rican Cultural Institute in order to downplay the existence of an indigenous Puerto Rican culture, but this move ran into strong popular opposition. Romero cooperated closely with the Reagan administration to make Puerto Rico an instrument of U.S. policy in the region. In addition to its military role, this meant using the Island to help promote the Puerto Rican model of foreign investment in other Caribbean countries.

Impact of Cerro Maravilla

On July 25, 1978, two young independence advocates, Carlos Soto Arriví, 18, and Arnaldo Darío Rosado, 24, were lured into an ambush by an undercover police agent posing as a member of their group. The two youths were encircled by heavily armed police at a remote mountain site called Cerro Maravilla, or Mountain of Wonder. There they were beaten and executed with high-powered rifles as they begged for mercy.

For five years the Romero administration covered up the truth, claiming that the youths had been on their way to blow up a communications tower and that the police had fired in self-defense. The U.S. Justice Department opened two investigations into the deaths but quickly closed them for "lack of evidence."[2] In 1983, however, the Puerto Rican Senate—controlled by the opposition Polulares—opened a series of public hearings on the affair. The hearings were televised, and Puerto Ricans watched in shocked fascination as three policemen testified to the planned murder of the youths. In August 1984, the Puerto Rican Senate opened a new investigation into the complicity of U.S. federal agencies in covering up the truth about Cerro Maravilla.

The Cerro Maravilla revelations became "Puerto Rico's Watergate." Evidence came tumbling out of high-level and pervasive corruption in the Romero administration: kickbacks to government officials, abuse of public funds, rampant corruption in the police, and the involvement of prominent NPP figures in an organized arms, drugs and stolen goods racket tied to the Mafia. It also became clear that the killing of Soto and Darío was planned at high levels of the NPP administration as part of an overall strategy to repress and discredit the independence movement.

Corruption, economic stagnation, and the impact of Cerro Maravilla combined to sink Romero's administration in the Puerto Rican gubernatorial election of November 1984. With Romero's image so thoroughly tainted by scandal, Washington quietly withdrew its support from the NPP in favor of Hernan Padilla, founder of the new Reformist Party. Padilla's candidacy split the NPP vote, with the result that the Populares returned to power and former governor Rafael Hernández Colón regained the office he lost to Romero in 1976.

The Populares stand for continued Commonwealth status. There is an *autonomista* wing of the party, however, which favors greater distance from Washington within the Commonwealth framework and is critical of Puerto Rico's role in the U.S. military build-up. This tendency is led by Severo Colberg, president of the Puerto Rican House of Representatives. The strength of the autonomista wing in recent years led Hernández Colón to condemn the U.S. invasion of Grenada, while Romero backed it enthusiastically.[3] Nonetheless, Hernández Colón's first foreign visit as governor was to Grenada, signalling acceptance of the invasion and support for the U.S.-backed Blaize government. In this and other areas, the Hernández administration appears to be continuing the Romero policy of promoting U.S. strategy in the Caribbean.[4]

Fish killed by chemical wastes discharged into a lagoon outside San Juan.

Claridad

The Populares Party's return to power is widely seen as an opening for the independence movement and the left in general to organize. This is true especially since two candidates of the Puerto Rican Independence Party, including PIP president Rubén Berríos, won unexpected victories in the election for at-large seats in the House and Senate. The independence movement as a whole has gained in sympathy and public respect since the revelations of Cerro Maravilla. Now that the extent of government repression and frame-ups of the movement is known, it is no longer so easy for the establishment to portray independence advocates as "terrorists" and "communist subversives."

Pollution and Militarism: Issues of the '80s

Notwithstanding this more positive public image, the independence movement is still narrowly based in professional and intellectual sectors and has had difficulty building strong ties to the mainstream. Factionalism within the movement, including tenuous relations between the Puerto Rican Independence Party and the Puerto Rican Socialist Party, has not helped. But over the past several years, a new phenomenon not overtly related to the status debate has been gradually transforming the political landscape: community-based organizing, focusing on issues of militarism and environmental destruction.

Puerto Rico is a dumping ground for the dirtiest industries in the U.S. economy. It has been called the "New Jersey of the Caribbean" because of the preponderance of heavy industries using highly toxic materials and producing large volumes of toxic wastes. Oil refineries, power plants and petrochemical factories have polluted the air, while along the northern coast, chemical and pharmaceutical factories have poisoned surface and subterranean waters and killed fish along the shore. In 1982, the U.S. Geological Survey tested eighteen wells on the Island and found all but one to be contaminated, ten so seriously that they had to be shut down. Among the chemicals found were carbon tetrachloride, trichloroethylene, tetrachloroethylene, mercury, benzene, dieldrin and phenols.[5]

The issue of environmental contamination and its visible health effects has become a political time bomb in Puerto Rico. Many industrial communities have experienced abnormal rates of respiratory diseases, cancers and birth defects. In Puerto Rico's own "Love Canal" incident, the government had to relocate the entire community of Ciudad Cristiana de Humacao when mercury contamination was found in the earth used for landfill under the houses. In response to such developments, communities across the Island have organized to fight against pollution in their areas. In Mayaguez, for example, the "Committee for the Recovery of Our Health" staged a march to protest pollution of the town with toxic gases. In the town of Yabucoa, where a Union Carbide plant manufactures electrodes, residents have been engaged in a long-running battle with the company and health authorities to prove that the town's high rate of respiratory diseases and throat-and-nose cancer are being caused by the heavy black soot emissions from the Union Carbide plant. The issue of pollution has turned into a catalyst for popular organization and is raising consciousness about the hidden costs of Puerto Rico's alliance with U.S. capital.

173

Air pollution from a south coast oil refinery.

Claridad

The other issue which has begun to politicize the mainstream is that of Puerto Rico's role as a base for U.S. military intervention in the region. Controversy has been growing since Reagan entered office, focusing on the bombing of Vieques by the U.S. Navy, the expansion of the U.S. military infrastructure on Puerto Rican soil, and the use of Puerto Rican National Guard (PRNG) in Central America and the Caribbean.

When units of the PRNG were sent to Honduras to take part in the Big Pine exercises, Puerto Ricans began to realize that they might one day find themselves fighting for the United States against other Hispanics in Central America. These fears grew when the PRNG took part in the U.S. naval maneuvers called Ocean Venture '84. In December of that year, it was announced that the PRNG would participate along with National Guard units from several states in five months of military maneuvers in Panama. This growing use of Puerto Rican troops in U.S. regional mobilizations has introduced a new and profoundly disturbing element into the militarism debate. Puerto Ricans are "a Caribbean and Latin American people," said Severo Colberg in urging the Hernández administration to resist Puerto Rican involvement in Central America. Miguel Hernández Agosto, president of the Puerto Rican

Senate, warned in a radio interview that Puerto Ricans would not willingly fight for the United States in Nicaragua. "The U.S. government," he said, "must understand that Puerto Rico is united to Latin America by what we call blood ties."[6]

This controversy was minor compared to the furor which erupted over the news that Washington has secret contingency plans to deploy nuclear weapons in Puerto Rico. The charges were first made in an August 1984 report by the Puerto Rican Bar Association, which stated that the Roosevelt Roads Naval Station is "prepared to function as a center for command and control operations for nuclear weapons, as well as a base from which nuclear weapons could be deployed." The report identified rooms in the Roosevelt Roads complex equipped as the operations control site for nuclear command, and stated that Puerto Rico is already being used as a center for communications related to nuclear activities.[7]

Six months later, the *New York Times* reported the contents of leaked documents confirming U.S. contingency plans to deploy nuclear weapons in Puerto Rico as well as in Canada, Bermuda and Iceland. The newspaper said U.S. officials had acknowledged the existence of nuclear weapons storage facilities in Puerto Rico, and that U.S. personnel there had been trained to handle nuclear operations.[8]

The revelations caused an uproar in Puerto Rico and to a lesser extent in the other three countries, none of whose governments had been informed of the U.S. plans. Public opinion was strongly negative, while dissension broke out within the party of Governor Hernández Colón, who insisted he had not known of the plans. It was pointed out that the deployment of nuclear weaponry in Puerto Rico would violate the 1967 Tlatelolco Treaty which makes Latin America, including Puerto Rico, a nuclear-free zone, and which the United States had signed on Puerto Rico's behalf. The fact that Washington could secretly scheme to violate the treaty and make Puerto Rico a nuclear target in case of war—and that Puerto Rico would be powerless to prevent this—drove home the Island's lack of sovereignty in a dramatic manner.

Search for Alternatives

On April 29, 1984, a crowd estimated at up to 50,000 turned out for a march through San Juan to protest militarism, specifically the involvement of Puerto Rico in Ocean Venture '84. The march was called by the Puerto Rican Independence Party, but the turnout far exceeded the small membership of either the PIP or the PSP. The escalation of popular protest around environmentalism and militarism means that while the independence parties have not expanded their ranks greatly, there is an incipient anti-colonial consciousness building at the grassroots level. People feel that the conditions of their lives—economically, environmentally, and otherwise—are worsening, and they no longer see the Commonwealth association with the U.S. as the answer to their problems. Yet there is no consensus on either of the alternatives, independence or statehood.

The pro-statehood NPP calls for a *jíbaro* (indigenous) statehood that would allow Puerto Rico to retain its culture and the Spanish language. But few people seriously believe this would be possible. The more likely outcome is that everything

Puerto Rican would be swallowed up by assimilation to the dominant U.S. culture.

In the short range, U.S. dominance and the dependency it has imposed seem to many Puerto Ricans like insurmountable obstacles to independence. The colonialist ideology is that Puerto Rico enjoys a high standard of living because it is "part" of the United States. This message is disseminated through the mass media, which is penetrated at high levels by North Americans and right-wing Cuban emigrés. It is taught in the schools, which ignore Puerto Rico's own history while emphasizing that of the U.S. From the time they are small, Puerto Rican schoolchildren sing both the U.S. and Puerto Rican national anthems and salute both flags. The schools actively assist in recruitment for the U.S. armed forces, and militarism permeates the society.

Repression against the independence movement has come from both local and federal authorities, led by the FBI. Pro-independence and socialist parties, labor unions and student groups have been the target of constant surveillance, including wiretapping, infiltration by agents, and interrogation of activists' friends and neighbors. Another form of harassment is the fabrication of criminal cases and the use of the federal Grand Jury to incarcerate Puerto Rican activists in U.S. prisons.

These pervasive ideological pressures, together with Puerto Rico's dependence on federal subsidies, limit the number of people who openly support independence. At the same time, however, many Puerto Ricans who say that independence is not *possible* or *practical* in the present situation continue to nurture a nostalgic reverence for the ideal of an independent nation. As contradictions increase in Puerto Rican society, the search for an alternative to colonialism will grow. One activist said:

We know independence will come. The important question is if we can make it happen in time to prevent the total destruction of our natural resources, our cultural heritage, our identity as a people.[9] ∎

Juan Ibáñez - *Claridad*

U.S. VIRGIN ISLANDS: TOURISM AND TENSION

If Puerto Rico is an industrial enclave of the United States economy, the U.S. Virgin Islands are its tourist playground. At least ten cruise liners dock daily at the duty-free port of Charlotte Amalie, St. Thomas, and Virgin Islanders must elbow their way through throngs of American tourists on downtown streets. Many North Americans also live in the Virgin Islands, where they own land, businesses, luxury condominiums and retirement villas facing onto private beaches. The best-known luxury resort is the Caneel Bay Plantation on St. John, built and operated by the Rockefeller family empire.

The Virgin Islands' economy is thoroughly controlled by U.S. corporations. The U.S.-based Amerada Hess Oil Co. is the largest private employer, operating the western world's largest oil refinery on St. Croix. The relationship between Hess and the Virgin Islands administration has been tense, with Hess threatening to leave in response to demands for greater benefits for the islands. Other U.S. companies include Martin Marietta, an aerospace giant which produces aluminum on St. Croix, and plants assembling items like watches. Most small businesses are owned by non-blacks, including North Americans, Syrians and Lebanese. The working class consists of native Virgin Islanders and West Indian immigrants from the "down islands," as the Leewards and Windwards are called. However, small business owners not infrequently hire transient white job seekers from the United States in preference to local blacks.

Not surprisingly, the island air is often laden with tension. The continuous tourist invasion, the economic dominance of foreigners and the extreme congestion of the islands has fueled a suppressed hostility which occasionally breaks to the surface, as in 1972 when nine tourists were murdered in St. Croix. There is also some tension between native Virgin Islanders and the down-island immigrants because of competition over scarce jobs. This has been exacerbated by the decline of the industrial sector, most recently with the closing of a Martin Marietta plant and cutbacks at the Hess Oil refinery in St. Croix.

As in other heavily touristed countries, however, most resentment is suppressed because everyone is acutely aware of the economy's dependence on tourism. The island government periodically launches "courtesy campaigns" to encourage more welcoming behavior toward tourists. In the

Struggling to define a Caribbean identity in an American tourist playground.

case of the Virgin Islands, however, there is an additional dependence on U.S. federal subsidies. For these reasons, there is little talk of independence, nor have the Virgin Islands traditionally had a well-defined sense of Caribbean identity. This is changing somewhat with the impact of the down-islanders who have helped to spread an interest in reggae and Rastafarianism among Virgin Island youth.

NEW DIRECTIONS FOR THE ATLANTIC COAST

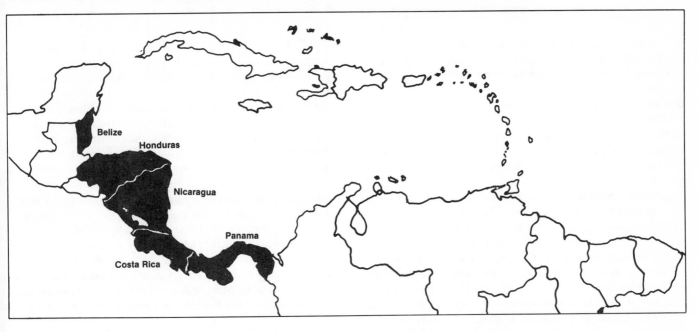

The people who migrated from the West Indies to the Atlantic rim of Central America formed the human link uniting the Caribbean and Central America in history. Today, the second, third and fourth generations of their descendants have few remaining direct ties to the Caribbean islands. At the same time, however, these Atlantic coast peoples have been marginalized from Central American societies by a long history of physical isolation, cultural rejection and extreme economic deprivation. No longer directly connected to the Caribbean, but only weakly integrated into the Central American nation-states, the *costeños*—or coastal people—live in isolated enclaves shaped by their traditional cultures and by foreign influences, especially that of the United States.

One result of this isolation from both the Caribbean and the rest of Central America is a history of cultural and economic links along the coast itself. Black, English-speaking people in Belize, Honduras, Nicaragua, Costa Rica and Panama share a common history as workers first for British and later for North American companies. They also share a common Caribbean culture. Esmeralda Browne, a Panamanian woman of West Indian descent, emphasizes this unity:

> There is a close connection between people of West Indian descent all along the Atlantic. For instance, you would find Panamanian blacks having relatives on the Atlantic coast of Costa Rica or Nicaragua.
>
> Because of the historic racism in our countries and the way West Indians have been marginalized, they haven't related closely to the national societies. Costa Rica is a good example: Limón has been totally isolated from the reality of San José. The people of Limón had a closer relationship with us in Colon [Panama] than with their own capital of San José. There's a kind of solidarity. If someone from Limón or from Bluefields [Nicaragua] comes to Panama, you feel like they're one of yours. When I go to the Atlantic coast of Nicaragua or Costa

Rica, people feel we speak the same language even though they identify my accent as Panamanian.

> I think there's been an attempt to keep us separate from the Caribbean. The dominant culture places more emphasis on being close to the U.S. and close to the "Madre Patria," Spain.

Since 1980, the isolation of the coastal enclaves has been steadily eroded as the high stakes of Central American geopolitics thrust the region into new prominence. Because of the coastal groups' traditional isolation from the rest of Nicaragua, the United States was able to manipulate their legitimate demands for self-determination into an integral part of the U.S. strategy for destroying the Sandinista revolution. This goal has also led to the militarization of Honduras and to a lesser extent Costa Rica—a military build-up taking place primarily in the Atlantic coast areas and adding a new chapter to their history of underdevelopment and exploitation.

Central American governments traditionally have done little to bridge the cultural separateness of the Atlantic coast, but in recent years several have made efforts to promote national integration. The Price government in Belize consciously attempted to build a multi-ethnic unity in that nation, and also strengthened Belize's political links to the Caribbean. The Torrijos government in Panama made ethnic integration a primary goal of its nationalist "revolution," breaking down barriers between Latino Panamanians and those of West Indian descent. More recently, the Sandinistas have attempted to reverse the isolation and underdevelopment of the Nicaraguan Zelaya through development projects and, since early 1985, by offering the coastal ethnic groups local autonomy within the revolution. Thus the potential for creative change is in the air even as the growing U.S. military presence along the coast draws the once-forgotten area deeper into the vortex of war. ■

Belize

Alone among the Central American countries, Belize faces the Caribbean. Its sparse population of 146,000 is concentrated on the coast, nearly one-third of the total living in the Caribbean port of Belize City. As a former British colony, Belize is a member of the British Commonwealth and of CARICOM, the English-speaking Caribbean community. Yet its politics are dominated by the threat from a neighboring Central American country—Guatemala—while rising U.S. influence may soon push Belize closer to the conflict in the region.

Belize's population is a kaleidoscopic mix typical of Central America's Atlantic coast. The numerically and politically dominant group is the Creoles, descendants of African slaves and British settlers, accounting for 40% of the population. Next in size are a Spanish-speaking mestizo population (33%); three Mayan Indian groups (10%); and the Black Caribs or Garifunas originally from St. Vincent (8%). In addition to these major sectors, there are several minority groups including a German-speaking Mennonite farming community, Belizean merchants of Lebanese, Palestinian, Chinese and East Indian descent, a garrison of British soldiers, and a few North American and Canadian entrepreneurs. In addition, since 1980, Belize has had to cope with thousands of newly-arrived and desperately poor Salvadoran and Guatemalan refugees.[1]

The population is, however, more integrated than such a demography suggests, as there has been extensive ethnic intermixing. Although the country is divided between those who speak English, Spanish, Garífuna or Indian dialects as their first language, nearly everyone understands and can communicate in a creole English dialect which is the country's main vernacular. In the late 1960s, the government of George Price took symbolic steps aimed at promoting "dialogue" between the various social groupings. The capital was moved from the Creole center of Belize City to Belmopan in the interior, symbolically bringing the government closer to the inland Mayan and mestizo populations. Laws were passed to restrain the pirating of Mayan artifacts by foreign art dealers, officially recognizing the Indian culture as part of the country's heritage. This integrative thrust increased after Belize's independence in 1981. In the government's commemorative booklet, *The Road to Independence,* Mayan and slave struggles were highlighted in a progressive class analysis of the country's history.

Belize's economic picture has much in common with the rest of the Caribbean. The country depends on sugar for about 60% of its export earnings, and the world sugar crisis has taken a heavy toll on Belize. As a result, Tate & Lyle, which formerly controlled all of Belize's sugar, threatened to pull out of the country if the government did not purchase 75% equity in the industry.[2] Belize does have a number of other exports including citrus fruits, bananas, beef, seafood and manufactured garments. But its two biggest foreign exchange earners are invisible: emigration and the ganja trade. Belizeans

Belize City in the 1920s shows British and American influences.

Belize Government Information Service

emigrate heavily—primarily Creoles going to the United States—and the remittances they send back are an important source of income. Even more crucial is the estimated $100 million a year marijuana crop, which makes Belize one of the most drug-dependent economies in the region.[3]

This economic weakness has not, however, dissuaded the Guatemalan government from continuing to lay claim to the whole territory of Belize, and fear of a Guatemalan invasion is a constant backdrop to Belizean life. Guatemala claims to have inherited sovereignty over Belize from the Spanish Crown, but neither Spain nor Guatemala ever actually occupied Belizean territory. An 1859 treaty between Guatemala and Britain—which Guatemala now refuses to recognize—defined the Belize/Guatemala border. Despite this, Guatemalans adhere to the slogan *Belice es Nuestra*—"Belize is Ours"—and official Guatemalan government maps depict Belize as a province of Guatemala. Given the neo-fascist nature of the Guatemalan military and oligarchy, the claim is no idle threat, and for this reason independent Belize begs Britain to keep its 1,800-man garrison on Belizean soil.

The Guatemalan threat has had a far-reaching impact on Belize, increasing the country's reliance on neocolonial protectors even beyond the normal dependence of Caribbean countries. The government of George Price, who dominated Belizean politics from the 1950s through 1984, carried out a political balancing act between various contradictory interests and pressures: Belize's identification with the Caribbean versus its geographic location in Central America; its desire for independence versus the need for a foreign military presence to deter the Guatemalans; and its desire for friendly relations with its progressive neighbors versus U.S. pressures to break such ties.

Belize's independence was held up for years by the unresolved dispute with Guatemala. Until 1976, all the Latin American countries except Cuba sided with Guatemala and voted against Belizean sovereignty in the United Nations and the Organization of American States. The first to break ranks was Omar Torrijos of Panama, after which a number of South American states—but no other Central American—were gradually won over to Belize's side. Beginning in 1979, both the new Sandinista government in Nicaragua and the Bishop government in Grenada made a particular point of solidarity with Belize. By the end of 1980, international support for a secure Belizean independence was nearly unanimous. The Organization of American States gave its formal support in 1981, influenced by its new English-speaking Caribbean members.[4]

In part because of gratitude for their strong support, and in part reflecting the influence of progressive elements within Price's social-democratic government, Belize moved after independence to strengthen friendly ties with Cuba, Nicaragua and Grenada. Belizean teachers participated in the literacy campaign in the English-speaking areas of Nicaragua's Atlantic coast, while members of Price's cabinet attended anniversary celebrations in Managua. Interchange with Cuba resulted in an offer of Cuban scholarships for Belizean students and the prospect of trade ties. But these offers had to be rejected, and relations with Nicaragua also cooled, when it became apparent that such ties would incur the wrath of the United States. One Belizean paper commented, "The two countries in the region—Cuba and Nicaragua—that have been most friendly to us are not allowed to have relations with us."[5]

Independence also brought stronger ties with the English-speaking Caribbean, which had supported Belizean sovereignty through CARICOM and the British Commonwealth. In April 1982, Belize hosted a meeting of the CARICOM foreign ministers, who issued principled statements calling for the "non-exclusion" of any country from the Caribbean Basin Initiative. The ministers also endorsed the Zone of Peace resolution initiated by the Caribbean Churches, in part reflecting sensitivity to Belize's invasion concerns.

Rising U.S. Influence

But behind the independence euphoria and growing Caribbean integration, clouds were gathering. Mexico's devaluation of its currency in 1982 had an immediate negative impact on the Belizean economy, already buffeted by low sugar prices. By 1984, the Price government was forced to turn to the International Monetary Fund for a $7 million loan and was leaning toward increasingly conservative economic policies.

The United States meanwhile was quietly expanding its presence in the country, stationing more diplomats (29 compared to only 9 from the U.K.), increasing radio broadcasts over the Voice of America and providing development assistance through USAID.[6] Cultural penetration also increased, due especially to the pervasive presence of American television. But the most important new links were military. The desire of the British to withdraw their garrison implied a future opening for a U.S. military presence to replace it. After independence, therefore, the U.S. began providing training for the small Belizean military force and also opened discussions with the government about the possibility of building a U.S. base in Belize. However, the Price government's balancing act" did enable it to avoid cooperating fully with U.S. military strategy in the region. Belize declined to join the U.S.-sponsored Central American Democratic Community in 1982, and also did not join the Central American Defense Council (CONDECA), revived under U.S. auspices to increase military coordination between the Central American states.

This precarious attempt to chart an independent course was soon to be upset by major internal changes in Belize. Price's People's United Party, which had not lost an election in thirty years, was ousted in a sweeping upset in December 1984 by the United Democratic Party (UDP) of Manuel Esquivel. Not only was Esquivel a relative newcomer, having led his party for less than two years; but the repudiation of the government was so complete that Price saw his own parliamentary seat fall to a 25-year-old businessman who was the youngest candidate on the ballot. Economic factors clearly were involved, centering on the declining economy and U.S. pressures on the government to resume paraquat spraying of the countryside, a prospect strongly opposed by small farmers. Beyond that, however, the change appeared in keeping with the conservative ascendency in the region and clearly favored the U.S. position in Belize.

The new government has announced a "definitely pro-West" foreign policy involving "the strongest links with the United Kingdom" and the "best of relations with the United States of America." It also favors more foreign investment and less government regulation—precisely the Reagan philosophy—and is preparing to liberalize the foreign investment code.

The UDP administration appears eager to structure its political alliances along lines acceptable to the United States. Prime Minister Esquivel personally represented Belize at the opening of Grenada's new Parliament after the election of the U.S.-backed Blaize government, but sent only a very low-level official to Daniel Ortega's inauguration in Nicaragua after that country's elections. At the same time, however, the new Belize government has stopped short of full collaboration with Washington, calling the U.S. sanctions against Nicaragua "ill-conceived and not justified." Esquivel also appears committed to maintaining strong ties with CARICOM.

The Esquivel government *says* it would not seek a U.S. military presence in Belize even if the British pulled out.[8] Such principles could melt rapidly under the heat of both U.S. and Guatemalan pressures, and most Belizeans probably would accept a U.S. presence out of the fear of a Guatemalan invasion. In 1985, however, the Guatemalan government announced it had dropped plans for a military takeover of Belize, instead favoring a negotiated settlement.[9] Like the upcoming Guatemalan elections expected to install a figurehead civilian president, this apparent shift reflects the Guatemalan military's desire to break through its international isolation in order to gain badly needed economic aid. The military also apparently believes that U.S. support for Britain in the Falklands/Malvinas war indicates that Washington would oppose Guatemala in a contest over Belize.

But extreme right-wing elements in Guatemala oppose a Belizean "deal," and it is highly uncertain how far they will allow any new Guatemalan government to go. Meanwhile, Guatemalan and Salvadoran refugees continue to pour over the Belizean border, and the desire of the U.S. for a military foothold in the country is growing all the time. The prospect remains that once-isolated Belize, the Atlantic coast microcosm, will find its fledgling independence and Caribbean friendships an insufficient bulwark against the growing regional war. ∎

Cutting sugar cane in the Orange Walk district of Belize.

Belize Government Information Service

Honduras

The quintessential "banana republic," Honduras became a foreign enclave as a result of Anglo-American control over its railroads, mining industry and banana production in the 1800s. The Rockefeller-owned Rosario Mining Company dominated the economy with silver exports in the 1880s. When the silver panic of 1892-93 hit, the mining boom ended and Rosario pulled out, having done little to benefit Honduran development. This stagnation set the stage for the arrival of the U.S. banana companies which were to dominate the country for many years.

After the turn of the century, the United Fruit Company and the Standard Fruit and Steamship Company expanded their control over the rich alluvial plains of Honduras' Atlantic coast. By 1929, United Fruit and Standard owned or controlled 650,000 acres of the best arable land,[1] along with railroads and ports (United Fruit controlling the port of Tela and Standard the port of La Ceiba). Their banana operations were run like private fiefdoms, in which the companies kept order and crushed labor organizing with their own security forces or by calling in U.S. troops.

Bananas came to represent some 88% of Honduran exports, focusing the economic activity of the country almost wholly in the Atlantic coast region. Honduras is the only Central American country whose economic center is not the capital (Tegucigalpa) but a town near the Caribbean coast (San Pedro Sula). A second result was that the population of the coastal region became predominantly West Indian, since the U.S. companies preferred to hire English-speaking laborers. In addition to those recruited from the Caribbean islands, there was a Garífuna (Black Carib) population concentrated on the Bay Islands off the coast and in the town of Trujillo, where the government had granted them 7,000 hectares of land in 1901. Other banana workers were Spanish-speaking mestizos who had migrated from the central highlands to the coast.

Honduras was distinguished from its neighbors by the totality of the banana companies' control. In contrast to El Salvador, Costa Rica and Guatemala, no native oligarchy arose in the 19th century to make its fortunes from coffee exports. Instead, the U.S. companies controlled the government, financing political parties which intrigued against each other. In 1903, 1907, 1911, 1919 and 1924, U.S. troops intervened in Honduras to protect the banana companies' property or to influence the outcome of internal political struggles. The United States also began training a Honduran army and air force which were commanded by U.S. officers and served primarily to protect the interests of the banana companies.

After World War Two, the predominance of the banana companies was somewhat lessened by the diversification of agricultural exports and the start of a limited manufacturing sector, underwritten by loans and aid from multilateral agencies such as the World Bank. Honduran landowners along the Atlantic coast began converting land taken from small peasants to export production, grazing cattle for beef and raising sugar cane, coffee and cotton. While exports of these commodities increased dramatically during the 1950s and '60s, production of beans and rice—the subsistence foods of the peasantry—declined. At the same time, the successful unionization of the banana workers in 1954 prompted the banana companies to implement labor-saving changes, reducing the banana labor force from 35,000 in 1953 to 16,000 in 1959.[2]

The banana companies cultivated only about one-third of their lands, meaning that much of the best arable land lay idle. In addition, corrupt officials frequently would appropriate large tracts of land, either keeping it for themselves or selling it to foreign companies.[3] One example occurred in Trujillo, where the local military commander, Col. Gustavo Alvarez, expropriated 2,000 hectares of the lands belonging to the Garífuna and distributed them to large landowners over the Garífunas' protests.[4] As a result of this decreasing land availability combined with rising unemployment, the Honduran peasants began peaceful land occupations in the 1960s. Marcial Caballero, head of the National Peasant Union, defends the takeovers as

> . . . *recuperaciones de tierra* (land recoveries) because we are claiming what was ours to begin with. The land in Honduras used to belong to the state and anyone who farmed it had a right to that piece of land.[5]

In 1964, the agricultural multinational Castle & Cooke took over Standard Fruit, continuing to market its bananas and pineapples under the Dole label. United Fruit became United Brands in a 1970 merger. In Honduras, as elsewhere in Central America, the banana companies had begun to return some of their lands to the government, but continued to market the bananas grown by small farmers or peasant cooperatives on the returned lands. This arrangement not only avoided the political problems of direct ownership, but placed all the risk of crop failure on the small growers while keeping virtually the entire profit for the companies. The banana giants fiercely resisted allowing anyone else to share this profitable marketing business. This brought them into conflict with the Union of Banana Exporting Countries, formed in 1974 to press for fair taxation and better terms from the companies.

In September of that year, Hurricane Fifi destroyed nearly 60% of Honduras' agricultural production, and Standard Fruit abandoned many of its plantations. The idled banana workers responded by organizing Las Isletas Peasants Enterprise, whose members planted and harvested bananas collectively and shared the profits. Las Isletas processed over one million boxes of bananas in 1976 and four million in 1977, selling the produce to Standard. But when Las Isletas decided to market its fruit through the Union of Banana Exporting Countries, Standard pressured the Honduran government to arrest 200 militant members of Las Isletas and ransack the association's headquarters. These strong-arm tactics were carried out by the Honduran army under the leadership of Lt. Col. Gustavo Alvarez, who was on the payroll of Castle &

Cooke, Standard's parent company.[6]

Few people then foresaw the shadow of war hanging over Honduras or the role which Gustavo Alvarez would play in this new period of Honduran history. After the Sandinista victory in Nicaragua in 1979, the Carter administration began to modernize the Honduran army, and by 1981, the United States was using Honduras as the staging ground for attacks against Nicaragua and against the FMLN guerrillas in El Salvador. The person chosen by Washington to head up the Honduran role in this counterinsurgency effort was none other than (by now) Brig. General Gustavo Alvarez, a loyal U.S. ally because of his past service to the banana companies.

Since that time, the Atlantic coast of Honduras has become the scene of an immense U.S. military buildup, including an airbase at La Ceiba, a naval complex at Trujillo and a regional training center at Puerto Castillo. By the end of 1984, some 33 U.S.-Honduran military maneuvers had been carried out. This has meant the virtual occupation of the country by U.S. troops, increased repression against the Honduran peasantry, and the destructive spread of drugs and prostitution.

Formerly backward, forgotten Honduras has thus moved center-stage as the primary U.S. counterinsurgency base for the region. In some ways it is now more important than Panama, site of the U.S. Southern Command. The economic enclave established by the mining and banana companies at the turn of the century has been transformed into a U.S. military enclave, dragging Honduras inevitably into war.

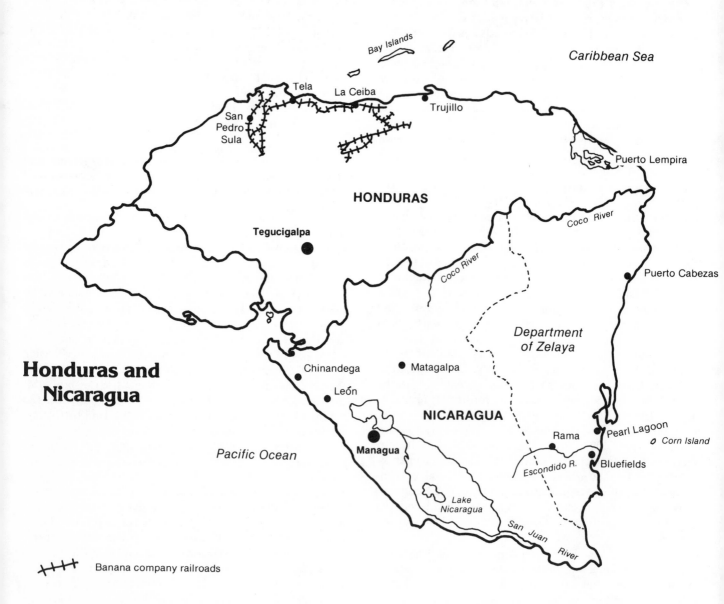

Honduras and Nicaragua

┼┼┼┼ Banana company railroads

Nicaragua

The department of Zelaya, commonly referred to in Nicaragua as *la costa atlántica*—the Atlantic coast—encompasses nearly half of the country's territory, yet contains only 10% of its population. Its long-standing isolation from the rest of Nicaragua is the product of its history as a British and then North American enclave, a reality reinforced by the Somoza dictatorship. Ironically, this very isolation and separate cultural identity have now thrust the Zelaya into the very center of the *contra* war to overthrow the Sandinista revolution.

The Miskito Indians were the dominant culture in the northern Zelaya during the 18th and 19th centuries, their traditional *Moskitia* domain straddling the Nicaraguan/Honduran border. Britain controlled the Zelaya during this time, using the Miskitos as local paramilitary forces to help hold back the line of Spanish colonization to the west. The profound antagonism between the Pacific and Atlantic regions of the country is rooted in this history:

> With little direct contact with the other Nicaraguans of the Pacific area, the Miskitos take great pride in having resisted the Spanish colonization. However, typical of many colonial situations, that resistance was related to their deep dependency on British colonialism . . .[1]

Along the southern part of the coast, British settlements at Bluefields, Pearl Lagoon and Corn Island brought in African slaves to work on plantations and in timber-cutting. These Africans gradually mixed with the Europeans and with the small mestizo, Indian and Chinese populations to produce a black and mulatto group known as the Creoles. Toward the end of the 19th century, North American entrepreneurs entered the area to export coconuts, bananas and precious woods. To service this growing business, two new groups of black workers were brought in from Jamaica and New Orleans.

Creole culture developed as typically Afro-Caribbean: English-speaking and heavily influenced by the British. Both the Creoles and the Indians viewed as outsiders the mestizo Nicaraguans from the Pacific region, whom they referred to as "Spaniards." This ethnic and cultural isolation of the coastal enclave was compounded by its physical isolation. The only way to reach the Pacific was to travel by boat up the Escondido River to Rama, with only a rustic overland connection between Rama and Managua. The coastal people thus developed a perspective which was both inward-looking (focusing on their indigenous cultures) and outward-looking (across the ocean to Britain and America), but did not relate closely to the rest of Nicaragua.

Britain's Miskito Reserve was finally reincorporated into the Nicaraguan state by President Zelaya in 1895 and renamed in his honor. His aim was a nationalistic attempt to unite the

Miskito Indians from village of Bismuna in northeastern corner of Nicaragua. The many rivers and creeks in the area make boat a common mode of travel.

Adriana Angel

183

country: "My government announces with rejoicing and enthusiasm, the absolute Reincorporation of the Mosquitia territory into the Republic . . . "[2] But a conservative revolt led by General Estrada overthrew President Zelaya with U.S. assistance in 1912. The conservatives favored foreign ties and thus left the Atlantic coast largely in the hands of U.S. business, maintaining its enclave nature.

The role of the Church was the other important factor in the social life of the Zelaya, but it too was dominated by foreign influences. While the rest of Nicaragua was predominantly Spanish Catholic, the main church among the Miskitos was the Moravian Church, directed initially by German missionaries. When this work was turned over to the American Moravians in 1916, the Church expanded its educational programs so that Moravianism came to prevail in the Creole communities as well. The Anglican Church, despite its long history among the Creoles, was much smaller and very traditional. Its mission work was taken over by the American Episcopal Church. Around the same time, the limited Catholic presence along the coast began to expand under the American Capuchins, quickly overtaking the Anglicans numerically. All three denominations concentrated their social ministry in education, with the Moravian high school becoming the center of higher learning for the whole Zelaya. The foreign orientation of the churches along the Atlantic coast reinforced the region's cultural separation from the rest of the country.

From 1912 through 1932, U.S. companies dominated the economic life of the Zelaya through banana exporting, lumbering and mining. This not only created jobs, but most of the coastal population purchased imported food, clothing and housewares from company commissaries, contributing to their pro-American outlook. But this corporate activity was short-lived. In the 1930s, a banana plague and attacks by Sandino's army prompted the banana companies to rip up their railroad tracks and leave, and the mining and lumbering industries also declined during the forties. Although the U.S. companies had exploited the area and reinvested almost nothing to benefit the local economy, many costeños still look back on that period as the "golden years" and view North Americans as benefactors.[3]

During the 1950s, Spanish-speaking mestizo peasants began to move into the Zelaya in large numbers, forced off their small plots in the fertile Pacific bottomlands by Somoza's army to make way for expanding cattle and cotton production. Today, the mestizos represent the largest group in the department, numbering some 120,000. Next in size is the Miskito Indian population, estimated at 80,000, which is concentrated in northeastern Zelaya. Third are the Creoles, numbering some 26,000 and found mainly in the towns of Bluefields, Pearl Lagoon and on Corn Island. The remainder include Sumu Indians in the northern interior highlands (8,000); Garífuna living along the coast north of Bluefields (1,500); and the Rama Indians in villages south of Bluefields (800).[4]

After World War Two, shrimp fishing along the coast grew into a major industry organized by a Chinese-American who then sold out to a firm jointly owned by Cuban capitalists and Somoza. Somoza maintained paternalistic relations with the coast, doing little to develop the area but occasionally

channeling donations through the churches. The U.S.-run churches developed almost all the social programs in the area, and during the 1960s, the U.S. government's Alliance for Progress and USAID channeled loans, aid and relief funds into the depressed Atlantic coast region. Until 1979, therefore, the primary loyalties of the people in the Zelaya were towards the Americans, Somoza and the churches. Except for a few individuals, the coastal groups were not involved in the struggle to overthrow the Somoza dictatorship, and hence the Zelaya largely escaped the repression which Somoza inflicted on the western regions of the country.

The Atlantic Coast and the Revolution

Although the Sandinistas carried out almost no organizing in the Zelaya before 1979, the FSLN declared that when it took power it would end the age-old isolation and backwardness of the region. Its platform included calls for ending the exploitation by foreign monopolies in the area and doing away with the hateful discrimination which the Indians and Creoles had long endured.

On November 15, 1979, the new Sandinista government, together with Indian organizations, created MISURASATA, an organization to serve as the political representative of the Indian peoples. A charismatic Indian leader, Steadman Fagoth, was elected coordinator of MISURASATA and as such was given a seat on the Council of State, the highest legislative body of the revolutionary government. In 1980, MISURASATA officially aligned itself with the revolution, saying:

> The Sandinista Revolution is founded on the basic principles of nationalism, anti-imperialism, internationalism, classism, and popular democracy. We, the indigenous peoples declare that these are the most significant and applicable principles for our national reality in general and our indigenous reality in particular.[5]

The Sandinistas initially held great hopes that this tactical alliance would finally overcome the centuries-old antagonism between the Atlantic and Pacific halves of the country and produce benefits for the impoverished peoples of the Zelaya. Literacy programs in English, Miskito and Sumu were carried out, along with the development of private cooperatives, housing and water systems, and the beginnings of some small industries under the auspices of the Nicaraguan Institute for the Atlantic Coast (INNICA). INNICA was to be headed by a tri-ethnic leadership consisting of Comandante William Ramírez of the FSLN (a mestizo), Com. Lumberto Campbell (a Creole), and the number two Miskito Indian leader, Brooklyn Rivera—although ultimately Rivera refused to participate.

These early initiatives of the Sandinistas, while motivated by idealism, were marred by their failure to understand or take seriously both the depth of traditional animosities and the importance of cultural differences between the Pacific and Atlantic coasts. When young Sandinista cadre from Managua were sent to the Zelaya, for instance, they showed little sensitivity to the local culture, to say nothing of being unable to

In a Miskito village.

communicate in the coastal languages. More than any one transgression of the Sandinistas, however, the costeños resented the arrogance of a revolutionary movement in which they had not been involved but which now sought to come into their communities to improve their way of life.

Meanwhile, Steadman Fagoth emerged as a power-seeking opportunist, whose influence among the Miskitos coupled with his demagogic skills made him a formidable force. He and Rivera claimed that *they* were responsible for the benefits brought by the revolutionary programs, while condemning the Sandinistas' errors as comparable to the worst the Indians had ever experienced at the hands of the "Spaniards." Fagoth began to promise the Indians that one day they would control the Zelaya, and in early 1981, it was learned that MISURASATA planned to present a demand for outright control of 33% of all Nicaraguan territory (3/4 of the Zelaya). This not only raised the possibility of splitting the country, but also posed a threat to the revolution since the Zelaya could then be used by Somoza's exiled National Guardsmen as a counterrevolutionary base. The Miskito proposal also antagonized some Creole communities which were told that when MISURASATA controlled the region, they would have to "go find an island somewhere."[6]

In February 1981, the government arrested Fagoth along with other Miskito leaders and published evidence showing him to have been an informer for Somoza while a university student in Managua in the 1970s. After he was released in response to Indian protests, Fagoth went to Honduras where he used the Somocistas' radio station to broadcast reports of Sandinista "atrocities" against the Indians, urging other Miskitos to join him in exile. Some ten thousand Miskitos did cross over into Honduras, and Fagoth publicly stated that "we took the decision to declare open war against Sandinismo." The Sandinistas responded by saying:

> Nicaragua is a single nation, territorially and politically, and cannot be dismembered, divided or damaged in its sovereignty and independence . . .

But the government also reaffirmed that

> . . . The popular Sandinista revolution will guarantee and legalize through property titles, the land on which the communities of the Atlantic coast have historically lived, be it in communal or collective form.[7]

Against this backdrop of Sandinista errors and Indian desires for autonomy, the stage was set for the Indian population to be swept into the growing conflict between the Sandinistas and Somoza's exiled guardsmen supported by the CIA. Some Miskitos willingly aided the counterrevolutionary

185

forces, but the *contras* also made many raids on Indian villages, kidnapping civilians and forcing them back into the Honduras base camps. As more and more unarmed Indians were killed in cross-border fighting—and their villages increasingly used as cover by the contras—the government decided to remove the Indians from the area, relocating about 8,000 in an area to the south called Tasba Pri.[8] While it is true that the Sandinistas burned the Indian villages after the people had left (to keep them from being used as counterrevolutionary bases), no one died in that forced march south, and none of the massacres charged to the Sandinistas by the U.S. has ever been proven.

The relocation to Tasba Pri marked the low point of Sandinista-Miskito relations. Since then, the Sandinista government has made great monetary sacrifices on behalf of Tasba Pri, providing housing, health clinics, churches, and farming assistance. More importantly, escalating attacks by the contras have killed more and more people in the Zelaya and disrupted vital food supplies. By 1983, growing numbers of Indians and Creoles were joining the Sandinista popular militia, representing a rejection of the contras even though those forces included some Indians. Finally, in July 1985, the Sandinistas allowed some Miskitos who wished to do so to return to their border villages.[9]

Initially many Creoles also were suspicious of or hostile to the Sandinistas. But the appointment of Creole leaders like Lumberto Campbell and support for the revolution by others such as the respected educator Ray Hooker gradually softened the opposition of the black community. In addition, contra violence also claimed Creole victims, including Ray Hooker who was kidnapped and released in 1984. A further factor was that the Moravian Church, some of whose pastors initially had inflamed tensions with anti-communist propaganda, eventually adopted a more conciliatory stance toward the revolution.

In the long term, the most important factor underlying the gradual shift in attitudes is the positive impact of the revolution's programs. Projects in the Zelaya include basic grain production and experimental development projects in African palm oil, rubber, cocoa, dairy farming, coffee, rice and plantains. Health care has improved greatly, with clinics and mobile medical units working to eliminate malaria, tuberculosis, and intestinal diseases. These programs and others have made progress toward winning over many costenos. Resentments and indifference remain for some, but the gradual intermixing with people from the Pacific region is helping to break down old prejudices.

In February 1985, the newly-elected Sandinista government announced a plan to grant political and social autonomy to the various ethnic groupings in the Atlantic coast region. The actual form of this "local autonomy" is still being developed: it does not mean political independence, but local control and participation by people of different ethnic origins in their own areas. This is in some ways already underway, with increasing numbers of indigenous people in charge of local offices of Sandinista programs on the coast. The Sandinistas believe that when individual ethnic groups are strengthened internally through local decision-making, "the revolution itself will be strengthened as well."[10] In granting such local autonomy, the Sandinistas have laid down a challenge to all the Central American governments in dealing with the ethnically diverse Atlantic coast.

Costa Rica

"That the [United Fruit] Company exploited the land and the people of Limón province for its own profit is undeniable. Its impact on the Atlantic Zone has been so great that it is impossible to imagine what course Limón's history might have followed without it."

— Paula Palmer, *What Happen*[1]

The province of Limón, Costa Rica is similar to the Nicaraguan Zelaya in that it encompasses the entire Atlantic coastal strip within a single department which has experienced grinding poverty under the dominance of foreign companies over the last 100 years. But Limón and the Zelaya are markedly dissimilar in other ways. Unlike Nicaragua, Costa Rica is heavily dependent on banana revenues, making its Atlantic coast region central to the national economy. Moreover, the Limón coast is linked to the rest of Costa Rica by an effective railroad system. So while Limón is a banana company enclave, its social history including aggressive labor organizing has played a critical role in modern Costa Rica.

The Costa Rica Railroad, completed in 1890, was built, owned and controlled by Minor C. Keith, the North American banana magnate. The original reason for building the railroad was not bananas, however, but coffee.[2] In order to ship Costa Rican coffee to Europe, a railroad was essential to get the crop from the central highlands to Puerto Limón on the Atlantic coast. To finance the construction, the government borrowed heavily from English trust houses in 1871 and granted Keith generous rights to land along the railroad line: 500 hectares for each mile of track completed. Keith also invested much of his own fortune in the venture and developed banana plantations on his newly acquired lands to offset his costs. While Keith became a member of the Costa Rican oligarchy through marriage, he over-extended his financial dealings, and the near-bankruptcy of his companies forced him to merge with the Boston Fruit Company in 1899 to form the United Fruit Company.[3]

Since the coastal region was sparsely settled by Amerindians, Keith and the Costa Rican government imported a foreign labor force to build the railroad. The first wave included 400 Chinese, 600 Jamaicans and 500 workers from the Cape Verde Islands off the coast of Africa. Another 1,500 workers came in the second wave, including 762 Italians, with the remainder consisting of Barbadians, Hindus and Chinese.[4] Working conditions on the railroad were harsh and dangerous due to malaria, yellow fever, snakes and the heat. The disgruntled Italians staged a major strike in 1888—the first organized labor protest in the country's history—but left the coast thereafter, many returning to Italy. The Chinese could not withstand the impact of malaria and most of them died, although some went to set up small businesses in Puerto Limón. As the railroad and banana plantations spread southward, the Amerindians retreated upland into mountain settlements along the slopes of the Talamanca range. Only the Afro-Caribbean peoples survived and remained, turning Limón into a black, English-speaking cultural enclave.

The rapid expansion of banana production after 1910 meant that almost all the Afro-Caribbean workers (often called "Jamaicans") worked for the United Fruit Company in one way or another: on the plantations, on the railroad, or loading cargo at the port. They were controlled by the company's rules and dependent on its wages, buying their supplies in company commissaries. As an imported foreign element, they were not recognized as citizens by the Costa Rican government, and most of the country was off-limits to them because of an unwritten color bar. Their culture and loyalties remained strongly West Indian, as the pan-Africanist Marcus Garvey discovered when he visited Costa Rica in 1910. Garvey's Universal Negro Improvement Association (UNIA) had an active branch in Puerto Limón and several other coastal towns, and old Jamaicans are proud of their participation in Garvey's movement. As one recalled:

> You had men come in from Limón, and afterwards they formed a branch [of the UNIA] with president from right here, and secretary, treasurer and all. Practically all the families around was in it. They was trying to unite the people, get all the Negroes together, say they was fighting to go to Africa, to go home back, for they claim that Africa was the home of the Negroes. But they didn't succeed in that part. But you had about two men come from Africa here visit all the UNIA branches.[5]

During the 1930s, significant changes took place in Limón. Because of a banana disease, United Fruit began pulling out of Limón, shifting its operations to the Pacific coast around Golfito. Some of the company's lands were bought or taken over by independent producers to grow bananas or cocoa. By 1935, only 25% of the bananas produced in Limón came from United Fruit's plantations, although most independent growers still sold their produce to the company.[7] But many other banana workers were left unemployed and destitute. They could not even travel to Golfito to work due to racist laws and attitudes. Indeed, trains from Limón regularly stopped at Turrialba, the half-way point, to change crews—from black to white—before continuing on to San José.

Nonetheless, linkages were developing between the Afro-Caribbean workers and the national labor movement, then led by the Costa Rican Communist Party (PCCR). This organizing started in the highlands among cobblers and bakers, then spread down along the rail line to the coast.[8] In 1934, the PCCR organized a successful strike among the banana workers through the Confederation of Workers of Costa Rica. The strike was supported even by many black workers who were not members of the labor confederation, giving the entire

Afro-Caribbean population a sense of power and lending impetus to further labor organizing.

The 1940 election brought to power the head of the Social Christian Party, Rafael Calderón Guardia, while the Communist Party's Workers and Peasant Bloc (BOC) received 11% of the vote, reflecting its strong trade union support. This led to a marriage of convenience between the two as Calderon, whose popularity soon ebbed because of his corruption and anti-democratic practices, turned to the BOC to shore up his failing popular base. Seeing the alliance as an easy way into power, the PCCR abandoned its class principles in favor of an anti-fascist tactical coalition. During the Second World War, such coalitions were coming into being all over Latin America, legitimized by the wartime alliance between the United States and the Soviet Union in their common fight against Nazi Germany.

This odd couple was joined together by the Catholic Church, which saw support for the government as a way to regain some of its long lost privileges.[9] The Church was motivated also by the spirit of the *Rerum Novarum,* the Papal Encyclical encouraging the Church to support trade unionism. This "triple alliance" between the Church, the communists and the government produced two unusual developments in 1943: the Catholic hierarchy approved Catholic participation in the PCCR's new Popular Vanguard Party—on condition that the party renounced its communist ideology—and the government passed a progressive Labor Code which infuriated the ruling class.

With the start of the Cold War in 1947, the triple alliance broke down. Street clashes in San José erupted between the Calderón/communist forces on the one hand and an organized mass resistance representing popular and middle-class sectors on the other. In 1948, these clashes escalated into a civil war that lasted for 40 days. It was won by José Figueres, whose Liberation Movement took control of Cartago in the highlands and then Limón on the coast, thus controlling the railroad. Figueres had a larger dream, however, of joining all the progressive forces of the region to eliminate the fascist dictators and construct a United Central American Republic. Toward this end, he had signed a pact with Juan José Arévalo, president of Guatemala, in 1947, and went to Europe to purchase arms. But the plan was thwarted by the threat of an invasion by Somoza and pressure from the United States.[10]

"Don Pepe," as Figueres often was called, won the respect and affection of the Afro-Caribbean population through his genuine concern about their poverty and the discrimination they suffered. His government allowed the blacks to apply for citizenship and to travel and settle anywhere in Costa Rica. In 1954, the government signed new contracts with the United Fruit Company calling for the construction of schools and hospitals, the eradication of malaria and the implementation of social security laws. Despite this pressure for better terms from the company, Figueres' government did not alter the underlying monopolistic control by United Fruit. In 1955 the company owned 500,000 acres of land in Limón and Golfito of which 75% law fallow, the company holding it in "reserve."[11]

During this twenty-year "dead period" of company inactivity (1940-1960), the workers were sustained primarily by their own production of bananas and cocoa. Many moved in on idle lands held by United Fruit, and some even took out loans from the government to purchase land for cooperatives.[12] The most successful—for a time—was the "Cooperative of Cocoa Producers of the Atlantic Zone," an independent marketing coop which had its best year in 1954 due to high cocoa prices. But eventually the banks gained control of the cooperative and it failed, deeply in debt.[13]

Failure of Developmentalism

In the 1960s, the government began attempting to develop Limón province under the supervision of the Administrative Board for the Development of the Atlantic Strip (JAPDEVA), which was also given management of the ports. A few small nationally-owned industries were begun in Limón, producing soap, soft drinks and coconut oil. At the same time, the Alliance for Progress sponsored a Regional Association for the people of southern Limón province, leading to a number of development projects including completion of a highway connecting Puerto Limón to the Talamanca coast. But by the end of the decade, the Regional Association had failed. Meanwhile, United Fruit had returned to Limón to start up production again, while Standard Fruit moved into the Estrella Valley, and together the companies doubled banana production between 1965 and 1970. The development of the sixties thus failed to break the hold of foreign control, as the banana firms continued to monopolize production at the expense of national producers and small farmers.

The oil crisis of 1973 dealt a severe blow to the Costa Rican economy and deepened poverty in the coastal region. As the result of a workers' strike that year, United Fruit agreed to sell the Costa Rica Railroad Co. to the government for $1.00, a giveaway which benefited the company since the railroad was in an advanced state of deterioration. This left the government with the task of maintaining a rail line that would continue to primarily serve the banana companies and the coffee elites at no cost to them. Furthermore, the banana companies began modernizing their cargo handling system with conveyor belts, relegating the stevedores to more menial jobs. The growing unemployment was little affected by the start of a small tourist industry in the area when the first highway was completed from San José to Limón. As a result, many costeños, particularly blacks, were forced to move to San José or migrate to Panama or the United States in search of work.

The skyrocketing price of oil in the late 1970s was accompanied by falling commodity prices for bananas and coffee, plunging the Costa Rican economy into deep distress. The government began to borrow heavily to finance its imports, but heavy interest payments and capital flight due to the growing regional turmoil caused dollar reserves to run out in 1980.[14] As a result, the economy went into uncontrolled inflation, with the value of local currency dropping from 9 to 60 *colones* per US$1 in 1980 alone. Because of the inflation, the Central Workers Confederation and the Unitary Workers Confederation (CUT) demanded pay hikes, leading to a series of strikes between 1979 and 1982 concentrated in the banana zone.

The pending collapse of the economy led to demands by the International Monetary Fund for a takeover, to which President Monge finally agreed in 1982. When the IMF conditions were imposed, they caused such widespread suffering that many families returned to eating corn tortillas instead of bread because of the high cost of imported flour. Although Monge appealed to Costa Ricans to "tighten their belts" and "return to the land," he ignored the demand for a much-needed agrarian reform. Many campesinos and banana workers began occupying fallow lands either privately owned or held by the fruit companies.[15]

In September 1982, the communist-backed CUT labor federation led a strike for a 17% wage increase at the Banana Development Company (BANDECO), a Del Monte subsidiary based in Limón. Widespread anti-labor advertising by BANDECO labelled the strikers Soviet-led terrorists, while President Monge threatened to declare the Communist Party illegal.[16] After 63 days, with the support of the banana workers on the Pacific coast, the CUT won its principal demands. However, its tendency to rely on crises rather than building a strong grassroots base has seriously weakened the CUT's influence. Most Atlantic coast workers are not members, although they sometimes support the labor federation's demands because of the economic crisis in the country.

As with multinationals elsewhere in the region, the banana companies not only forced the government to control labor unrest, but have pressed for greater and greater concessions, using the threat of their withdrawal as a bargaining chip. In the case of Standard and United Fruit, such mobility is easy because of the extent of their holdings throughout Central America. The two companies have constantly pressured Costa Rica to reduce its nominal taxation, which is still higher than the taxes the companies pay to Panama or Honduras. In the fall of 1984, United Fruit (now United Brands) began laying off its workers in Golfito, taking its equipment out of Palmar Sur and moving it into Panama. Fearing riots of unemployed workers, the Costa Rican government was forced to buy the Pacific coast plantations—$1.24 million for 4,200 acres of the country's own land.[17] The exploitative attitude of the banana companies is summed up bitterly by one Costa Rican popular organization: "If you serve me, I rob you; if not, I leave."[18]

In Limon today, the Afro-Caribbean population is dying out, moving away or intermarrying as mestizo Costa Ricans increasingly move in. While English language and customs are still very common in Limón, the future of this Caribbean link is uncertain. The remaining "Jamaicans" look at the past nostalgically and at the future with a sense of resignation:

Limón will always be different from the rest of Costa Rica. As a matter of culture I think we should stick to our English language. I think in Limón they should give classes in English to people who want it, of course not forgetting Spanish as the language of *our* country. But we need to continue the English as a matter of culture and of international communication. Costa Rica should be proud that they have a group of Costa Ricans that speak English. But as a matter of time I think the Protestant churches will go. The grandchildren will drop away from it, and at the end I think it will be all Catholic, as a matter of convenience, not conviction.[19]

Panama

With the exception of Belize, Panama is the Central American nation with the strongest historical links to Africa and the Caribbean. These links arose, firstly, from the long history of African slavery in Panama, although the number of slaves was small by comparison to Caribbean plantation societies. The second and more important link came from the thousands of West Indian immigrants who came for the building of the Panama railroad and canal, giving birth to the modern Panamanian working class.

After the initial conquest by Spain at the beginning of the 16th century, Panama became the principal passageway through which the Spanish shipped gold from Peru to Spain. Having decimated the indigenous Indian population of Cunas, Chocos and Guaymís, the Spaniards were forced to bring in African slaves to transport the gold and work on small farms near the transport zone. A letter to the Spanish Crown in 1583 stated that . . .

> . . . in this Kingdom there is no other service but that of the blacks and without them no one can live in this land.[1]

However, many of the slaves escaped and formed rebel communities of *cimarrones* (Maroons) in the eastern mountains. They were led by the "Black King" Bayano, who defied the authority of the Spanish and collaborated with English pirates against them.[2]

Over the next 300 years, the small population of Panama remained concentrated in the narrowest part of the isthmus—the transport zone—with an important commercial center at Portobelo. Many of the slaves were freed through manumission, while the diminished Amerindian population lived free although isolated in the jungles and mountains and on the San Blas islands. Unions between Africans, Spaniards and Indians gradually produced a predominantly black and mulatto population which identified itself as Panamanian.[3] It was a society ridden with racial and class animosities, in which the Indians were at the bottom of the social ladder and the "elite" bragged of its one-quarter Spanish blood. Notwithstanding this stratification, racial intermixing supported a growing cultural unity which formed the basis for the independence struggle from Spain in 1821. Descendants of the freed blacks, especially in Portobelo, held considerable prestige within the society and played an important role in defining this national Panamanian culture. The native black population came to be referred to as *negro colonial* to distinguish it from the *negros antillanos* (Antillean blacks) who arrived after independence.

In the mid-19th century a new era of Panamanian history began as North American capital virtually took over the country, importing its own foreign labor force. Three thousand Chinese and four thousand other foreign laborers entered around 1850 for the building of the Panama railroad.[4] From 1881, when the French began digging the canal, to 1914 when the U.S. completed the project, some 83,000 foreign workers entered Panama, the majority coming from the English- and French-speaking Caribbean islands [see Part I, Ch. 4]. A final, smaller wave entered during the Second World War to work on U.S. military bases in the Canal Zone.

Large numbers of the canal construction workers died—over 20,000 during the French digging alone. Others eventually returned to their countries or migrated to the United States. But those who remained and their descendants were numerous enough to have a permanent impact on Panamanian society, especially in the port cities of Colón and Panama City.

With the completion of the major work on the canal in 1913, some 5,000 canal workers were transferred to the United Fruit Company's banana plantations in the western province of Bocas del Toro.[5] This became a secondary U.S. enclave, also using mainly West Indian labor. By around 1929, there were some 24,000 West Indians in Bocas, although their number fell when United Fruit transferred most of its operations to Chiriquí province on the Pacific.[6] In addition to the West Indians, the banana company used the labor of the Guaymi Indians, perhaps the poorest and most exploited ethnic group in Panama.

Most of the West Indians, however, congregated in Panama City and Colón, the terminal points of the canal. In the heavily West Indian city of Colón, people were called "Jamaicans"—meaning that they came from the English-speaking Caribbean—or "French," referring to those from Haiti, Martinique and Guadeloupe. Their food consisted of typical Caribbean dishes such as rice with coconut and red beans, a dish of Jamaican origins. Their music was calypso and their language Creole English or French. One Panamanian recalls her childhood in Colón:

> My great-grandmother came from Martinique, and my great-grandfather from Guadeloupe. They came for the building of the Panama railroad. My maternal grandparents came from Jamaica for the building of the canal. They lived in the Canal Zone during the construction, and afterwards went to live in Colón.
>
> The culture in Colón was very rich, very Caribbean. There was always what they called the "French" community, and in fact French Creole was the first language I was taught. Although the people were very poor, they had a Caribbean tradition of hospitality and would always welcome you into their houses and offer food. The mestizo Panamanians even adopted some of our West Indian culture, such as the food and the calypso.
>
> But the Caribbean community was also marginalized from the larger Panamanian reality. My great-grandparents, for instance, never spoke Spanish, although they lived in Panama for years and years and had their children there.
>
> The Caribbean people always talked about going back to their countries, but most of them never were able to. Many did keep in contact with their relatives at home, for forty or fifty years in some cases.[7]

This cultural separateness of the West Indians and their special position as workers for the North Americans led to friction with the native Panamanians. The West Indians felt

Costa Rica and Panama

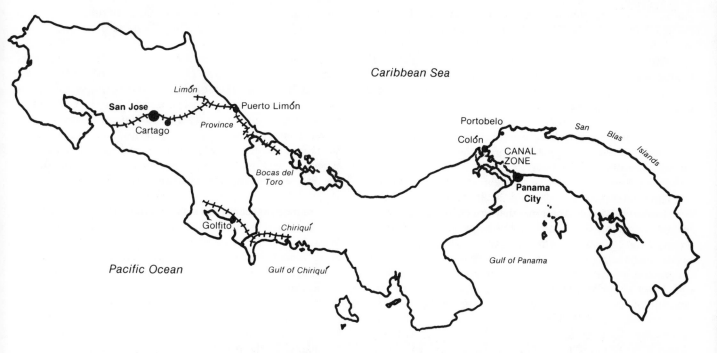

they had little in common with the latinized Panamanian campesinos, even though the majority of them also were black. They attempted to preserve their English language and culture by setting up special schools for their children with instruction in English. The Panamanians, on the other hand, tended to view the *antillanos* as pawns of the Americans who had facilitated the takeover and division of the country by the United States. Thus the West Indians were resented for their special "privileges," such as being welcome in the U.S.-run Canal Zone while native Panamanians were not. This was true even though the West Indian blacks were clearly second-class citizens in the Zone by comparison with the white North Americans or "Zonians."

Growing Unity Under Torrijos

During the Second World War, the Canal Zone became the scene of a mammoth U.S. military build-up. Fourteen military bases and 130 air and intelligence facilities were installed, ostensibly for defense of the canal but in fact as a permanent U.S. military presence in the region. This build-up highlighted Panama's lack of sovereignty over the Zone, a U.S.-controlled strip five miles wide on either side of the canal which effectively cut the country in two. U.S. laws held sway in the Zone, which had its own schools, postal system, police and courts, all run by North Americans.

In the late 1950s, U.S. domination of the canal enclave was challenged by a growing nationalist movement centered in the student population. Frequent strikes and protest marches culminated in the "Flag Riots" of 1964, which began when Panamanian students attempted to fly the Panamanian flag (as specified by law) beside the U.S. flag at a high school in the Zone. They were attacked by North American students and Zone residents, leading to a riot and intervention by U.S. Marines which resulted in dozens of deaths and injuries. Angry

Panamanian protests in the wake of the Flag Riots unified the diverse sectors of Panamanian society into a nationalism never before seen in the country.

On the strength of this unity, General Omar Torrijos came to power in a 1968 coup, advancing the canal-sovereignty issue as a key part of his "revolution." His program as defined in the new 1972 constitution was not radical, but it challenged the political power of the oligarchy and brought working-class and campesino sectors into an alliance with the government. Reforms included nationalizing the U.S.-owned Power & Light Company, establishing a state banana corporation and creating farmers' cooperatives around the country. New laws included a progressive Labor Code and an agrarian reform, and state services were extended to previously neglected areas of the country.

Most importantly, Torrijos launched a major campaign to integrate the country's diverse ethnic sectors into a unified society. The National Assembly was reorganized with 505 local representatives chosen democratically at the grassroots level. Torrijos repealed laws which had hindered West Indians from becoming citizens, and he facilitated their promotion within the government and civil service. Panamanian "national" culture was heavily emphasized in the schools, and the special English schools were eliminated so that all schoolchildren were educated in Spanish.

While promoting cultural and political nationalism, however, Torrijos also opened the door to increasing foreign economic penetration. The Banking Law of 1970 turned Panama into the "Little Switzerland" of Latin America, with 87 offshore banks paying almost no taxes and exempt from the scrutiny of U.S. agencies. He expanded the free port system at Colón, allowing ships of any country to "transnationalize" their cargo on paper as they passed through the Canal (thus reducing taxes in both the shipping and receiving countries). He also opened up huge land tracts in Chiriquí for copper mining by the Texasgulf Corporation at Cerro Colorado, with the state providing 80% of the investment capital and Texasgulf only 20%.

Although Torrijos challenged the political influence of the United States, therefore, he also permitted greater economic influence by foreign banks and transnationals, a strategy shaped by his conservative economic advisor Nicolas Ardito Barletta. This contradictory approach produced social programs for the poor but also greater wealth for Panamanian elites linked to foreign capital, polarizing the society between the demands of these two classes.[8]

When Torrijos died in a small plane crash in 1981—under suspicious circumstances—both his social programs and the tentative national unity he fostered fell apart.[9] He was followed over the next three yeas by three different presidents and three heads of the National Guard, who vainly attempted to hold onto Torrijos' popular support while retreating from his progressive policies. By 1983, the General's reformist constitution had been replaced, while many popular programs and laws still on the books were no longer being implemented.

In 1984, Ardito Barletta became president in an election tainted by the intervention of the Panamanian National Guard.[10] An economist trained at the University of Chicago who served as a vice-president of the World Bank for six years, Ardito Barletta is a favorite of Reagan administration policymakers and an enthusiastic proponent of the economic austerity preached by the World Bank and the IMF. He has attempted to deal with Panama's $3.7 billion debt by implementing a program of tax increases, cutbacks in public employment and services and elimination of subsidies on food and other necessities, demanding great sacrifices from Panamanians.

Reaction to these austerity measures and to the gutting of the Torrijos reforms has fostered a renewed unity among Panama's class and ethnic sectors. The government's attempts to raise food prices triggered a nationwide march on the capital in 1984, as Panamanians—led by several left parties—let the government know they would not tolerate "what happened in the Dominican Republic" under IMF austerity. These growing protests have raised the spectre of a new military coup should the Ardito Barletta government appear incapable of maintaining control.

Young Panamanians of West Indian descent are active in this popular movement, putting an end to the days when the West Indian community remained aloof from national struggles. This is the result of both a generational change and the integrative thrust of the Torrijos era, which together have led to the nearly total assimilation of younger West Indians. While their grandparents may still speak mainly or exclusively English, they are bilingual, with many more comfortable in Spanish than English. Reflecting this assimilation, the term "antillano" is falling into disuse as most West Indians no longer see themselves as a distinct group nor identify with U.S. interests in Panama. Today, the entire youth and student population is highly politicized, challenging the economic and military policies backed by Washington. While the United States remains a physical presence in Panama, the unified national challenge to its role appears likely to grow. ■

Panamanians celebrate Carnival.

Marcelo Montecino

NOTES TO PART SIX

Trinidad & Tobago

1. Eric Williams, *History of the People of Trinidad & Tobago* (London: Andre Deutch, 1964), p. 40.
2. Gordon K. Lewis, *The Growth of the Modern West Indies* (New York: Monthly Review Press, 1968), p. 69.
3. Prime Minister Chambers, Budget speech, January 1984.
4. Dr. Trevor Farrell, "Mr. Chambers' First Year," *Caribbean Contact,* November 1982.
5. *Caribbean Contact,* April 1983.
6. Prime Minister Chambers, Budget speech, January 1982.
7. Prime Minister Chambers, Budget speech, January 1982.
8. *Caribbean Contact,* August 1984.
9. OWTU, "The 1984 Budget: The Workers' Response."
10. Raphael Sebastien, "State-Sector Development in Trinidad and Tobago, 1956-1982," *Contemporary Marxism,* No. 10 (1985), p. 110.

St. Vincent and the Grenadines

1. *The Farmer,* bulletin of National Farmers Union, February 1984.
2. Projects Promotion Ltd. (St. Vincent), "Conjunctural Analysis" (mimeographed paper, 1984).
3. *Ibid.*
4. EPICA interview with Fr. Denis Hebert, Commission for Development of Peoples, St. Vincent, August 1982.
5. Caribbean/Central American Action, *Investing in St. Vincent and the Grenadines.*
6. *Ibid.*
7. *Unity* (St. Vincent), April 4, 1984.
8. *Unity,* March 7, 1984.
9. Interview with James Mitchell, *Caribbean Contact,* May 1985.
10. EPICA interview with member of the St. Vincent Union of Teachers, July 1984.

Barbados

1. "A Briefe Discription of the Ilande of Barbados," in Vincent T. Harlow, ed., *Colonising Expeditions to the West Indies and Guiana, 1623-1667* (London: Hakluyt Society, 1925), pp. 42-43.
2. U.S. Department of State, *Congressional Presentation: FY 1982 Security Assistance Programs,* p. 389.
3. Central Bank of Barbados, *Annual Reports 1981* and *1982.*
4. *Caribbean Contact,* September 1984.
5. "Barbados 1984," *Business Week,* April 1984, p. 39.
6. *Ibid.,* p. 33.
7. *New York Times,* May 18, 1984.
8. EPICA interview with Branford Taitt, president of Democratic Labour Party, May 1984.
9. Central Bank of Barbados, *Annual Report 1984,* p. 3.
10. *Barbados Advocate,* November 17, 1984.

Dominican Republic

1. Alan Howard, "A Report on Gulf + Western in the Dominican Republic," presented at the Dominican Republic 10th Anniversary Seminar, New York, April 1975.
2. Interview with Narciso Isa Conde in *Areito,* Vol. X, No. 38, 1984, p. 9.
3. *Breves Dominicanas,* Vol. II, No. 3, September 1979 (Centro Dominicano de Intercambio de Informacion, Santo Domingo), p. 11.
4. *El Sol,* February 23, 1980.
5. *La Noticia,* January 31, 1980.
6. *Miami Herald,* April 5, 1984.
7. Letter from President Ronald Reagan to President Jorge Blanco, March 23, 1984.
8. *Washington Post,* May 2, 1984; *El Nuevo Diario,* April 26, 1984; *La Noticia,* April 28, 1984; and other press reports.
9. *Washington Post,* May 2, 1984.
10. *La Noticia,* April 28, 1984.
11. *Caribbean Contact,* March 1985.

Haiti

1. Jean Jacques Honorat, "The Political Economy of the Haitian Refugee Crisis" (mimeographed paper, 1982), p. 60.
2. *Ibid.,* pp. 33-46.
3. *Ibid.,* p. 49.
4. Suzy Castor, "The Impact of Duvalierism on Socio-Political Dynamics," paper presented at Hunter College, New York, August 29, 1984.
5. *Miami Herald,* December 20, 1982.
6. *Latin America Regional Reports—Caribbean,* December 4, 1981.
7. Washington Office on Haiti, "Human Rights Violations in Haiti, 1984."
8. Amnesty International, "Haiti: Briefing" (A.I., March 1985), p. 14.
9. Interview with Gregoire Eugene by Don Foster, June 1984.
10. Pastoral letter from Bishops of Haiti, January 27, 1983.
11. *Washington Post,* March 10, 1983.

12. Declaration of Msgr. Francois Gayot, S.M.M., Bishop of Cap-Haitien at the Bishops' Conference, Port-au-Prince, December 12, 1984.
13. EPICA interview with Fritz Longchamp, director, Washington Office on Haiti, March 1985.

Jamaica

1. *Daily Gleaner,* August 16, 1983.
2. Carl Stone, "Continuing Crisis of Jamaica's Economy," *Caribbean Contact,* December 1984.
3. The Resource Center, "Jamaica: Open for Business" (Albuquerque: The Resource Center, 1984), p. 30.
4. Jamaica National Investment Promotion figures.
5. Caribbean Development Bank, *Annual Report 1983.*
6. Jamaica Bauxite Institute figures.
7. Carl Stone, "Continuing Crisis of Jamaica's Economy." Quote from EPICA interview with Jamaican peasant farmers, September 1983.
8. EPICA interview with Jamaican economist, September 1983.
9. Bank of Jamaica Statistical Digest, July 1984.
10. *Daily Gleaner,* May 7, 1984.
11. *Workers Time,* August 1984.
12. Interview by Don Foster with Horace Levy, Kingston, June 1984.
13. *Caribbean Contact,* February 1985.
14. *Caribbean Contact,* April 1985.
15. *Sunday Gleaner,* May 5, 1985.

Guyana

1. Guyana Human Rights Association, *Guyana Human Rights Report 1984,* p. 3. The official population figure used by the Guyanese government is 922,000. However, reliable estimates are lower. The GHRA uses the figure 645,000.
2. Walter Rodney, "Contemporary Political Trends in the English-Speaking Caribbean," *The Black Scholar,* September 1975, pp. 15-21.
3. Walter Rodney, "People's Power, No Dictator" (Working People's Alliance, 1979).
4. *Guyana Human Rights Report 1984,* p. 3.
5. *Washington Post,* November 18, 1983. "Rabbi Washington," whose real name is David Hill, fled the U.S. in 1966 after being convicted of extortion in Cleveland.
6. *Caribbean Contact,* January 1981.
7. Dr. Clive Thomas, "Collapse of Guyana's Economy," *Caribbean Contact,* January 1982; Caribbean Development Bank, *Annual Report 1983;* Central Bank of Barbados, *Annual Report 1984;* Caribbean Development Bank, *Annual Report 1984.*
8. *Guyana Human Rights Report 1984,* pp. 47-48.
9. *Ibid.,* p. 34.
10. *Caribbean Contact,* April 1985.
11. Rickey Singh, "Guyana: The Way Forward," *Caribbean Contact,* May 1985.

French Antilles

1. *Latin America Regional Reports—Caribbean,* July 6, 1982.
2. *Caribbean Contact,* March 1985.
3. C.L.R. James, *Spheres of Existence* (London: Alison & Busby, 1980), p. 152.
4. *Guadeloupe 2000,* July/August 1982, p. 2.
5. EPICA interview with UPLG, Guadeloupe, August 1982.
6. EPICA interview with Fr. Serge Plocoste, Jeunesse Ouvriere Chretienne, Guadeloupe, August 1982.
7. EPICA interview with Gilbert Bienville, Christians for the Liberation of the Guadeloupean People, August 1982.
8. UPLG, *Pou Nou Vanse au Chimen a Lendepandans,* June 1981.
9. *Le Monde,* March 1, 1985.
10. *Le Monde,* March 2, 1985.
11. *Jakata* (Guadeloupe), October 1981.
12. *Le Monde,* March 2, 1985.
13. M. Claude Makouke, secretary-general of UPLG, quoted in *ibid.*

French Guiana

1. Frank Schwarzbeck, "Recycling a Forgotten Colony," *Caribbean Review,* Spring 1984, p. 23.
2. *Ibid.,* p. 23.
3. *Washington Post,* August 5, 1984.
4. *Latin America Regional Reports—Caribbean,* May 10, 1985.

Netherlands Antilles

1. Dr. J. Hartog, *Curacao: Short History* (Aruba: De Wit Stores, 1979), p. 4.
2. Dr. J. Hartog, *Aruba: Short History* (Aruba: Van Dorp, 1980), p. 19.
3. *Ibid.,* p. 53.
4. *Ibid.,* p. 3.
5. *Antillen Review,* May/June 1984, pp. 5-7.
6. *Antillen Review,* December 1983/January 1984, p. 7.
7. EPICA interview with member of Teachers' Union, Curacao, April 1984.
8. *Antillen Review,* May/June 1984, p. 5.
9. *Antillen Review,* August/September 1983, p. 19.
10. EPICA interview with member of Teachers' Union, Curacao, April 1984.

Puerto Rico

1. National Ecumenical Movement of Puerto Rico, "Inside Puerto Rico 1984: Colonialism and Intervention in the Caribbean and Central America," *Prisa International,* April 1984, p. 3.
2. *New York Times,* August 19, 1984.
3. Harry Turner, "Elections in Puerto Rico," *Caribbean Today,* Spring 1984, p. 4.
4. *Claridad,* April 19-25, 1985, p. 2.
5. *San Juan Star,* March 1, 1983.
6. *The Militant,* January 11, 1985.
7. Judith Berkan et al., "Violating the Treaty of Tlatelolco," *Arms Control Today,* January 1985.
8. *New York Times,* February 13, 1985, p. 1.
9. *Prisa International,* p. 1.

Belize

1. Milton Jamail, "Belize: Will Independence Mean New Dependence?", *NACLA Report on the Americas,* July-August 1984, p. 13.
2. *Mesoamerica,* Vol. 4, No. 6, June 1985 (Institute for Central American Studies, San Jose, Costa Rica).
3. *Washington Post,* January 27, 1985.
4. Government of Belize, *The Road to Independence* (September 1981).
5. Jamail, p. 15.
6. *Washington Post,* January 27, 1985.
7. Manuel Esquivel, statement to the press, cited in *The New Belize,* January 1985.
8. *Ibid.*
9. *Mesoamerica,* Vo. 4, No. 6, June 1985; *Enfoprensa,* June 14, 1985.

Honduras

1. "Banana Diplomacy: The Development of U.S.-Honduran Relations," *El Salvador Bulletin,* Vol. 2, No. 7, May 1983 (Berkeley, CA: U.S.-Salvadoran Research and Information Center), p. 4.
2. *Mesoamerica,* May 1983, p. 7.
3. *Honduras Update* (Sommerville, MA), Vol. 3, No. 6, March 1985.
4. Interview with Juan Ambrosio Sabio, leader of Honduran Professional Teachers' Training Guild, in *Honduras Update,* Vol. 3, No. 8, May 1985.
5. *Honduras Update,* Vol. 3, No. 6, March 1985.
6. "Honduras: On the Border of War," *NACLA Report on the Americas,* Vol. XV, No. 6 (November-December 1981), p. 24.

Nicaragua

1. Roxanne Dunbar Ortiz, "The Miskito People, Ethnicity, and the Atlantic Coast," *Nicaraguan Perspectives,* Number 3, Winter 1982.
2. Eduardo Perez-Valle, *Expediente de Campos Azules, Historia de Bluefields* (Managua, 1978), pp. 238-39.
3. Centro de Investigaciones y Documentacion de la Costa Atlantica (CIDCA), *Trabil Nani: Historical Background and Current Situation of the Atlantic Coast* (Managua: CIDCA, 1984), pp. 11-12.
4. *Ibid.,* pp. 8-14. The figures were updated by CIDCA in the summer of 1985.
5. MISURASATA, "Lineamientos Generales," 1980.
6. *Trabil Nani,* p. 23.
7. Declaration of Principles Regarding the Indigenous Communities on the Atlantic Coast, August 21, 1981.
8. *Trabil Nani,* p. 3.
9. *Washington Post,* July 27, 1985.
10. Statement by Ray Hooker, newly elected member of the Council of State from Bluefields, in Washington, DC, February 19, 1985.

Costa Rica

1. Paula Palmer, "*What Happen*": *A Folk-History of Costa Rica's Talamanca Coast* (San Jose Ecodesarrollos, 1977), p. 157.
2. Carolyn Hall, *El Cafe y el Desarrollo Historico-Geografico de Costa Rica* (San Jose: Editorial Costa Rica, 1979), p. 23.
3. Jeffrey Casey Gaspar, *Limon 1880-1940; Un Estudio de la Industria Banamera en Costa Rica* (San Jose: Editorial Costa Rica, 1979), p. 23.
4. Rodrigo Quesada Monge, "Ferrocarilles y Crecimiento Economica: El Caso de la Costa Rica Railroad Company." *Annuario de Estudios Centroamericanos* (Instituto de Investigaciones Sociales, Universidad de Costa Rica), Vol. 8, 1983, p. 98.
5. Palmer, p. 200.
6. Gaspar, p. 322.
7. *Ibid.,* p. 91.
8. John A. Booth, "Representative Constitutional Democracy in Costa Rica," in Steve C. Ropp and James A. Morris, *Central America: Crisis and Adaptation* (Albuquerque: University of New Mexico Press, 1984), pp. 161-163.
9. Comite Patriotico Nacional (COPAN), Revista Teorica (Costa Rica), August 16, 1984, p. 40.
10. Carlos Schifter, *Costa Rica 1948* (San Jose: Editorial Universitaria Centroamericana, 1984), chapter 4.
11. Carlos Araya Pochet, *Historia Economica de Costa Rica 1950-1970* (San Jose: Editorial Fernandez Ara, 1975), p. 41.
12. EPICA interview with cooperative leader, Siquirres, Costa Rica, July 1985.
13. Palmer, pp. 274-283.
14. Booth, p. 177.
15. Marc Edelman and Jayne Hutchcroft, "Costa Rica: Resisting Austerity," *NACLA Report on the Americas,* Vol. XVIII, January/February 1984, p. 38.
16. Ibid., p. 39.
17. *Washington Post,* March 31, 1985.
18. COPAN, *Revista Teorica,* August 6-12, 1984, p. 6.
19. Palmer, p. 324.

Panama

1. Juan Materno Vasquez, *El Pais por Conquistar* (Panama: J.M. Vasques, 1974), p. 36.
2. Luis A. Diez Castillo, *Los Cimarrones y los Negros Antillanos en Panama* (Panama: L. Diez Castillo, 1981), Chapter 2.
3. Materno Vasquez, p. 39.
4. Diez Castillo, p. 63. See also: Xabier Gorostiaga, "La Zona del Canal y su Impacto en el Movimiento Obrero Panameno," *Tareas* (Panama), #32, July/August 1975, pp. 34-35.
5. Jorge Arosemena, "Ls Panamenos Negros Descendientes de Antillaos: Un Caso de Marginalidad Social?" *Tareas,* #32, July/August 1975, p. 57.
6. Diez Castillo, p. 91.
7. EPICA interview with Esmeralda Browne, Washington, DC, May 1985.
8. *Dialogo Social* (Panama), January 1985, pp. 6-7.
9. *Dialogo Social,* August 1984, pp. 27-28.
10. *Washington Post,* August 27, 1985.

PART SEVEN
In the Shadow of the Empire

Introduction

The dramatic political reverses triggered by the Grenada invasion must be understood in light of the gradual spread of progressive ideals in the period before 1983. In the wake of the Grenada revolution in 1979 and Reagan's election in 1980, progressive and right-wing trends vied for influence in the region. The election of Seaga and other conservative victories, plus the announcement of the Caribbean Basin Initiative reinforced bilateral allegiances to the United States. Simultaneously, however, sectors such as trade unions, grassroots groups, intellectuals and some Christians were stepping up their efforts toward regional unity and social change. The revolution in Grenada played a pivotal role in this regard. In no other country was a Grenada-style revolution imminent, nor were left-wing parties expanding rapidly. But Grenada served as a rallying point and inspiration, providing a model for change in many social and economic areas. Equally important, the Bishop government served as a voice for popular concerns and positions within the context of regional governmental institutions. These factors helped build unity between progressive sectors and bring their concerns closer to the mainstream of political debate.

The long period of dormancy in the regional integration movement came to an end in 1982 as two meetings of the CARICOM heads of government were held in the space of less than a year. At these meetings, the prime ministers rejected attempts by the U.S. and Barbados to expel Grenada from CARICOM, a move which would have set implicit ideological limits on the body's membership. Thus the concept of ideological pluralism in the region was gradually winning legitimacy and acceptance.

The rebirth of the integration movement came at a time when Washington was wooing individual governments through its Caribbean Basin Initiative. While most Caribbean leaders hoped to get something out of the CBI, neither they nor others in the region could ignore its negative implications. The exclusion of certain countries from CBI benefits and favoritism toward others raised questions about a U.S. attempt to "divide and rule," with ominous implications for regional unity. Furthermore, the CBI's promotion of the old Puerto Rican model of foreign investment reopened the question of foreign economic control versus self-reliance. Trade unions were among the main critics of the CBI, based on their past experiences with exploitative foreign companies. While raising some hopes for a quick fix, therefore, the CBI also helped to provoke debate on more profound issues.

A similar process took place in regards to the militarization of the region under the Reagan administration. The growing U.S. military involvement in Central America and its echoes in the Caribbean made the region extremely nervous. While conservative governments went along with the military build-up, progressive sectors began popularizing the concept of a Caribbean Zone of Peace, a non-militarized, non-aligned region which would be protected from involvement in superpower conflicts. Initiated by the Caribbean Conference of Churches, the Zone of Peace concept received strong support from the Bishop government and was gradually working its way into the CARICOM agenda, although other regional governments gave lip service far beyond any concrete commitment to action.

Although conflicting trends continued to pull at the region, these ideals—regional unity and pluralism, greater local economic control, and a Caribbean Zone of Peace—slowly gained currency at various levels of Caribbean society. That fragile process was shattered in 1983, first by the shock of the Grenada revolution's self-destruction, then by the U.S. invasion. Afterwards, the Reagan administration moved quickly to consolidate a "new Caribbean order" which closed off the opening for the progressive forces and imposed what some feared would soon become a recolonization of the Caribbean by the United States. ∎

Barbadian group protests presence of U.S. nuclear- powered aircraft carrier Dwight D. Eisenhower in Caribbean waters.

Monali

Left Under Fire

The year 1984 was a crucible for the Caribbean progressive movement. Whirled in controversy, under pressure from the establishment, and burning with mutual recriminations and self-reproach, the left began the process of forging a new unity. All agree that the destruction of the Grenada revolution set back the movement, probably by years. The process of recovery has barely begun. But that process holds out hope: hope that through questioning and defining basic principles, and opening them to public debate, the left will emerge from its crisis with a new clarity and stronger ties to its popular base.

Two factors combined to produce the crisis for the progressive movement. One was the split within the New Jewel Movement, culminating in the executions of Maurice Bishop and the other leaders. The other was the U.S. invasion. Both contributed to the sudden, dramatic strengthening of the regional right wing, but it can be argued that the significance of the first factor outweighed that of the second. Invasions by the United States against popular Caribbean movements are not new, and an aggression against Grenada had long been expected. Indeed, if the U.S. invasion had occurred *without* the executions, it most likely would have strengthened the left and hurt the right by again proving the truth of allegations about U.S. imperialism in the region.[1]

The invasion did, of course, prove that, but the political waters were greatly muddied by the events which came before. For many people, the execution of the immensely popular Bishop destroyed the revolution from within and made the invasion a justifiable, almost inevitable consequence. In the Dominican Republic, where the largest protests against the U.S. action took place—due to the island's own history of U.S. invasion—one progressive leader wrote:

> Solidarity with Grenada could have been 100 times more powerful if the events there had not been so difficult to understand, owing to the murder of Bishop and his comrades. Had that situation not arisen, the imperialists would have encountered not only much greater resistance from the Grenadian people, but also far more serious mass protests in all the countries of the region.[2]

Paradoxically, however, one effect of the invasion was to partially restore the revolution's positive image after it had been so severely tarnished by the killings. The superpower attack on a tiny island once again cast Grenada in the role of innocent victim. In the process of coming to terms with this reality of U.S. imperialism, many people were prompted to recall what the Grenada revolution stood for and why it had been important for the Caribbean. As Fidel Castro stated on November 14, 1983:

> . . . The United States wanted to kill the symbol of the Grenadian revolution, but the symbol was already dead. The Grenadian revolutionaries themselves destroyed it with their spirit and their colossal errors. We believe that, after the death of Bishop and his closest comrades, after the army fired on the people and after the [New Jewel Movement] and the govern-

ment divorced themselves from the masses and isolated themselves from the world, the Grenadian revolutionary process could not survive.

> In its efforts to destroy a symbol, the United States killed a corpse and brought the symbol back to life at the same time.[3]

Repression Against the Left

The destruction of the Grenada revolution by a faction labeled "ultraleft" opened the entire Caribbean left movement to bitter attack. Simultaneously, the invasion bolstered the confidence of conservative sectors, including ruling politicians, elements of the Church, the business elite, and the middle class. They seized the opportunity for a crusade against the left in its moment of division and weakness.

The result was a flurry of red-baiting and false allegations reminiscent of the worst days of McCarthyism in the U.S. The label "communist" was promiscuously applied to any sort of dissent. Regional politicians took advantage of the widespread horror and grief over the killing of Maurice Bishop by accusing all the region's left parties of being capable of similar acts. The leaders' underlying motive was to entrench themselves in power, using the Grenadian affair to discredit their own domestic opposition (Seaga, for instance, tried to suggest that Michael Manley might be murdered by the left wing of the PNP).

A central theme was that Cuba had been behind the killing of Bishop and was now working hand in hand with leftist parties to overthrow Caribbean governments. Seaga, for instance, claimed that the Cuban government had given instructions to the Workers Party of Jamaica to "step up action" against his government. He went on television and named 25 Jamaicans who he said had traveled to Cuba or the Soviet Union, and he threatened to launch a "shattering offensive" against "saboteurs and traitors." He also claimed that a Soviet plot existed to kill a member of the civil service, and dramatically expelled four Soviet diplomats and a Cuban journalist from the country.[4] These sensational accusations diverted public attention from Jamaica's worst economic crisis since Seaga came to power, allowing him to call and win a snap election several weeks later.

Antigua's prime minister, Vere C. Bird, attacked the Antigua Caribbean Liberation Movement, describing them as "persons with totalitarian aspirations and communist affiliations."[5] Prime Minister John Compton of St. Lucia proclaimed that the invasion was a "message" to revolutionary groups in the region that no armed force could ever take power again because "we now have the Stars and Stripes here to protect us against them."[6] Other regional politicians made similar statements.

These allegations of Cuban responsibility and armed subversion were an ironic reversal of the truth. One point on which inside observers of the Grenada tragedy agree is that Cuba was not involved in the split with the New Jewel

(continued on page 200)

GRENADA'S TRAGEDY

How and why the Grenada revolution fell apart will be the subject of debate for years to come. Some of the internal process has come to light through interviews with surviving members of the New Jewel Movement, especially former government ministers Kenrick Radix and George Louison. Further information may eventually become available if Bernard Coard and his supporters, presently in prison in Grenada, are allowed to tell their story. Meanwhile, a number of published accounts are available to those who wish to study the subject in greater depth.

The conflict which developed within the New Jewel Movement (NJM) apparently hinged on both personal rivalries and political disputes. Some observers say that Coard, who was minister of finance and deputy prime minister in the government headed by Maurice Bishop, envied Bishop's power and popularity. However, larger issues were also involved. All of the leadership, including Bishop and Coard, saw the New Jewel Movement as a vanguard party structured along Leninist lines, with decision-making by majority vote within the party's Central Committee (CC). For Bishop, however, it was the Grenadian people, not the party, who ultimately were key to the revolutionary process. He assigned great importance, for instance, to the building of organs of "popular democracy," village and parish councils where the people could have a direct voice in government. The tendency led by Coard showed less interest in these structures and favored tight party control through a disciplined and "ideologically advanced" Central Committee.

Coard's faction grew out of a Marxist study group called OREL which he led in the 1970s, bringing a number of young Grenadians under his influence at a time when the New Jewel Movement was in formation. Although OREL joined the NJM in 1973, some of its members continued to form a clique around Coard within the party, concentrated in the NJM's youth arm.[11]

By the end of 1982, two identifiable factions had emerged within the party, although it appears that Bishop was not aware of the split or at least not convinced of its seriousness. According to Radix and Louison, Coard used his influence to stack the Central Committee with former OREL members, some of whom were also officers in the People's Revolutionary Army. The perception of a military threat from the United States contributed to this tendency toward enlarging the army and bringing its officers into important party positions. Most of the original founders of the NJM, meanwhile, remained loyal to Bishop, including foreign minister Unison Whiteman, education minister Jacqueline Creft, Radix, Louison and a number of others.

It is important to recognize that the issues at stake did *not* primarily concern the programs or goals of the revolution. Both Bishop and Coard saw the revolution's ultimate goal as building socialism in Grenada.[12] Both also understood the need to manage the economy on a capitalist basis in the near term. Indeed, Bernard Coard was widely praised by economists and bankers in the region for his competence as a financial manager and his harmonious dealings with international lending agencies such as the International Monetary Fund, the Caribbean Development Bank and the World Bank. Both Bishop and Coard wanted normal relations with the United States and other capitalist countries, although not at the price of giving up the revolution's principles. It is erroneous to suggest, as some have, that Coard wanted "instant socialism" while Bishop favored a reconciliation with the capitalist world.

The Party and the People

Rather, the conflict was over the nature and leadership of the party and its relationship to the people. By mid-1983, there was a perception in the party that popular enthusiasm for the revolution was flagging and that many government programs were disorganized. While the latter at least was probably partly true, the Central Committee's reaction seems to have been grossly out of proportion to the actual problems. While everyone agreed there was a crisis, the party split over how to deal with it. Bishop argued for strengthening the party's "weak links" with the masses and for greater accountability of the party. Coard supporters, on the other hand, blamed Bishop himself, accusing him of weak leadership and attacking him and his supporters as "petty bourgeois" and "right opportunist." The heavy ideological tone of these accusations contributed to the later theory of an "ultra-left" group within the party, but it does not appear that any substantive ideological debate took place.

Since Bishop remained extraordinarily popular among the Grenadian people, the move against him within the Central Committee marked the party's alienation from the mainstream sentiment in the country. Indeed, as the crisis deepened, the Central Committee's disdain for popular wishes seemed almost vengeful. Bishop's decision to question the Central Committee order to share leadership with Coard may have violated the norms of a Leninist party, as some argue.[13] But the far more important reality was that Bishop's stature as a leader in Grenada and internationally and the affection Grenadians held for him were crucial elements enabling the revolution to go forward. For the Central Committee members to consider stripping such a figure of his leadership, to say nothing of backing up their decision with murder, was to blindly cast away the only basis for the revolution's survival—its popular support.

Further Reading

Latin America Bureau, *Grenada: Whose Freedom?* (London: LAB, 1984) (1 Amwell St., London, ECIR 1UL, England).

Hugh O'Shaughnessy, *Grenada: Revolution, Invasion and Aftermath* (London: Sphere Books Ltd., 1984).

Catherine Sunshine and Philip Wheaton, *Death of a Revolution: An Analysis of the Grenada Tragedy and the U.S. Invasion* (Washington, DC: EPICA, 1984).

Department of State and Department of Defense, *Grenada Documents: An Overview and Selection.* (Although the authenticity of the captured documents cannot be vouched for, most analysts have regarded the party records as authentic.)

Don Rojas, interview, December 26, 1983; George Louison, interview, April 16, 1984; Kenrick Radix, interview, April 30, 1984. *Intercontinental Press,* 410 West St., New York, NY 10014.

ernard Coard, left, and Maurice Bishop in happier times.

Barbados *Nation*

Movement. Fidel Castro had deep personal links of friendship with Maurice Bishop—almost a mentor relationship of the veteran revolutionary to the younger one. Bishop's charismatic leadership, moreover, was closer to Cuba's kind of revolution than was the more doctrinaire, party-oriented approach of Bernard Coard. For both reasons, Cuba made little secret of its sympathy for Bishop when it learned of the split.

In an October 15 message to the Central Committee, which had just placed Bishop under house arrest, Castro reaffirmed Cuba's respect for Bishop and warned that divisions in the party would result in heavy damage to the image of the Grenada revolution. This repudiation came as a blow to Coard and his supporters.[7] Later, after Bishop had been killed, Cuba censured the Revolutionary Military Council in extremely harsh terms, and rejected their request for help in defending the island against the expected invasion. Instead, Castro instructed the Cuban construction workers to defend only their own work camp and not to coordinate with the Grenadian armed forces in any way.

Secondly, accusations of plots to overthrow governments were woven out of whole cloth by leaders anxious to divert attention from severe economic problems. There is presently no organized armed threat to any Caribbean government, nor are there signs of any developing soon. Most left-wing parties in the region participate in electoral politics as soon as they are strong enough to do so.

Regional politicians nonetheless profited from the general hysteria to enact measures curbing civil liberties and the right to dissent. In Dominica, for instance, the Eugenia Charles government passed a "Treason Act" and a "State Security Act" which impose harsh punishments (including death by hanging) for a series of vaguely worded offenses, including "forming an intention to overthrow the state." The St. Vincent government brought criminal charges against Renwick Rose, a leader of the United Peoples Movement, for possession of several Soviet magazines. The incident was symptomatic of the erosion of civil liberties, especially freedom of expression, in the post-invasion period.

Nowhere was this more true than in Barbados, whose government spearheaded Caribbean participation in the U.S. invasion. In that island, anticommunism became tinted with xenophobia as the Adams government accused "foreign elements" of fostering subversion. By "foreign elements" Adams meant people from other Caribbean countries resident in Barbados. In an act which came to symbolize the new drive for conformity, Adams expelled Guyanese journalist Rickey Singh from Barbados for writing articles critical of the invasion. Singh had been editor of the regional monthly *Caribbean Contact,* published by the Caribbean Conference of Churches at its headquarters in Bridgetown. In a speech to the Barbadian Parliament, Adams charged that the CCC was full of "foreign elements" and threatened to expel other CCC officials who were non-Barbadians.

In an anguished response, the Rev. Allan Kirton, general secretary of the CCC, wrote:

> [Our] first concern is about democracy. This term became the rallying cry of recent operations. In the name of "democracy," disagreement has been characterized as treachery worthy of death.[8]

Barbadian group protests Reagan/Adams collaboration in front of U.S. Embassy in Bridgetown. Such dissent came under attack after the Grenada invasion.

Likewise, the president of the opposition Democratic Labour Party, Branford Taitt, stood up in the Barbados Parliament and reminded his colleagues that people in a democracy were free to express their ideas even when they conflicted with those of the existing state power. Another Member of Parliament warned Barbadians, "Do not fall into the trap of believing that you are unpatriotic because you do not agree with the Prime Minister."[9]

Time brought a gradual cooling of emotions in Barbados and around the region. By mid-1984, more people were finding the courage to express their disagreement or doubts about the invasion. This dissenting view became more respectable after Errol Barrow, former Barbadian prime minister and present leader of the opposition, wrote a critique debunking the U.S. pretexts for the invasion and warning of divisions it implanted in the region.[10] Another factor was the realization that through its prominent participation in the invasion, Barbados had isolated itself as a U.S. pawn and was now regarded with disdain by some Caribbean countries and much of the Third World. Two diplomatic defeats, Barbados' failure to gain a seat on the U.N. Security Council and to win the post of Secretary General of the Organization of American States, drove this lesson home.

In spite of this gradual reappraisal, the "witch hunt" against dissenters left deep scars all over the Caribbean. There is a persistent fear to disagree with the majority opinion, and a readiness to label anyone who does disagree a communist. Freedom of thought and speech, one of the Caribbean's proud ideals, stands sadly tarnished in the wake of the Grenada affair.

Debate Within the Movement

Most people in the region viewed the specific fabrications against the left as lacking in proof, if not downright absurd. There was, nonetheless, a new pressure on progressive groups to define where they stood in terms of basic ideology and models. This caught some groups unprepared as they had never really achieved any clarity on these issues, despite having very specific platforms of economic and social reforms. No longer could parties claim to be simply "popular movements" advocating progressive change. Especially in the case of the stronger opposition parties, people demanded to know what they believed, how they operated, and how they would govern.

This was particularly the case in Jamaica and Guyana, where the search for alternatives to Seaga and Burnham made the character of opposition parties a matter of pressing concern. The Workers Party of Jamaica (WPJ), for example, published a letter from a reader in its newspaper, *Struggle,* which read in part:

> . . . Now many people are looking for your Party's activity in youth and community development here in southern Trelawney. The JLP [Seaga's party] showing themselves as very strong but they do not do much work toward the poor only the rich. So your party supporters are asking you to contest the next General Elections in Southern Trelawney.
> . . . I know your Party's policy is very strong towards our economy. But I don't think many Jamaicans fully understand the intention of the Party because they think you would take away their freedom and democracy from them and also hold no elections. So I am asking you to hold meetings and give the people the fullest idea of your Party so they cooperate with it.[14]

Similarly, a columnist in the Guyanese weekly the *Catholic Standard* wanted to know:

> What is the position of the WPA [Working People's Alliance] on the Grenadian debacle?
> Did it support the Bishop faction or the Coard faction? Has that issue provoked debate within the party?
> Arising out of this, is the WPA a Marxist-Leninist party and what does that mean in practice?[15]

In part, such questions were stimulated by the anticommunist histrionics of conservative leaders. But at the same time, they reflected concern about the real differences existing among the progressive forces—differences which had developed over a period of time and which emerged publicly in response to events in Grenada.

In analyzing the debate which erupted within the left, it is important to recognize that broad and substantial points of agreement continued to characterize the movement. *No progressive party or group in the region supported the U.S. invasion of Grenada.* All opposed it in the strongest terms, no matter what their position on internal events in Grenada. The invasion was condemned even by liberal and social democratic politicians like Michael Manley in Jamaica and Errol Barrow in Barbados. Moreover, all recognized that while a crisis existed in Grenada after the death of Bishop, this crisis merely presented the Reagan administration with an opportunity to implement long-standing intervention plans. For example, the Oilfields Workers Trade Union (OWTU) in Trinidad wrote:

The Reagan administration has always wished to see an end to the process of new democracy in Grenada. They wanted to put an end to the efforts of the Grenadian people who were building a free country that was an inspiration to the entire working people of the Caribbean. Indeed the records will show that over the past four years the Reagan administration secretly decided on a military rather than a political solution and therefore had developed sophisticated plans for the military invasion of Grenada.[16]

Like many others, however, the OWTU also bitterly condemned the Coard faction for Bishop's death and blamed their actions for opening the door to invasion:

> Freedom was first highjacked by the Butchers of St. George's and this laid the foundation for the invasion of foreign troops.[17]

On the other hand, several groups in the region argued that the regional condemnation and isolation of the Revolutionary Military Council (RMC) had encouraged the United States to invade. These groups sent solidarity messages to be read on Grenadian radio during the period the RMC was in control. Their line of reasoning blamed Bishop for disobeying the decision of the Central Committee on joint leadership, and saw this as provoking the violence. A few even questioned whether the killings at Fort Rupert had really been a massacre or execution as widely reported:

> . . . If[Bishop] was executed and if he was assassinated, then we cannot agree with such a thing, we are against it and we condemn it.[18]

Persons espousing such views quickly ran into a confrontation with the overwhelming weight of public opinion in the region, which was distraught over Bishop's murder and uninterested in arguments about party prerogatives. As a result, several small parties which had initially sided with the Central Committee backed off when it became obvious that this was a profoundly unpopular position.

The perception remained, however, of a split within the left over reaction to Grenada. The shock of the violent finale to the region's showcase revolution caused latent divisions within the movement to surface. These divisions concerned fundamental issues such as the role of the party versus that of the people; the nature and pace of social change in the Caribbean; and the role of democratic institutions in a revolutionary process.

Coard's tendency within the NJM placed high priority on the principle of *democratic centralism,* or party decision-making by majority vote in which lower levels of the party are bound by decisions of higher organs. This in turn is linked to the Leninist concept of the vanguard party, the elite group which uses its theoretical understanding of social forces to "lead" the masses to socialism.

After the death of Bishop, left-wing parties around the region began taking a closer look at these concepts and how they had been used by a ruling party. Democratic centralism had been used by the Coard faction to justify the removal of Bishop, on the basis of a party majority but in direct defiance of popular wishes. This betrayed a serious misunderstanding of the Grenadian revolutionary process by some of its own leaders, for, as Barbadian novelist George Lamming put it,

Bishop "existed in the popular consciousness of the Grenada people as their most organic link to the revolution."

Even those who had remained doubtful about the revolutionary process had found in Maurice Bishop a symbol of national pride with which they could identify. In the context of that political culture, the question we ask is this:
"How do you put such a leader under house arrest without arresting the revolution itself? By what failure of the imagination could such an act be separated from its consequences?"[19]

The question of vanguardism was pertinent because the New Jewel Movement was in fact a very small party, with less than 300 members, of whom only about 65 were "full members." The Central Committee numbered 17. Since the People's Revolutionary Government enjoyed mass support, the narrow composition of the decision-making organs attracted little attention until the crisis hit. Clive Thomas, a Guyanese political economist and a member of the collective leadership of the Working People's Alliance, comments:

One of the issues which comes out of these events is the failure of the [New Jewel Movement] regime to recognize that the very development of the idea of vanguardism during the period of its control was leading in effect to a certain type of *depoliticization* of the people and the rise of authoritarianism—whatever might have been their well-meaning intentions to the contrary.
When one reads the [Central Committee] record, one sees for example such ridiculous statements as "the position of the Central Committee and of the masses of workers do not always coincide, because in many instances we have the advantage of science." It shows how divorced a small vanguard group had become from the very people and situations they were seeking to represent.[20]

The realization of the NJM's isolation from the Grenadian people raised new questions as to whether the people and the party had seen the revolutionary process in the same way. One Grenadian trade union leader later reflected:

The socialist aims of the revolution were a long way off. In the short term, the PRG was bringing immediate benefits to the workers, especially the right to organize. That's why they supported the revolution.
Socialism was being discussed by a broad cross section of the working class, but they weren't convinced yet. We needed time, a lot more time.[21]

The popular roots of the Grenada revolution were not socialist but primarily democratic and anti-dictatorial. The revolutionary leadership agreed that the revolution in its initial stages was merely "oriented" toward the goal of socialism. In his "Line of March for the Party" of September 1982, Bishop outlined the reasons why Grenada could not build socialism quickly, emphasizing the small size of the Grenadian working class (as opposed to the peasantry) and the underdevelopment of production in the country.

While there is little evidence that Coard or his supporters actually thought they could speed up the transition to socialism, the *perception* that they sought to do so was an important factor in the regional debate. Since the Grenada tragedy, progressive parties have moved to define more precisely their position on the transition to socialism. Representing one tendency in the region, Tim Hector of the Antigua Caribbean Liberation Movement writes:

At this juncture, ACLM proposes not a socialist economy in Antigua, but a national economy, based on three pillars: the Public sector, 2) the Private sector, and 3) the Cooperative sector. For the question at this time is not overcoming capitalism, but first and foremost, overcoming the root cause of our historical woe, absentee ownership or foreign domination.[32]

Even for those parties which identify themselves as strictly Marxist-Leninist, a guarded tone has entered the debate. For example, the Bloque Socialista in the Dominican Republic states:

The Socialist Bloc defines itself as a Marxist-Leninist revolutionary organization . . . Its program of revolutionary transformations has a socialist perspective, although it is not fully committed to the immediate construction of socialism.[23]

A final area of debate concerns the role of elections, the multi-party system, and constitutionality in the process of social change. The New Jewel Movement had rejected these structures, at least in the short term, as incapable of bringing about true democracy. This analysis was rooted in Grenada's history, since Gairy had used fraudulent elections to maintain his dictatorship. Because of this, few progressives in the region criticized the NJM for deferring elections and attempting to build a new political system. But when that effort fell apart, the left reopened debate on the problem.

The discussion is not about whether left parties should contest elections while in opposition, since most do as soon as they are strong enough to capture a few percent of the vote. The question is whether these structures of "Westminster democracy"—opposing parties, a Parliament, a Constitution, periodic national elections—should be the model which progressive parties advocate and perpetuate once in power.

One response to this question has come from the opposition parties in Guyana. Like Eric Gairy, Guyanese president Forbes Burnham holds regular fraudulent elections to legitimize his rule. Moreover, Burnham was installed after the U.S. and Britain deposed the socialist government of Cheddi Jagan who had *twice* been constitutionally elected by the Guyanese people. So elections in Guyana's history have been neither a guarantee of democracy nor a protection against destabilization. But rather than "throwing the baby out with the bathwater," both the Working People's Alliance and Jagan's PPP are calling for genuine electoral democracy to replace Burnham's fraud. In a March 1984 statement, the WPA said:

The WPA believes in free and fair elections, fully elected representative bodies and legislature at all levels of the state, the freedom of special interests to campaign for due process and the constitutional behavior of all who exercise authority.
The WPA in respect of Guyana does not support a one-party state, formal or informal.[4]

Reflecting this new emphasis, the WPA made "free and fair elections" the theme of its 1984 Walter Rodney Freedom Festivals honoring the slain WPA leader.

Despite the Westminster model's tendency toward stagnation and its vulnerability to abuse by a Gairy or a Burnham, it has retained a legitimacy and importance in Caribbean popular culture which cannot be easily ignored. There is a growing consensus, therefore, that some form of the electoral process is in the Caribbean to stay. At the same time, few people in the region think that the NJM could have avoided U.S. destabilization simply by holding elections, as some outsiders have suggested. Gordon K. Lewis, an historian at the University of Puerto Rico, writes:

> Even if the PRG regime had held elections after 1979—which might at least have been a prudent move—that in itself could not have guaranteed safety, for British Guiana [Guyana] showed that imperialism will destabilize a leftwing regime even though it has been constitutionally elected.[25]

While some parties reacted to the Grenada debacle by edging closer to traditional Caribbean social democracy, others argue that this approach has failed in the past to bring lasting change. This is the view of the Workers Party of Jamaica (WPJ), which argues that two terms under Michael Manley's social democratic PNP failed to break the hold of the Jamaican ruling class, now ascendent again under Seaga's right-wing regime. The WPJ states:

> No voting alone, no election alone can force the Jamaican big people to give up their ill-gotten gains nor to change the system for the benefit of the masses. Imperialism and the big people have never allowed themselves nor their oppressive system to be voted out. Before that [happens], they destabilize and sabotage like what they did to Allende in Chile and Manley in Jamaica.[26]

The new reflections on democracy thus deal not with protecting against external pressures, but with internal strengthening of the social change process. The violent collapse of the New Jewel Movement revealed that while old, unsatisfactory structures had been dispensed with, the new ones which replaced them had not provided a framework for resolving internal differences peacefully. Nor had they created adequate channels for popular input into the governmental process. The question of *institutionalizing* a successful revolution has thus become a crucial one. Tim Hector reflects:

> We have to begin to review the role of the party: not in an anti-Leninist way, but we are in a dynamic changing situation and there is a need for changing theory. We need to look at the *concept* of the vanguard party. The transformation of party leaders into a ruling elite can and must be avoided.
> Party building must be based in productive activity—cooperatives, agriculture, education. We need to understand the problems of organizing the masses. In Grenada, the people responded enthusiastically to the parish and village councils, but the whole state machinery worked to negate it.[27]

Themes of Hope

Out of the painful time of reassessment which followed the invasion, some positive hope for the future has emerged.

First, there is now a more sober and realistic understanding of the constraints that a progressive government will face in attempting to transform a Caribbean society. The economic crisis affecting the region, the attacks from Washington, the underdeveloped physical infrastructure and the shortage of trained persons in the country all place limits on what a revolutionary government can expect to accomplish in its first years. At the same time, popular expectations of immediate benefits place the new leadership under tremendous pressure to "deliver." The Grenada experience dramatized how serious the impact of these combined pressures could be, and the level of political and personal maturity needed to survive them.

Secondly, there is a new stress on the need for honesty in political relations. Most left parties in the region did not know of the divisions within the New Jewel Movement, just as most Grenadians did not know, and many share the Grenadian people's sense of betrayal. It is clear that the NJM's secrecy about its problems stemmed in part from the siege mentality which developed in response to hostility from the United States. But it is also evident in retrospect that such secrecy allowed internal differences to build up to the point of explosion. Concludes one party: "The tragic events of October 19 raise a question that all serious parties will have to face: whether or not differences which develop inside the party should be put out for public discussion before they get out of hand."[28]

Linked to this is a heightened respect for the role of the people in social change. While a well-organized party is obviously a necessity for leading such a process, the Grenada debacle convinced many observers of the dangers in allowing the role of the party to overshadow the opinions, desires and creativity of the masses. It is increasingly recognized that this popular creativity and grassroot democratic input was at the heart of the Grenada revolution's success—a recognition which can only strengthen the progressive movement in the region.

Finally, the Grenada revolution is by no means completely discredited in the minds of Caribbean people. Rather, its image has been personified in the memory of Bishop, who has become even larger in death than in life. Many persons who were skeptical or undecided while the NJM was in power now characterize Bishop as the force for "good" behind the revolution. While this polarized view of Bishop-good/Coard-evil has been counterproductive in many ways, it has nevertheless opened many minds to the fact that the revolution did have positive and successful elements. Bishop is increasingly portrayed as a representative of an indigenous Caribbean progressive tradition which includes such figures as George Padmore, C.L.R. James, Marcus Garvey, and most recently, Walter Rodney. All based their political philosophy on empowering the masses of people through direct involvement in governing themselves. This positive message is one final lesson of Grenada. ∎

Religious Challenge and Conformity in the 1980's

Ecumenism in the Wake of the Grenada Invasion

Religion in the Caribbean traditionally has both shaped and mirrored the values and class structure of the society. This meant that the churches were at once deeply affected by the Grenada invasion and agents in furthering the social divisiveness caused by the event. This was all the more true because of the latent tensions between the conservative religious tradition and the liberal perspective of the ecumenical movement, embodied in the Caribbean Conference of Churches. This division within the Church between the roles of guardian and changer of the social order came dramatically to the surface in response to the events of 1983.

Developments during the 1970s had seemed to justify and reinforce the ideals behind the founding of the Caribbean Conference of Churches. While the protests of the 1960s challenged the neocolonial order, the seventies saw a growing search for and experimentation with alternatives. The formation of CARICOM in 1973 symbolized a new official commitment to regionalism which paralleled the ecumenical unity of the churches. The Manley experiment with democratic socialism in Jamaica, the opening of diplomatic relations between four English-speaking states and Cuba, and the choice in favor of non-alignment by Guyana signaled an openness to ideological pluralism in the region. The Grenadian and Nicaraguan revolutions, coming at the climax of the decade, reinforced the impact of these changes.

Furthermore, a decade of innovative thinking had begun gradually to affect the perspective of the traditional Church. The untimely death of Trinidadian theologian Idris Hamid in August 1981 left deep sorrow but not a vacuum. Others, such as Leo Erskine of Jamaica, Roy Neehall of Trinidad, Leslie Lett of Antigua, Sergio Arce of Cuba, and Francisco Reus Froylan of Puerto Rico—to mention only a few—continued to work toward a decolonizing of Caribbean theology.[1] Pastors and laypersons were becoming more familiar with this new thinking, which was frequently explored in the pages of the CCC's widely-read newspaper *Caribbean Contact*.

At the same time, the seventies had shown that resistance to change was still deep-seated within the churches. In the fall of 1981, the Rev. Ashley Smith of Jamaica asserted that "ecumenism must succeed" as part of the larger task of freeing the Caribbean from its colonial past. But he added:

> There is covert mistrust of the regional ecumenical body by rank and file Christians of the respective churches, a situation created largely out of the disparity in the use of language between those in the pew and the ecumenical bureaucrats who often speak on behalf of the churches . . .[2]

This mistrust sometimes took the form of tensions between the CCC and the local Christian Councils, which were especially conservative in the small Eastern Caribbean islands. There were also occasional differences between agencies and levels of the CCC, with the board of directors of CADEC—the

CCC's development arm—often taking a more traditional developmentalist perspective. Thus when the Dominica Christian Council objected to the hiring of two local activists as CADEC field staff in that island, the CADEC hierarchy in Bridgetown backed up their objections. Together with other factors, this led to the collapse of the CADEC program in Dominica, with the progressive staffers leaving to found their own grassroots development group (the Small Projects Assistance Team). Around the region, clergy and lay Christians working toward self-organization of the poor or speaking out on social issues encountered opposition both from some church hierarchies and from governments. This led to instances of progressive priests and pastors being removed from their congregations or transferred from one island to another when their activities were deemed controversial.

So while the CCC had succeeded in bringing about various forms of interdenominational cooperation since 1973, many of the local churches remained tied to old colonial patterns and middle-class conservatism. As the CCC General Secretary, Dr. Roy Neehall, admitted shortly before his retirement:

> Ecumenism has not led to any basic transformation within the heart of the churches themselves . . . There is a limit to how far you can push an institution like the Church.[3]

"Politics Dividing the Church"

This tenuous unity around the ecumenical project of the seventies was soon to come under seige from opposing political forces at the start of the 1980s. The daring experimentation of the Grenada and Nicaragua revolutions on the one hand, and the reactionary militancy of the newly-elected Reagan administration on the other produced a growing polarization in the region. This disunity deeply affected the churches, leading Dr. Neehall to warn that "politics and ideology are dividing the Church."[4]

In its reaction to the Grenada revolution of March 1979, *Caribbean Contact* hailed the removal of the Gairy regime—as did many in Grenada and in the region—and pointed out that the "blind eye" which Caribbean governments had turned to Gairy's abuses had contributed to closing off non-violent avenues for change. By November of that year, however, *Contact* voiced editorial criticism of the Bishop government for closing the *Torchlight* newspaper and for failing to hold elections. It found the latter especially perplexing In view of the fact that the Bishop government could "easily have won" an election on the basis of its popularity in the country.

During the years of the revolution, *Contact* gave basic support to the Bishop government while expressing strong reservations and sometimes criticism regarding certain of its actions. But even this balanced approach exacerbated tensions with conservative church leaders. This was all the more true

Pentecostal church service in Barbados.

because the Conference of Churches of Grenada soon hardened its opposition to the People's Revolutionary Government, citing the lack of elections, censorship of the press and political detainees. *Contact* continued to comment on these negative issues, but also highlighted the positive accomplishments of the revolution in bringing about social and economic change.

By 1981, the Reagan administration's growing military involvement in Central America and its militaristic posturing in the Caribbean were alarming many Caribbean Christians. While the Ocean Venture '81 naval maneuvers were underway, the CCC convened a "Working Conference on Peace" at a Catholic retreat center in Trinidad, where representatives from churches in the English, Spanish, French and Dutch-speaking Caribbean hammered out proposals to be submitted to the CCC's Third General Assembly the following month. This "Zone of Peace" initiative was finally ratified by the CCC's General Assembly in October 1982, calling for:

- The CCC to request the United Nations to declare the Caribbean a Zone of Peace
- The CCC to request governments of the Caribbean to commit themselves to:
  - non-participation in the development of nuclear weapons and their emplacement in the Caribbean and Latin America

- pursuance of a genuine policy of non-alignment
- work for the elimination of all foreign military bases in the region and for an end to foreign military maneuvers in the area
- a policy of military non-intervention among Caribbean territories and from outside the region.[5]

Along with the issue of militarism, the divide-and-rule tactics of the Reagan White House troubled Caribbean Christians who saw the goal of ecumenism as linked to the overall strengthening of unity between the people and countries of the region. The Caribbean Basin Initiative, announced in the spring of 1982, favored U.S. client states like Jamaica and El Salvador while excluding Cuba, Nicaragua, and Grenada. Soon after the announcement of the CBI, President Reagan made an Easter vacation visit to Barbados where he met with selected "friendly" Caribbean leaders and invited them to join him in a verbal attack on Grenada and Cuba which he launched from Barbadian soil. Reflecting on this bid to turn Caribbean countries against each other, *Contact* wrote:

> The Reagan administration has indeed offered a great challenge to CARICOM's resolve . . . a serious testing of the region's governments' determination to make of their people not "fellow Americans," as the President feels, but citizens of One Caribbean.[6]

As U.S. attacks on Nicaragua and Grenada escalated during Reagan's first term, *Contact* outspokenly urged Caribbean peoples and governments to reject the U.S. approach. The newspaper dismissed as hypocrisy Reagan's professed concern about freedom in Grenada, noting that "the Reagan White House can live with Burnham's brand of 'cooperative socialism,' Duvalier's Haiti, or South Africa's apartheid system; but not, apparently, with Bishop's PRG."[7] After President Reagan's "Star Wars" speech of March 1983, in which he called Grenada a threat to the U.S., *Contact* said:

> When a head of state of one of the superpowers vilifies, as President Reagan has done, a tiny and vulnerable tourist island of the Caribbean as being a threat to the 'national security' of the USA, without offering a shred of evidence, then, irrespective of ideological differences and chosen paths of development, member governments and organizations of the Caribbean Community should, as a matter of principle, express publicly their concern—if not support for Grenada.[8]

The CCC's defense of Grenada, Cuba and Nicaragua along with its other progressive positions brought the ecumenical body up against powerful forces gathering on the right of the religious spectrum. The wave of conservatism accompanying Reagan's election saw "moral majority" types gain influence in various U.S., European and Caribbean churches, affecting both the CCC and its funding partners overseas. By mid-1982, there was pressure within some sectors of the CCC to remove Rickey Singh as editor of *Contact*. There were also attacks on the CCC from the U.S. right wing, such as a Heritage Foundation report which called CADEC "anti-U.S. and Marxist." Potentially the most far-reaching threat, however, came from the growth of the conservative evangelical sects—the so-called "television evangelists"—which were rapidly expanding from their U.S. bases into ambitious activities throughout the Caribbean and Central America.

Rise of the Right-Wing Sects

Several factors came together in the mid-1970s to produce an explosion of right-wing evangelical religion in the Caribbean, influencing political culture and posing a direct challenge to the mainline churches. One factor was the intrinsic appeal of fundamentalist religion to many Caribbean people. After World War II, Pentecostal churches had filled the gap between the historic churches (such as Catholic, Anglican and Methodist) and the traditional African and Revivalist religions. Whereas the mainline churches tended to be reserved and "proper" in their style of worship, the Pentecostals appealed to the fervent religiosity of the Caribbean masses with an emphasis on singing, collective emotion and "closeness" to God. These same qualities also drew people to the new North American sects* which resembled the Pentecostals in their fundamentalist style but were distinguished from them by their right-wing politics and tight organizational control from the top.

---

*Called "evangelicals" in the English-speaking Caribbean.

The second factor was a reaction against the emerging social consciousness of the historic churches marked by the formation of the CCC in 1973. Some people who had difficulty accepting this concept of social action ministry and who found the mainline churches becoming "too secular" were drawn to the sects, which stressed personal piety, individual salvation, and future hope rather than concrete action in the present.

Thirdly, the expansion of the ultra-conservative sects was linked to the ascendence of right-wing forces leading up to the election of Reagan. Based mostly in the southern United States, they expanded throughout the U.S. in the 1960s and early '70s, and by the latter part of the seventies were sending numerous missions into Central America and the Caribbean. There they bought land and established churches with local or sometimes North American pastors. With their U.S. backing, the sects had virtually limitless funds and purchased enormous amounts of radio and television time for religious programming patterned after the Christian Broadcasting Network's "700 Club."

In the deepest sense, the explosive growth of the new sects reflects a profound popular discontent with the status quo. But the remedy they propose for this discontent is a fundamentally passive one, which precludes any action to challenge social injustice. The sects assert that mankind is basically evil, that the present world is beyond redemption, and that the only hope lies in the reward of salvation in the hereafter. The faithful are exhorted not to think about their worldly problems because involvement in "politics" equals sin. This message reaches the poorest and most remote corners of the Caribbean through ubiquitous radio programs with names like "Gospel Hall" and "Streams of Power," permeating political and religious attitudes at the grassroots.

Despite this formal renunciation of politics, the sects have not hesitated to translate their popular following into political leverage. In Puerto Rico, for example, where the sects have grown much more rapidly in the last decade than the historic Protestant or Catholic churches, their pastors increasingly serve as intermediaries between the government and the people. Led by the "four evangelists" of Puerto Rico, they warn elected officials that they are monitoring their performance and will force a reckoning at election time.

The close ties of the conservative sects to the Reagan administration and the New Right network in the United States has had a definite impact on politics in the region. Right-wing religious leaders like Jerry Falwell and Billy Graham formed the link between the Reagan White House and General Efraín Ríos Montt in Guatemala, whose "born-again" government slaughtered thousands of peasants in the Guatemalan countryside in 1982. In Jamaica, the rise of the right-wing sects helped prepare the political climate for the election of Edward Seaga in 1980:

> The evangelicals definitely played a role in helping to remove Manley. They came into Jamaica in large numbers from about the end of 1979 and into 1980. You could see their tents mushrooming around the city and along the main highways, and in the countryside.
> The message they carried was anti-socialist, anti-communist. They included the Manley government, in some cases

quite openly, under the label communist, which was by no means an objectively correct classification at all.

Seaga has attempted to split the churches between the mainstream denominations and the evangelicals, lining up the evangelicals behind him. He has tried to isolate the Jamaica Council of Churches, the older established churches which were mostly supportive of the Manley government.[10]

The sects operate entirely outside the structure of mainline ecumenism and the CCC, whose social action concerns they brand as "communist." They have rejected invitations to engage in dialogue with the mainline denominations or join local Christian Councils. On the other hand there is a high degree of cooperation among the different evangelical sects, and ongoing contact between the Caribbean missions and their U.S. sponsors.

Despite these divisions, many Caribbean people have retained their membership in one of the historic churches while simultaneously participating in some activities of the North American sects. Partly in response to the fundamentalist challenge, the Catholic Church (and to a lesser extent, the Anglican Church) has developed within its structure a "charismatic" movement with an exuberant, fundamentalist style which has helped keep people within the Church. Nonetheless, the growth of the sects continues, fueled by economic suffering which causes people to seek relief in an emotional faith. Given the already existing divisions between liberal and conservative influence within the mainline denominations, these religious trends combined to place a majority of church-goers somewhere on the right of the political/religious spectrum at the time of the invasion of Grenada.

Impact of the Invasion

When it became known that Grenada was suffering an internal political crisis in October 1983, the CCC offered to mediate between the Bishop and Coard sides of the dispute. Before that could happen, however, the October 19 killings occurred and the CCC immediately cut off all relations with the military junta of Coard and his supporters. At the same time, the CCC called for the crisis to be resolved without external military intervention into Grenada.[11]

On October 25, 1983, as U.S. forces were overrunning Grenada, the CCC declared:

The Caribbean Conference of Churches, reaffirming its principled stance against military intervention in the Caribbean by forces external to the region, strongly deplores the events of the past few hours leading to this morning's invasion of Grenada. The fact of a Caribbean presence among the invading forces by no means alters the principle . . . [12]

In addition to invoking its previous commitment to the Zone of Peace resolution, the CCC justified its position by pointing to CARICOM's own endorsement of the principle of non-intervention reached at the Ocho Rios summit in November 1982. It also noted the breach of the "unanimity" requirement in the charter of the Organization of Eastern Caribbean States, contradicting the U.S. claim to have been legally invited to invade by the OECS.

The statement by CCC General Secretary Allan Kirton came as the Caribbean churches were being swept up in the regional controversy over the U.S. action. In the Eastern Caribbean islands (St. Vincent, Barbados, St. Lucia, Dominica, and Antigua) the local Christian Councils strongly supported the invasion to which their governments had lent troops and political support. In Trinidad, conversely, both the government and the churches opposed the invasion, and an ecumenical service for Maurice Bishop and the other slain leaders was held in Trinity Cathedral in Port-of-Spain. The main exception to the pattern of church/government parallelism was Jamaica, where the Jamaica Council of Churches opposed the invasion despite the Seaga government's involvement. Support for the CCC position also came from the churches in Curaçao, Cuba, the Dominican Republic, and Haiti.

There was more than deference to political authority behind the pro-invasion enthusiasm of the Eastern Caribbean churches. Many conservative church leaders had long opposed the Grenada revolution, but had refrained from attacking it openly for fear of antagonizing relations between the PRG and the Grenadian churches. Other factors contributing to their restraint were the relationship with the CCC which supported the Grenadian process; and finally, guilt about not having spoken out against Gairy before the revolution. Once the revolution had been overthrown, however, these clergy welcomed the opportunity to vigorously condemn the entire Grenadian experiment.

This brought to light the churches' underlying ambivalence toward a social change process which had delivered obvious benefits to the people but which also undercut the privileges and status of the middle and upper class—and by extension, of the churches rooted in these classes. Nowhere was this more evident than in Grenada itself. Ironically, the Grenadian churches were among the most conservative in the region, remaining (with a few exceptions) largely unaffected by the social upheavals of the 1960s and '70s. In 1979, the Grenadian Catholic Church broke its ties to its one progressive project, the Pope Paul Ecumenical Center. During the revolution, the churches did not respond beyond their traditional activities in education, and they were sometimes critical of projects the CCC sponsored in Grenada (through the local CADEC committee) for following too closely the development policies of the government. Relations between the PRG and the Conference of Churches of Grenada became increasingly suspicious and finally hostile. Church leaders expressed their disapproval in terms of concern about press freedom, detainees and elections, while the government accused the churches of working to turn Grenadians against the revolution.

After the invasion, therefore, the Grenada churches expressed gratitude to "the American and Caribbean forces who responded to the call for help," and called for a return to "respect for law, persons and property as enshrined in the Constitution."[13] Under the direction of the Anglican Archdeacon Hoskins Huggins, the churches distributed toys and candy sent from the U.S. to the "poor children" of Grenada. The Catholic Church handed over the site of the Pope Paul

Rickey Singh, editor of
Caribbean Contact *from
1974-1983.*

center to the conservative Catholic organization SERVOL to offer employment training for Grenadian youths. These and other initiatives represented support for the post-invasion rebuilding which had not been offered for the building of a new society after the fall of Gairy.

The Grenadian church statement offered "thanks to God" that the country could again look forward to peace and freedom. Other voices in the region also thanked God for the invasion, including the Barbadian churches which held a "Thank You" mass at which it was claimed that the invasion was "in full accordance with the principles of Christianity." This suggestion of divine inspiration for the U.S. action dismayed progressive Christians with its overtones of neo-colonial dependency. The Roman Catholic Archbishop of Port-of-Spain, the Rev. Anthony Pantin, warned against allowing any Caribbean country to become a "toy" in superpower conflicts. Dr. Leslie Lett, an Anglican priest from Antigua, commented on what he called the "parachute incarnation" theology used to justify the notion that the U.S. had come to Grenada on a rescue mission:

> From the colonial perspective, the story of the Incarnation was and continues to be distorted to mean that the "inherent inferiority" of black people always requires a miraculous Rescuer, Invader, Big Brother, to parachute down in our midst to sort things out and save us from ourselves . . . [14]

The Grenadian churches' support for the invasion placed the CCC in a difficult position. So did the extreme pro-invasion stance of the Barbadian churches and government, which launched verbal attacks on the CCC's Bridgetown headquarters. In response to the outcry, the CCC reiterated that it was upholding the Zone of Peace resolution which its member churches had approved one year earlier; but this support for principle was shouted into the storm winds of regional hysteria. Dr. Lett wrote;

> Suddenly, "principle" is being openly ridiculed by many leaders in both State and Church . . . One gets the distinct impression that principles are applicable only when they do not interfere with the ambitions and fears of these same leaders. [15]

The Barbados government's withdrawal of Rickey Singh's work permit was a victory for regional conservatives, who saw the invasion as an opportunity to silence the outspoken *Contact* editor. In a strong response, Rev. Kirton emphasized that the CCC would continue to speak out on its principles and welcomed controversy as preferable to the tradition of silence:

By our silences in the past, we have connived in and condoned many of the elements that have led to the benighting of our Christian community . . . Politics is concerned with people, not only influencing but also determining their lives. As long as this is true, silence on our part will be irresponsible and indefensible. [16]

The strengthening of the regional right has brought pressure on the CCC to abandon its commitment to the poor in favor of a more "balanced" position which would accommodate the historic bias of the Church toward the elite. For instance, the Grenadian Archdeacon Huggins commented:

> [The CCC] seems to preach only liberation theology and theology of the poor. I don't think that Christ was the Christ of the poor alone, He is also the Christ of the rich. So there must be a happy balance. [17]

The controversy over its values and direction prompted the CCC to undertake an internal reflection in the first months of 1984. This produced a clear reaffirmation of the CCC's commitment to a theology of solidarity with the poor. At the same time, it was made clear that *Caribbean Contact* is not the official voice of all the churches but an open forum for dialogue, thus removing some of the grounds for criticism of its editorial line.

"Little did we know that the end of ten years would mark the end of an era," wrote the Rev. Kirton in December after the invasion. [18] He was referring to the ten-year anniversary of the founding of the CCC which was celebrated, amid both joy and sadness, in November 1983. The era which has ended is that of the progressive 1970s, with its opening for new ideas and models of development. Today, there is a determination to push ahead with the ecumenical project but also an awareness that the CCC is "swimming against the tide" of the current political climate. The CCC has continued to speak out, most recently on issues such as the U.S. war against Nicaragua and the lack of democracy in Burnham's Guyana. Progressive Christians know that adherence to principle will not be easy in the 1980s, but that it is more necessary than ever before.

The Region Recolonized: Reagan's New Caribbean Order

The Grenada invasion marked the high point of the Reagan administration's Caribbean strategy. From October 1983 through the summer of 1984, everything seemed to be falling into place for the White House in its campaign to make the region an anticommunist bastion of U.S. influence. Grenada's revolution had been destroyed, and Washington credited the invasion with dealing a blow to the Cubans as well. The dismal failure of the Jamaican economy was temporarily masked by invasion fever, allowing Seaga to win a new electoral mandate. The participation of the Eastern Caribbean states in the invasion cemented bilateral alliances and gave the U.S. a foot in the door to militarize the area. And in Grenada itself, the election of a U.S.-backed government seemed to offer the opportunity for a new showcase of capitalist development which might succeed where Jamaica's had failed.

Behind these impressive gains, however, lay unresolved contradictions which made the White House victories more fragile than they appeared. One paradoxical effect of the U.S. success in pursuing its Caribbean strategy is a growing understanding in the region of what that strategy really is. By late 1984 invasion fever was waning, allowing Caribbean leaders and people to take a closer look at the implications of the "new order."

Military Strategy: The Regional Picture

The Greater Antilles of Cuba, Jamaica, Haiti, the Dominican Republic and Puerto Rico have historically played a dominant role in Caribbean geopolitics because of their relative size and closeness to the United States. The latter four have taken on additional importance in this century because of their proximity to Cuba and positions astride the "sea lanes" leading to the Panama Canal.

Since 1959, U.S. military strategy in the Caribbean has had as its primary goal the encirclement and intimidation of Cuba. The U.S. maintains a large naval and air base on Cuban soil at Guantánamo Bay. There is a U.S. base on Andros Island off Cuba's northern coast, and the U.S. Caribbean Command stares at Havana across the Florida Straits. Key West forms the northern tip of a rough diamond enclosing Cuba whose other points are the U.S. Southern Command at the Panama Canal Zone with land, air and naval facilities; Honduras to the west and Puerto Rico to the east, both bristling with U.S. bases. In addition, there are U.S. bases on Bermuda in the Atlantic and Antigua in the Eastern Caribbean.

Puerto Rico remains the main bastion of U.S. military power in the Caribbean Sea. The nerve center is the Roosevelt Roads Naval Station, site of the Naval Forces Caribbean and prepared to function as a center for the launching of nuclear weapons in time of war [see Part VI, Ch. 10]. Other major military installations in Puerto Rico include the Ramey Air Force Base, the Salinas National Guard Camp, and Vieques Island, which the Navy uses for bombing practice and war games. In addition, Puerto Rico is home to the Caribbean Police School, where the FBI has trained police from Trinidad, Jamaica, Panama, Honduras and El Salvador.[1]

Among independent countries of the Caribbean, the largest recipient of U.S. military assistance is the Dominican Republic. The U.S. has been building up the Dominican armed forces since the 1965 insurrection and they are now the largest in the Caribbean after Cuba's. Recently, the Reagan administration has increased aid to the Dominican military because of the threat of political instability connected with the country's economic crisis. The Dominican army is also seen as insurance against any uprising in neighboring Haiti.

The second largest recipient of U.S. military assistance is

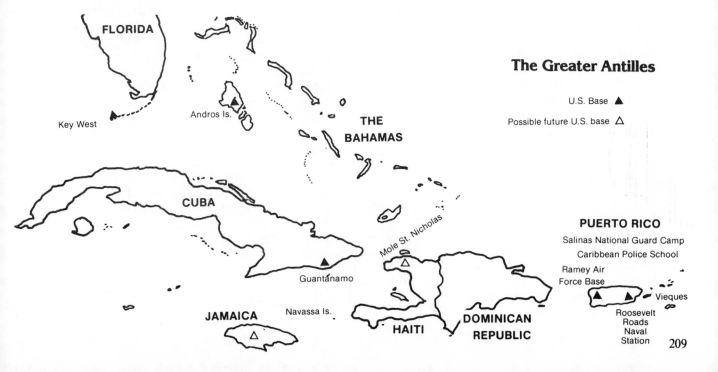

The Greater Antilles

U.S. Base ▲

Possible future U.S. base △

PUERTO RICO
Salinas National Guard Camp
Caribbean Police School
Ramey Air Force Base
Roosevelt Roads Naval Station
Vieques

FLORIDA
Key West
Andros Is.
THE BAHAMAS
CUBA
Guantánamo
JAMAICA
Navassa Is.
Mole St. Nicholas
HAITI
DOMINICAN REPUBLIC

Jamaica, which also receives more U.S. economic aid than any other Caribbean country.[2] As in the Dominican Republic, this heavy aid program reflects Washington's desire to keep the lid on rising social unrest. Jamaica also figures in the regional picture through its participation in the occupation of Grenada and in the Eastern Caribbean defense pact. The Jamaica Defense Force is the largest army in the English-speaking Caribbean.

Because of Haiti's poor human rights image, it receives only a small amount of U.S. military aid, mainly equipment for the Haitian Navy to aid in the interdiction of the boat people.[3] Haiti's real military support comes from Israel, as in several other areas where the U.S. prefers not to arm a repressive regime directly. Nonetheless, Washington has been eyeing the northwest corner of Haiti for a possible military base, since the lease on Guantánamo expires at the end of the century and is hardly likely to be renewed by the Cubans. Located across the narrow Windward Passage from southeastern Cuba, the Mole St. Nicholas peninsula is an obvious choice for Guantánamo's replacement.

It is not the only choice, however. The U.S. government has for some time been making covert overtures to the Seaga government about the possibility of a U.S. base on Jamaica. The Pentagon also plans an "expeditionary airfield" on Navassa Island, a U.S. possession midway between Jamaica and Haiti.[4]

Since they are under direct colonial control, the French and Dutch Antilles are of less concern to Washington. The fact that France and Holland have troops stationed on these islands is, nonetheless, a factor in the regional picture. The Dutch troops on Curaçao and Aruba have participated in most of the U.S.-NATO exercises in the Caribbean, along with additional troops from Holland. The port of Willemstad, Curaçao has the largest dry-dock and bunkering facilities in the western hemisphere, with obvious strategic value. England sought to use the port during the Falklands/Malvinas conflict, but Curaçao refused due to pressure from its close and powerful neighbor, Venezuela.[5] But no one doubts that the U.S. could secure the use of Curaçao's port under NATO accords in case of a regional conflict or intervention.

The French departments of Guadeloupe, Martinique and French Guiana are perhaps the least subject to U.S. influence of any Caribbean territories. France is not a member of NATO and therefore does not usually participate in U.S.-NATO maneuvers. As in Europe, however, U.S. strategists assume France would cooperate with western forces should a military crisis arise.

Government Boots

With the Grenada revolution out of the way, Washington's continuing military interest in the Eastern Caribbean is aimed at preventing "another Grenada" in neighboring islands. Immediately after the invasion, U.S. Green Berets were dispatched to Barbados, Antigua, Dominica, St. Vincent, St. Lucia and Jamaica to train elite police units as a first line of defense against internal political unrest.

The smell of cordite hardly had time to dissipate in Grenada when special forces training teams from Fort Bragg, North Carolina began landing on neighboring islands with new weaponry. Although unnoticed by the outside world, the Green Berets did not go unnoticed by opposition political parties on the islands, the first to reveal their presence . . . The six-week training include[d] becoming familiar with the new weapons, learning to shoot straight with live ammunition, map reading, and basic military field operations and procedures.[6]

The initial training of an 80-man "Special Service Unit" (SSU) on each island took place in the spring of 1984, with graduates rotated into Grenada to join the occupation force. The training was highly secretive, taking place in concealed areas of the islands without public announcement. The public was alerted, however, when U.S. military transport planes began unloading sophisticated weaponry at island airports. In St. Vincent, for example, incoming arms included M16 automatic rifles, sub-machine guns, grenade launchers, mortars and anti-aircraft guns. The New Democratic Party (then in opposition) echoed the general sentiment: "We want roads and an international airport for St. Vincent. We want university scholarships abroad. We want food, technology and cash, not guns please."[7]

The new elite units clearly are insufficient to deter a foreign attack, raising questions about whom they are supposed to fight against. Police on several islands already have a reputation for brutality, especially toward youth and Rastafarians. And the danger of building up an army has been driven home by the deaths of Grenada's leaders at the hands of the military. Another Vincentian party complained:

> . . . This army in disguise is likely to be used as an instrument of political oppression of the people. And when this back-door army sees itself as the arbiter of national politics, its more ambitious members will make a bid for direct political power . . . This army nonsense must stop before it stops us and democracy as we understand it.[8]

Except in Jamaica and Barbados, the trainees are members of the islands' police forces. U.S. law, however, expressly prohibits using U.S. funds to train foreign police. The statute, section 660 of the 1974 Foreign Assistance Act, was passed after it was revealed that the U.S. had trained Latin American police in torture techniques in the 1960s. To get around the law, the Reagan administration has designated the Caribbean trainees as "paramilitaries."[9]

Another question being raised in the region has to do with spending scarce resources on militarization rather than economic development. "The government won't provide skills training for employment or transport for crops, when such things are quickly made available for the military," notes Atherton Martin, a former agriculture minister in Dominica.[10] A Barbadian calypso, "Boots," became a region-wide hit when it criticized expenditures on the Barbados Defense Force:

Left, right, left, right!
The government boots, the government boots!
It is necessary to have so much soldiers in this small country?

U.S.-trained Caribbean soldiers board U.S. helicopter in Grenada.

Department of Defense

No, no, no, no!
Is it necessary to shine soldiers boots with taxpayers money?
No, no, no, no!
Well don't tell Tommy, he put them in St. Lucy*
Unemployment high and the treasury low
And he buying boots to cover soldiers toe
I see them boots, boots, boots and more boots
On the feet of young trigger-happy recruits
Marching, threatening army troops
Tell Tom I say, that wouldn't do
He's got to see, about me and you
Can we afford to feed an army
When so many children naked and hungry . . . ?

Irregardless of such popular criticism, Prime Minister Adams went ahead after the invasion to draw up plans with Washington for a 1,500-man standing army involving all the countries of the Eastern Caribbean. There was little mystery about the purpose of the army, which Adams plainly stated was to protect against "external aggression and domestic revolution."[11] But by 1985, the idea had been quietly shelved and the Reagan administration was protesting its innocence, declaring that "Nobody is advocating the militarization of the [Eastern Caribbean] area."[12]

This reversal reflected growing fears in the Caribbean regarding militarization and its cost. Regional politicians were having second thoughts by the summer of 1984, when they took advantage of a meeting hosted by the White House to cautiously rebuke the administration for paying too much attention to military security and not enough to the region's economic plight. John Compton, the staunchly pro-U.S. prime minister of St. Lucia, told the gathering that " . . . Our problems are not military; they are social and economic."[13] Echoing this theme, the prime minister of St. Kitts-Nevis said, "Security can't be won with force of arms."[14]

Their concerns were reinforced when voters in St. Vincent and the Grenadines threw out the long-entrenched Cato government and replaced it with the New Democratic Party of James Mitchell in July 1984. Although Mitchell had supported the Grenada invasion more strongly than Cato did, Cato's government was resented for its internal repressiveness and blamed for economic stagnation. The outcry against the Special Service Unit was loud in St. Vincent. After the election, Mitchell rejected the idea of the regional army, saying that "not one cent" of his government's money would go to militarization while food, jobs and housing needs were still unmet. One of his first acts as prime minister was to have the Special Service troops take off their green army fatigues and resume wearing police uniforms.

Cato's ignominious defeat was the handwriting on the wall for other conservative island leaders. They could no longer afford to ignore the rising criticism about spending money on armies while development languished. It became clear, moreover, that while the U.S. would pay for setting up the regional army, the cost of its upkeep would come out of island budgets.

While the controversial army idea was dropped, a new defense pact between the Eastern Caribbean governments achieves the same goal by allowing the leader of one country to call for military intervention by the Special Service Unit of another.[15] The training of the SSU's meanwhile has become more sophisticated. Members of the units reportedly have traveled to the U.S. training facilities in Panama and at Fort Bragg for instruction in urban warfare, crowd control, demoli-

---

*Former U.S. naval base in Barbados, now headquarters of the Barbados Defense Force. "Tommy" refers to Prime Minister Tom Adams.

tion, counterinsurgency and psychological warfare.[16]

The Economic Strategy

If the administration's military strategy departs from past policies mainly in the level of U.S. involvement, its economic program must be regarded as its own, profoundly ideological creation. Important elements of the strategy include:

- Definition of the private sector as the key to development and support for foreign investment in the Caribbean, primarily through the Caribbean Basin Initiative (CBI);
- Encouraging right-wing countries such as Israel, South Korea and Taiwan to become involved in the region, giving technical assistance and promoting their models of industrialization;
- A shift from multilateral to bilateral aid, giving the U.S. more political leverage over aid recipients;
- Promotion of a "showcase" of capitalist development, first Jamaica, and now—the White House hopes—Grenada.

The deeply ideological bias in favor of private enterprise—the "magic of the market," as President Reagan has described it—permeates the administration's economic and development aid efforts in the Caribbean. The reality, however, is that the bulk of the indigenous private sector consists on the one hand of peasants, and on the other of merchants, who import goods rather than produce them. There are relatively few industrial entrepreneurs in the region who could lead an industrialization process. The Reagan policy therefore translates into support for *foreign* private investment—the old Puerto Rican model.

The U.S. Agency for International Development (USAID) is the main instrument of this economic thrust. While USAID has traditionally built infrastructure for foreign investors, its approach during this administration has become a highly politicized emphasis on "privatization" and private sector support.[17] USAID funds have paid for many of the factory shells occupied by foreign manufacturers in the region, and the agency has hired the U.S. consulting firm of Coopers & Lybrand to seek out potential investors for the region.

The current economic strategy is based on a specific assumption: that the Caribbean can replicate the rapid industrialization process achieved in the 1960s by Far Eastern countries such as Taiwan, South Korea and Singapore. The Caribbean does have the advantage of proximity to U.S. markets and corporate headquarters. As wages have risen in some Asian countries such as Taiwan, those Caribbean countries with very low wages may present a marginal advantage.

© 1981 *The Miami Herald.* Reprinted by permission.

212

A few U.S. investors have moved their plants from the Far East to the Caribbean. MacGregor Sporting Goods, for example, has decided to move its production of basketballs and volleyballs from Taiwan to Haiti.[18] In addition, some Asian industrialists appear interested in building plants in the Caribbean to take advantage of duty-free entry to the U.S. market under the Caribbean Basin Initiative. Thus encouraged, various Caribbean leaders have toured the Far East to drum up investment and explore trade, technical assistance and diplomatic ties. Jamaica has opened an investment promotion office in Hong Kong that will also cover Japan, South Korea and Singapore. The prime ministers of Antigua and St. Lucia have likewise toured the Far East, and South Korea has sent its first resident ambassador to Barbados.

To jump to the assumption, as does the director of Coopers & Lybrand, that "we are witnessing an historic shift of investment from the Far East to the Caribbean,"[19] is, however, farfetched. In addition to the small size of Caribbean populations and the islands' lack of infrastructure, there are other reasons why the Caribbean could not repeat the Asian experience, even if such a course were desirable. Taiwan's export boom in the 1960s came only after self-sufficiency had been achieved in food production and stable food prices made it possible to hold wages down. Foreign investment was not initially the motor force; rather, there was huge *public* sector investment in infrastructure in the 1950s, much of it financed by U.S. economic aid. Unions were very weak and political dissent scarcely permitted.[20]

The political intent of the administration's aid program is also reflected in the way it distributes aid in the region. In the 1970s, most U.S. economic aid to the Eastern Caribbean was channeled through the Caribbean Development Bank (CDB), a regional institution which receives and distributes aid to the Eastern Caribbean countries. The Reagan administration, however, reversed this practice. According to a report by the U.S. General Accounting Office, the turning point came in June 1981 when USAID offered the Bank a $4 million "basic human needs" package for the region on condition that Grenada be excluded from benefits. The project would have improved roads, water supplies, and health clinics throughout the Eastern Caribbean. Stressing that its charter prohibits interference in the political affairs of members (in this case Grenada) and that it could not appear to be an instrument of U.S. foreign policy, the CDB refused the aid.[21]

In apparent retaliation, the U.S. has since shifted most of its aid to the Eastern Caribbean into bilateral programs. These allow the administration to favor some countries over others and to direct funding into programs which fit its ideological mold. The GAO report comments:

Immediate beneficiaries of AID's projects appear to be well-established business concerns in the region, such as the national chambers of commerce, corporations, and affluent businessmen.[22]

Ironically, many Caribbean businessmen also have been disappointed with the results of "Reaganomics." In Jamaica, where USAID has been given nearly free rein to restructure the economy, policies designed to attract foreign investors have worked against domestic producers, forcing many Jamaican-owned businesses to close their doors.

The situation is so desperate that the Reagan administration no longer talks about the miracle to take place in Jamaica. It has pinned its hopes on a new showcase of development: Grenada. USAID arrived in Grenada "almost with the troops," according to one U.S. official.[23] Its mission is to privatize everything that was publicly owned in Grenada and allow Reagan's "magic of the market" to remake the island.

Grenada: New U.S. Client State

The centerpiece of the U.S. campaign to purge progressive trends from the Caribbean is the transformation of Grenada. No sooner had the U.S. won the shooting war in October 1983 than the ideological war began. While the White House had sold the invasion to the American public on the basis of the need to "rescue" the American medical students, U.S. troops stayed in Grenada after the students were long gone, running a sophisticated police operation intended to wipe out any remaining sympathy for the Maurice Bishop government.

The first part of this operation consisted of humiliating the Cubans on the island who had survived the U.S. military assault. Although Havana was anxious for the return of its nationals, the 600-odd airport workers were detained for days in barbed-wire enclosures exposed to the elements, where they were interrogated by U.S. intelligence personnel. This was followed by the rounding-up of some 1,000 Grenadians who, according to U.S. press reports, were "suspected or accused of sympathizing or having had ties with the government of slain prime minister Maurice Bishop" or the Revolutionary Military Council.[24] During their interrogation by U.S. Army Intelligence, the detainees were held in wooden packing crates at the Point Salines airport. The information gathered was fed into U.S. computers. General Jack Farris, commander of the U.S. 82nd Airborne Forces in Grenada, explained the strategy to reporters:

You develop a human-intelligence network, whereby you have your police and your agents throughout the country and find out who the bad guys are . . . You build a data base on those people, on thousands of them, and bring them all in and pick up all these people and question them. You put them all in a data base, and that's how you stamp out something like that.[25]

Most of the Grenadians were eventually released, but some 40 remained detained without charge at Richmond Hill Prison. They included Bernard and Phyllis Coard, Hudson Austin, and most of the other former members of the Central Committee accused of being behind the killing of Bishop. Murder charges were finally brought against 19 persons in February 1984. Held virtually incommunicado, the prisoners were denied adequate access to lawyers, and Amnesty International expressed concern about reports that they had been beaten and mistreated in prison.[26] As of the summer of 1985, their trial had not yet begun.

Meanwhile, psychological warfare specialists from Fort Bragg mounted a propaganda campaign which used radio broadcasts and wall posters to stir up hatred against the NJM. This message found fertile ground in Grenada because of the shock and outrage over the killing of Bishop. Most although not all Grenadians initially welcomed the invasion, seeing it as deliverance from the Revolutionary Military Council and the shoot-on-sight curfew after the killings at Fort Rupert. "The overwhelming factor causing people to welcome the invasion was the desire for revenge," says a teacher who was in Grenada at the time. These emotions of anger and betrayal were easily channeled along broadly pro-U.S. and anticommunist lines.

Part of this ideological campaign was carried out by the American Institute for Free Labor Development and its main Grenadian agent, the Seamen's and Waterfront Workers Union (SWWU). SWWU cadre were hired to drive around the island painting out revolutionary slogans on walls and billboards, and the union also cooperated with AIFLD in a series of classes for Grenadian workers on "Political Theories and Systems"—a thinly disguised process of anticommunist indoctrination. The SWWU launched a red-baiting campaign against unions which had supported the revolution, accusing them of being "communist-infiltrated" and "pro-Coard."[27]

Another reason many Grenadians initially welcomed the occupation was the expectation that the U.S. presence would bring a windfall of aid, jobs and investment. "Uncle Sam is here—so where's the payoff?" was how one visitor characterized the mood. The Reagan administation encouraged these hopes by touting the "opening" of Grenada to U.S. investors, who were to be lured with special tax breaks and a US \$4.50 a day English-speaking work force. Grenada was declared eligible for the CBI, and the White House and USAID sponsored a red-carpet tour to the island for potential investors in January 1984.

In keeping with the push for foreign investment, AIFLD was given the task of "restructuring" the Grenadian labor movement to prevent a resurgence of labor radicalism.[28] It worked primarily through the SWWU, which made raids on the membership of other unions in order to weaken their influence. A British trade union delegation which visited Grenada in December 1983 reported "[attempts] by American-trained and backed Grenadians to remove elected Union officers and take over some unions" which had supported the revolution. This included, for example, a takeover of the executive of the Technical and Allied Workers Union (TAWU). The report states:

> Rank-and-file members of the union to whom we spoke claimed that this group [attempting to take over] was being organized by the AIFLD-trained Grenadian who had just returned to Grenada from the United States.[29]

The attempt at a right-wing takeover of Grenadian labor was only partly successful, however. As of 1985, AIFLD had failed to gain control of the main labor federation, the Trade Union Congress.

Along with the effort to attract investors, the economic strategy being administered by USAID includes the dismant-ling of the so-called "Marxist" structures of the revolution. The interim government which ran Grenada for the U.S. during 198 shut down numerous state-owned enterprises such as the Agro-Industry plant, the coffee-processing plant, and the Sandino prefabricated housing plant. Funds for new farm cooperatives were frozen, and the National Cooperative Development Agency (NACDA) was downgraded to a division in the Ministry of Agriculture. Price controls on essential foodstuffs were relaxed so that profits could be returned to the merchants. A number of state-owned farms were returned to private landowners who had previously allowed their lands to lie idle, and the government sought private buyers for other state enterprises, primarily hotels.

U.S. officials also supervised the closure of many social programs, particularly those involving Cuban assistance or reflecting any revolutionary ideology. The Centre for Popular Education, for instance, was shut down because the Reagan administration found its literacy and adult education materials politically objectionable. With the departure of the Cuban doctors and dentists, the revolution's expanded health care system collapsed, to be replaced by medical treatment on a far more limited scale by the Project Hope boat and a Swedish charity.

This attempt to "cleanse" Cuban influence from Grenada and substitute U.S. influence was particularly ironic in the case of the new Point Salines airport, on which 600 Cuban "internationalists" had worked alongside Grenadians to complete 80% of the construction. The U.S. invasion was partly rationalized by President Reagan's assertion that the airport was really intended as a military base. After the invasion, however, the Grenada Chamber of Commerce and virtually everyone else informed the U.S. that the airport was badly needed. Responsible now for the island's economy, the Reagan administration announced that the airport was needed for tourism—precisely the argument the Bishop government had consistently made to justify the project.

U.S. companies were contracted to finish the job, and on October 29, 1984, as smiling U.S. officials stood by, ribbons were cut on the new Point Salines International Airport in a ceremony to which no Cuban representative was invited. The dedication speech did not thank or even mention Cuba, and also failed to mention the name of Maurice Bishop, to the annoyance of many Grenadians. "Give credit where credit is due," said one.[30]

The decision to complete the airport came as the White House was begining to realize that the task of remaking Grenada's economy would not be easy. By the start of 1985, only two U.S. businesses had actually started up in Grenada— a wooden toy factory and a nutmeg novelty outfit. Despite generous tax breaks and non-union shops, both failed and left the island within a few months.

The investment campaign is foundering on the reality that there is little for foreign corporations to exploit in Grenada. Like most of the Eastern Caribbean, Grenada has a primitive infrastructure, little flat land, and no natural resources other than its rugged beauty. The few projects still going forward primarily involve investment in tourism, such as the luxury condominiums being planned by U.S. investors in the former

Cinnamon Hill hotel. "It certainly is a lovely piece of real estate," commented Secretary of State George Shultz upon arriving on the island.[31]

By the first anniversary of the invasion, Grenadians' hopes for a U.S.-funded economic boom had largely given way to disappointment. The dismantling of the economy set much of the workforce adrift, so that unemployment rose again to around 40%, near where it had been before the revolution began. The U.S. allocated $54 million in aid over two years (mostly for completion of the airport) but the expected bail-out never appeared. Many Grenadians, especially youth, became bitter and disillusioned, and there were increasing incidents of rock-throwing and hostile name-calling against the occupying U.S. and Caribbean soldiers.

Those Grenadians who felt things were improving came mainly from the traditional business class. The *New York Times* reported "signs of an economic revival" in March 1985, citing the example of Geoffrey Thompson, a Grenadian importer who is vice-president of the island's Chamber of Commerce.[32] He plans to build Grenada's first shopping mall on land he owns in downtown St. George's. Such activity does not involve new production, the key to any real economic recovery, but merely reverts to the traditional import-export profitmaking of the Caribbean merchant class. "The businessmen here are engaged in what we call invoice capitalism," said George Louison, one of the surviving ministers from Bishop's government. "Anyone who places their future in the hands of Grenada's merchants will be in for a rude shock."[32]

The return of economic power to the landowners and merchants is paralleled by the return of political power to the same hands. Herbert Blaize, who became the new prime minister in December 1984, represents Grenada's old bour-geoisie. He twice served as prime minister in the 1950s and '60s, when his Grenada National Party represented middle and upper-class interests closely linked to British colonialism.

The election was central to U.S. strategy and image-making around Grenada. It legitimized the invasion and dramatically symbolized the "return to democracy" which the Reagan administration promised for Grenada. While this symbolism received heavy play in the U.S. press, behind the scenes the U.S. was maneuvering feverishly to put together a party which could turn back challenges both from Gairy's party and from the survivors of Bishop's cabinet, regrouped as the Maurice Bishop Patriotic Movement. The White House initially hoped to have anticommunist Grenadian exiles step into this role, but the plan was scrapped when it became apparent that they had no popular backing in Grenada.

Washington therefore aimed for a coalition led by Blaize and including the other contending "centrist" parties: the Grenada Democratic Movement of the exiles and the National Democratic Party of liberal intellectual George Brizan. The three parties were brought together in August 1984 on Union Island near St. Vincent, where an electoral coalition called the New National Party (NNP) was hammered out under the supervision of Eastern Caribbean leaders close to the U.S.

There was no doubt in the minds of Grenadians that the NNP enjoyed Washington's support. U.S. officials made it clear that future U.S. investment depended on the outcome of the election, and openly hinted that the U.S. might suspend its aid program if the wrong party were to be elected. In addition, the NNP received funding and technical assistance from the New Right network in the United States, including two campaign advisors hired with funds raised by direct-mail appeal to wealthy conservatives. This effort was spearheaded

Comic book titled "Grenada: Rescued from Rape and Slavery" circulated on the island in the weeks preceding the election. Printed in the United States, it was among the propaganda materials which sought to smear the Maurice Bishop government and stir up anti-communist hatred among Grenadians.

by the Council for National Policy, a secretive organization linking such New Right luminaries as Jerry Falwell, Joseph Coors of the Adolph Coors Co., Phyllis Schlafly, Senator Jesse Helms and Phillip Nicolaides, head of Accuracy in Media. The CNP's director is Louisiana legislator Louis "Woody" Jenkins, whose Friends of the Americas group has been one of the leading sources of private funding for the Nicaraguan contras.[34]

The New National Party was able to give away large quantities of promotional items such as t-shirts, buttons, and ball-point pens, and even had a plane trail campaign banners across Grenada's skies. More importantly, it had the active backing of the Grenadian middle class and faced a divided and unpopular opposition. Most Grenadians greatly feared a return of Gairy to office. (True to form, Gairy's campaign platform called for planting "beautiful floral designs" in traffic circles, ensuring a permanent U.S. military presence in Grenada, and reviving horse racing "on a much larger scale than ever before.") And while Maurice Bishop himself continued to be held in high regard by Grenadians, their feelings for the slain leader did not translate into electoral support for the Maurice Bishop Patriotic Movement. Although its leaders Kenrick Radix and George Louison were recognized Bishop loyalists, the lingering shock of the NJM's self-destruction was too great for anyone associated with the party to be elected in Grenada in 1984.

The NNP thus won almost total victory with 14 of the 15 Parliamentary seats. Prime Minister Blaize promptly confirmed his allegiance to Washington (and his own insecurity) by requesting that the U.S. military remain in Grenada indefinitely. Withdrawal of the troops nevertheless took place in the spring of 1985, reflecting Washington's desire for a lower profile in Grenada and confidence that the "security" situation was under control. The process of voter registration before the election was used to fingerprint and photograph all adult Grenadians, facilitating surveillance of the population. A new Grenadian police force was being trained by the British, and U.S. Green Berets trained an 80-man Special Service Unit.

In some ways, Grenada is where Jamaica was in 1980 after Seaga was elected with U.S. backing. Many people are resigned to the surrender of sovereignty, hoping that with a U.S.-approved government in office their economic future will be secure. Like Jamaicans, however, Grenadians are already facing disappointment. The economic consequences of the U.S. takeover have been acute joblessness and the loss of many social programs Grenadians had become accustomed to. It is doubtful that the Reagan administration intends to continue subsidizing Grenada, seeing it instead as a chance to prove that the private sector can turn the economy around. However, Grenada is far less developed than Jamaica and is even less likely to succeed as an experiment in free market magic. The administration therefore will have to make a choice: support Grenada as a client state, or watch the Blaize government fall prey to the same frustrated expectations and economic desperation as its counterparts in the region.

The New Political Order

While many people in the Caribbean approved of the invasion as a "rescue" from the Revolutionary Military Council, doubts rose as the occupation troops stayed and stayed. The spectacle of Grenada being transformed into an American-run fiefdom was profoundly disturbing to many, driving home the essential weakness of all the islands' newly-won independence.

The invasion put the region on notice that the U.S. had moved decisively into the vacuum created by Britain's departure. British Prime Minister Margaret Thatcher was not consulted on the invasion nor even informed of the plan until hours before the action. About to invade a former British colony and present member of the British Commonwealth, Washington was not interested in Britain's opinion, and indeed took pains to conceal the pending invasion from its supposed ally. While protesting the slight, London had little choice but to acquiesce to this new reality of power.

The invasion also formalized bilateral alliances which had been emerging for some time in contrast to the larger, stated commitment to regionalism. The U.S. had determined events in collusion with Jamaica, Barbados, etc.; while CARICOM, the regional institution, was bypassed and excluded from the decision about how to handle a crisis involving a member state. Moreover, the four leading members of CARICOM—Trinidad Jamaica, Barbados, and Guyana—were split down the middle, with Trinidad and Guyana opposing the invasion while Jamaica and Barbados were major participants.

Although the breach within CARICOM was eventually papered over, it left a legacy of divisions. These rest less on real ideological differences than on the degree of support for the invasion and U.S. regional dominance in general. The idea of ideological pluralism which had been gaining acceptance in the region was shelved abruptly, as few wanted to risk being labeled "communist" by allowing for the possibility of socialism in the region. Similarly, progress toward the Zone of Peace ideal was suspended as governments were swept up in U.S.-sponsored militarization.

The dramatic advance of the regional right and retreat of the left seemed initially to be the most far-reaching impact of the invasion on regional politics. With the left traumatized and divided, conservative prime ministers who had collaborated with Washington gained an artificial security and moved to entrench their control. Two prime ministers, Seaga of Jamaica and Vere Bird of Antigua, seized the opportunity to renew their mandates with snap elections (under the Westminster system, a ruling party may call an election at any time and secure a new five-year term if it wins.)

The campaign slogan of Bird's Antigua Labour Party in April 1984 was: "It's Safer With Labour." The message was not that the ruling party had any positive plans for the country, but merely that the opposition was to be feared—a subtle form of red-baiting. A further factor was the collapse of a tenuous alliance between the three opposition parties due to the unwillingness of the official opposition to join forces with the Antigua Caribbean Liberation Movement.

Campaign posters of the Antigua Labour Party promote candidacies of Prime Minister Vere C. Bird's sons, Lester and Vere Jr.

The Antiguan election marked the nadir of post-invasion politics. The voter turnout of 61% was the lowest in Antigua since 1971. Few issues were raised in the listless campaign, and a palpable apathy hung over the island as the polling day approached. When the votes were counted and the ruling party's victory announced, the streets remained eerily silent, in contrast to the rowdy celebrations normally staged by supporters of the winning party.

The year which followed was to show both the persistence of this pattern of conservative entrenchment and its underlying fragility. Dominica's Eugenia Charles won reelection in July 1985 in much the way Bird won in Antigua—through an anticommunist harangue against the (non-communist) opposition, and by touting her U.S. connection. In Dominica, as in Antigua, the opposition was plagued by an image of factionalism, although the Dominican opposition parties had managed to form a tenuous unity shortly before the election.

The election was not a great victory for Charles nonetheless. Those elected from the opposition included its most progressive candidates, among them two from the former Dominica Liberation Movement—precisely the ones Charles had attempted to smear as "communists." Similarly, the aging Bird may appear to have the political scene locked up in Antigua, but this actually masks an unstable situation in which the traditional opposition has collapsed and the only viable opposition is the progressive ACLM. As long as economic and social problems remain unsolved, none of the Reagan allies enjoys a secure political future.

Finally, the death of Tom Adams of Barbados is important on both a real and a symbolic level. His replacement, former Deputy Prime Minister Bernard St. John, is known a a technocrat and a manager, someone more interested in economic issues than geo-politics. Although he presumably will adhere to Adams' basic politics until the 1986 election, he clearly will not pursue the role of U.S. surrogate and regional mini-power with the same determination that Adams did.

At 53, J.M.G.M. "Tom" Adams was a respected Caribbean statesman. His unexpected death from a heart attack stunned and grieved Barbadians and the region. But on a deeper, almost subliminal level, it also fueled doubts and speculation about his controversial actions. Photographed as he bid the invading troops farewell from the Grantley Adams International Airport, Tom Adams was more closely identified with the Grenada invasion than anyone else except Ronald Reagan. Just as Cato's fall to Mitchell signaled the unpopularity of repression, Adams' sudden death symbolically closed the episode of the Grenada invasion and encouraged a growing reassessment in its wake. ∎

Caribbean Unity, The Frustrated Dream

The fragmentation of the Caribbean dates back to the origins of modern Caribbean society. The colonial legacy was one of artificial divisions and rivalry—of being "chopped up like a loaf of bread," in the words of Maurice Bishop. Geographic distance, language barriers, and nationalism (or insularity) all play their part in perpetuating these divisions. And while the role of the historic colonial powers is waning, the growing involvement of the United States in the region today poses new obstacles to unity.

The building of a "united Caribbean" is a loosely defined but nonetheless fundamental part of the progressive vision in the region. Given the small size and economic weakness of most Caribbean countries, their only hope for escaping permanent neocolonial dependence is to link their economies—a fact long recognized if not acted upon successfully. Moreover, the political independence achieved with the departure of the colonial powers has proven feeble and vulnerable for the Caribbean mini-states. Maintaining independence in the shadow of a superpower, it is realized, will be virtually impossible for the Caribbean countries individually. Only united do they stand a chance.

While governmental efforts to achieve such unity have been dogged by failure, efforts at the popular level have been going forward quietly and with modest short-term goals. Among the major groups involved are intellectuals and cultural workers; grassroots sectors such as women, trade unions, farmers, and development workers; and the Church. Through regional meetings and action projects linking different countries, they are building bridges to span the old divisions and work toward a common philosophy of change.

Historic Divisions versus Popular Desire for Unity

Before the arrival of Columbus, the most far-flung corners of the Caribbean were linked by the migratory sweep of the Carib and Arawak Indians. Although the Amerindians did not create a unified state, their network of settlements and inter-island trade encompassed the entire Caribbean archipelago, as well as areas of the mainland which are now Belize, the Yucatan peninsula, Venezuela, and Guyana.

With European colonization, the situation changed. Individual islands became the pawns of European power politics, to be snatched back and forth as plunder in the interminable wars between Spain, Holland, England and France. Four separate empires developed, each locked in an iron embrace with the colonizer through the monopoly system. Under the system of plantation slavery each colony was a separate entity, although groups sometimes were administered together for the sake of convenience. Relations between the islands were always suppressed in favor of each island's tie to the "mother country," and a fiercely insular mentality arose among the West Indian planters and middle class.

At the popular level, racial and color differences were used to create divisions. As Europeans and Africans intermingled over generations, a wide range of color gradations appeared and became the basis for a complex social stratification. In Trinidad and Guyana, where over half the popular is of East Indian descent, African/Indian rivalries were used to split the working class to the ultimate benefit of those on top.

Despite this colonial legacy, the desire for some kind of unity has been a persistent if submerged theme of popular Caribbean thought. "The people are one people; it's the politicians who are keeping us apart" is a common sentiment rooted in the shared history of the Caribbean working class. Or as the calypsonian Black Stalin put it:

Them is one race - the Caribbean man
From the same place - the Caribbean man

That make the same trip - the Caribbean man
On the same ship - the Caribbean man

But on closer examination this concept of unity turns out to be limited in scope. It relates specifically to black Caribbean people, whose shared history includes African origins ("one race from the same place") and the slavery experience ("the same trip on the same ship"). This definition leaves open the role of other groups such as East Indians and Hispanics who make up part of the larger Caribbean working class. More than this, however, the concept of "Caribbean Man" which evolved as part of the Black Power movement in the 1960s is usually, though not exclusively, defined in terms of the English-speaking Caribbean. This double qualification is evident in a calypso by Explainer:

So if you born in Kingston
Or if you born in Bridgetown
If you is Bajan or Jamaican
Once you black you's my brother man
The Vincentian feller
That's my black brother
So if you's Bajan or Vincentian
Once you black, you's my brother man.

The countries named by Explainer—Jamaica, Barbados, and St. Vincent, are all former British colonies, even though the Spanish, French and Dutch-speaking territories also have large black populations. The concept of a black Puerto Rican or Martiniquan as "brother" to a black Jamaican is articulated only rarely, usually in a self-conscious attempt to broaden the concept of Caribbean unity.

Divisions between the English, Spanish, French and Dutch areas of the region are unquestionably the biggest hindrance to a united Caribbean. Language barriers play a part, especially for people in the non-English-speaking countries. While second languages are taught in some Caribbean

Prime Minister Eric Williams of Trinidad, left, and Fidel Castro. Photo dates from the early 70s, when four Commonwealth Caribbean states established diplomatic relations with Cuba.

Puerto Rico's lack of sovereignty on the one hand and the U.S. attempt to isolate Cuba on the other have combined to break down the historic unity of the Spanish-speaking Caribbean. As a U.S. "associated state," Puerto Rico cannot maintain diplomatic relations or direct trade ties with any Caribbean countries, nor can it participate in regional bodies as an independent nation. The Reagan administration considers that its ban on U.S. citizens visiting Cuba applies to Puerto Ricans. In 1982, nearly 200 Puerto Ricans sports fans defied the ban in order to attend the 14th annual Central American and Caribbean Games being hosted by Cuba that year. When they arrived home in Puerto Rico, U.S. customs officials seized the Cuban books and records they had purchased as souvenirs.[1]

Washington encourages links between Caribbean countries when those links serve U.S. policy interests and take place under U.S. control. The Reagan administration favors the admission of the Dominican Republic and Haiti to CARICOM—where they would be the first non-anglophone members—in order to strengthen U.S. influence within that body. Puerto Rico is urged to enter into a "twin-plant" relationship with countries like Haiti, but that twinning is performed by U.S. corporations. And while Washington pressured Caribbean countries to isolate revolutionary Grenada, it is anxious to gain regional acceptance for the U.S.-backed Blaize government. Puerto Rican governor Hernández Colón's first overseas visit was to St. George's in April 1985 to discuss a twin-plant relationship between Puerto Rico and Grenada.

Regional Integration in the Commonwealth Caribbean

You try a Federation, the whole thing end in confusion
Caricom and then Carifta, but somehow ah smelling disaster
Mister West Indian politician, you went to big institution
How come you can't unite seven million
When a West Indian unity I know is very easy
If you only rap to you people and tell them like me.

— Black Stalin, "Caribbean Man"

While no one has yet sought to unite the entire Caribbean, the many attempts to unite the English-speaking countries are the subject of Black Stalin's cynical verse. The concept of such a union has emerged repeatedly throughout Caribbean history, in part because the territories colonized by Britain—with the exception of Guyana—are particularly small. Yet despite their common language and history, the countries of the Commonwealth Caribbean have found regional unity a most elusive goal.

The principal attempt was that of the West Indies Federation, whose short life span (1958-62) established a

schools, there is no serious attempt to compensate for linguistic diversity. The result is that there has been a negligible flow of communication and contacts across the linguistic/cultural barriers.

Colonial divisions also are perpetuated by visa barriers. Citizens of the English-speaking countries can go anywhere within the Commonwealth Caribbean, but must have visas to enter the French, Dutch or Spanish-speaking islands. Any Frenchman can travel across the Atlantic Ocean and enter Guadeloupe, Martinique, or French Guiana with scarcely a nod from customs officials; but citizens of island just a few miles away must have visas to get in.

Where U.S. politics are involved, the problems multiply. To get into Puerto Rico one must apply for and receive a U.S. visa, a process increasingly politicized under the Reagan administration. The U.S. State Department has denied entry to a number of Latin American and Caribbean progressives seeking to visit Puerto Rico. A young Catholic woman from Grenada, Suzanne Berkeley, was harassed and finally deported from Puerto Rico by U.S. authorities in 1982 when she arrived to attend a "Theology in the Americas" conference as an invited guest.

backdrop of failure to the subsequent regional integration movement. Initially pushed by the Caribbean labor movement in the 1940s, the Federation was to include ten English-speaking territories of which the largest were Trinidad and Jamaica. The original plan called for the Federation to have a strong central government which could stand up to imperialist pressures and plan industrialization on a regional basis.

This vision ran up headlong against the interests not only of Britain, but of politicians and businessmen in the larger islands who were jumping on the bandwagon of "industrialization by invitation." Key among them was Norman Manley, who took office in Jamaica in 1955 and promptly yielded to British pressures for changes in the Federation's constitution. Richard Hart, then secretary of the Caribbean Labour Congress, describes Manley's role:

> The reason for this change of policy was that Mr. Manley's whole conception of how to industrialize had changed. He now saw industrialization not as a process to take place under local ownership and against the interests of imperialism, but as a process actually to be performed by foreign investors . . . He therefore no longer wanted a strong federal government with power to control investment in the entire area. Instead he wanted a weak central government, so that he would have the right to pursue an independent policy of attracting foreign capital by tax and other incentives to Jamaica.[2]

A similar mentality prevailed in Trinidad, while the smaller islands were willing to accept federation on any terms. The result was that the strong central government was scrapped and the Federation was born in a fatally weakened condition.

Jamaica and Trinidad both received internal self-government from Britian in 1959. After this, the idea that West Indian unity was a precondition for self-government lost its mystique. The politicians of each island began looking toward

Anti-Federation propaganda of the Jamaica Labour Party claimed that Jamaica would have to subsidize the smaller islands.

national independence, and Manley pulled back from the Federation in order to prepare for his role as prime minister of an independent Jamaica. Meanwhile, the Jamaica Labour Party headed by Bustamante whipped up a propaganda campaign against the Federation, claiming that Jamaica would have to subsidize the smaller islands. Finally, in a referendum held in 1961, Jamaicans voted to pull out.

As soon as Jamaica left, Trinidad prime minister Eric Williams made his famous pronouncement that "One from ten leaves zero," and Trinidad followed Jamaica in abandoning the regional body. The Federation thereupon collapsed, and with it the hopes of many working-class Caribbean people for a strong and united West Indian nation. Many people felt that the politicians had sold them out, or at least had shown short-sightedness in allowing selfish insularity to destroy the Federation. The Trinidadian calypsonian The Mighty Sparrow captured these feelings of scorn and disappointment in his "Federation" calypso:

> *Federation boil down to simply this*
> *It's dog-eat-dog, and survival of the fittest*
> *Everybody going for independence*
> *Singularly, Trinidad for instance*
> *And we'll get it too, boy, don't bother*
> *But I find we should all be together*
> *Not separated as we are*
> *Because of Jamaica.*

The break-up of the Federation left each island facing independence weak and alone. Foreshadowed by the United States' refusal to yield its Chaguaramas military base in Trinidad for the Federation's capital site, the failure of West Indian unity opened the door to U.S. domination of a fragmented and quarreling region.

Convinced that a political union could not work, regional politicians began exploring possibilities for a more limited economic association. In 1968, the Caribbean Free Trade Association (CARIFTA) was established with the original ten countries from the Federation plus Guyana. Its purpose was to stimulate production in its member territories by lowering trade barriers between them—that is, by creating a common market.

Free trade alone, however, failed to bring about any substantial increase in production. The next step was to attempt to link production in the various territories so as to cut the costs of industrializing which were a heavy burden on small countries. In 1973, CARIFTA gave birth to the Caribbean Community and Common Market, known as CARICOM. In addition to creating production linkages, CARICOM was to oversee cooperation in areas such as tourism development, regional transport, health care, and scientific research. It was also supposed to coordinate the foreign policies of member states.

But CARICOM's most important projects were stillborn, and dreams of unity again faded. The most ambitious joint production scheme involved two collectively-owned aluminum smelters which would use Trinidad's natural gas and Guyana's hydro-power to turn Jamaican and Guyanese bauxite into aluminum. But the project became entangled in a dispute between Jamaica and Trinidad, and was abandoned after Jamaica and Guyana pulled out.

Another project, the Regional Food Plan, was built on the attractive premise that the region could reduce its food import bill by having each country produce and share what it was best suited to grow. But the plan was never taken seriously, as agriculture in general remained the neglected stepchild of most Caribbean governments.

The real problem was not that production linkages weren't feasible, but that production under local control and using local resources hardly existed in most of the islands. Furthermore, there was little attempt to involve the people who knew most about production—the workers and farmers—in the planning process. Key questions of land ownership and class structure were never addressed.

Attempts at production linkages gradually fell by the wayside, and CARICOM became limited to the free trade area and functional cooperation. There have been achievements in the latter, especially in health and education. But by the late 1970s, CARICOM had fallen into the doldrums and was frequently reported in the regional press to be "on its last legs," "dying," or "merely in need of a decent burial."

The role of Trinidadian prime minister Eric Williams was key during this period. With its oil-rich economy, Trinidad was both a source of aid to weaker CARICOM states and the largest market for manufactured goods within the free trade area. Williams had a strong idealistic commitment to regionalism, but became disenchanted with the shortcomings of CARICOM and what he saw as ingratitude for Trinidad's aid. Although he personally had helped to institutionalize the annual CARICOM summits, after 1975 he refused to attend them, and from 1976 through 1982 the CARICOM heads of government did not meet at all.

1980s: The Rift Widens

CARICOM was officially revived in November 1982 when the heads of government gathered in Ocho Rios, Jamaica for their third summit meeting. It was the first time in seven years that the leaders of the English-speaking Caribbean had come together, and there was an air of optimism and self-congratulation as the politicians proclaimed their belief that "the maintenance and deepening of the Caribbean community... provides the only certain way for the survival of our States as independent, free and developing societies."[3]

A year and a half later, however, as the regional heads met for their fifth summit in July 1984, these words seemed empty. Summing up the dismal state of CARICOM, Trinidadian journalist Jeremy Taylor wrote:

> There is no free movement of labor, no waiving of entry restrictions and no common currency. The Caricom Secretariat, starved of funds, operates in the depressed Guyanese capital of Georgetown with no physical presence elsewhere.
> There has been no serious coordination of foreign policy, no attempt to form a parliament, and trading has become a bitter battle against regional protectionism.
> A regional clearinghouse, established to simplify trade,

has been choked with work for two years. More Caricom states are turning to bartering, and the joke is that nothing is left of regionalism except the University of the West Indies—now being decentralized—and the West Indies cricket team.[4]

On the surface, the issues which have all but destroyed CARICOM belong in two categories. Ideological differences between the members have been blamed for division, culminating in the split within the body over whether to invade Grenada. On the other hand, economic difficulties have severely eroded intra-CARICOM trade and threatened to sink the regional movement. But on a deeper level, these issues are related. The root cause in both cases has to do with fundamental questions of sovereignty versus dependence in the context of imperialist pressures on the Caribbean.

Following the Grenada revolution in 1979, CARICOM spent much energy debating the question of "ideological pluralism" and its effect on integration. This was the first time that ideological differences were seen as a problem, even though Jamaica and Guyana had both announced pro-socialist paths in the 1970s.[5] Indeed, the four "more developed" members of CARICOM—Jamaica, Guyana, Trinidad, and Barbados—jointly established diplomatic relations with Cuba in 1972. They did so less for ideological reasons than out of a simple conviction that the larger states of the Caribbean should have relations—and a willingness, in the optimistic early days of the regional movement, to chart their own course even at the risk of conflicting with U.S. wishes.

A decade later, things had changed. Soon after taking power in 1980, Seaga severed Jamaica's relations with Cuba at the behest of Washington. At the Ocho Rios summit in 1982, Seaga and Adams led an attempt to expel Grenada from CARICOM by proposing a "human rights" amendment which would make "free, fair, and regular elections" a requirement for membership.

The invitation to line up with the U.S. against Grenada raised many embarrassing questions which the leaders would have preferred to avoid. For one thing, everyone knew that Forbes Burnham maintained himself in power through unfair, fraudulent elections; should Guyana, site of the CARICOM Secretariat, be censured for its behavior? And just what *was* the state of human rights in the other member countries? No leader wanted to open his or her own performance to scrutiny. Grenadian prime minister Maurice Bishop played on these doubts by offering a counter-amendment which would have included the right to life, jobs, food, education, electricity, and running water—that is, to "rights" which if used as criteria for membership would have left CARICOM with no members at all.

A further problem was that no fault could reasonably be found with Grenada's behavior within CARICOM. Indeed, Bishop was an outspoken proponent of regionalism, and Grenada played an active and constructive role in CARICOM and in other regional bodies such as the Organization of Eastern Caribbean States, the Caribbean Development Bank, and the University of the West Indies. The authors of the prestigious Demas Report, commissioned in 1980 to examine CARICOM's problems, stated that they did not view ideological differences as a major obstacle to integration. Clearly, then, the ideological question was being inflated to serve private agendas.

In the final communique which went out to the world from Ocho Rios, the leaders rejected the Seaga/Adams amendment and affirmed . . .

> . . . the right of self-determination of all peoples including the right to choose their own path of social, political, and economic development, and we insist that there can be no justification for any external interference with the exercise of that right.

The communique went on to declare "inadmissible" the "use of force in international relations" and called for conflicts to be resolved "by peaceful means based on respect for sovereignty, independence and territorial integrity."[6]

Less than a year later, the brave ideals of Ocho Rios were thrown to the winds as six CARICOM governments assisted a foreign invasion of one of CARICOM's smallest member states. At the very least, the Grenada invasion marked the failure of the attempt to coordinate the foreign policies of CARICOM members. At a deeper level, it symbolized the weakness of the commitment to regionalism in the face of incentives and pressures on each country to seek a "special" relationship with the United States.

Many people feared that the invasion had dealt a fatal blow to the regional integration movement. But at the July 1984 CARICOM summit held in Nassau, the Bahamas, the heads of government surprised the region by avoiding fractious discussion of their invasion roles. The Nassau summit managed to avoid reopening the wounds of the previous months by putting on a back burner subjects such as ideological pluralism, militarism and the Zone of Peace. Instead, their discussion focused on CARICOM's other pressing problem—the steep decline of intra-regional trade.

The root of the problem lies in the desperate condition of the Caribbean economies and the measures individual countries have taken to cope with the crisis. Basically, the emphasis on attracting foreign investment and exporting to markets outside the region has come at the expense of intra-regional trade. Currency devaluations in Jamaica and Guyana have cut their buying power and drastically reduced their imports from other CARICOM states. Trinidad, CARICOM's largest market, has tried to conserve its dwindling oil revenues by erecting trade barriers, including licensing requirements for imports from within the CARICOM free trade zone. This turn to protectionism has caused bitter disputes within CARICOM.

A major factor in the decline of trade has been the collapse of the CARICOM Multi-Lateral Clearing Facility (CMCF), a credit device for regional trade. After the CMFC suspended operations in 1983, bankrupted by debts Guyana owed the facility, countries with different currencies had to use scarce foreign exchange to settle their trade accounts. There has been some experimentation with direct barter to avoid this—Guyanese rice for Jamaican manufactures, for example.

The trade crisis has brought some of the structural weaknesses of CARICOM into sharper focus. Basing integration on a shared history and language does not necessarily lead to a dynamic economic arrangement or one able to survive hard times. A market of 5 million people—the population of the CARICOM countries—may in fact be too small to provide a basis for modern agricultural or industrial production. But entrenched colonial divisions prevent the region from taking advantage of its potential market of 30 million represented by the English, Spanish, French and Dutch-speaking countries together.

"Industrialization by invitation has resulted in invasion by invitation," commented one Caribbean critic after the Grenada episode. In the past, there was no pretense at sovereignty as each Caribbean territory was dominated politically and economically by a colonial power. Today, the trappings of sovereignty are there: prime ministers, parliaments, national budgets and armies. But the underlying pattern of domination by the western powers has not been broken, merely redirected toward the United States as first Spain, then Britain departed from the region.

The formal independence of the Caribbean is a boon rather than a hindrance to U.S. neocolonialism. It means that the U.S. is not forced to support colonies; economic aid may be promised but need not materialize. And it multiplies their value as allies in the international arena. Washington is now trying to cash in on its relationship with some Caribbean countries to garner support for its unpopular war against the government of Nicaragua. When Caribbean leaders met with President Reagan in South Carolina in July 1984, they pressed for more U.S. economic aid, while he exhorted them to join the United States in isolating and pressuring Nicaragua. After the White House announced its economic embargo against Nicaragua in 1985—a move scarcely supported even by Washington's right-wing allies in Latin America—the CARICOM foreign ministers denounced the embargo at their meeting in St. Kitts. But after intensive U.S. lobbying, the CARICOM heads of government backed away from the foreign ministers' position. The result was a deafening silence on the subject of the embargo when the leaders met for their sixth CARICOM summit in Bridgetown in July 1985.

Popular Unifiers: Cricket, Carnival, Migration and Music

The majority of West Indians know little about the workings of CARICOM and other regional bureaucracies. Nor, oftentimes, do they see them as particularly relevant to the question of unity. The average person in the Caribbean experiences regionalism in a different way: as something based on people-to-people contacts and the informal ties they promote. These linkages have always existed in the Caribbean and are deeper and stronger than the formal integration mechanisms.[7]

The most important unifier is inter-island migration, rooted in the phenomenon of male migration for employment. Caribbean men have always traveled to where opportunities beckon: to build the Panama Canal, to cut sugar cane in Cuba, to work in the oil fields of Trinidad and the Netherlands Antilles, or in the tourist industry of the Virgin Islands. While away, men marry and have children, creating families with dual-island loyalties. It is entirely normal for a person to have blood relations in several territories and to have lived in more than one. A typical example is George Headley, one of the region's famous cricketers:

Born in Panama on May 30, 1909, to a Jamaican mother and a Barbadian father, George Alphonso Headley was taken to Cuba at the age of five and to an aunt in Jamaica at nine.[8]

Such kinship networks are the basis for many informal economic ties between countries. A boat leaves Grenada every week loaded with fresh fruits and vegetables which Grenadian farmers send to their relatives in Trinidad to sell on the Trinidad market. The profits return to Grenada, part of the web of informal ties which bind the two islands. Similarly, a man from Dominica who has found work in neighboring Guadeloupe will be likely to send back part of his earnings to his family at home.

Migration is the only unifier which consistently straddles the colonial divisions between the English, Spanish, French and Dutch territories. To cite a prominent example, former Grenadian prime minister Maurice Bishop was born in Aruba to Grenadian parents while his father was employed in the Aruban oil fields. Although Aruba is part of the Dutch-speaking Netherlands Antilles, many English-speaking West Indians have lived there because of the oil industry. Migration sometimes creates enduring cultural links. Around the turn of the twentieth century thousands of West Indians, especially Jamaicans, migrated to eastern Cuba to work in the sugar industry. They left a West Indian cultural stamp on that part of the island, so that Santiago de Cuba, the eastern provincial capital, is now "the most Caribbean city in Cuba"—meaning that it has the most African and West Indian cultural influences and a predominantly black population.[9]

People-to-people ties, of course, are strongest within each cultural/linguistic block. Within the English-speaking Caribbean a number of cultural elements serve as unifiers, of which the most important is undoubtedly the sport of cricket.

"Whoever and whatever we are, we are cricketers," writes C.L.R. James.[10] Cricket was an upper-class British game introduced into the Caribbean (and into Australia, India, South Africa and New Zealand) by the colonial settlers. But class and color distinctions on the cricket field eventually gave way before the growing superiority of black and brown players, who dominated West Indies cricket by the 1940s. The West Indies won its first test series against England in 1935, and since the 1960s has dominated world cricket—the colonized beating the colonizers at their own game.

Cricket is important to unity because the West Indies competes internationally as a single team, although individual island teams also play each other. The West Indies Cricket Team is made up of the best players from each island, and is the focus of boundless regional pride. Moreover, the Caribbean's supremacy in cricket allows it to enforce an anti-apartheid policy against South Africa. All the Commonwealth Caribbean nations are signatories to the Gleneagles Agreement which discourages sporting links with South Africa, and the West Indies Cricket Board of Control has banned South African cricketers from the region. In 1983, however, a group of "rebel cricketers" mainly from Barbados sparked an acrimonious regional debate by going on a lucrative unofficial tour of South Africa. The West Indian governments were unable to agree on action to be taken against the mercenary sportsmen, although the cricket board has barred them from future competition in the Caribbean.

What cricket is to West Indians, baseball is to the Spanish-speaking Caribbean. Cubans, Dominicans, and Puerto Ricans are passionate baseball fans, and the three

West Indies versus England in a cricket test match.

Everybody's Magazine

countries have produced some of the best players in the world, including many in the U.S. major leagues. Examples include Luis Arroyo of Puerto Rico, Felipe and Matty Alou of the Dominican Republic, "Mini" Minozo of Cuba and many others. The famous Roberto Clemente, centerfield for the Pittsburgh Pirates until his death in 1972, was born in Puerto Rico and is regarded as a hero in his homeland.

Love of baseball not only unites the Spanish-speaking Caribbean peoples; it also builds bridges between the Caribbean and other parts of Latin America where baseball is played, such as Mexico, Nicaragua and Venezuela. National teams frequently play against each other, and all compete in the Pan American games. In this arena, political barriers are bypassed. Puerto Rico competes as an independent nation. Cuba, which is isolated in political and diplomatic settings, participates fully and is highly respected for its sports prowess.

Calypso: Voice of the Small Man

In the eyes of the outside world, two cultural phenomena have come to represent the Caribbean and symbolize the vibrancy of its culture. Both have their origins in the West Indian working class: reggae/Rastafarianism, originating in Jamaica, and carnival/calypso, originating in Trinidad. Although strongest in their countries of origin, both of these cultural "complexes" have spread throughout the Caribbean and are claimed by West Indians as the region's original creations.

Calypso is one of the earliest authentic West Indian art forms. It is rooted in the African oral tradition, in which songs of praise or derision were sung as a form of pointed social comment. In the modern Caribbean, calypso serves as the "voice of the small man," who enjoys a vicarious social protest through the scathing commentary of the calypsonian. The dominant characteristics of calypso are wit (preferably spicy), colorful language, and opinionated reference to social or political events of the day. For instance, a calypso composed in the 1930s commented on the abdication of Edward VIII from the British throne.

Believe me, friends, if I were King
I'd marry any woman and give her a ring
I wouldn't give a damn what the people say
So long as she can wash, cook and dingolay.

Many calypsos were banned by the colonial authorities in the 1930s for being "profane." Although sex was a popular topic, what the authorities actually objected to was the boldness of calypsonians in mocking and embarrassing the ruling class. A 1950 calypso by the Growling Tiger, for example, broke social taboos by denouncing the misdeeds of a British expatriate official in Trinidad:

The Assistant Director of Education
He found himself in confusion
Drunk and driving his motor car
Dangerous to the public, what behavior!

He is a disgrace to my native land
So the public should demand his resignation.

Calypsonians are usually of working-class origins, traditionally from the poor areas of Port-of-Spain. As part of their humorous personae they adopt sobriquets borrowed from British nobility or from the roster of history's great conquerers: The Mighty Duke, King Solomon, King Obstinate, Atilla the Hun, Black Stalin, Lord Nelson, Lord Kitchener (Kitchener, along with The Mighty Sparrow, dominated Trinidad calypso for decades; he is named for the commander of the British overseas forces in Africa and India during the 19th century).

The period during and after World War Two saw the marriage of politics and calypso. This was linked in part to the emergence in 1956 of The Mighty Sparrow, whose career in turn paralleled the political rise of Dr. Eric Williams and his People's National Movement in Trinidad. Sparrow was a strong supporter of Williams, but he did not fail to air popular dissatisfaction when Williams was seen to be breaking his promises:

They raise up the taxi fare
No, Doctor, no

Lord Kitchener and The Mighty Duke, in a photo probably dating from the 1950s.

Jamaica Journal

And the blasted milk gone up so dear
No, Doctor, no
But you must remember
We support you in September
You better come good
Because I have a big piece o' mango wood.

Inevitably, calypso goes beyond mere commentary to become a potent political weapon. By highlighting an issue or scandal it fans the flames of public controversy, often with direct results. The calypsonian's true role is that of a catalyst for mass expression: he gives voice to a vague but widespread sentiment, and in so doing helps to galvanize it into a definite protest. This happened, for example, with the calypso "Boots," which helped make militarization a regional issue. Politicians dread ridicule at the hands of the calypsonians, and within the past few years several calypsos aimed at incumbent governments have been banned from the airwaves in Barbados and Antigua.

Calypso's unifying power comes from its effectiveness as a means of mass communication. The most popular numbers receive air play all over the region, informing people in other territories of current issues in the country where the song originates. While the official version of events is contained in the news media, the average person's interpretation (which may be quite different) is publicized through the calypso.

Calypso is closely linked to Carnival, the festival held in the days leading up to Lent. Carnival is biggest in Trinidad, but also is traditional in Grenada, St. Vincent, Antigua, Aruba, and Brazil. The Carnival season begins in January with the opening of the calypso tents. Here the public gets to hear the season's new crop of calypsos and size up contenders for the title of Calypso Monarch. In the "pan yards," steelbands rehearse for their competition, which in Trinidad's past often took the form of a violent clash. The climax comes on the two days before Ash Wednesday. Sunday night is "Dimanche Gras," when the Calypso King and Queen are chosen. In the dawn hours of Monday morning begins J'Ouvert (*jour ouvert*, or open day), when costumed masqueraders converge on Port-of-Spain for two days of unbroken revelry.

Up on the Hill Carnival Monday morning breaks upon the backs of these tin shacks with no cock's crow, and before the mist clears, little boys, costumed in old dresses, their heads tied, holding brooms made from the ribs of coconut palm leaves, blowing whistles and beating kerosene tins for drums, move across the face of the awakening Hill, sweeping yards in a ritual, heralding the masqueraders' coming, that goes back centuries for its beginnings, back across the Middle Passage, back to Mali and Guinea and Dahomey and Congo, back to Africa where Maskers were sacred and revered . . .

The music burst forth from the steelband; shouts went up, and the steelband and the masqueraders . . . the robbers and the Indians and the clowns—the whole Hill began moving down upon Port-of-Spain . . .

From *The Dragon Can't Dance* by Earl Lovelace
(Essex: Longman Group Ltd., 1969)

Carnival has become more commercialized since the 1960s, losing some of its original spirit of rebelliousness and mock violence. In becoming a major tourist attraction, however, it also has become a Caribbean unifier, as people from the other islands and from Caribbean communities abroad flock to Trinidad for the yearly event.

Reggae and the Sufferer Culture

At the opposite end of the island chain, Jamaica is the birthplace of Rastafarianism and the reggae music it helped inspire. Their evolution is closely bound to the Afro-Jamaican experience. Yet they have taken on significance for people all over the Caribbean, above all for black youth; and they form an important cultural link between West Indians in the Caribbean and those living abroad.

At one level, reggae is an international commercial success, the first Caribbean music ever to make it big in the white music world. "Reggae is a victorious thing for arts in the Caribbean," proving to Caribbean youth that their culture produces something valued by the outside world.[11] This international recognition is closely tied to the ascendency of Jamaican superstar Bob Marley, who dominated the reggae world until his death from cancer in 1981.

It is at the deeper level of meaning, however, that reggae and Rastafarianism take on their true importance. Ironically, this has little to do with reggae's international success, since reggae's popularity with white listeners is almost entirely due to its compelling rhythms and melodies. Nor does the rather voyeuristic interest in Rastafarianism among tourists to Jamaica and others necessarily imply an understanding of the religion's meaning in the Afro-Caribbean context.

Rastafarianism speaks to the historical experience of black peoples in Jamaica and the rest of the New World. As international capital penetrated Jamaica in the 1950s and a materialistic middle class emerged, Rastafarianism gained strength as an alternative creed for those shut out of this process. Rooted in the Pan-African tradition of Marcus Garvey, Rastafarianism promised redemption through repatriation to Africa for black people suffering in the white man's world [see Part I, Ch. 6].

Early Rastafarian music incorporated elements of Afro-American spirituals, hymns, and rhythm and blues, which were popular among poor Jamaicans. When reggae burst forth at the end of the 1960s, these elements were woven into the new music, along with references to Africa, Garvey, Zion (the promised land) Babylon (the white world), and Jah (God). Marley's "Zion Train" is essentially a transformation of an old Baptist spiritual, illustrating how black Christian religiosity is one of the strains feeding into the evolution of Rastafarianism:

Zion train is coming our way
Zion train is coming our way
Oh people better get on board
You better get on board
Thank the Lord, praise Fari
     [Ras Tafari, or Haile Selassie, worshipped
     as divine by Rastafarians]

The "Peace Concert": Reggae superstar Bob Marley brings together rival party leaders Michael Manley, left, and Edward Seaga, right, for a symbolic reconciliation onstage in Kingston in 1978. With the 1980 election approaching, violence was rising between warring factions of the Jamaica Labour Party and People's National Party. Over 800 persons died in political violence by the time the election was held.

The dominant influence, however, is Pan-Africanism and the Garveyite theme of repatriation.

Africa unite
Cause we're moving right out of Babylon
And we're going to our fathers' land

Although Rastafarianism predates and influenced reggae, reggae in turn has served as a vehicle for the spread of Rastafarianism. There are now Rastas in every country of the English-speaking Caribbean, as well as in West Indian communities abroad. In addition, many youth affect some aspects of the Rasta style but do not fully adhere to it as a religion. Reggae's appeal is nonetheless far broader than that of Rastafarianism. The music's wide popularity among black

West Indian youth reflects its portrayal of the reality they live—the "sufferer culture" in a world of economic hardship, racism and injustice.

They made their world so hard
Everyday we got to keep on fighting
They made their world so hard
Everyday the people are dying
It dread, dread for hunger and
Starvation dread dread, dread on dread
Lamentation dread dread
But read it in revelation dread dread
You'll find your redemption.

Rastafarians traditionally regard political struggle as

irrelevant, seeing salvation as possible only through a future "redemption" or repatriation. Reggae, however, departs from this. Marley in particular is forceful and positive in urging the downtrodden to stand up and reclaim their rights. In the song "Wake Up and Live," he echoes Garvey's call for united struggle by the black race:

Rise ye mighty people
There is work to be done
So let's do it little by little
Rise from your sleepless slumber

Another theme pervading Marley's music is the need for black people to triumph over the divide-and-rule tactics of the establishment. He sings of the struggle for unity and liberation of the African continent (*"Africans a liberate Zimbabwe"*). Closer to home, he denounces the internecine violence which the political parties have encouraged within the Jamaican working class:

Would you let the system
Make you kill your brotherman
No dread no

While this message is directed especially toward Jamaicans, it touches a nerve in black youth all over the Caribbean and even outside it. In one of his last compositions before his death, "Redemption Song," Marley urges black youth to transcend the history of slavery, and voices his faith in the new Caribbean generation:

Old pirates yes they rob I
Sold I to the merchant ships
Minutes after they took I
From the bottomless pit
But my hand was made strong
By the hand of the Almighty
We forward in this generation
Triumphantly

The song goes on to echo the black liberation philosophy of Frantz Fanon:

Emancipate yourself from mental slavery
None but ourselves can free our mind

Marley thus articulates for Caribbean youth an activist and progressive alternative to the passivity of the "sufferer" or the self-destruction of the ghetto fighter. This has provided the seed for a new awareness and pride among Caribbean youth, including an emerging concept of unity. As the calypsonian Black Stalin argues, this popular vision may prove more solidly grounded than the formal attempts at integration.

A man who don't know his history can't form no unity
How could a man who don't know his history form his own
*   ideology*
If the Rastafarian movement spreading and Carifta dying slow

Den is something dem Rastas on dat dem politicians don't
*   know.*

Building Bridges

We broke language barriers and declared them no longer a limitation to our unity. On a very personal, human level we enjoyed with our Caribbean sisters the sameness within our cultures. We enjoyed dancing to Antiguan music in the same way we dance in Cuba. Our foods are also very similar as are our gestures when speaking. We share a common sense of humor. We worked hard and talked about everything that affects us as Caribbean women.

— Cuban delegate at First Caribbean Women's Encounter

The First Caribbean Women's Encounter, held in Antigua from October 18-20, 1984, brought together women from the four corners of the Caribbean. They came from English-speaking Antigua, Barbados, the Bahamas, Belize, Dominica, Grenada, Guyana, Jamaica, St. Lucia, St. Kitts-Nevis, St. Vincent, and Trinidad & Tobago; from Spanish-speaking Cuba, Puerto Rico and the Dominican Republic; from French-speaking Haiti; and from Dutch-speaking Curaçao and Suriname. The encounter was organized by the Antigua Women's Movement, the women's arm of the Antigua Caribbean Liberation Movement. Because the ACLM was involved, the Antiguan government of Vere Bird responded with paranoid harassment, stationing police in and around the convention hall to record the proceedings on film and tape.

Progressive political parties are one of the main sectors working to promote dialogue and interaction between the disparate parts of the Caribbean. Others include unions, development workers, cultural workers, intellectuals (academics, writers and journalists), women's groups, and church and ecumenical organizations. These categories are not separate and distinct, but overlapping, with the same individuals often involved at several levels—a university professor who leads a left political party, for example, or a woman working with a church-sponsored development project who also leads a drama workshop for youth.

The link between the political left and university intellectuals is a central element of this fusion. The University of the West Indies has long been considered one of the most successful examples of regionalism, with its three campuses—in Trinidad, Jamaica and Barbados—serving the entire Commonwealth Caribbean. Now, however, the University is being "decentralized." This move will transfer political and financial power over each campus to the government of the territory where it is located, rather than continuing to share it among all the participating countries in the region. Opposed primarily by Bishop's government in Grenada, which argued that the smaller islands would be placed at a disadvantage, and by the West Indies Group of University Teachers (WIGUT) and other student and teacher associations, the plan nonetheless went into effect in 1984. The dismantling of UWI has been greeted with dismay in many quarters—not only because of its implications for regionalism, but because of fears that the governments of the "campus" territories, most notably Seaga's, may use their control to move against radicals on the university faculty.

Contacts between intellectuals and academics of the region take place within the formal structure of the University and its programs, as well as in professional associations such as the Association of Caribbean Historians. At the same time, there exists outside the university structure an independent movement of progressive intellectuals. Grenada became a pole of attraction for this group during the revolution. In November 1982, Grenada hosted the first Conference on Culture and Sovereignty, which issued a call for "a sovereign Caribbean Nation-State embracing the entire archipelago." Out of this conference emerged the Regional Committee of Caribbean Cultural and Intellectual Workers, headed by Barbadian novelist George Lamming and drawing from many Caribbean countries, including Cuba. Papers of the group have been published by Casa de las Americas, the Cuban publishing house which sponsors competitions for Latin American and Caribbean writers and regularly publishes works from the English-speaking Caribbean.

"Cultural workers" including artists, musicians and dramatists also tend to take a pan-Caribbean perspective. Popular theater, especially in Jamaica and the Eastern Caribbean, has been used as a consciousness-raising tool and a means of promoting dialogue between the people of various islands. The People's Action Theater of Dominica, for instance, has performed in the neighboring French colony of Martinique, using the French Creole or patois language spoken in both territories (while Dominica's main language is English, patois is a cultural survival from the island's early history as a colony of France.)

Probably the most consistent work in intra-regional cooperation is being carried out by the Church, particularly the Caribbean Conference of Churches. The CCC funds development projects in most of the Caribbean territories, and CCC-funded workshops frequently bring together participants from different areas of the region. *Caribbean Contact* attempts to include news from the French, Dutch and Spanish-speaking countries, although the emphasis is on the Commonwealth Caribbean. The newspaper has begun to include several articles in French or Spanish in each issue.

The churches and the ecumenical movement have been willing to tackle some of the most difficult problems in intra-regional relations. In the early seventies, the ecumenical movement was the first to call for ties between Cuba and other Caribbean states. The CCC's inclusion of the Cuban churches has been important in keeping alive what few ties survive between Cuba and the region; in September 1983 Cuba hosted a meeting of the CCC's Continuation Committee, its highest decision-making body between general assemblies.

Another area where the Church has taken on the task of trying to heal historic divisions is in the troubled island of Hispaniola, where Dominicans and Haitians co-exist in uneasy and sometimes hostile proximity. In February 1984, the Conference of Bishops of the Dominican Republic and Haiti called for an "urgent" solution to the "inhuman and unjust" persecution of Haitian immigrants in the Dominican Republic. In a joint communique released in both countries and translated into French, Spanish and Creole, the bishops announced the creation of a pastoral center for Haitian immigrants to be located in Santo Domingo. The bishops' statement criticized both the repression in Haiti and the discrimination against the refugees in the Dominican Republic. Given the long-standing animosity between Dominicans and Haitians, the Church's initiative represents a significant positive step.

Increasingly, regional cooperation sponsored by the CCC and other progressive organizations has focused on analysis of the crisis which faces the region in the 1980s. While language, culture, and politics divide the region's peoples, their problems are increasingly similar. These negative realities have sparked a dialogue which holds the potential of bringing the region closer together.

In December 1983, the CCC and the Santo Domingo-based EDOC (Caribbean Center for Research and Documentation) held a regional seminar to discuss the impact of the International Monetary Fund in the Caribbean. The Dominican Republic was chosen as the venue not only because of its experience with the IMF, but also as a means of building ties between the English-speaking and Spanish-speaking Caribbean.[13]

The following year, Puerto Rico was the site for a conference on "Threats to Peace in the Caribbean and Central America." It was sponsored by the Caribbean Project for Justice and Peace, a program in Puerto Rico of the Philadelphia-based American Friends Service Committee. More than 70 activists and scholars attended, representing four distinct cultural blocks: the Spanish-speaking Caribbean, the English-speaking Caribbean, Central America, and North America/Europe.

"Our main objective was to link people from Central America and the Caribbean and provide a space for them to meet and discuss the situation they face," said Awilda Colón, one of the organizers. Washington's use of Puerto Rico as a base for regional intervention hung as a somber backdrop to the conference. In organizing the event, said Colón, "an issue we discussed was the possibility that Puerto Rico, which is presently a springboard for militarism in the region, could be converted into a springboard for communication and peace."[14]

If the experience of shared crises is a factor strengthening the regional dialogue, a weakness of the process is its tendency to take place at the level of conferences and other temporary events, rather than ongoing organized cooperation. This is more the case for the dialogue among intellectuals and less so at the developmentalist level, where both Caribbean and outside organizations frequently fund small-scale projects spanning more than one territory. This is the level at which popular sectors like the peasantry are most likely to participate in inter-island cooperation.

So far, the building of ties between popular organizations in different countries is in its infancy, but it holds promise. One example is the work of the Farmers' Union in Dominica, which is trying to find markets for crops other than the main export, bananas. Hoping to enable the farmers to control the marketing themselves, the union has purchased its own boat, with help from a Dutch government agency, to transport produce to lands such as Trinidad where fruits and vegetables must be imported. The long-term goal is to link up with farmers' unions in Grenada and St. Vincent to cooperate on the marketing project, building ultimately toward regional self-sufficiency in food.[15]

Because the leadership of the Farmers' Union includes activists who have been involved on the left, the Charles government has brought pressure on the project. But the Farmers' Union nevertheless has raised its membership from about 200 to nearly 1,000.

"We need to manage the growth of progressive move-ments so that the popular base always provides a solid foundation of support," comments Atherton Martin, an organizer of the Dominican marketing project. Increasingly, activists are finding that such support comes through pur-poseful activity at the grassroots level, building a movement from the base up rather than the top down. To many governments, such grassroots cooperation may be at best irrelevant, at worst a threat. But as the formal integration movement founders, these cautious beginnings may point the way to a new regionalism more solidly grounded in the creativity and strength of the Caribbean people. ∎

Building a cooperative bakery in Dominica.

Conclusion

As we go to press at the end of summer 1985, events are racing ahead in the Caribbean, deepening the dominant regional trends developed in this book. Threats to the economic survival of Caribbean people continue to produce intense social unrest—indeed, so acute has the crisis become in several countries that explosions now appear inevitable unless rapid and major changes are made. Popular struggles (although not armed struggle) continue to challenge colonialism, dictatorship, militarism and the IMF. And the issue of sovereignty is increasingly sharply defined as Caribbean governments and people face the implications of the Reagan administration's neocolonial political order.

In Jamaica, workers staged an island-wide general strike in June which disrupted water supplies, electricity and communications and paralyzed much of the economy. Led by the six major unions in the country, including the one affiliated with Seaga's own party, the strike marked the transition from spontaneous to organized national protest against the Seaga/IMF policies of layoffs and devaluations. The prime minister refused to negotiate, instead calling in members of the security forces to operate key public services, and the strike fizzled without achieving its goals. With a bitter and frustrated population increasingly united against him, Seaga stated flatly that he would not run the country on the basis of public opinion, and there were dark rumors of a possible "military solution" to Jamaica's agony.

In the Dominican Republic, also suffering in the grip of the IMF, popular protests achieved a temporary victory when President Jorge Blanco raised the minimum wage from US$58 to $83 per month. As in Jamaica, however, a mood of helplessness, anger and desperation prevailed as it appeared that the country's policies were being entirely made in Washington and that none of the national leaders or would-be leaders had any alternative solution to offer. Alluding to the deepening poverty and repression, Caribbean observers spoke of the "Haitianization" of other countries in the region. "The spectre of Haiti is haunting our brothers and sisters in Jamaica, as it is haunting Guyana to the south," warned a Trinidadian economist.

In Haiti itself, President-for-Life Jean Claude Duvalier staged a July "referendum" as part of his series of paper reforms designed to impress foreign aid donors, particularly the U.S. Congress. It was, however, such a mockery of the democratic process that even the U.S. Embassy in Haiti was too embarrassed to endorse it. Although independent sources estimate that 60% of the electorate boycotted the poll, the Duvalier government claimed that 99.9% voted "yes" to constitutional amendments affirming the institution of the presidency-for-life and giving the president the right to choose his successor. The new laws also provide for the establishment of "political parties," but only if they pledge loyalty to the Duvalier presidency-for-life. The confrontation between the government and the Church also continued to grow. On July 23, assailants—presumed to be government security forces—clubbed to death a 78-year-old Belgian priest, Albert Desmet, while the government expelled three other Missionhurst priests from the country for criticizing the referendum. Yet the United States made no move to suspend its planned $55 million in aid to Haiti for 1986.

In Guadeloupe, the anti-colonial movement continued to gain momentum. Violence convulsed the island for six days in late July as demonstrators demanded the release of Georges Faisans, an imprisoned independence activist. Protesters' barricades sealed off the capital of Pointe-a-Pitre, while the French government rushed in military reinforcements from France to assist police in battling the demonstrators. Faisans was finally released while his case remained on appeal; he had been sentenced to three years in prison for assaulting a white teacher who had kicked a black student while saying "Negroes must be driven by kicks." This confrontation with French racism and colonialism came against the ironic backdrop of the French government's announcement in July of official sanctions against the South African apartheid regime.

In Puerto Rico, more than 4,000 young people marched 35 miles from San Juan to the Roosevelt Roads Naval Station to protest the presence of U.S. nuclear weapons facilities on the island. Governor Hernández Colón's increasingly close collaboration with Reagan administration strategy was highlighted by his speech to CARICOM in Barbados, in which the colonial governor lashed out against "international communism" and praised the invasion of Grenada as having "written a new chapter in the history of freedom in the region." His speech was sharply criticized by progressive forces in Puerto Rico as anti-colonial consciousness among Puerto Ricans continued to advance.

Far from being isolated incidents, these social upheavals and quickened protests are symptomatic of a profound region-wide instability overtaking the Caribbean. At the deepest level this instability stems from the impending *collapse of the old models*—the crisis and failure of colonialism (as in Guadeloupe and Puerto Rico), dictatorship (as in Haiti), and U.S. neocolonialism (as in the Dominican Republic and Jamaica). The desperation which has characterized the protests reflects the fact that while people can no longer survive under the old models, the paths to more socially just and economically viable societies appear ill-defined and blocked. Alternative models lack clarity, and two important attempts have either fallen short of expectations (Manley's Jamaica) or ended disastrously (Grenada). At the same time, attempts to develop alternative models of progressive change are blocked by the United States, which has crushed such efforts through militant intervention in the past and shows every indication of continuing to do so.

In the days of gunboat diplomacy at the beginning of the century, the U.S. strategy for maintaining control in the Caribbean relied on outright force—invasions and occupations followed by the installation of dictatorships or puppet governments. In recent years, invasions and destabilizations have continued, but have been followed by the more liberal strategy of attempting to fashion pseudo-democratic, elected "show-case" governments supported by heavy U.S. aid. Examples of this approach include the Dominican Republic under Balaguer, Jamaica under Seaga and Grenada under Blaize. But far from promoting prosperity or democracy, such neocolonial regimes have blocked real change, creating a time bomb of failed expectations and economic decline.

The failure of the liberal strategy raises the ominous possibility of a return to tactics of blunt local repression and direct U.S. military intervention. The Reagan administration has moved in this direction, although the model or showcase strategy has not been completely abandoned. The Caribbean is thus heading backward toward the days of gunboat diplomacy. But as one Caribbean leader aptly said, "Security can't be won with force of arms." The United States may succeed in barring progressive paths to Caribbean development, but this will lead neither to prosperity nor to greater U.S. security. Instead, this policy will plant the seeds of greater misery and future social explosions.

Caribbean - North American Dialogue

In response to such an impasse, the perennial question arises: "What can we do?" One answer lies in a process like that which has taken place over the past five years between North Americans and Central Americans: people-to-people dialogue.

Such a dialogue could take as its starting point those specific issues which are most well-known and controversial in the Caribbean and the U.S. These include, for example, the Cuban revolution and its impact on the region, the Grenada revolution and invasion, the U.S. invasion of the Dominican Republic, the failed Jamaican "miracle," Puerto Rico's status as a U.S. colony, and U.S. support for the Duvalier dicta-torship in Haiti. From such discussions can grow a more holistic and critical reevaluation of U.S. policy in the region.

A key part of this dialogue should be interchange with Cuba, aimed at a better North American understanding of this important Caribbean society. Whether Americans agree with the ideology of the revolution or not, the Castro government enjoys popular support in Cuba, and has valuable expertise to lend the region in many areas of development. Moreover, the U.S. vendetta against Cuba is poisoning the atmosphere in the Caribbean and blinding many North Americans to the real causes of the region's problems.

Secondly, North Americans must break free of the old ideologies and myths which have dominated our concept of the Caribbean for so long. This concept is rooted in the gunboat diplomacy era, when the North American elite coveted the Caribbean islands as additions to the growing empire. The continuing influence of such ideas in U.S. thinking is sym-bolized by Senator Barry Goldwater's suggestion, after the Grenada invasion, that Grenada, Puerto Rico, the U.S. Virgin Islands and any other Caribbean territory so wishing form an 'archipelago state" to be admitted to the Union. Clearly, the North American dream of a Caribbean empire is far from dead.

The Caribbean is not a U.S. appendage, tropical state or empire; it is a group of sovereign nations which have the right to determine their own political and economic forms. It is natural that trade, aid and tourism will take place between the United States and the Caribbean, but they must take place on a basis of mutual respect, as difficult as this concept may be for a superpower. This includes respect for the desire of Caribbean people to build a regional movement necessary for their survival and to become a non-aligned zone of peace. Although perhaps more difficult for the U.S. to manipulate, a self-reliant and united Caribbean, with diverse ties to Latin America, Western Europe, Canada, the socialist bloc and the United States, would be more in the long-term interests of this country than a poor and conflict-ridden region, however subserviant.

Specific myths which must be confronted include the notion that every attempt at social change in the Caribbean comes from Cuba or will provide an opening for communism. The Cold War mentality has become so prevalent that today one can scarcely discuss the process of social change without becoming enmeshed in the issue of the "communist threat." It is true, on the one hand, that socialist attitudes have influenced the majority of social change experiments in the Caribbean since the 1950s. However, these socialist currents have been just one factor in an eclectic mix whose other elements include anti-colonialism, democratic and constitutional impulses, Black Power, and Third World non-alignment. Progressive experiments in Guyana, Cuba, the Dominican Republic, Jamaica, Grenada and Nicaragua have had some elements in common, but in other ways they have been very different. In all cases they represent genuinely Caribbean (or Central Amer-ican) processes, and the myth of Soviet or Cuban instigation is false.

Another myth which must be challenged is the Reagan ideology that export-oriented economies and foreign exploi-tation of cheap Caribbean labor will bring prosperity to the region. The Caribbean Basin Initiative has faded from the news; little mention is made of the disastrous conditions in Seaga's Jamaica; and even the recent "rescue" of Grenada's economy from Marxism is no longer touted by the White House since economic conditions have deteriorated there. Rather than letting these failures slip by unnoticed while rhetoric continues at a high pitch, we need to critically examine the reasons for them and the implications for the U.S. neocolonial model.

Finally, inspired by the growth of the Central American solidarity movement, we affirm the value of personal visits to and exchanges with the Caribbean. These must go beyond tourism and all that it represents to encompass dialogue with people from all social sectors, but particularly from the majority sector of rural and urban working people. While such people-to-people exchanges may not produce immediate or radical breakthroughs, they can lead us to a deeper under-standing of the Caribbean and its problems, the prerequisite for any change in U.S. actions. We believe that the Black community in the U.S., the Hispanic community, the labor movement, concerned Christians and the Central American solidarity movement are all key elements in building this critical dialogue. ∎

NOTES TO PART SEVEN

Left Under Fire

1. Clive Thomas, address at Queen's University, Kingston, Ontario, May 9, 1984.
2. Interview with Octavio Rivera, member of the Political Committee of the Bloque Socialista, Dominican Republic, in *Intercontinental Press,* April 16, 1984.
3. Fidel Castro, public address in Havana, November 14, 1983.
4. Edward Seaga, address to the Jamaican Parliament, November 1, 1983.
5. *Latin America Regional Reports-Caribbean,* December 9, 1983.
6. John Compton, public address in St. Lucia, November 5, 1983.
7. Interview with Kenrick Radix, *Intercontinental Press,* April 30, 1984.
8. *Caribbean Contact,* December 1983.
9. *Caribbean Contact,* December 1983.
10. Errol Barrow, "The Danger of Rescue Operations," *Caribbean Review,* Fall 1983.
11. Interview with Kenrick Radix, *op. cit.;* interview with Don Rojas, *Intercontinental Press,* December 26, 1983.
12. Bishop's vision of the revolution's trajectory is spelled out in "Line of March for the Party," presented to a general meeting of the NJM, September 13, 1982.
13. See for example Richard Hart's introduction to *In Nobody's Backyard: Maurice Bishop's Speeches, 1979-1983: A Memorial Volume* (London: Zed Books Ltd., 1984).
14. *Struggle,* February 10, 1984.
15. *Catholic Standard,* February 26, 1984.
16. Oilfields Workers Trade Union, "Statement Condemning the Invasion of Grenada," November 1, 1983.
17. *Ibid.*
18. *Struggle,* November 11, 1983.
19. George Lamming, address at University of the West Indies, Cave Hill, Barbados, November 17, 1983.
20. Clive Thomas, address at Queen's University, *op. cit.*
21. *The Militant,* December 30, 1983.
22. *Outlet,* December 23, 1983.
23. Interview with Octavio Rivera, *op. cit.*
24. Letter from WPA to *Catholic Standard,* March 4, 1984.
25. *Caribbean Contact,* December 1983.
26. *Struggle,* September 16, 1983.
27. EPICA interview with Tim Hector, May 1984.
28. *Dayclean,* November 5, 1983.

Religious Challenge and Conformity

1. Other important figures include Dale Bisnauth and Mike McCormack of Guyana, Pablo Marichal of Cuba, William Watty of Dominica and Jamaica, Luis Rivera of Puerto Rico, and David Mitchell of Grenada and Barbados—among others.
2. *Caribbean Contact,* September 1981, p. 2.
3. EPICA interview with Dr. Roy Neehall, Trinidad, August 1982.
4. *Ibid.*
5. *Caribbean Contact,* December 1981, p. 1.
6. *Caribbean Contact,* May 1982, p. 9.
7. *Caribbean Contact,* August 1981.
8. *Caribbean Contact,* April 1983.
9. Moises Rosa Ramos, "Analysis of the Church in Puerto Rico," Church and Theology Project of the National Ecumenical Movement of Puerto Rico, 1985.
10. Interview by Don Foster with Horace Levy, SAC Ltd., Kingston, Jamaica, June 1984.
11. EPICA interview with Michael James, CCC, Bridgetown, Barbados, May 1984.
12. CCC statement, October 25, 1983, cited in *Caribbean Contact,* November 1983.
13. Conference of Churches, Grenada, "Message addressed to all people in Grenada, Carriacou, and Petite Martinique," signed by Rev. Sydney Charles, acting chairman.
14. Dr. Leslie Lett, "Grenada: A Churchman's View," remarks presented to Caribbean Studies Association, St. Kitts-Nevis, June 2, 1984.
15. *Ibid.*
16. *Caribbean Contact,* May 1984.
17. Interview with Archdeacon Hoskins Huggins, in *The Grenadian Voice,* April 28, 1984.
18. *Caribbean Contact,* December 1983.

Region Recolonized

1. EPICA interview with Jorge Rodriguez Beruff, Caribbean Project for Justice and Peace, Rio Piedras, PR, October 1984.
2. U.S. Department of State, "Congressional Presentation: Security Assistance Programs FY 1986."

3. *Ibid.*
4. William Arkin, remarks at conference "Threats to Peace in the Caribbean and Central America," Aguas Buenas, PR, October 1984.
5. EPICA interview with Angel Salsbach, member of Parliament, Curacao, April 1984.
6. Bernard Diederich, "The End of West Indian Innocence: Arming the Police," *Caribbean Review,* Spring 1984, p. 11.
7. *Ibid.,* p. 11.
8. *Unity* (newsletter of Movement for National Unity, St. Vincent & the Grenadines), December 29, 1983 and May 9, 1984.
9. Council on Hemispheric Affairs, press release, July 19, 1984.
10. EPICA interview with Atherton Martin, Washington, DC, April 1985.
11. Barbados *Nation,* January 23, 1984, p. 1.
12. U.S. Department of State, "Aid and U.S. Interests in Latin America and the Caribbean," March 5, 1985.
13. *Washington Post,* July 19, 1984.
14. *Washington Post,* July 26, 1984.
15. *Washington Post,* June 12, 1985.
16. EPICA interview with Atherton Martin.
17. U.S. General Accounting Office, "AID Assistance to the Eastern Caribbean: Program Changes and Possible Consequences," July 22, 1983.
18. *New York Times,* February 20, 1984.
19. *New York Times,* February 20, 1984.
20. Bernardo Vega, "The CBI Faces Adversity: Lessons from the Asian Export Strategy," *Caribbean Review,* Vol. XIV, No. 2, Spring 1985, pp. 18-19.
21. U.S. General Accounting Office, "AID Assistance to the Eastern Caribbean," pp. 12-19.
21. *Ibid.,* pp. 30-31.
23. The Resource Center, "Focus on the Eastern Caribbean" (Albuquerque: Resource Center, 1984), p. 20.
24. *Washington Post,* November 13, 1983.
25. *Philadelphia Inquirer,* November 7, 1983, p. 14.
26. *Amnesty International Report 1984* (London: Amnesty International Publications, 1984), pp. 153-157.
27. "Grenada: Report of a British Labor-Movement Delegation, December 1983" (4 Grays Inn Bldg., Roseberry Ave., London EC1R, U.K.), p. 18.
28. U.S. Government Interagency Team on Commercial and Private Sector Initiatives, "Prospects for Growth in Grenada: The Role of the Private Sector," p. 21.
29. "Grenada: Report of a British Labour-Movement Delegation," p. 23.
30. *Everybody's Magazine,* December 1984, p. 9.
31. Caribbean News Agency, February 8, 1984.
32. *New York Times,* March 27, 1985.
33. *New York Times,* July 29, 1984.
34. Cathy Sunshine, "How the New Right Engineered the Elections," *The Guardian* (New York), December 26, 1984.

Regional Unity

1. EPICA interview with Eunice Santana, National Ecumenical Movement of Puerto Rico (PRISA), San Juan, September 1983.
2. Richard Hart, "Trade Unionism in the English-speaking Caribbean: the Formative Years and the Caribbean Labour Congress," in Susan Craig, ed., *Contemporary Caribbean: A Sociological Reader,* Vol. II (Trinidad: Craig, 1982), p. 89.
3. From the Ocho Rios Declaration, cited in *Caribbean Contact,* December 1982.
4. Jeremy Taylor, London Observer Service, July 2, 1984.
5. Dr. Neville Linton, "Facing Up to Ideological Pluralism in CARICOM," *Caribbean Contact,* July 1983.
6. Ocho Rios Declaration.
7. Rosina Wiltshire-Brodber, "Informal and Formal Bases of Caribbean Regional Integration," presented at Hunter College, September 1, 1984.
8. David Frith, "Salute to George Headley," *Outlet,* April 6, 1984.
9. *Cuba Internacional,* July 1983.
10. C.L.R. James, "Garfield Sobers," in *The Future in the Present* (London: Allison & Busby, 1977), p. 225.
11. EPICA interview with Barbadian artist Omowale Stewart, August 1982.
12. *Outlet,* November 2, 1984.
13. *Caribbean Contact,* March 1984.
14. EPICA interview with Awilda Colon, Puerto Rico, October 1984.
15. EPICA interview with Atherton Martin, Washington, DC, April 1985.

FE